Regional
Italian
Cuisine

Regional
Italian
Cuisine

Typical recipes and culinary impressions
from all regions.

Authors: Reinhardt Hess and Sabine Sälzer
Introduction: Franco Benussi
English Translation and U.S. Adaptation:
Elisabetta A.G.Castleman
Recipe Styling and Food Photography:
Foodfotografie Eising

BARRON'S

Contents

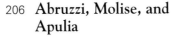

About This Book

No other country is so closely tied to our longing for sun, mild breezes, and blue ocean, as Italy. Images and memories come to mind of cuisine, of uncomplicated patio dining under the open sky, of steaming pasta, of the aroma of freshly grated Parmesan cheese, and of good country wine. To eat here means to absorb with all one's senses the culture of a creative people. Can a cookbook actually convey the strong impressions and recreate them with enough energy? We believe that we have been able to do so. The unique and beautifully photographed recipes sparkle under the southern sun, with shadows like branches appearing over the plates, and with wineglasses reflecting color accents. The preparation steps for many of the recipes show in a simple way how the dish is prepared. Even beginners will feel the urge to go immediately to the kitchen to begin cooking.

We have collected 230 typical recipes from throughout the country that are as authentic as the modern market allows them to be. We are sure that many of these recipes will soon count among your favorites, because they authentically reflect the genuine pleasure of the people of the region who have prepared them every day and have perfected them. For each region you will find a complete menu sequence, from appetizers to desserts, so that you will have no trouble putting together an authentic menu. Information on each dish includes topics of conversation and tips on drinks, while the wine page will help you to select a suitable accompaniment.

This cookbook can also be a guide to a tour through Italy showing the natural origins of each culinary region, the landscapes that bring forth delicious products for regional cooking: the fishing industry, farming, the unique aspects of the country, and above all, the people in their daily lives, during their meals, and enjoying various celebrations. Here, we try to explain those factors that influence the regional cuisines, including the geographical, historical, and human components that make up their traditions. This book should accompany any visitor to Italy; as it inspires interesting culinary tours to museums, craft shops, and food-and-drink-related events, regional specialties will become familiar. And of course, the Italian products—olive oil, sausage and cheese, pasta, fish and seafood typical of each region—come to life with impressive pictures. We feel we have been able to depict the real Italian cuisine in a new and unique way. You be the judge.

The Authors and the Publisher

The Diversity of Italian Cuisine

Today you can enjoy Italian food in many restaurants and, by reading books, go on culinary tours and explorations. Due to the availability of Italian products in most supermarkets and farmers' markets, it is also easy to follow instructions on how to prepare Italian dishes. Perhaps you are even one of those fortunate people who like to spend a vacation in Italy while you become familiar with the local dishes. If so, you will have noticed that many recipes included in cookbooks can be found only in certain regions of Italy, and that they are often prepared differently than what you are familiar with from home cooking.

The gastronomic culture of a country is tightly interwoven with the geographical conditions, historical events, and social peculiarities. This is also the case with Italian cuisine. It is common, but not completely accurate, to speak of a universal Italian way of cooking. Each region, as a result of its own multifaceted cultural evolution, has its own cuisine. Discovering these various culinary cultures requires the willingness to go back in time to before 1860, before the unification of the Italian states, when classic recipes and regional culinary traditions came into existence. Few recipes were influenced by the cuisines of the courts and the aristocratic families that were connected with the French and the Central Europeans, especially the Transalpine royal courts.

The traditional dishes reflect the farming culture of the people; they are genuine, simple, and delicious. Since the regions are climatically and geologically very different from each other, the products and the palates of the inhabitants are diverse; therefore, one can find that a dish that originated in a certain region tastes different in another and is prepared differently from place to place.

It is possible to speak of a classic cuisine only if one considers a few common and very popular recipes. The center of culinary tradition, however, is to be found in the regional way of cooking. After all, the land extends from north to south, and the major climatic differences influence the main ingredients, one very important reason for the differences between northern and southern regional cuisine. Consider that in the Aosta Valley, in Piedmont, in Lombardy, in Veneto, and Venezia Giulia, as well as in the northern areas of the country, the tomato was not well known, while in the southern areas these New World fruits figured much earlier in the important local ingredients. In the Alpine regions, olive oil and chili peppers are not used in the traditional cuisine, while in the flat lands, central, and southern regions, they are included in many specialties.

Pasta, of course, is typical of Italian cuisine. Each region has its own tradition, its own way to prepare it, so that even in the case of pasta, one cannot speak of one common denominator.

Due to the passion for travel of contemporary society, certain regional dishes can also be found today in other areas. This is partly due to the desire of cooks to meet their guests' expectations, but is not proof that Italian cuisine has become uniform. Today, local culinary traditions are mostly kept in home cooking. It is only through the rendition of the main regional recipes that the individual aspects of Italian cuisine, which are so rich with flavors, unique specialties, and extraordinary culinary traditions, become evident.

Professor Franco Benussi

The Culinary Regions

For many of us, Italian cuisine has been long represented mainly by pizza and spaghetti, as if people in Italy always eat the same food. One should add here that the first pizza restaurants appeared mainly due to important reasons: They were often started by immigrants who came from areas around Naples and who searched abroad for a new source of income. Pizza originated in Naples, and, with its basic ingredients, it reflects a region where inhabitants had to eat in a simple way. The other regions also have their typical specialties that are only found there. Culinary traditions have never followed the laws of administrative border politics, but have more often shown how rock formations and soil, ocean and land, agriculture and fishing, as well as history, have affected regional daily cooking.

Comparable culinary basics were the main reason why twenty-one Italian regions have been turned here into eight culinary chapters that present a big picture. Each chapter includes an introduction to the region, a background of the regional cuisine, a glance into the mentality of the people, and tips for culinary sightseeing and events. Finally, typical regional recipes are presented, from *antipasti* (appetizers), *primi piatti* (pasta, rice, and soups) and *secondi piatti* (fish, meat, poultry, venison, and egg dishes), to *dolci* (desserts), all of which can be easily prepared at home.

These eight chapters are:

Liguria and Coastal Tuscany

The menu here, as in many other coastal regions, is shaped by the fishing industry; however, something special is added, herbs that intensify and add to the aroma of every dish. Pesto, an intensely aromatic paste of basil, garlic, pine nuts, cheese, and olive oil, is native to Liguria. Also, cooking is done with olive oil; for this reason, we will discuss this ingredient here. The cuisine is above all based on vegetables; this is a *di magro* quality (vegetarian), as Italians call it. They are grown on narrow terraces or in small gardens and have intense flavors. Loving and patient methods of preparation make these specialties with simple ingredients worth your while.

The Po Basin

The vast fruitful landscape in the regions of Emilia-Romagna, Veneto, and Southern Lombardy is the area of rice specialties, such as *risotto*, which is prepared in many ways. This is not surprising, as rice cultivation finds its best conditions in the foggy fields found in this area. An intensive farming economy delivers meat, milk, and cream; favorites are cheese, ham, and sausage, as well as dishes prepared with veal and beef, which are simmered and stewed with wine and tomatoes, such as *ossobuco*, veal shanks prepared according to the Milanese style of cooking. The use of butter is more common here than olive oil. Emilia Romagna is the region where homemade pasta, *lasagne, tortellini,* and *tagliatelle* are most commonly found.

The Alpine Regions

These are the most complicated to describe. Almost every valley has its tradition, its own specialties. A common denominator is a simple and hearty cuisine based on mountain dairy products. Butter, bacon, cheese, and bread are the main ingredients. Large and small dumplings made with potato dough demonstrate the connection to northern regions, fish are from mountain brooks, not from the ocean, and desserts play an important role. Famous delicacies are white truffles from the Piedmont and, of course, the favorite *grappa*.

Tuscany, Umbria, and Le Marche

Sophisticated simplicity and country heartiness characterize the cuisine of these regions, which cover an area from gentle hills to the rugged mountain peaks of the Apennine Range. Olive oil is used here for cooking, and hams and sausages are served as appetizers. Tomatoes and legumes play an important role. The people here eat a lot of meat, prepared mainly grilled or on a spit such as *bistecca alla fiorentina*, a huge steak cut from Chianina beef grilled over open wood charcoal. Instead of pasta, they eat white bread with a crunchy crust. One of the most popular of all Italian wines, Chianti, is native to Tuscany. Delicious fish chowders are prepared along the coast, while throughout the mountainous region, sea and river trout and carp are staples.

Latium and Sardinia

Latium focuses on Rome, where traditional, hearty, robust specialties predominate. Meat is often stewed in gravies, or roasted with lard and bacon. Coffee is very important here. The cuisine of Sardinia is based on a few main ingredients, and the region shares with Latium the love for sheep milk products: *pecorino* and *ricotta* cheeses.

Abruzzi, Molise, Apulia

A common denominator among these regions is the shepherds who move throughout these areas with their herds, and who have brought not only meat and cheese, but also new ways to prepare regional dishes. Together with olive oil from Apulia, spicy peppers are also used in the simple and original regional specialties, which thus acquire a fiery taste. Vegetables and homemade pasta play important roles, as well as fish caught along the coasts.

Campagna and Basilicata

Characteristic of this cuisine are simple ingredients used in spicy and interesting specialties, of which pizza is a good example. The diversity of the pasta, exemplified by the different types of noodles used, is highlighted especially by the cuisine of Naples. Vegetables, tomatoes, and cheese are part of every meal. The use of basil adds greatly to the cooking of pork and sausage and incredibly spicy chili peppers.

Calabria and Sicily

The farther south, the scantier and more deserted the regions become. Here, sheep and goat raising becomes more important, with the production of cheese, originally the only way to preserve the milk of these animals. The sharp bite of various spices is also appreciated. Along the coast, the fishing industry, and in the interior, pork and sausages, represent the basics of the local cuisine. Favorite main course vegetables are tomatoes and eggplant, while the rich desserts and the dishes containing cinnamon and raisins demonstrate an Oriental culinary influence on these regions.

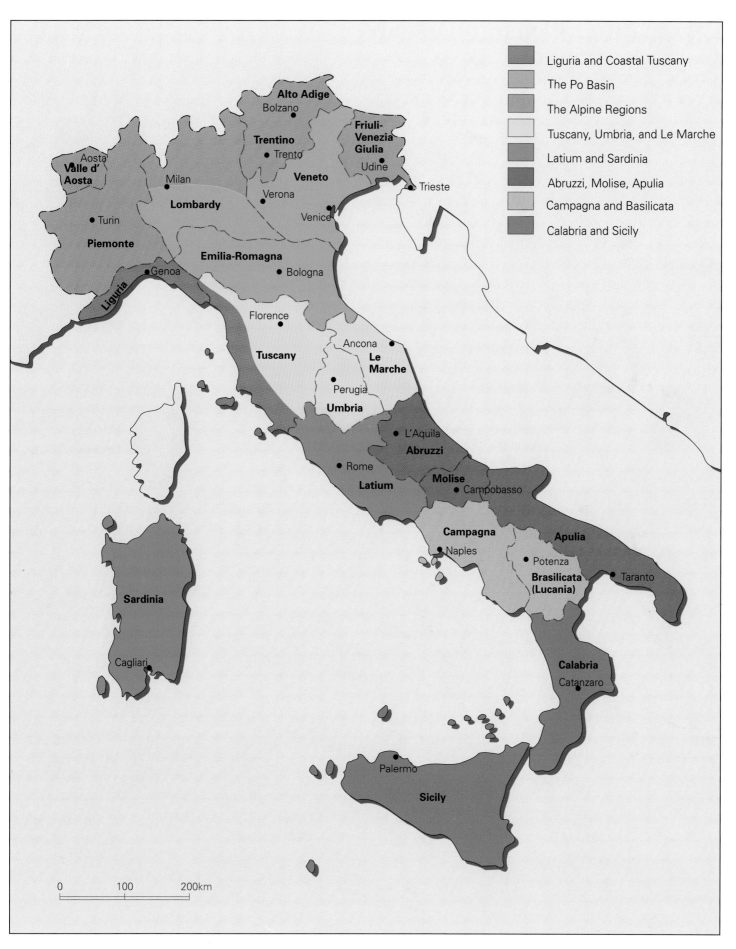

Liguria and Coastal Tuscany

The Po Basin

The Alpine Regions

Tuscany, Umbria, and Le Marche

Latium and Sardinia

Abruzzi, Molise, Apulia

Campagna and Basilicata

Calabria and Sicily

Alto Adige
Bolzano

Trentino
Trento

Friuli-
Venezia
Giulia
Udine

Aosta
Valle d'
Aosta

Milan

Veneto

Verona

Trieste

Lombardy

Venice

Turin

Piemonte

Emilia-Romagna

Genoa

Bologna

Liguria

Florence

Ancona

Tuscany

Le
Marche

Perugia

Umbria

L'Aquila

Abruzzi

Rome

Molise

Latium

Campobasso

Campagna

Apulia

Naples

Potenza

Taranto

Brasilicata
(Lucania)

Sardinia

Cagliari

Calabria

Catanzaro

Palermo

Sicily

0   100   200km

Liguria and Coastal Tuscany

Cliffs and Ocean:
Vernazza, one of the villages
of Cinqueterre.

The Regions and Their Products

dried only during the past century. Before that, its inhabitants painstakingly carved their farming soil out of the poor mountainous land. The Maremma is now a rural region, and sheep raising has been replaced by growing wheat and olives, and by a wine industry.

The fishing industry, cultivation of olives, and, above all, herbs that grow in the mountains, determine the Ligurian cuisine. It has always been simple and predominantly vegetarian—*di magro* in Italian. Loving and patient methods of preparation, and the use of simple ingredients, make Liguria's specialties outstanding.

Liguria is located in the Northwest, where the boot of Italy forms its open fold, facing the Gulf of Genoa. The coastal regions of Tuscany are attached to it, from the marble quarries of Carrara as far as the Maremma, the marshland in the Southeast. The narrow southward-reaching coast of Liguria, which is ragged and climbs suddenly into the mountains, leaves little space for raising animals or extensive farming. As if to compensate for this, the area is full of beautiful coastal scenic sites with tiny gardens and narrow terraces where fresh fruit and vegetables grow and almost seem to shine among the green foliage. The mild local climate makes everything grow earlier here, while it helps in the abundant growth of flowers (especially carnations and roses), asparagus, and citrus fruits.

From the peaks of Mesco to those of Montenero is the portion of the Riviera known as Cinqueterre, five locations along the steep coastal chain that turn into a closed, hard-to-reach region in which the Ligurian culture has remained almost untouched.

The Tuscan coast is made of intermittent long beaches, rocky mountainous projections, and curved strips of sand. The rivers have sand planes at their outlets; in the past, the ocean took up much more of the land. In the Middle Ages, when Pisa was one of the strongest sea powers, the Arno River was navigable up to the city. Today, a long arm reaches out to the sea, the Arno's alluvial land. Its delta contributes one of Pisa's specialties, *le cee*, young, still transparent eels that are caught with large nets from the pier and fried with sage leaves in olive oil.

The Maremma, also called "the bitter one" until a few years ago has its own peculiar character. The original marshland was

What sheep in Liguria love as fodder are also favorite culinary ingredients: fragrant mountain herbs. The fishing industry is also important to the cuisine of the area.

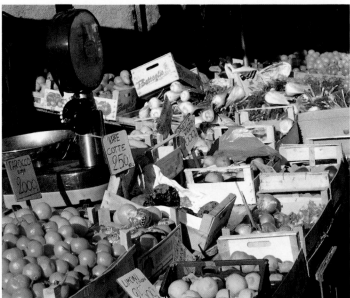

Top: Catch of eels at the outlet of the Arno River. Fried eels in olive oil and sage are a Pisa specialty called le cee.

Above: Fruits and vegetables for Liguria's markets are cultivated laboriously but bring higher profits because the climate allows everything to grow earlier.

Flavorful Ligurian olive oil is usually used for cooking. Two main ingredients characterize the cuisine of this region: fish, and herbs that grow either wild throughout the hills or gardens. Fish is considered good only if it comes from the Gulf of Genoa, although the catch is often somewhat meager and

guests are sometimes served frozen fish. The coast of Tuscany along the Tyrrhenian Sea also provides fresh fish and shellfish. The fish chowder prepared in Leghorn (Livorno), *cacciucco*, is among the finest of the region's seafood dishes. Hunting also plays an important role in the area, and recipes for

preparing rabbit are popular. Specialties with regional pasta variations are not common.

Ligurians' love for a cuisine filled with the aromas and perfumes of herbs is easily understandable if one considers the traditional image of fishermen coming back from the ocean,

where they ate monotonous foods such as salted fish and biscuits. They rejoiced at the fragrant scent of basil, sage, rosemary, and marjoram, and at the sight of fresh vegetables growing in the gardens. Pesto, made with basil, olive oil, garlic, pine nuts, and cheese, is among the most popular

Above: Zucchini squash, and especially their blossoms, are culinary favorites that are prepared with fish or mushrooms, or filled with mashed potatoes and herbs.

Top left: Despite these days' relatively lean catches from the Mediterranean Sea, fish shopping always begins at the fish market.

Middle left: Dried codfish stoccafisso is a prominent, unusual ingredient. Its use in Ligurian cuisine demonstrates how courageous fishermen reached northern Europe, and returned with this specialty.

Above: There is no dish without herbs. Where else are sprigs of thyme for a stew, or abundant sage and rosemary for grilled lobster mandatory? Ligurian cuisine without pesto, prepared in a mortar and pestle with garlic, cheese, and minced basil, is almost unthinkable.

sauces; nowhere does pesto taste better than here. Ligurian basil is small-leafed and fragrant, much different than the large-leafed type that is common elsewhere.

Among Ligurians, three ways to use pesto are popular: in the hearty and thick *minestrone* (soup), as sauce over hot *trenette* (a type of flat pasta), and as a sauce over *trofie* (a type of Genoa dumpling).

Fragrant herbs are also important in Genoa's *cappon magro*, or lean capon salad, which is somehow a contradiction, since the specialty is prepared not with poultry, but with fish and shellfish and a lot of vegetables.

People, Events, Sightseeing

Ligurians are as diverse as their region's landscapes. Along the coast they are friendly and progressive, ever open-minded and in search of new lands; therefore, it comes as no surprise that Christopher Columbus was one of Genoa's sons. Ligurians often seem to have mixed emotions: They love adventure and faraway places, but at the same time they have a great attachment for their land, their friends, and their own culture. Ligurian cuisine, also nicknamed *cucina del ritorno*, the cuisine of home-coming, is marked by the mariners' longing for their homeland, for herbs and greens.

The inhabitants of the interior, on the other hand, are serious, quiet, reserved, and marked by struggle. The villages are sometimes built like hawk nests on rugged cliffs, the houses tight, the roads narrow and steep. Rarely does a tourist, once inland, get lost; however, that may happen on the coast, which is buzzing with life during the summer months.

Tuscans are very attached to their land. Their ways are expressed everywhere. With frugality and a love of order, they modify nature with their own stamp. Some say they are stingy and suspicious, but also alert and with a good sense of humor. Along the entire coast, there are villages and cities in which good eating can be enjoyed under open skies.

Names like Finale Ligure, San Remo, Portofino, Cinqueterre, Viareggio, Pisa, and Livorno have become synonymous with tourism and a tourism-based economy. For those who wish to avoid the hustle and bustle, however, only a few miles away toward the interior there are wonderful villages where it is possible to live well and inexpensively. Part of the lifestyle experience here, undoubtedly, should be a visit to a bar, since Italy is ultimately known for its numerous aperitifs that precede the typical menu.

Worthwhile visits include in Pontedassio (Liguria), the Spaghetti Museum in the residence of Agnesi, a prominent pasta manufacturer. Displayed here are old and modern machines for the making of pasta, as well as documents on various varieties that date back to the thirteenth century.

Above: Relaxing on a terrace in Monterosso, Cinqueterre, looking at the ocean, and enjoying Ligurian culinary specialties—who would want to miss this opportunity?

Above: A farinata is baked in a wood-burning oven. This Ligurian version of pizza is prepared with garbanzo beans, oil, and water. It is served only with lettuce.

Above: This peaceful image can be deceptive, as Portofino is a Ligurian yacht port for jetsetters. Although the prices in restaurants and bars reflect this, the atmosphere and the style mixed with natural beauty make a visit here memorable.

In Cassago there is a farmers' museum put together by students who wish to preserve the lifestyles of their grandparents. Worthwhile visits include the market in Chiavari, which is held every Friday. It is among the best and most colorful anywhere.

Celebrations: On March 19, Santa Margherita Ligure, near Genoa, celebrates a Spring Festival. On the beach, one can enjoy crepes with fish, herbs, honey, and apples. In Camogli, on the weekend around May 13, a big fish feast is held during which tons of fish are deep-fried in huge frying pans. On August 14, Lavagna celebrates a popular event called "La Torta

Above: An old olive press in the Oil Museum of Toirano. It used to produce cloudy and fruity oil.

Above: May singing in Varese Ligure. During the traditional performance of old songs, no one would think that the local people are usually quiet and reserved.

Left: During the Fish Feast, tons of fish are deep-fried. The frying pans have a diameter of 16 feet and are called padellone.

dei Fieschi," during which a huge cake distributed to all attendees is served in remembrance of a noble wedding party from 700 years ago. In Belstrino (Province of Savona), 17 different varieties of olives are grown. Locally this is enough reason for a March celebration with tastings and quality awards for the best olives and oils, and everyone is invited to sample them. Massa on the Tuscany coast annually celebrates a Vintage Event in August during which typical wine from Candia is offered. This is a wine that is produced regionally in only limited quantities. In the Maremma, during the second weekend of October, a *butteri* rodeo is held. During the event, which is highly publicized for incoming visitors, cowherders ride bulls. It takes a great deal of skill to ride the wild animals with huge horns and lead them to the *marcatura*, a branding ritual.

The Wines

Ligurians usually drink their own wines, the *nostralini* ("our small wines"). They are country wines, scratched out of terraces located on steep cliffs. Many vineyards are now abandoned, but wine production is still practiced in villages; grapes bought in Tuscany, Piedmont, and southern Italy are used to make home wines.

A common simple wine is the *Barbarossa Ligure*, a rosé that is light red in color, light, and dry. The white wines from Cinqueterre are popular; they are straw yellow with green highlights, dry, with a slightly bitter aroma. They are suited for fish and shellfish. They should all be consumed while young, although sometimes, good vintages can be consumed later. *Sciacchetrà,* a heavy dessert wine, also comes from this region. *Pigato*, made from the same type of grapes, is a pale yellow, dry white wine that is refreshing though fairly heavy.

Vermentino, named after the grape variety, is a light yellow white wine. Also marketed as

Above: Ligurian vineyards are often steep and hard to reach, such as this one in Cinqueterre.

Coronata, it is dry, refreshing, almost sparkling, and suitable for fish and such appetizers as *frutti di mare.*

Rossese Dolceacqua, according to legend, was Napoleon's favorite wine. This red wine has body but is not heavy, has a lot of character with a delicate, almost peppery aftertaste, and a light aroma of strawberries and roses. It is suitable for white and dark meats, poultry, and

roasts; it is also good if stored for a few years.

The wines of Tuscany are less renowned; however, they include several varieties that are worth trying. One is *Montescudaio,* named after the city and the eastern region of Cecina. As a white wine, it is pleasantly dry, straw yellow, mostly made with Tuscan Trebbiano grapes. The red wine is intensely red, mellow, and fruity with a dry, slightly tannic aftertaste. *Morellino di Scansano* has a ruby red color that tends to turn garnet red when older and has a bouquet that becomes more interesting with age. It is robust, full – bodied, and slightly acidic. It can also be kept for more than eight years, especial-

ly if, after two years of maturity, it is labeled Riserva. As recently as 1982 *Bolgheri* was entered among the wines with DOC (recognized zones of origins). The original vineyard region is located in the province of Livorno.

Rosato (rosé) is dry, balanced, and best served chilled with appetizers, seafood, and fish. *Parrina*, from the northeastern region of Orbetello, is available as red and white wine. The white wine is dry with a delicate aroma of almonds and should be consumed young; the red is smooth, balanced, and keeps

Above: Creative farmers make their work easier with a type of elevator.

well. *Bianco di Pitigliano,* from the area of Pitigliano, is made with four white grape varieties. It is dry and slightly bitter, and is perfect for fish. Red and white wines from the Isle of Elba should also be mentioned. The white wines are pale yellow with a delicate aroma and should be served while they are young. The red wines tolerate only medium-length storage times; they are dry, light, and aromatic.

Wines of this region: from left Pigato (Ramoino), Vermentino, Bolgheri Rosato (Scalabrone), Cinqueterre, Rossese Dolceacqua, Morellino di Scansano.

Regional Recipes

Torta pasqualina
Savory Easter Pie (Liguria)

Serves 8

<u>For the dough:</u>
4 cups all – purpose flour +
   enough flour to roll out the
   dough
2 tablespoons olive oil +
   enough oil to brush the
   baking pan
Salt

<u>For the filling:</u>
2 pounds leaf spinach
1 to 2 teaspoons marjoram
   (either fresh or dried)
1 stale roll
3 ounces or 1 1/3 cups freshly
   grated Parmesan cheese
1/2 cup milk
1 pound or about 2 cups ricotta
   cheese (you may substitute
   drained cottage cheese)
2 ounces or 3 tablespoons
   butter
8 small eggs
Salt and pepper

<u>Approximate preparation time:</u>
   3 hours;
   620 calories per serving.

Let's confess, this extraordinary specialty pie from Genoa, prepared lovingly once a year at Easter time, takes some time to make. In the past, no fewer than 33 layers of thin crispy dough, representing the 33 years of Jesus's life, were mandatory for this dish. Today, this pie is prepared with less work and meticulousness. One easy trick that is acceptable is the use of frozen and thawed philo dough.

A favorite variation in Italy is made with separate layers of ricotta cheese and cooked vegetables instead of mixing the cheese with the vegetables.

Very important: Do not serve this pie directly from the refrigerator; this dish tastes best if it is slightly warm.

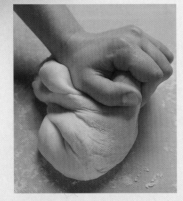

1 For the dough: on a clean surface combine 4 cups flour with a pinch of salt, mix the olive oil and enough water (about 1 cup) to make a smooth, silky dough. Knead about 10 minutes. Cut the dough into 12 even portions, shape into small rolls, and set aside on a well – floured surface. Cover with a slightly moist dishcloth and let rest for about 1 hour.

2 For the filling, trim and clean the spinach leaves. Salt and cook the rinsed and drained spinach in a large pot. Set the cooked spinach aside to cool and drain. Squeeze it to remove excess moisture before using it. Chop it, season it with pepper and more salt, if necessary, and flavor it with the marjoram.

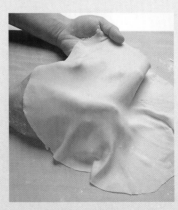

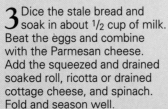

3 Dice the stale bread and soak in about 1/2 cup of milk. Beat the eggs and combine with the Parmesan cheese. Add the squeezed and drained soaked roll, ricotta or drained cottage cheese, and spinach. Fold and season well.

4 On the work surface, roll out the dough as thin as possible. The dough should be very thin. If necessary, finish pulling it by hand to make a very thin sheet, as if it were a sheet of philo dough.

5 Brush a round baking pan (10-inch diameter) with oil and position the thin dough so that it overlaps the rim of the pan by 1/2 inch. Brush the dough with oil. Repeat this procedure with 5 additional layers of dough, laying each on top of the other. Brush each layer of dough, except the last one, with oil.

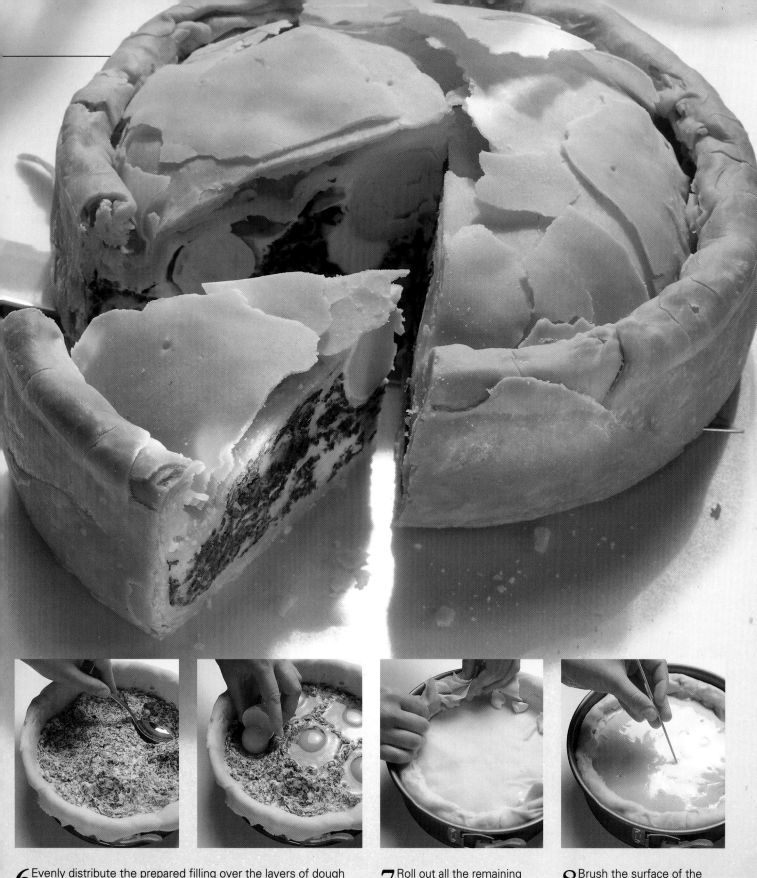

6 Evenly distribute the prepared filling over the layers of dough and drizzle with oil. With the back of a large spoon, press 6 indentations at even distances throughout the filling. Add a pat of butter in each indentation. Without breaking the egg yolk, gently break one egg into each indentation. Season each raw egg with salt and pepper, and cover with the remaining cheese. Preheat the oven to 400°F.

7 Roll out all the remaining dough rolls, again very thinly. Place them as before in the baking pan and brush them with oil. Line each edge with pats of butter. Roll and press inward the overlapping edges of dough along the rim of the pan.

8 Brush the surface of the final layer of dough with oil. Carefully pierce it with either a cake tester or toothpick (do not pierce the eggs underneath!) to let the steam out during baking. Bake in the preheated oven for about 75 minutes or until golden brown. Serve warm or at room temperature.

Sardenaira
Tangy Sheet Cake with Anchovies (Liguria)

Serves 8 to 10

For the dough:
4 cups all – purpose flour
1 ounce fresh compressed
   yeast (or 2 1/4 ounce
   package active dry yeast or
   about 5 teaspoons active
   dry bulk yeast)
4 tablespoons milk
4 tablespoons olive oil plus
   enough to brush the pan
Salt

For the topping:
2 pounds fresh ripe tomatoes
1 to 2 teaspoons oregano
   (fresh or dried)
Fresh stemless basil leaves
2 white onions, chopped
3 1/2 ounces black olives
3 1/2 ounces canned anchovy
   fillets, drained and minced
3 cloves of garlic, sliced
6 tablespoons olive oil

Approximate preparation time:
   2 hours;
   310 calories per serving.

1 Dough: Prepare a well with the flour. Add the fresh yeast (or active dry yeast) dissolved in the lukewarm milk. Work into the dough 1/2 teaspoon salt, olive oil, and 7 tablespoons of lukewarm water; knead until you obtain a smooth, silky dough. Cover with a dishcloth and let rise for 1 hour.

2 Topping: Blanch tomatoes for 15 seconds in boiling water; peel, and chop. In a medium saucepan, sauté the onions in the hot olive oil. Add the tomatoes and anchovies. Simmer until the liquid evaporates. Preheat the oven to 350°F.

3 Brush a baking sheet with oil. Stretch the dough until it fits into the pan. Top with the tomatoes. Distribute the garlic, black olives, and oregano over the layer of tomatoes. Bake 45 minutes. Top with the chopped basil before serving.

Focaccia al formaggio
Cheese Focaccia (Flat Cheese Bread) (Liguria)

Serves 6

9 ounces fresh goat cheese
   (you may substitute soft,
   fresh blue cheese)
7 ounces or 1 1/2 cups bread
   flour
Approx. 1/3 cup + 2 tablespoons
   pure olive oil
1/2 teaspoon salt

Approximate preparation time:
   1 1/2 hours;
   360 calories per serving.

1 Dough: Knead the dough with the flour and 1/4 cup + 1 tablespoon of olive oil. Add enough cold water to obtain a smooth, silky ball. When the dough is ready, wrap it in plastic wrap and set it aside to rest for 1 hour.

2 Knead the dough for a few minutes; cut it into 2 portions, and set it aside again to rest for 5 minutes. With a rolling pin, roll one portion of the dough into a thin sheet. Preheat the oven to the highest possible temperature.

3 Line a large rimmed pizza pan with the dough sheet (in Liguria, homemakers use pans that are used in wood-burning ovens and that are 20 inches in diameter). You may substitute a rimmed baking sheet for the large Ligurian pan.

4 Crumble the goat cheese and distribute it evenly over the sheet of dough in the pan. Cover the sheet with the second portion of dough rolled out like the first one. Pinch the two dough sheets together along the rim of the baking pan. Lightly press indentations on the upper sheet of the focaccia. Sprinkle it with salt and drizzle the remaining olive oil over it. Brush the oil evenly over the whole surface of the focaccia. Bake for 10 minutes in the preheated oven.

Torta di biete e carciofi
Swiss Chard and Artichoke Pie (Liguria)

• This Ligurian specialty is called *formaggetta*. If you cannot find goat cheese, you may use fresh blue cheese; however, whatever cheese you use, make sure it is very fresh.

• The ideal way to bake this specialty is in a wood-burning stone oven. At home, make sure that the door of your residential electric or gas oven is kept closed until the end of the baking process.

Serves 8 to 10

For the dough:
4 cups all-purpose flour + enough flour to roll it out
4 tablespoons olive oil
Salt

For the filling:
2 pounds fresh Swiss chard, cleaned and trimmed
12 fresh artichoke hearts (or canned, drained artichoke hearts)
1 teaspoon fresh stemless marjoram or 1/2 teaspoon dried
2 cups grated Parmesan cheese
3 tablespoons butter
5 tablespoons olive oil + enough to brush the pie crust
1 onion, chopped
3 tablespoons unseasoned breadcrumbs
Salt and freshly ground pepper

Approximate preparation time: 2 hours; 360 calories per serving.

1 Dough: Prepare a well with the flour. Add 1 teaspoon of salt, the olive oil, and 1 cup of cold water. Knead until you have obtained a smooth dough. Cover and set aside.

2 Filling: Rinse and trim the Swiss chard. Remove the thick and stringy stems. Spin the leaves dry and chop them.

3 Remove the outer leaves of the artichokes until the hearts show, and cut off the leaf tops. Remove the middle thistle. Slice artichoke hearts very thin. Heat 3 tablespoons of oil and sauté the onions and artichoke until limp (add canned artichoke hearts only at the end of the sautéing process). Add the Swiss chard and simmer briefly until it looses its fresh consistency.

4 Melt the butter in a frying pan. Toast 2 tablespoons of breadcrumbs. Add the Parme-

san cheese and breadcrumbs to the artichokes. Add 2 tablespoons of olive oil and 1 teaspoon of marjoram; mix well. Season with salt and pepper. Preheat oven to 400°F. Brush a round, 10-inch baking pan with oil.

5 Divide the dough into two portions. Roll out each portion to a thin sheet that fits the baking pan. Line the pan with one sheet. Distribute the breadcrumbs over this first sheet. Add the filling and cover with the second sheet of dough. Pinch both sheets together along the rim of the pan and overlap the dough inward if necessary.

6 Brush the piecrust with oil and pierce with a fork. Bake in oven for 55 minutes. Serve lukewarm or cold.

Ravioli alla genovese
Ravioli, Genoa Style (Liguria)

Serves 6

<u>For the dough:</u>
3 cups + 2 tablespoons
  all-purpose flour
  flour to roll out the dough
4 eggs, lightly beaten
Salt

<u>For the filling:</u>
5 ounces calf's sweetbreads
5 ounces ground veal
3 1/2 ounces mild ground
  sausage
7 ounces fresh stemless Swiss
  chard leaves
5 ounces fresh parsley and
  basil leaves
3 tablespoons grated Parmesan
1/3 cup + 2 tablespoons veal
  stock
4 eggs
1 stale roll
1/2 teaspoon dried marjoram
Salt and freshly ground pepper

<u>For serving:</u>
1 tablespoon fresh stemless
  marjoram leaves
3 tablespoons butter
2/3 cup grated Parmesan

<u>Approximate preparation time:</u>
  70 minutes;
  570 calories per serving.

Pasta lovers never fail to mention Ligurian ravioli when they speak about pasta specialties. This dish has been famous since the Middle Ages. The most refined variations, according to original recipes, include a selection of meat varieties and delicate veal added to a combination of fresh aromatic herbs, which grow in abundance throughout the coastal area.

This version has been simplified to a more modern cooking style; however, in case you make larger quantities of these ravioli, you might find it worthwhile to add other variety meats such as calf's brains and kidney.

1 For the dough: make a well and, one at a time, add the 4 beaten eggs and salt to the well. Drawing the flour around the center, knead until you obtain smooth and springy ball-shaped dough. Set aside to rest under a clean, moist dishcloth.

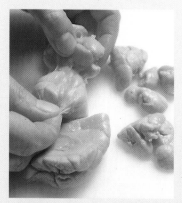

2 Filling: Wash the Swiss chard, parsley, and basil leaves thoroughly. Blanch them in boiling salted water for 3 minutes. Remove the leaves with a slotted spoon and rinse them in cold water. Drain them well and, when cool enough to handle, squeeze them to remove excess moisture. Chop them and set them aside.

3 Blanch the variety meats in boiling salted water for 5 minutes in a large pot and dip them into iced water. Remove the skins and the membranes, and mince. Add to the greens.

4 Grate the stale roll to make breadcrumbs. Soak these in the veal stock.

5 Add the ground veal and sausage meat to the vegetables. Add the 2 eggs, breadcrumbs, and Parmesan cheese, and mix well. Season with salt, pepper, and dried marjoram.

6 On the floured work surface, cut the dough into two portions. Roll out each portion of dough to a thin sheet (about $1/16$ inch). With a pastry wheel, cut each sheet of dough in 2-inch-wide strips. On half of the wide pasta strips, spacing the filling about $1–1\ 1/2$ inches apart, place small portions of filling (no larger than a teaspoon). Lay a second layer of pasta over those strips with the filling and cut out the ravioli. With your fingers, press the borders of the ravioli to seal them.

7 In a pot, cook the ravioli in boiling salted water for 3 to 4 minutes; remove and drain well. Serve topped with melted butter, fresh marjoram leaves, and grated Parmesan cheese. If you wish, you may add marjoram-flavored butter.

Trenette col pesto
Flat Pasta with Basil Sauce (Liguria)

Serves 4

1 large bunch of fresh basil
3 tablespoons romano or
    Parmesan cheese
2 tablespoons pine nuts
1 pound trenette (Ligurian flat
    noodles) or linguine
3 cloves of garlic, minced
1 cup olive oil
Salt

<u>*Approximate preparation time:*</u>
    30 minutes;
    710 calories per serving.

1 Pesto: Wipe the basil leaves clean, but do not wash. In a small frying pan, roast pine nuts until lightly golden. Combine the basil, pine nuts, garlic, and salt in a mortar and pestle or mixer and purée until they form a paste.

2 In a medium-size bowl, combine the basil paste with 1 cup olive oil and romano or Parmesan cheese. Fold oil into the mixture until you get a smooth cream.

3 In a large pot, bring 1 gallon of salted water to a boil, and cook the trenette until they are *al dente* (still firm). Add 2 to 3 tablespoons of the trenette water to the pesto.

4 Drain the trenette. Place the noodles together with ³/₄ of the pesto in a warm serving bowl. Fold the pesto into the noodles and top them with the remaining sauce.

• Trenette are long, narrow, flat noodles that are very similar to linguine and that are so called only in Liguria. And pesto? The most remarkable sauce combination made with fresh basil, garlic, and olive oil!

Pansooti con salsa di noci
Pasta Triangles with Walnut Sauce (Liguria)

Serves 4

3 ¹/₂ ounces fresh stemless borage
    leaves (or Swiss chard)
5 ounces fresh stemless basil
    leaves
¹/₂ cup ricotta cheese
¹/₂ cup grated Parmesan cheese
4 tablespoons half-and-half
³/₄ cup walnuts + garnish
¹/₂ cup dry white wine
1 egg, lightly beaten
2 cloves of garlic, crushed
4 tablespoons unseasoned bread-
    crumbs
2 ¹/₂ cups all-purpose flour + flour
    to roll out the dough
4 tablespoons olive oil
Salt and freshly ground pepper

<u>*Approximate preparation time:*</u>
    1 ¹/₂ hour;
    740 calories per serving.

1 Filling: Wash the herbs. Blanch them in boiling salted water for 3 minutes. Remove the leaves with a slotted spoon and rinse them in cold water. Drain them well in a colander, and when cool, squeeze to remove excess moisture. Mince them and set aside.

2 In a bowl, mix the garlic with the herbs, ricotta cheese, egg, and Parmesan cheese. Season with salt and pepper.

3 Dough: Form a dough with the flour, wine, salt, and enough water. Cover and set aside to rest for 20 minutes. Roll out the dough to a sheet ¹/₈ inch thick and cut into 2-inch wide squares.

4 On each square place a portion of filling. Brush the borders with water; fold them over to make triangles, and pinch together to seal them.

5 Sauce: Drop the walnuts into boiling water in a saucepan. Remove them with a slotted spoon and peel them by hand. Soak the breadcrumbs in water, drain, and squeeze them dry. In the mortar, with the pestle, make a paste the walnuts and salt (or mince them in a food processor). Pass the paste

Trofie con salsa di funghi
Spiral-shaped Dumplings with Wild Mushroom Sauce (Liguria)

through a fine strainer and add olive oil and half-and-half.

6 In a pot, bring salted water to a boil. Cook pansooti about 15 minutes. Remove them with a slotted spoon, drain them well, and mix them with the sauce. Serve them hot, topped with the remaining Parmesan cheese. You may garnish the dish with whole walnut halves.

• The remarkable flavor of this dish is due to its dough, prepared with wine. The flavor of the herbs and minced walnuts make it unique and wonderful.

Serves 4

7 ounces fresh porcini or cepes mushrooms (or 1/2 to 1 ounce or 3/4 cup dried, soaked in water for 2 hours, drained)
14 ounces fresh ripe tomatoes
2 ounces or 2/3 cup grated Parmesan cheese
2 tablespoons tomato paste
1 small onion, minced
1 clove garlic, minced
2 1/2 cups + 2 tablespoons all-purpose flour
3/4 cup wheat bran
3 tablespoons olive oil
1 ounce or 2 tablespoons butter
Salt and freshly ground pepper

<u>*Approximate preparation time:*</u>
80 minutes;
520 calories per serving.

1 Dough: Make a dough with the flour, wheat bran, 1/2 tablespoon salt, and approximately 1 cup of lukewarm water. Cover with a moist dishcloth; set aside to rest for 20 minutes.

2 Sauce: Wipe and clean the mushrooms thoroughly. Slice thin. Drop tomatoes in boiling water in a large pot; remove them with a slotted spoon. When they are cold enough to handle, peel them, seed them, and dice them.

3 In a medium saucepan heat the olive oil, and add the onion, garlic, tomatoes and tomato paste. Season with salt and pepper. Sauté until all ingredients are limp. Add the mushrooms and let simmer while covered.

4 Tear small pieces from the dough and shape them like short, 2-inch-long pieces of rope. With a thick knitting needle, shape the dough into twisted spiral-shaped curls. Set the dumplings aside to dry.

5 In a large pot, bring 1 gallon of salted water to a boil. Gradually drop the twisted

dumplings into the water. Let them cook until they rise to the water's surface. Remove them with a slotted spoon, drain them well, and place them in a large warm serving bowl.

Add the butter, melted, half of the grated Parmesan cheese and the mushroom sauce, which, if necessary, can be diluted with some of the pasta water. Top the dumplings with the remaining Parmesan cheese.

• Trofie are a type of *gnocchi*, which can be found only in the region of Genoa. The regional dumplings are usually served with pesto, but here they are prepared as a variation with vegetables.

Minestrone col pesto
Hearty Vegetable Soup with Pesto (Liguria)

Serves 4 to 6

11 ounces or 1 ½ cup fresh
   borlotti beans, shelled
   (or 1 cup dried beans)
4 small potatoes
   (preferably a waxy variety)
2 carrots
2 small leeks
2 stalks of celery
2 small zucchini
1 onion
2 tomatoes
1 bunch of fresh borage (preferably with blossoms)
4 tablespoons grated Parmesan
   cheese
5 ounces or 1 cup elbow
   noodles
4 tablespoons olive oil + extra
   virgin olive oil to drizzle
2 tablespoons pesto
Salt and freshly ground pepper

<u>Approximate preparation time:</u>
*1 ½ hours (excluding time
for soaking the beans);
290 calories per serving.*

1 If you use dried beans, soak them in water overnight. Wash, peel, trim, and slice the potatoes, carrots, leeks, celery, zucchini, and onion.

2 In a large pot, bring ¾ of a gallon of salted water to a boil. Add the vegetables and beans. (If you use dried beans, cook them first separately for about 15 minutes before adding them to the other vegetables.) Add the olive oil, mix, and cover. Simmer for about 30 minutes.

3 Bring the water to a boil in a second large pot, drop the tomatoes into the boiling water, remove them with a slotted spoon, and when they are cool enough to handle, peel them. Seed and dice the peeled tomatoes. Thoroughly wash the fresh borage, drain it, and chop it. After the soup has been simmering for at least 30 minutes, add the borage and the toma-toes and allow the soup to simmer for 15 more minutes. Shortly before serving, add the elbow noodles to the soup.

4 Mix the pesto in a ladle filled with soup, then add the mixture to the soup and serve immediately. At the table, drizzle with the extra virgin olive oil, and top with Parmesan cheese. Garnish with open borage blossoms if you have any.

• You may substitute borlotti beans with either white Great Northern, pinto, or pink beans.

Pesto—a Green Delicacy

Ligurians are familiar with three basic uses for pesto: as a floating island in minestrone, and as sauces for *trenette* and for *trofie*, the twisted dumplings that are a Ligurian version of *gnocchi*. Pesto was named for the verb *pestare*, which means to mince and crush with the mortar and pestle. The classic recipe calls for two types of cheeses: Parmesan, and freshly grated, sharp pecorino cheese. Tip: While fresh basil is in season, prepare a larger batch of pesto for later use. If you don't use it sooner (is this possible?), you can keep pesto frozen until next season!

Zuppa di cozze
Mussel Chowder (Liguria)

Serves 4

4 pounds fresh mussels
1 whole, unpeeled lemon
1 bunch of fresh Italian parsley
2 cloves garlic
3 tablespoons olive oil
3/4 cup dry white wine
1/2 cup clear stock
1 tablespoon butter
1 tablespoon all – purpose flour
8 small slices plain white bread
Salt

Approximate preparation time:
*   45 minutes;*
*   450 calories per serving.*

1 Clean and thoroughly brush the mussels under running water. Discard those mussels that stay open when tapped with your finger.

2 In a large pot, heat the olive oil and press the cloves of garlic over it. Mince the fresh parsley and sauté half of it with the garlic.

3 Add the rinsed and cleaned mussels and simmer until all remain open (about 5 minutes). Pour the clear stock and white wine over them, and season with salt. Let simmer 10 more minutes.

4 Mix the butter with the flour to make a paste; whisk this mixture into the clear stock. Season the mussel liquid. Cut the lemon into eight pieces. Toast small slices of bread. Place the open mussels in serving bowls, drizzle them with the mussel liquid from the pan, and top with the remaining fresh minced parsley. Serve with the lemon wedges and toasted bread slices.

• Variation: Shortly before serving, you can add 1 pound of peeled and pureed ripe tomatoes to the mussel liquid in the pan. Bring the final liquid to a rapid boil and drizzle this over the mussels.

Zuppa alla genovese
Soup with Herbed Pancake Strips, Genoa Style (Liguria)

Serves 4

1 head of Belgian endive
*   (about 2 to 4 ounces)*
1 mixed bunch of fresh herbs
*   (basil, chives, parsley,*
*   borage, and thyme), minced*
1 teaspoon lemon juice
3 tablespoons grated Parmesan
*   cheese*
3 eggs, lightly beaten
1 small onion, minced
3 tablespoons olive oil
4 cups clear meat stock
Salt and freshly ground pepper
Nutmeg

Approximate preparation time:
*   45 minutes;*
*   230 calories per serving.*

1 Trim and thoroughly wash the endive and blanch in boiling salted water in a large saucepan for 2 minutes. Remove with a slotted spoon and rinse in cold water to stop it from cooking. Drain well in a colander.

2 In a large frying pan, heat the oil, and sauté the herbs and the onion until limp. Squeeze the endive to remove excess moisture, and slice thin. Add 3/4 of the endive to the onion and herbs, and simmer for about 10 minutes. Season with 1 teaspoon of lemon juice and salt, pepper, and nutmeg.

3 Whisk together the eggs and Parmesan cheese. Pour the mixture over the vegetables. Carefully fold in all the ingredients, and cook until a type of pancake has formed. Remove from the pan and let cool. Bring the meat stock to a boil.

4 Cut the pancake into thin strips and add, with the remaining endive, to the boiling stock. Briefly simmer and serve.

• If fresh borage is available, use this in the soup instead of endive!

Cacciucco alla livornese
Seafood Chowder, Leghorn (Livorno) Style (Tuscany)

Serves 6

3 pounds fresh mixed fish
(such as flounder, rockfish,
mullet, cod, halibut, and
mackerel)
1/2 pound squid
1 pound mussels
2 celery stalks
1 1/ pound fresh,
ripe tomatoes
1 bunch fresh Italian parsley,
washed thoroughly
1 carrot
1 large onion
5 cloves garlic
1 cup dry white wine
1/3 cup + 2 tablespoons olive oil
Fresh white bread, sliced
Salt and pepper

<u>Approximate preparation time:</u>
1 3/4 hours;
500 calories per serving.

The extraordinary selection of
fish and shellfish is the secret
of this specialty and will contribute to the unique flavor of
the dish. Try any selection of
fish and crustaceans that are
available at your market; the
aroma here will always be determined by the selection you
decide to use.

Tip: With this specialty, take
advantage of the special fish
offers from your market!

During this cooking process,
pay close attention to the type
of fish and shellfish you use; to
prevent their overcooking and
falling apart, add the delicate
types of fish at the end and
simmer them only briefly.

• Wine serving suggestion: dry
white wine, such as *Bianco di
Pitigliano* or white wine from
Cinqueterre.

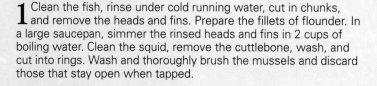

1 Clean the fish, rinse under cold running water, cut in chunks,
and remove the heads and fins. Prepare the fillets of flounder. In
a large saucepan, simmer the rinsed heads and fins in 2 cups of
boiling water. Clean the squid, remove the cuttlebone, wash, and
cut into rings. Wash and thoroughly brush the mussels and discard
those that stay open when tapped.

2 Chop the celery, carrot, 1/2
onion, and 2 cloves of garlic,
and add to the simmering
heads and fins of fish. Add 1/2
tablespoon to the fish stock
and let simmer 30 minutes.
When the stock is ready, drain
it through a fine strainer, and
keep the liquid.

3 Heat 6 tablespoons of olive oil. Add the remaining ¹/₂ onion and minced garlic. Add the squid. Blanch the tomatoes and when they are cool, peel them and dice them. Simmer tomatoes with wine for 15 minutes. Season with salt and pepper.

4 To the tomato mixture, add first the firmer types of fish (rockfish, billfish, cod, halibut, or mackerel), then half of the fish stock, and let simmer gently for 10 minutes.

5 Finally, add the mussels, mullet, and flounder, and the remaining fish stock. Simmer 10 to 15 minutes more. Mince the fresh parsley and add to the chowder. Season with salt and pepper.

6 Toast the slices of white bread and rub them with the remaining cloves of garlic. Drizzle these with the remaining olive oil. Serve with the fish chowder.

Stoccafisso
Codfish Stew (Liguria)

Serves 4

1 to 1 1/2 pounds dried codfish
1 pound fresh ripe tomatoes
1 celery stalk, minced
1 carrot, minced
2 medium potatoes
1/2 bunch fresh Italian parsley
1/2 bunch fresh basil
3 tablespoons pine nuts
1 small onion, minced
2 cloves garlic, minced
5 tablespoons olive oil
About 4 cups vegetable stock
Salt and freshly ground pepper

Approximate preparation time:
    2 1/4 hours;
    760 calories per serving.

1 Soak dried cod overnight, or for 24 hours; change the water twice while soaking. Thoroughly clean and rinse the soaked fish. Remove the skin and all the membranes, and debone it. Cut it into bite-size chunks.

2 Bring the water to a boil in a large pot, drop the tomatoes into the boiling water, remove them with a slotted spoon, and when they are cool enough to handle, peel them. Seed and dice the peeled tomatoes.

3 Heat the olive oil in a large saucepan. Sauté the celery, carrot, onion, and garlic until limp. Add the codfish and cook until all sides are golden brown and sealed. Add the tomatoes, and stock, and season with salt (not too much!) and freshly ground pepper. Simmer, covered, for about 1 hour.

4 Peel and dice the potatoes. After cooking for 1 hour, add the potatoes to the fish and let everything simmer for 30 minutes. Season the stew and top it with parsley, basil, and pine nuts.

Sarde in marinara
Marinated Sardines (Liguria/Tuscany)

Serves 4

1 1/2 pound fresh sardines (or
*   smelts or whitefish)*
1 lemon
1/2 bunch fresh Italian parsley
1/2 bunch fresh basil
2 cloves garlic, minced
1 small onion, minced
1 bay leaf
1 teaspoon dried rosemary
1/2 cup dry white wine
1/2 cup white wine vinegar
2 tablespoons all-purpose flour
5 tablespoons olive oil
Salt and pepper

Approximate preparation time:
    25 minutes;
    380 calories per serving.

1 Thoroughly clean and wash the fresh sardines (or smelts) and cut off their heads. With a paper towel, pat the sardines dry, drizzle with the juice of 1/2 lemon, and dust them on both sides with the flour. In a large frying pan, heat the olive oil and fry the fish for about 2 minutes on both sides.

2 Marinade: Place the garlic and onion in a medium saucepan, together with the white wine, the white wine vinegar, bay leaf, dried rosemary, and 1/2 tablespoon of salt. Bring to a boil and cook for 2 minutes. Mince the parsley, and cut the basil leaves in strips. Remove from the heat, add the fresh herbs, and season with pepper.

3 Slice thin the remaining 1/2 lemon. With a slotted spoon, remove the sardines, place them in layers, together with the lemon slices, in a suitable container. Pour the marinade liquid over them, cover, and set aside for later use.

• You may use this dish also as a warm or cold appetizer for 6 to 8 people.

Moscardini alla genovese
Stewed Squid, Genoa Style (Liguria)

Triglie alla livornese
Red Mullet, Livorno Style (Tuscany)

Serves 6

2 pounds squid
³/₄ cup dried mushrooms
1 to 1 ¹/₂ pounds fresh, ripe
  tomatoes
1 bunch fresh parsley
¹/₂ bunch fresh basil
1 cup dry white wine
¹/₂ cup fish stock
2 onions, minced
3 cloves garlic, minced
4 tablespoons olive oil
Salt and freshly ground pepper

<u>*Approximate preparation time:*</u>
  1 ¹/₂ hours;
  230 calories per serving.

1 In a small mixing bowl, soak the dried mushrooms in the white wine. Thoroughly clean and rinse the squid. Remove the membranes, cuttlebones, ink sacs, and eyes, and cut the tentacles from the mantle. Cut into wide rings.

2 Bring water to a boil in a pot. Blanch the tomatoes, re-move them with a slotted spoon, and when they are cool enough, peel them. Seed and dice them.

3 In a large frying pan heat the olive oil. Sauté the onions and garlic until limp. Squeeze and drain the mushrooms to re-move excess moisture, setting aside the remaining liquid. Chop the mushrooms and sauté them briefly. Add the tomatoes and mushroom liquid. Season with salt and pepper. Simmer for 10 more minutes, stirring occasion-ally as necessary.

4 Add the squid and cook, cov-ered, for about 50 minutes. Occasionally stir in some fish stock.

5 Mince the parsley, and cut the basil leaves into thin strips. Season the squid and add the fresh herbs.

• Serve with toasted garlic bread.

Serves 4

8 small mullets
1 pound fresh, ripe tomatoes
2 celery stalks, minced
¹/₂ bunch fresh Italian parsley
3 cloves garlic, minced
5 tablespoons olive oil
2 to 3 tablespoons all-purpose
  flour
Salt and freshly ground pepper

<u>*Approximate preparation time:*</u>
  40 minutes;
  360 calories per serving.

1 For the sauce, bring water to a boil in a large pot, drop the tomatoes into the boiling water, remove them with a slotted spoon, and when they are cool enough to handle, peel them. Seed and dice the peeled toma-toes. In a large saucepan, heat 2 tablespoons of olive oil and sauté the celery and garlic. Add the tomatoes, season with salt and pepper, and simmer for about 15 minutes. If necessary, moisten with more water.

2 Thoroughly clean and rinse the mullets. Pat the fish dry with a paper towel. Dust with the flour. In a large frying pan, heat 3 tablespoons of olive oil and fry the mullets for 1 minute on both sides.

3 Remove the tomato sauce from the saucepan and, when it is cool enough to han-dle, pass it through a fine strainer. Return the sauce to the saucepan and add the fried mullets. Let simmer for about 5 minutes. Season to taste. Serve topped with fresh stem-less parsley leaves.

• Mullets do not have bladders; therefore, especially in the case of small mullets, they don't need to be emptied like other fish varieties while you rinse them.

Cima ripiena alla genovese
Stuffed Breast of Veal, Genoa Style (Liguria)

Serves 6 to 8

1 whole deboned breast of veal
  (2 to 2 1/2 pounds)
6 ounces calf's brains
6 ounces ground veal
1 ounce or 1 cup dried
  mushrooms
2 to 3 ounces or 3/4 cup fresh
  shelled or frozen peas
1 medium carrot, chopped
1/2 bunch fresh Italian parsley,
  minced
1 teaspoon fresh, stemless
  marjoram leaves
1/2 tablespoon dried
  marjoram
2 tablespoons pine nuts or
  shelled pistachio nuts
3 tablespoons grated Parmesan
  cheese
3 eggs
1 ounce or 2 tablespoons butter
2 cloves garlic, minced
8 cups vegetable stock
Salt and freshly ground pepper
Nutmeg

Approximate preparation time:
  3 hours;
  400 calories per serving.

The preparation of this dish is
open to culinary creativity; in
Italy, for example, another variation of this dish is prepared
with ground pork and bacon,
chopped spinach leaves,
onions, and mixed herbs, and
sometimes, with the addition of
hard-boiled eggs.

This dish is usually served cold
and thinly sliced. The resulting
broth is either served on the
side or used for other purposes
(for example, for preparing
risotto). In order to obtain clean-
ly cut slices without shredding,
you may want to cover the
meat with a large heavy platter.

It is, of course, obvious that
this breast of veal is also delicious warm and sliced thick, at
least the variation without the
hard-boiled eggs.

• Wine serving suggestion:
Rosé or light red wine.

1 In a small bowl, soak 1
ounce or 1 cup of dry mushrooms in water. On a flat cutting
board, slice a large horizontal
pocket with a sharp and pointed
knife into the piece of meat (or
ask your butcher to prepare the
breast of veal for stuffing).
Rinse the meat thoroughly and
pat dry with paper towels.

2 Blanch the calf's brains in
salted boiling water in a
large pot for 5 minutes. Remove the cooked brains with a
slotted spoon and dip in iced
water to stop from cooking.
Carefully peel the membranes,
remove the vessels, and dice
the cooked lobes.

3 Heat the butter in a large
frying pan, and lightly stir-fry
the brains. Remove from the
pan and place in a large mixing
bowl.

4 Drain and chop the mushrooms, setting aside the mushroom liquid. Add garlic, parsley, and carrot to the brains in the mixing bowl.

5 Add the ground veal, peas, pine nuts or shelled pistachio nuts, and 1 teaspoon of marjoram. Mix well. Whisk the eggs together with the Parmesan cheese. Season with salt, pepper, and fresh grated nutmeg.

6 Stuff the breast of veal with only two-thirds of the mixture since the mixture will expand in the meat pocket during cooking time. With a trussing needle and string, sew the ends of the meat pocket together. In the meantime, heat the vegetable stock with the mushroom water in a large pot.

7 Lower the breast of veal into the hot stock shortly before the boiling point. Simmer, covered, for at least 2 hours. Remove from the heat, but keep the meat in the stock for 30 minutes. Remove the meat. When it is cold, slice and serve.

33

Spezzatino con zucchine
Stewed Veal with Zucchini (Liguria)

Serves 6

1 1/2 pounds veal meat for
  stewing (shoulder or breast)
2 celery stalks
1 carrot
1 pound potatoes (preferably
  waxy)
9 ounces fresh, ripe tomatoes
9 ounces fresh, small zucchini
1 teaspoon fresh stemless
  rosemary leaves
1 onion
2 cloves garlic
5 tablespoons olive oil
1/2 cup dry white wine
About 1/2 cup hot clear stock
 Salt and freshly ground pepper

Approximate preparation time:
  1 hour;
  330 calories per serving.

1 Dice the veal. Mince the celery, carrot, and garlic. Peel
and dice the potatoes.

2 In a large pot, heat the olive
oil. Gradually add the meat,
and brown evenly. Add the vegetables and cook with the meat.
Moisten with the white wine
and hot stock. Add the rosemary and potatoes. Cover and
cook.

3 Bring some water to a boil in
a separate large pot. Drop
the tomatoes into the boiling
water, remove them with a slotted spoon, and when they are
cool enough to handle, peel
them. Seed and dice the peeled
tomatoes, and add them to the
stew. Season with salt and pepper. Simmer for about 20 minutes, or until potatoes are done.

4 Wash and trim the zucchini.
Slice them into 1/4-inch-thick
rounds. Add them to the stew,
and cook for 10 more minutes.

• A summertime specialty that
can be prepared creatively with
many varieties of fresh mixed
vegetables.

Bollito freddo
Cold, Boiled Beef (Liguria)

Serves 4

12 ounces cooked lean beef
  (you may use a leftover piece
  of a larger portion of boiled
  beef)
1/2 bunch fresh Italian parsley
4 to 5 tablespoons dry white
  wine
4 canned anchovy fillets, drained
2 tablespoons capers
2 stale rolls
6 tablespoons extra virgin
  olive oil
3 tablespoons wine vinegar
Salt and freshly ground pepper

Approximate preparation time:
  20 minutes;
  430 calories per serving.

1 Slice the rolls and place them
on a platter; drizzle them with
the white wine.

2 Rinse the anchovy fillets under running water, pat them
dry with a paper towel, and slice
them in half lengthwise.

3 Thinly slice the cooked lean
beef and place on the bread
slices. Top the meat and bread
with the anchovies. Refrigerate
for later use.

4 Mince the capers and cream
with the olive oil, wine vinegar, a pinch of salt, and freshly
ground pepper. Mince the parsley
and add to caper-cream mixture.
Spread over meat and bread.

Coniglio in umido
Stewed Rabbit (Liguria)

Vitello all'uccelletto
Braised Veal with White Wine and Green Olives (Liguria)

Serves 6

1 ready-to-use rabbit
    (about 3 pounds)
1 pound fresh, ripe tomatoes
1/2 bunch fresh Italian parsley
1 teaspoon fresh stemless
    rosemary leaves or 1/2 table-
    spoon dried rosemary
3 sage leaves
2 tablespoons pine nuts
1/2 to 1 cup dry white wine
4 tablespoons olive oil
2 tablespoons butter
2 cloves garlic, sliced thin
2 bay leaves
Salt and freshly ground pepper
Nutmeg

<u>Approximate preparation time:</u>
    1 1/4 hours;
    520 calories per serving.

1 Cut the rabbit into 8 to 10 pieces, rinse under running water, and pat dry with paper towels.

2 In a large Dutch oven or casserole, heat the sliced garlic together with the olive oil, butter, rosemary, sage leaves, and bay leaves.

3 Add the rabbit pieces, and brown on each side. Season with salt, pepper, and nutmeg. Moisten with the white wine, bring to a rapid boil, reduce the heat, and let simmer.

4 In a large pot, bring some water to a boil, drop the tomatoes into the boiling water, remove them with a slotted spoon, and when they are cool enough to handle them, peel them. Seed and dice the peeled tomatoes, and add to the rabbit. Simmer covered for 45 minutes. If necessary, occasionally moisten with additional wine. Serve topped with pine nuts and fresh stemless parsley leaves.

Serves 4

About 1 1/2 pounds lean veal
    (sirloin tip or loin)
3 ounces or 3/4 cup small pitted
    green olives
6 sage leaves
1/4 cup dry white wine
4 tablespoons olive oil
1 ounce or 2 tablespoons butter
1 bay leaf
Salt and freshly ground pepper

<u>Approximate preparation time:</u>
    30 minutes;
    330 calories per serving.

1 Cube the veal. Heat olive oil in a large frying pan, and add the butter, allowing it to melt. Add the sage leaves and bay leaf. Heat.

2 Raise the heat, gradually add each piece of meat, and brown well, stirring constantly.

3 Season with salt and pepper, moisten with the white wine, and simmer 10 minutes. Add the pitted green olives and heat them. Season with salt and pepper, and serve.

• Wine serving suggestion: Full-bodied, dry white wine, such as a *Ligurian Pigato*.

Fiori di zucchini ripieni

Stuffed Zucchini Blossoms (Liguria)

Serves 4

8 large zucchini blossoms
6 ounces zucchini or summer
   squash
2 potatoes (about 5 ounces,
   preferably baking variety)
1 bunch fresh basil
1 tablespoon fresh marjoram
   leaves (or 1/2 tablespoon
   dried)
1 tablespoon freshly grated
   Parmesan cheese
1 egg
2 cloves garlic
5 tablespoons olive oil
Salt and pepper

Approximate preparation time:
   1 hour;
   220 calories per serving.

Ligurians love vegetables, especially those that can be stuffed. No wonder, therefore, that the brightly colored large blossoms of zucchini are often prepared and served in this region. The delicate blossoms are harvested often, from spring to early fall, either singly or attached to a young, pale green piece of stem. The blossom is cut open like a fan, shortly before baking it or frying it, in order to simultaneously cook the stuffing and the blossom.

Zucchini blossoms, filled with herbs and mushrooms, ground meat, pureed vegetables, pesto, or as described here, can make a wonderful appetizer or a fine side dish. To make a small main course for 2 people, it can also be served with crispy white bread.

Tip for a quick garnish: Dress fresh, ripe, chopped tomatoes with extra virgin olive oil, salt, and pepper. Use this salsa to top the blossoms or to serve with them.

1 Remove the stems from the blossoms. Dip the blossoms in cold water, then remove, and carefully shake them, and let them drain thoroughly in a colander.

2 Cook the potatoes in salted boiling water in a large saucepan until soft. Finely chop the zucchini. In a separate saucepan, cook these for about 5 minutes, covered, with some water and a pinch of salt.

3 Drain the zucchini, and when cool enough to handle, puree and place in a mixing bowl. Peel and rice the potatoes while they are still warm. Add the potatoes to the zucchini. Mix and set aside to cool.

4 Thinly slice the basil leaves and mince the fresh stemless marjoram leaves. Add both ingredients to the potatoes and zucchini.
Crush the garlic into the mixture. Add the Parmesan cheese, egg,
and 2 tablespoons olive oil. Mix thoroughly. Season with salt and
pepper.

5 Preheat the oven to 475°F.
Brush a large baking dish
with 1 tablespoon of olive oil.
Cut and remove the inside centers of the zucchini blossoms.

6 Fill the zucchini blossoms
with the vegetable mixture
and place them side by side in
the greased baking dish. Drizzle
again with 2 tablespoons of oil
and bake about 3 minutes.
Serve hot.

Fagiolini alla genovese
Green Beans, Genoa Style (Liguria)

Serves 4

About 1 ¹/₂ pounds fresh,
*   young green beans*
1 bunch fresh Italian parsley,
*   minced*
4 canned anchovy fillets,
*   drained and minced*
2 cloves garlic, minced
4 tablespoons olive oil
1 tablespoon butter
Salt and freshly ground pepper

<u>*Approximate preparation time:*</u>
*   25 minutes;*
*   160 calories per serving.*

1 Trim and clean the green beans. Blanch them in salted boiling water in a medium saucepan for 5 minutes. With a slotted spoon, remove them and dip them in iced water to stop them from cooking. Drain them thoroughly.

2 Rinse the anchovies and, with a paper towel, pat them dry. Thoroughly wash the parsley and remove the leaves from the stems. Mince the anchovies, garlic, and parsley.

3 Heat the olive oil in a large frying pan and melt the butter. Add the anchovy mixture and briefly sauté, stirring constantly.

4 Add the drained green beans, and simmer, briefly. Season with salt and pepper, and serve.

• This is a splendid side dish for broiled meats and cutlets, such as veal cutlets or steaks, juicy lamb cutlets, grilled rabbit, or poultry.

Frittata di carciofi
Artichoke Frittata (Artichoke Omelet) (Tuscany)

Serves 4

4 young fresh artichokes
2 tablespoons lemon juice
4 eggs
2 tablespoons milk
4 tablespoons olive oil
2 tablespoons butter
1 tablespoon all-purpose flour
Salt and pepper

<u>*Approximate preparation time:*</u>
*   20 minutes;*
*   290 calories per serving.*

1 Snap off all leaves of the artichokes that are woody and cut off the points. Cut the artichokes into eighths. Scoop out the central portion of the heart. To prevent discoloration, place the artichokes in cold water mixed with lemon juice.

2 Heat the olive oil in a frying pan. Drain the artichoke wedges, pat them dry, and sprinkle them with salt and pepper. Dust them with flour on both sides, and fry them in the hot oil. Remove the artichokes and set them on paper towels Wipe the pan.

3 Beat the eggs with the milk. Season with salt and pepper. Using the same pan used for frying the artichokes, melt the butter, place the artichokes on the bottom of the pan, and pour the egg mixture over them. Fry until the bottom is golden. Carefully turn the omelet onto a large platter, then return it to the pan, and fry the other side. Serve hot.

• Omelets, called *frittata*, prepared with vegetables and fresh herbs, are often served as appetizers or cold finger foods.

Scorzonera fritta
Fried Scorzonera (Liguria)

Serves 4

*1 1/2 pounds fresh scorzonera
    (or salsify)
Juice of 1/2 lemon
1 ounce or 1/2 cup grated
    Parmesan cheese
2 tablespoons dry white wine
2 eggs
3/4 cup all-purpose flour
Enough oil for deep-frying
Salt*

*Approximate preparation time:
    45 minutes;
    430 calories per serving.*

1 Under running water, and with a potato peeler, clean, scrape thoroughly, and peel the scorzonera. Cut the peeled pieces into 1 1/2-inch-long chunks and dip them immediately into cold water mixed with the juice of 1/2 lemon. Drain, and simmer in boiling water in a large saucepan for 10 to 15 minutes or until done.

2 Separate the eggs. Combine in a medium bowl and beat the egg yolks with the flour, grated Parmesan cheese, dry white wine, and 2 tablespoons of cold water. In a separate small bowl, beat the egg whites to a stiff peak, and fold carefully into the egg batter. Pour enough oil into a deep frying pan or a fryer, and heat the oil.

3 Rinse the scorzonera thoroughly, drain, and pat dry with paper towels. Dip the scorzonera into the batter and fry in the hot oil until golden and crispy. With a slotted spoon, remove the fried scorzonera, and place them, piece by piece, on more paper towels to drain any excess oil. Serve as a side dish to meats.

• Very important during the deep-frying process: Do not use old oil and make sure the oil is sufficiently hot. How to make sure that the oil is hot? Simply dip the handle of a wooden spoon in the hot oil, and, if you see small bubbles raising to the surface, you may begin frying.

Scorzonera in umido
Stewed Scorzonera (Liguria)

Serves 4

*1 1/2 pounds fresh scorzonera (or
    salsify)
Juice of 1 lemon
1 onion, minced
1 bunch fresh Italian parsley,
    minced
4 tablespoons olive oil
1 teaspoon all-purpose flour
1 cup good stock
2 egg yolks
Salt*

*Approximate preparation time:
    45 minutes;
    290 calories per serving.*

1 Brush the scorzonera under running water. With a potato peeler, peel them, and dip immediately into cold water mixed with the juice of 1/2 lemon.

2 Wash 1/2 bunch of parsley. Mince the onion and parsley. In a large frying pan, heat the olive oil and sauté the onions and parsley, stirring periodically.

3 Drain the scorzonera and cut into thumb-size pieces. Add them to the ingredients in the pan, season with salt, and sauté for 5 minutes. Sprinkle with the flour, continue frying until they are pale brown. Moisten with the stock. Simmer 15 to 20 minutes.

4 In a bowl, mix egg yolks, remaining lemon juice, 2 tablespoons of stock, and a pinch of salt. Drop the mixture into the sauce but do not cook further. Sprinkle with the remaining parsley.

• Peeling scorzonera is a lengthy procedure. Try this alternate method: Wash and brush them and drop, unpeeled, into boiling salted water. Blanch 10 minutes. Remove from hot water, drain, dip in iced water and peel. With this method, the cooking time is obviously reduced.

Canestrelli
Almond Cookies (Liguria)

Latte dolce fritto
Fried Milk Flan (Liguria)

Yield: 60 cookies

11 ounces or about 2 1/4 cups
  blanched, peeled almonds
6 ounces or 3/4 cup + 2 tablespoons granulated sugar
5 to 6 tablespoons orange blossom water (or 2 tablespoons
  orange-flavored liqueur
  + 3 to 4 tablespoons water)
Enough oil to grease a cookie
  sheet
Commercial orange syrup
  for glazing

<u>Approximate preparation time:</u>
  *50 minutes;
  50 calories per cookie.*

1 Grind the almonds, and, in a
medium mixing bowl, com-
bine them with the sugar. Mix
thoroughly with a spoon. Add
the orange blossom water to
the mixture, until you get a
dough that is fairly smooth.

2 Preheat the oven to 300°F.
By hand, shape the dough

into small, finger-thick pieces.
Form small crescents and place
them on the cookie sheet.

3 Bake each sheet of cookies
separately, placing each on
the highest possible oven rack
position, for 15 to 20 minutes;
these cookies are so delicate
that they need more time to dry
than to bake thoroughly. When
you remove them, glaze them
with orange syrup while they
are still hot. Let them cool in
small, multicolored, petit-four-
size paper cups.

• To glaze these almond cookies, instead of using commercial orange syrup, you may use
6 to 8 tablespoons of heated orange marmalade diluted with 1
tablespoon of lemon juice.
Tip for storing: Keep these almond cookies in a well-sealed
metal jar; in time these crescents will soften.

Serves 6 to 8

8 eggs
Peel from 1 organic lemon
1/2 cup granulated sugar
4 cups milk
1 cup + 2 tablespoons
  all-purpose flour
8 tablespoons unseasoned
  breadcrumbs
Enough oil for deep-frying
Enough cinnamon and sugar
  to dust

<u>Approximate preparation time:</u>
  *45 minutes (plus 30 minutes
  to set aside and approximately 1 hour to cool completely);
  430 calories per serving.*

1 Separate 4 eggs. In a deep
mixing bowl, beat 4 egg
yolks with 4 whole eggs, the
grated peel of 1 lemon, and 1/2
cup of sugar. Add and whisk, al-
ternately, the milk and flour until you get a smooth mixture
without lumps.

2 Allow the mixture to set for
30 minutes. While stirring
constantly, bring the mixture
just to a boil (the best way to
do this is to use a double boiler). When the mixture is
cooked, remove it from the
heat, and set it aside, allowing
the cream to set. Rinse a flat
container or a rimmed baking
pan with cold water, and pour
the thick mixture into it about 1
inch high. If necessary, spread
it evenly with a spatula. Allow
the cream to cool off thoroughly until solid.

3 Slice the solidified cream into squares or diamonds approximately 2 inches long. Beat
the egg white with a fork, dip
the cold cream pieces into it,
and coat it with the breadcrumbs.

4 In a large, deep frying pan,
heat enough oil to fry. (Temperature Test: Dip the handle of
a wooden stirring spoon into

Ravioli dolci

Sweet Ravioli (Liguria)

the oil and, when small bubbles rise to the surface of the oil the oil is ready for frying). Fry the breaded cream until golden brown on both sides. To remove excess oil, place the fried slices on a layer of paper towels. Serve warm on a preheated platter dusted with cinnamon and sugar.

• This dessert can be glorious with a fruit treat on the side, such as pureed raspberries flavored with lemon juice and vanilla sugar.

• The best wine for all these desserts should be sweet and full-bodied, such as the *Sciacchetra* from Cinqueterre.

Serves 6 to 8

Peel from 1 orange
5 ounces or 3/4 cup candied fruit
6 ounces or 3/4 to 1 cup ricotta cheese
9 ounces pastry dough that is ready to use
Enough flour to roll out the dough
Enough oil to deep-fry
Enough confectioners' sugar to dust

<u>Approximate preparation time:</u>
30 minutes;
290 calories per serving.

1 Thoroughly drain the ricotta cheese. Wash the orange in hot water and pat dry. With a fine, mesh grater, grate the peel of the orange. Mince 5 ounces or 3/4 cup of candied fruit and mix with the ricotta cheese and grated orange peel.

2 On a well- floured surface roll out the pastry dough (if you use frozen and thawed dough, place the layers next to each other. On half of the pastry dough, spacing the filling evenly at about 1 to 1 1/2 inches apart, place a teaspoon of ricotta cheese filling and carefully lay the other half of the pastry dough on top of the sheet with the filling. With a glass, cut out round ravioli shapes with filling and seal each of the borders by hand.

3 In a large pot, heat enough oil to deep-fry. (Temperature Test: Dip the handle of a wooden stirring spoon into the oil and, when small bubbles rise to the surface of the oil the oil is ready for frying.) Fry the ravioli, a few at a time, until golden brown on both sides. To remove excess oil, place the fried ravioli on a layer of paper towels. Serve warm and dusted with confectioners' sugar.

• *Ravioli dolci* is a typical Mardi Gras specialty that is prepared with a variety of fillings and with different types of dough. Frozen and thawed pastry dough is a suitable and quick option, if you are in a hurry.

• If you wish to prepare this dish the original way, make this flaky pastry dough: Knead 1 1/2 cup flour, 5 ounces or 1/2 cup butter, and 1 egg yolk with a pinch of salt to make a smooth dough. Refrigerate for 30 minutes, roll out in a thin sheet, and use as described above.

Olive Oil—The Golden Nectar of Bitter Fruits

Olive trees, obstinate and gnarled, have been a part of history since ancient times. They are considered among the oldest plants, and their oil, obtained from their fruit, has for centuries symbolized wealth, peace, and hope. It is not an easy profit that can drive a farmer to plant an olive tree—only after five years will the tree produce its first fruit, and it will take fifty years before the tree is at its production peak. Child and grandchild will harvest what the father has left for posterity. If no hard frost comes to disrupt this cycle, the great-grandchild will also reap the trees' fruit. As frugal as the olive tree might be for its soil condition needs, it is difficult when it comes to climate—the average year's temperature must stay between 52 and 65°F, while even a few degrees of frost during long periods, or strong winds, can cause great damage and interrupt the fruit production. A good harvest can be expected if the temperature during the winter drops only to around the frost point, if the summer sun is strong, and if, during the time of the fruits' maturation, up to November, there is little rain. And, of course, if the farmer, throughout the year, takes care of the trees: pruning the stems to prevent the branches from being too dense and the tree

For good oil, olives should be harvested during the "red" maturity stage, when the fruits turn from green to a purple-red color.

Ligurian olive trees grow on rocky soil. In spite of their rugged and robust appearance, olive trees require special climatic conditions. Long periods of frost or strong winds can damage them and interrupt fruit production for quite some time. On the other hand, a good harvest can be expected when there is light frost during the winter and intense sun during the summer. Also, there should be limited precipitation up to the harvest time.

growing too rapidly, and hoeing and fertilizing the ground around the roots. Insecticides are rarely used, since the oil in the fruit would immediately absorb every foreign flavor, making the oil unusable.

The most important part of the oil production, the harvest, begins in November if all conditions for good oil production are met. For consumption, green or fully ripe black olives are harvested; for the production of oil, the olive's color must be just turning from green-blue. During this stage, olives do not seem to snap easily from the branch.

The Obstinate Fruit of the Olive Tree

Olives are picked laboriously by hand (this method provides fruit for the finest olive oil), or they are knocked down with long sticks, falling from the branches onto large nets spread out under the tree. Skilled pickers can gather up to 80 pounds a day, which, during a good season, can produce roughly about 2 gallons of oil. It should therefore not be surprising if 70 percent of the production costs are due to the harvest operation.

Since quality decreases while acid content of the oil increases after 24 hours, olives need to be processed as soon as possible. They are immediately taken to the oil mills where millstones weighing several tons crush them to a gray-brown mush. The mush paste is spread on round mats of straw, which are stacked in layers to form a tower. To stabilize the tower, plates of metal are placed between the layers, and even before any pressure is applied to the tower, the first drops of the best oil drip from the mats. When a pressure of up to 400 tons is applied by a modern hydraulic press, a green-golden and cloudy liquid flows vigorously. It is at this point that tasting occurs; color and aroma are

By November, at harvestime, the nets are spread under the trees. If the olives fall by themselves, they are too ripe for good oil varieties, as the texture would be too greasy and the oil would have a lingering aftertaste.

tested, as well as consistency and flavor. The flavor of the raw juices of the mush can vary according to region, time of harvest, and mill. Some have an aroma of almonds or peaches; others are stronger and even slightly bitter. Even if the fat content remains unchanged, tasters differentiate between "rich" and "lean" oils. Freshly toasted bread drizzled with oil, seasoned with salt, and served with wine, can become a refined delicacy. The new and "virginal" fluid can not yet be bottled as *Olio Vergine Extra*; the water content needs to settle on the bottom and certain press residues, called *sansa* need to be removed. In the past, this

step was executed with simple filtering through cotton sheets. Today, both steps are done with a centrifuge. This much clearer oil can come in colors that range from bright yellow to light green. If the oil turns out too green, it might be due to too heavy pressing.

The best olive oils carry the European Common Market approved word "Extra" (it is specifically the word "Extra" that counts here). In order to evaluate quality, the content of acids is measured: no more than 1 gram of acid per 100 grams are allowed; the best (and the most expensive) varieties are under 0.5 gram acid per 100 grams. The "original

olive oil," without the "Extra," can contain up to 2 grams of acid per 100 grams. The remaining original oil obtained after the production of the very refined oil (after the removal of the impurities), with an acid content of 1.5 grams per 100 grams is simply labeled olive oil. The labeling is still no indication of flavor, which, in the case of Tuscany's oil, is strong, almost wild, among the oil produced throughout the Maremma, and in the area of Lucchesia around Lucca, the oil is refined and light, possibly the finest of all. As to the Ligurian olive oil, it is considered by many to be the best, since it is mellow, light, fruity, and sometimes very mild without any bitterness.

Above: The first olives are already in the net; a long day is still ahead. The advantage of the nets is that the fruit is not damaged, and small, unripe olives automatically fall through the net.

Above top: Farmers of the area deliver their harvest to the oil mill. The processing will have to take place immediately, as after 24 hours, acidity content in the fruit will increase and quality will decrease.

Above: In the past, olives were pressed by pure physical strength, as shown here with these old press plates at the Masseria in Massafra (near Taranto).

Middle top: Heavy granite wheels crush the fruit to mush. During this very noisy process, it is hardly possible to have a conversation. The round straw mats on which the olive concoction will be spread are ready nearby.

Above: A look at the crushing rollers. The wheels, which reduce the olives to a pulp, weigh 8 tons. The mush is spread on the straw mats as soon as the pulp reaches the proper consistency. Modern mats are usually made of plastic and are used only for the duration of one harvest.

Left: Before the freshly squeezed oil can be poured into bottles, small particles of fruit and the remaining water need to be removed; the oil is passed through filters and centrifuges. Finally, a laboratory will evaluate the color, aroma, flavor, and acid content of the oil.

Left: Smaller operations still leave the oil alone in cool cellars in large clay containers, while they wait patiently for the lighter oil to separate from the remaining water, and for all impurities to be deposited on the bottom. Whoever has the good fortune to know of a good olive oil dealer in Italy will notice that the price will be higher than for bottled oils, but the quality will be remarkable.

Above: To balance the straw mats, metal plates are positioned between them. The finest oil from the pulp flows even before the hydraulic press applies its force of several hundred tons.

The Po Basin

Emilia-Romagna, Veneto, Southern Lombardy

Flatlands and Foggy Fields:
Rice cultivation in the Province of Pavia.

The Regions and Their Products

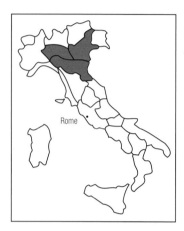

The Po Basin, which stretches over 300 miles, is certainly not as uniform as its geographical name might imply. In the western region, the area extends as far as the hills of the

The humid regions of the Po Basin are best suited for rice cultivation. Here, with a planting machine, young rice plants are planted.

Monferrato; in the southern part of Vicenza, the volcanic formations of the Colli Euganei and of the Monti Berici rise gradually. The modern levels were ancient oceans. Later, during the Ice Age, with sedimentary material brought forth by rivers flowing mainly from the Alps, the water gradually became fertile land. This process continues to this day, with the many branches of the Po Delta gradually reaching into the Adriatic Sea. Ancient and past port cities, like Adria and Ravenna, are today far away from the sea.

Seen from the north, the Po Valley extends southward from the Alps with a dry and hilly area that is only partly used. Attached to this area is an expansion of farmland that is intensely cultivated with wheat and corn.

Further down, reaching the direction of the Po, are more humid and marshy areas. Rice is grown here, especially throughout the area of the Po Basin of southern Lombardy. Therefore, it should not come as a surprise that this is the home region of *risotto*, especially around the area that borders the Piedmont. Almost all homemakers in Lombardy have their own special recipe. The cultivated fields have also created the basis here for an intensive cattle and dairy industry that provides the cheese, cream, and butter that are used more than olive oil in the Po Basin. Favorite specialties are dishes with beef and veal, with a lot of herbs, tomatoes, and wine. A specialty here is *ossobuco*, shanks of veal that have been cooked, according to typical Milanese style, very slowly and at a low temperature. Almost as prominent as this dish is the *costoletta alla Milanese*, a breaded veal

chop fried in butter that is the forerunner of the *Wiener Schnitzel*. In addition, many types of cold cuts originated here, especially from the area of the Brianza.

To provide food for the most important industrial cities of Milan and Turin, fruits and vegetables that are important ingredients of many dishes are grown here, for example, peppers, tomatoes, and onions, ingredients for the *peperonata* that is prepared here as well as in Sicily. In Cremona, the city of violins, *mostarda di frutta*, fruit preserved in a sugar-mustard sauce, is served with boiled meat.

Top: Canals determine the pace of life in Venice, where food, wine, and housewares are transported by boats. The palaces commemorate the past wealth of this city.

Above: Padova's market, Prato della Valle. A specialty of this university city that is full of tradition is fiori di zucca alla Padovana, *a delicacy made with the blossoms of a special variety of squash.*

The marshlands of the delta where the Po divides into many branches reaches from Ferrara to the Adriatic Sea. The coast is full of lagoons and areas of water separated more or less evenly by sandbanks where prominent tourist centers are located. Venice is located in the largest lagoon, which, in the past, belonged to the most

powerful cities in the eastern Mediterranean Sea. Modern Venice is the capital of the province of Venezia. It has a classic dish, *risi e bisi*, rice and peas, which according to the purists, should be made only in the spring, with peas that are grown in fields located between Chioggia and Burano, along the shores of the Venetian lagoon.

The coastal bodies of water that form a background to the beach areas, the largest of which is in Comacchio, are an ideal place for the fishing industry. Eel farming is especially well developed here. Comacchio, and the nearby villages located within the region of Ferrara, are surrounded by fertile farmland created by draining

the coastal swamps. Apples and pears such as the Passagrassana variety are also grown here in large orchards.

Balsamic Vinegar

The balsamic vinegar produced throughout the area of Modena has little in common with the vinegar routinely used in salad dressings. Thick, dark brown, and tasty, it is used as a flavoring. It is made with the best white wines that are cooked down and fermented with a special vinegar starter. As it ages, the vinegar is transferred into gradually smaller barrels made with different woods such as chestnut, cherry, ash, and finally mulberry, and, only for the finest vinegars, into small $3\frac{1}{2}$-gallon barrels made of juniper wood. The most expensive varieties can be between 50 and 100 years old.

From the southern side of the river toward the northern part of the Apennine range, the landscape is even. Across a narrow tongue of hilly land, the basin draws near to the mountains, divided by rugged valleys cut into the land by the Fiumara, which has water only when it rains. Emilia-Romagna is the native home region of such pastas as *lasagna, tortelli, tortellini, tagliatelle, anolini,* and *agnolotti.* At least on Sunday, these are still prepared at home from scratch. Fillings and sauces include, apart from meat (usually ham), Parmesan cheese, and ricotta cheese, typical products of the region. Everything is prepared with time and patience; the food is rich and substantial. Emilia-Romagna is a leader in the production of processed pork meat; not only does the world-famous *mortadella* originate here (Bologna), but also *prosciutto* (Parma) and *coppa* (Piacenza).

Top: Cultivation of corn, the basis for polenta.

Above, middle: Emilia-Romagna is a sausage and cheese paradise.

Below, left: Radicchio *from Treviso, with its oblong leaves, has a somewhat pungent and bitter flavor. The rounder variety from Castelfranco has a milder flavor.*

Above: Culatello, *a gourmet specialty made with the center cut of Parma* prosciutto, *and homemade* cappelletti, *small "hats" filled with cheese, poultry, or ham and cooked and served in broth.*

People, Events, Sightseeing

Since ancient times, the Po River has been the most important navigable water connection between the Adriatic Sea and the Alps. According to historical tradition, it was navigable up to Pavia near the Ticino River, serving as a very lively commercial parallel two-way conduit through the Basin. The Gulf of Venice's wide bend, together with the port city of Adria, has also long been a very important commercial center.

Today, tremendous amounts of money are needed to restore Venice's palaces, with their crumbling facades, walls, and supporting pilings, but this does not seem to worry Venetians too much. Relaxed and smart, they appear courteous and not at all bothered. Even along narrow paths, Venetians manage to pass each other without bumping into one another. A glimpse into the past wealth and love for amusement is still visible in the Ca' Rezzonico Museum, as well as, obviously, the legendary Carnival with its masks and performances filled with bright colors and fantasy.

No less impressive is the historic Regatta along the Grand Canal, held at the beginning of September, with beautiful old Venetian ships called *bucintori*, and participants in costumes representing famous personalities.

Above: Venice—a gondola on the Grand Canal, which Göethe called "the most beautiful street in the world." Today it is a museum, and at the same time, a waterway.

Above: Venice's palaces commemorate the power and wealth of this city, which once held a monopoly on trade in coffee, spices, sugar, and salt, and delivered these goods throughout Europe.

Above, top: Café Pedrocchi in downtown Padova, where Galileo once was a teacher, is famous for its coffee, from the pitch-black espresso to the pale cappuccino. Here you may also order the café alla Borgia with apricot liqueur and cinnamon.

Above: Pub in the area of Colli Euganei. The interior of Venice is still entrenched in the traditions of a farming community typified by frugality and "few words spoken."

Above, right: Galleria Vittorio Emanuele II in Milan, the most beautiful and most prominent shopping mall in the world, with ceiling frescoes and marble pavements, elaborate columns, and covered by a huge glass cupola. It is possible to buy the latest fashions here, and it is the meeting spot of the elegant Milanese. Not far away, on Corso Matteotti, is Sant Ambroeus, the finest pastry shop in Milan, famous for its pastry and handmade candy.

On Carnival Friday, Verona celebrates the Bacanal del Gnoco, the dumpling festival. A parade of costumes, led by "Papà del Gnoco," then moves to the Piazza del Duomo, where, at twelve o'clock, tons of dumplings are cooked and served to all. During the middle of October, Teolo (near Padova) celebrates a chestnut festival. In Treviso, in the middle of December, an annual *radicchio* show is held along the arcades of Palazzo dei Trecento.

In contrast to the countryside that is marked by the tradition of the Po Basin, Milan, the capital of Lombardy, is called by some the "regional capital of Europe." Time and business regulate the pace here: "Rome eats, Milan works." Here can be found international businesses and fashion houses and designers. The heart of the city beats around Piazza Duomo, La Scala, and Galleria Vittorio Emanuele II, the world-famous shopping mall.

Cities in Emilia-Romagna, like Bologna, capital of the historical province of Emilia, are conveniently located across the main traffic line of the Po Basin along the east coast and toward the south. Somehow, Bologna has been able to keep some of its provincial charm. The old downtown section, the Centro Storico, with 21 miles of porticos and galleries, is the second largest after Venice.

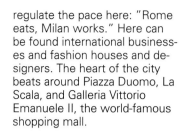

Many festivals are celebrated here: In the middle of September, in Castel San Pietro Terme near Bologna, the braciola festival is held with food, wine, and entertainment; they are also at the Artusiana festival in June in Forlimpopoli. In Cattolica, a huge grill festival is held in the middle of July, followed by a grape festival in September.

In Dovadola, a truffle festival with an annual market is held in the middle of October, and Cesenatico hosts the Garibaldi festival on the first Sunday in August. In Brisighella, an olive festival with stands offering regional specialties is celebrated at the beginning of December.

Above: Piadina—an Emilia-Romagna specialty— is baked on a hot stone plate. It is a flat disk made of flour, water, salt, and lard, and is eaten instead of bread.

Left: The famous checkers tournament in Marostica, which is held every two years. Since the early fourteenth century, special events have been celebrated in the Venetian region with tournaments and public games.

Right: Carnival in Venice is more serious and artificial than relaxed and joyful.

The Wines

Left: The Colli Euganei, a wine island in the Po Basin. Here, wines are labeled "Superiore" if they reach a certain alcoholic content and if they have been allowed to mature for 6 to 12 months.

One might tend to conjure up images of hearty wine that comes in large bottles, rather than a precious drink when thinking of Venetian *Valpolicella*. However, the traditional dry, slightly velvety, ruby red Valpolicella, originally made in 20 counties located north of Verona, suitable while young to accompany pasta dishes and meats, is still available. Venetian *Bardolino* was served in the past even at the French royal court, while today it is usually associated with an image of cheap wine. The attempts of committed winemakers located on the eastern shore of the Lake of Garda to avoid mass marketing could in time elevate the product, which certainly has a better quality than its popular image. A good Bardolino is a solid popular wine that needs to be consumed young and fresh. It goes best with pasta dishes with meat sauces, for light meat such as veal, poultry, and rabbit; as a mature Bardolino, the *Classico Superiore* is also quite suitable for venison and cheese.

The white *Soave*, produced east of Verona, has had fewer problems. If the wine is produced from original grapes from the Soave area, it is allowed to be labeled "Classico." It has a straw yellow color, sometimes with green refractions, and has a typical dry flavor slightly reminiscent of almonds. It goes very well with fish and seafood.

A recent trendsetter is the *Prosecco*, a wine from around the province of Treviso, made with prosecco grapes, a variety that should be included among the sparkling *spumante* types.

These straw yellow, slightly fizzy, sparkling wines are pleasantly bitter and refreshing. They go well as aperitifs, or with appetizers, fish specialties, and pungent cheeses. The fruity and sweet varieties labeled *amabile* are best suited for desserts.

The Colli Euganei are wine islands in the Po Basin, where white, red, and moscato grapes grow and ripen on volcanic soil. The white wines here are straw yellow and dry or mild; the red wines, predominantly from Merlot grapes, are ruby red, also dry, or slightly sweet.

Below: After pruning, vines are tied with willow twigs.

Southern Lombardy has the *Oltrepò Pavese,* red and white, both dry and of good quality.

The most renowned wine of Emilia-Romagna is the *Lambrusco,* destined to undergo a similar fate to that experienced by the Valpolicella. Especially produced throughout the areas of Modena, Reggio Emilia, and Parma, it never tastes the same, since every village has its own wine-making tradition. From the region around Piacenza come the *Barbera* and the *Gutturnio.* The *Albana di Romagna* is a white wine, which is available in both dry and *amabile* (fruity and mild) versions. A well-balanced red wine is the *Sangiovese di Romagna.*

Wines of the Region: From left, Lambrusco Grasparossa di Castelvetro, Recioto della Valpolicella, Bardolino Classico Superiore, Soave Classico *and, served in a fancy wineglass, a pearled sparkling* spumante *wine,* Prosecco di Valdobbiadene.

Regional Recipes

Risotto alla milanese
Creamed Saffron Rice, Milan Style (Lombardy)

Serves 4 to 6

1 bone with marrow
2 1/2 ounces or 1 cup freshly grated Parmesan cheese
12 ounces or 2 cups short/round-grain Vialone, Avorio, or Arborio risotto rice
Approx. 4 cups stock (beef or chicken)
5 tablespoons butter
1 envelope saffron (1/2 to 1 teaspoon saffron in bulk)
1 small onion, minced
Salt and freshly ground pepper

Approximate preparation time:
35 minutes;
360 calories per serving.

A true risotto is not like a conventional rice dish, where kernels are fluffy and clearly distinguishable from each other. It is more similar to a semiliquid, creamed rice-mush, which is juicy and has a wonderful aroma. After cooking, the kernels must still have a pleasantly semifirm texture; for this reason a risotto must be served right after it is prepared.

The home city of risotto is Milan, where each restaurant has its own secret recipe. Only the method of preparation remains the same: Round/short-grain rice (also labeled risotto rice) is sautéed in butter until it is evenly shiny on all sides, gradually moistened with liquid, and cooked slowly while being stirred constantly. The finest variety of risotto rice is called Carnaroli, the classic is the Vialone, and the most popular is the Arborio, also marketed as Avorio. Not everyone agrees on the type of fat that should be used for sautéing the rice; purists use only butter with the addition of bone marrow to enhance the flavor.

In the classic recipe, only minced onion is added to the fat. Those who wish to make it more elaborate sometimes add one carrot and a stalk of celery, both minced. Garlic is also allowed. For moistening, hot beef, veal, or chicken stock is used. A dash of white wine can

also be added toward the end of cooking. An important point is that only a limited amount of a very hot liquid should be gradually poured into the rice; otherwise, the cooking process will be interrupted. If one is into rich flavors, whipping cream can be stirred into it toward the end.

1 Dip the bone with the marrow briefly into iced water and press the marrow out of the bone. Pat dry with paper towels. Dice the bone marrow. In a small saucepan, dissolve the saffron in 2 tablespoons of boiling water. Remove and set aside. Heat the stock in the same saucepan.

2 In a large pot, melt 2 tablespoons of butter and the bone marrow, add the onion, and sauté until glossy, stirring constantly.

3 Add the rice and sauté lightly until it is evenly shiny on all sides, stirring constantly to prevent it from becoming dark. Add a good amount of stock (approximately 1 cup) and continue stirring.

4 As soon as the liquid is almost absorbed by the rice, add more stock, and let simmer, stirring constantly. Make sure to have only enough stock in the rice to barely cover the mixture.

5 After approximately 15 minutes, add the dissolved saffron. Cook 7 more minutes, stirring constantly and continuing to add stock.

6 Taste. If the kernels are almost done but still firm, add the remaining butter and freshly grated Parmesan cheese. Season with salt and pepper.

7 At this point, the risotto should be so moist and creamy that it tends to flow out if you tip the pot. Remove from the heat, cover, and set aside for 1 to 2 minutes, allowing the rice to set. Serve immediately and sprinkle with more Parmesan cheese to taste.

Risi e bisi
Risotto with Peas (Veneto)

Serves 4 to 6

2 thick slices bacon
1 pound young peas (or frozen and thawed peas)
1 bunch fresh Italian parsley
1 1/4 cup grated Parmesan cheese
1 1/2 cup short/round-grain Vialone, Arborio, or Avorio risotto rice
3 tablespoons butter
About 4 cups hot stock
1 onion
Salt and freshly grated pepper

<u>*Approximate preparation time:*</u>
45 minutes;
380 calories per serving.

1 Mince the bacon, onion and 1/2 bunch of parsley. In a saucepan, melt 2 tablespoons of butter. Add the minced bacon, onion, parsley, and sauté until glossy.

2 Add the peas and 1 cup of hot stock. According to the type of peas you are using, sim-mer 5 to 15 minutes (young peas will require less time). Gradually add the remaining stock.

3 Add the rice and simmer about 20 minutes, stirring occasionally. Season with salt and pepper. When ready to serve, fold 1 tablespoon of but-ter and 2/3 cup of Parmesan cheese. Mince the remaining parsley. Sprinkle the rice with. Serve topped with Parmesan cheese.

• When served abroad, this specialty is fairly grainy and dri-er than the original, which is commonly served like a semi-liquid dish.

• Wine serving suggestion: a not too dry white wine, such as a white wine of the Colli Eu-ganei region.

Risotto nero
Black Squid Risotto (Veneto)

Serves 4 to 6

1 2/3 pounds squid with the ink sacs (available at your special-ized fish market)
Juice of 1 lemon
1 1/2 cups short/round-grain Vialone, Arborio, or Avorio risotto rice
1 bunch fresh Italian parsley
1 onion, minced
2 cloves garlic, minced
7 tablespoons olive oil
1 cup white wine
3 cups hot fish stock (or ready to use fish demi-glace)
Salt and freshly ground pepper

<u>*Approximate preparation time:*</u>
1 1/4 hour;
360 calories per serving.

1 Clean the squid. Peel off the membranes, remove the cut-tlebone, and set aside, in a small cup, the squids' ink sacs. Rinse the squid and cut the mantle and the tentacles into strips. Mix the garlic with 3 tablespoons of olive oil and the lemon juice. Use the mixture to marinate the squid for about 20 minutes.

2 In a pot, heat 4 tablespoons of olive oil, and sauté the onion until glossy. Add the squid. Cook until limp, stirring constantly. Moisten with the marinade and with the white wine. Snip the ink sacs open and drop them into the mixture. Cook for 20 min-utes, and if necessary, add some more fish stock.

3 Add the rice and, while stir-ring constantly, gradually add the remaining stock. Cook and moisten with stock until the rice is done. Season with salt and pepper. Mince the parsley, sprin-kle it on the rice, and serve.

• You may also serve this dish topped with thin, curled lemon peel.

Risotto con asparagi
Asparagus Risotto (Emilia-Romagna)

Serves 4 to 6

18 ounces fresh asparagus
1 $\frac{1}{2}$ ounces or $\frac{2}{3}$ cup freshly
    grated Parmesan cheese
9 ounces or 1 $\frac{1}{2}$ cups
    short/round-grain Vialone, Ar-
    borio, or Avorio risotto rice
$\frac{1}{2}$ cup dry white wine
6 tablespoons olive oil
1 tablespoon butter
1 onion, minced
Salt and freshly ground pepper

<u>Approximate preparation time:</u>
    1 $\frac{1}{4}$ hours;
    290 calories per serving.

1 Clean the asparagus and remove all the woody parts. Cut
and set aside the tender tops.
Chop the remaining parts of the
asparagus and cook for 25 minutes in 4 cups of boiling salted
water in a large pot. With a slotted spoon, remove and drain the
asparagus (keep the water for later use). With a hand blender,
puree the cooked asparagus, or

press it through a fine strainer,
and return this puree to the hot
asparagus water.

2 In a large pot, heat the olive
oil. Sauté the onion in the hot
oil until limp and golden. Add the
tender tops of asparagus and
sauté them lightly. Add the
short/round-grain Vialone, Arborio, or Avorio risotto rice and stir-
fry until all sides are shiny. Moist-
en with the dry white wine and
gradually, while stirring constantly, add the asparagus stock
(about 3 cups) and allow to cook
until done.

3 When the rice is ready to
serve, fold in the butter and
Parmesan cheese. Season with
salt and pepper.

• This idea might not be truly a
classic, but you can serve this
rice topped decoratively with
broiled shrimp flavored with a
touch of garlic and freshly ground
pepper.

Risotto con fegatini
Risotto with Chicken Livers (Veneto)

Serves 4 to 6

9 ounces chicken livers
2 ounces or 2 thin slices bacon
$\frac{1}{2}$ to 1 ounce or $\frac{3}{4}$ cup dried
    porcini or cepes mushrooms
4 tablespoons freshly grated
    Parmesan cheese
9 ounces or 1 $\frac{1}{2}$ cup
    short/round-grain Vialone,
    Arborio, or Avorio risotto rice
$\frac{1}{2}$ cup dry white wine
4 cups hot chicken stock
1 onion
3 tablespoons butter
Salt and freshly ground pepper

<u>Approximate preparation time:</u>
    45 minutes;
    330 calories per serving.

1 Soak the dried mushrooms
for about 2 hours in the
white wine.

2 Mince the bacon and onion.
In a large pot, melt the butter. Drain the mushrooms and
set aside the liquid for later

use. Chop the mushrooms and
sauté them briefly with the bacon and the onion. Add the rice
and stir-fry until all sides are
shiny.

3 Gradually moisten the rice
with the hot chicken stock,
and cook until the rice is done.
Season with salt and pepper.
Fold in the freshly grated
Parmesan cheese.

4 In the meantime, finely chop
the chicken livers. Melt 1 tablespoon of butter in a small
frying pan. Add the livers and
brown on both sides for 3 minutes. Season with salt and pepper. Add the wine-mushroom
liquid and bring to a boil. Top
the rice with the chicken livers
and with the remaining Parmesan cheese.

• Another refined variation: Prepare this dish with fresh porcini
mushrooms!

Lasagne verdi al forno
Green Baked Lasagna (Emilia-Romagna)

Serves 4 to 6

For the dough:
5 ounces fresh, stemless
   spinach leaves
2 eggs
1/2 cup + 2 tablespoons
   semolina flour
1 1/2 cups all-purpose flour +
   enough flour to roll out the
   dough
Salt

For the ragù:
3 1/2 ounces lean pork
3 1/2 ounces beef
3 1/2 ounces prosciutto (you
   may substitute country ham)
2 thin slices bacon
3 1/2 ounces chicken livers
1 medium carrot
1 celery stalk (or a small piece
   of celeriac)
2 tablespoons butter
2 tablespoons tomato paste
1 cup meat stock
1 onion
1 teaspoon dried oregano
Salt and freshly ground pepper

For the bèchamel/white sauce:
2 tablespoons butter
2 lightly heaped tablespoons
   all-purpose flour
2 cups milk
Salt and nutmeg

To finish:
3 1/2 ounces or 1 2/3 cups freshly grated Parmesan cheese
3 tablespoons butter to grease
   the baking dish and to top
   lasagna.

Approximate preparation time:
   1 3/4 hours;
   690 calories per serving.

This is, of course, a rather elaborate recipe, but the completed
dish will be a pasta delight without equal.

The details of this dish include:
three varieties of meat and raw
ham—a must in the ragù, which
will require very little seasoning.
The freshly grated Parmesan
cheese will add flavor; at the end,
the pats of butter used to top the
lasagna will add the final touch for
a golden brown, crispy, baked top.
Obviously, store-bought lasagna
noodles and mixed ground beef
will cut the preparation time,
but it will not be the original.

1 For the dough: Clean the
spinach leaves; wash, rinse,
drain, and steam them briefly.
When they have cooled off,
squeeze them to remove all the
excess moisture, and chop or
mince them through either a
manual grinder or an electric
food processor.

2 Mix and knead the semolina
flour, all-purpose flour, 1 teaspoon of salt, the spinach, and
the eggs to obtain a smooth
dough. Set the dough aside,
covered for later use.

3 For the ragù: Grind and
process the pork, beef, and
prosciutto (or country ham)
through either a manual grinder
or an electric food processor.
Dice the bacon, onion, carrot,
and celery.

4 In a medium frying pan, heat
the butter, and sauté the bacon and the vegetables. Add
and brown the ground meat.
Add the tomato paste, dried
oregano, and stock. Season
sparingly with salt and pepper.
Simmer, covered, for about 20
minutes.

5 For the béchamel sauce: In
a saucepan, make a light
roux with 2 tablespoons of butter and 2 tablespoons of flour.
Remove from the heat, and after 1 minute, whisk the milk into the mixture. Return to the
heat and let simmer for 10 minutes, stirring constantly. Season
with salt and ground nutmeg.

6 In a pot, boil salted water. On a floured surface, cut the dough into three portions. Roll out each portion to a thin sheet of dough. Cook pasta for 3 minutes in the boiling salted water. To stop the pasta from cooking, dip it in iced water and drain. Dry the sheets by placing them on a clean dishcloth.

7 Trim and chop the chicken livers and add to the meat ragù. Season with salt and pepper; set aside for later use. Grease a large lasagna pan. Preheat oven to 400°F.

8 In the greased baking pan, place, in alternate layers, a layer of pasta, an evenly distributed portion of ragù, a portion of béchamel sauce, and some Parmesan cheese, alternating the layers until there are no more ingredients.

9 The final layers will be béchamel sauce and grated Parmesan cheese topped with small pats of butter. Bake 30 minutes until golden brown.

Tagliatelle al prosciutto
Ribbon Pasta with Ham Sauce (Emilia-Romagna)

Serves 4 to 6

5 ounces or 3 slices Parma prosciutto (you may substitute
   cooked ham)
2 ounces Parmesan cheese,
   freshly grated
3 eggs
1 small onion
2 ounces or 3 tablespoons
   butter
2 cups all-purpose flour +
   enough flour to roll out
   the dough
Salt and freshly ground pepper

Approximate preparation time:
   1 1/2 hours;
   480 calories per serving.

1 Dough: Make a smooth and
   springy dough with the flour,
eggs, and 1 pinch of salt. Cover
with a moist dishcloth and set
aside to rest for 30 minutes.

2 On a floured work surface,
   roll out the dough to a thin
sheet and cut it into strips 1/8

inch wide and 4 inches long. In
a large pot, bring 3 quarts of
salted water to a boil.

3 Trim the fat from the ham
   and set aside. Dice the
trimmed ham. In a large frying
pan, melt the butter and sauté
the trimmed fat until crispy.
Mince the onion, add to the
pan, and sauté until glossy. Add
the trimmed, diced ham and
sauté until limp.

4 In the meantime, cook the
   pasta in water in a large pot
until done but still firm, drain,
and add to the sautéed ham in
the frying pan. Toss thoroughly,
and season with salt and pepper. Serve with the freshly grated Parmesan cheese.

• A specialty of the city of Parma, this, of course, can also be
prepared with store-bought
tagliatelle.

Malfatti
Spinach-cheese Dumplings (Lombardy)

Serves 6

1 1/3 pound fresh stemless
   spinach leaves
5 ounces or 3/4 cup ricotta
   cheese
1 2/3 cups Parmesan cheese,
   freshly grated
2 eggs
1 egg yolk
3 1/2 ounces or 6 tablespoons
   butter
1 1/2 cups all-purpose flour
1 small onion
Nutmeg
Salt and freshly ground pepper

Approximate preparation time:
   1 hour;
   480 calories per serving.

1 Trim and clean the spinach
   leaves. Cook briefly in a
large pot until wilted. Set the
cooked spinach aside in a
colander. When the spinach has
cooled off, squeeze out the excess moisture, and mince.

2 Chop the onion and sauté in
   2 tablespoons of melted butter in a medium saucepan. Add
the minced spinach, remove
from the heat, mix thoroughly,
and set aside to cool.

3 Cream the ricotta cheese
   with the cooled spinach mixture and half of the Parmesan
cheese. Add and mix the whole
eggs and 1 egg yolk, season
with salt, pepper, and nutmeg.

4 Add the flour to the spinach
   mixture, tablespoon by tablespoon and mix until you get
a soft dough. Season again to
taste. In a large pot, bring 8
cups of salted water to a boil.
With a spoon, form the spinach
dough into dumplings. Drop
these into the boiling water, reduce the temperature, and let
the dumplings simmer until
they float up to the water's surface. Preheat the oven to
350°F.

Maccheroni alla bolognese
Macaroni with Meat Sauce, Bologna Style (Emilia-Romagna)

5 With a slotted spoon, remove the dumplings from the water, drain, and place in a baking dish. Melt the remaining butter and drizzle it over the dumplings. Bake in the preheated oven for 5 minutes. Sprinkle with the remaining Parmesan cheese and serve immediately.

• Curiously enough, the name of this specialty, *malfatti*, has a rather unpleasant connotation; it means something that has not turned out very well. However, be aware that with this term, Italians mean to express the degree of ease in preparation associated with these dumplings; that is, a very simple way of preparing dumplings in comparison to other numerous and elegant pasta competitor varieties. Flavor-wise, the spinach dumplings should be considered top quality!

Serves 6

1/2 pound ground beef
1 chicken liver (1 ounce)
3 ounces or 2 thick slices
  bacon, minced
1 carrot, minced
1 celery stalk, minced
2/3 cup Parmesan cheese,
  freshly grated
1 pound macaroni noodles
1/2 cup beef stock
2 tablespoons butter
1 teaspoon all-purpose flour
1 onion
1 whole clove
1 whole bay leaf
Nutmeg
1 pinch cayenne pepper
Salt and freshly ground pepper

Approximate preparation time:
  1 hour;
  520 calories per serving.

1 Add the minced carrot, celery, and bacon to the melted butter in a large frying pan, and stir-fry lightly.

2 Add the ground meat and brown. Dust the meat with 1 teaspoon of flour and moisten it with the beef stock. Season with salt, pepper, and freshly ground nutmeg. Add the clove and bay leaf. Simmer, covered, for about 20 minutes.

3 In a large pot bring 8 cups of salted water to a boil. Add the macaroni and cook until done but still firm.

4 Mince the chicken liver, add to the ground beef and cook 3 to 4 minutes. Season the sauce with salt, pepper, and a pinch of cayenne pepper. Remove the bay leaf and clove.

5 Drain the cooked macaroni, distribute in portions on preheated plates, and top with the meat sauce. Serve with the Parmesan cheese.

• In the original *Ragù Bolognese* recipe, no ground beef but very finely minced meat, cut extremely small with a sharp knife, is actually used. In this way, there is no meat juice coming from the beef and the flavor of the meat is easily retained.

• Variation: Peel and seed 11 ounces of tomatoes. Chop them and cook together with the sauce. You can enhance the flavor with tomato paste.

Tortellini

Chicken Meat-filled Tortellini (Emilia-Romagna)

Serves 8

<u>For the dough:</u>
4 cups all-purpose flour +
 enough flour to roll out the
 dough
2 eggs
2 tablespoons olive oil
1 teaspoon salt

<u>For the filling:</u>
11 ounces boneless chicken
 breast
1 cup chicken stock
5 tablespoons Parmesan
 cheese, freshly grated
1 tablespoon crème fraîche
 (you may substitute sour
 cream)
2 egg yolks
Peel of $1/2$ lemon
Salt and freshly ground pepper
Nutmeg
Enough clear meat broth to
 cook the tortellini (about 1
 gallon)

<u>Approximate preparation time:</u>
 75 minutes;
 450 calories per serving.

Although their culinary origin cannot be accurately established, *tortellini* play a very important role in the cuisine of Emilia-Romagna. In Bologna, they are traditionally included as a first course on the Christmas menu.

Regarding the origin of *tortellini*, people in Bologna refer to Ostilio Lucarini's play, *The Inventor of Tortellini*, in which a cook, who saw the sleeping wife of his master, fell in love with her. In celebrating the navel, he invented small and round pasta pockets.

Tortellini can be filled with ground pork, ham, sausage, cheese, or eggs and served in clear beef broth. They can be served with Ragù Bolognese (see recipe on page 63) or simply with pats of butter and sprinkled with Parmesan cheese.

• Wine serving suggestion: *Lambrusco* or *Gutturnio* from Colli Piacentini.

1 Dough: Mix and knead 4 cups of flour with $1/2$ cup of water, the eggs, 1 teaspoon salt, and 2 tablespoons of olive oil until you get a smooth and springy dough that is not sticky. Dust with flour, cover with a clean dishcloth, and set aside to rest for 20 minutes.

2 Filling: Simmer the boneless chicken breasts in the chicken stock in a medium saucepan for 15 minutes. Remove from the water and drain. With either a sharp chef's knife or in a food processor, mince the chicken meat and fold in the crème fraîche (or sour cream).

3 In a medium mixing bowl, combine the freshly grated Parmesan cheese, egg yolks, lemon peel, salt, pepper, and a pinch of freshly ground nutmeg. Mix everything thoroughly.

4 Divide the dough into four portions, and roll out 1 portion into a thin sheet.

5 On the sheet of dough, cut out circles of 2 inches in diameter. In the center of each circle, place ½ teaspoon of chicken-cream mixture.

6 Moisten the borders, fold each circle in half, and pinch them together along the borders.

7 Form round pasta pockets by pulling both corners of the half-circle together around the index finger and pinching them together. Place the shaped tortellini on a floured, clean dishcloth. Proceed as before with each dough portion.

8 Bring broth to a rolling boil and add tortellini. Stir them carefully as they reach the broth. Simmer 8 minutes. Serve with the broth as you would a soup with dumplings or remove tortellini from broth, drain, and serve with Ragù Bolognese (page 63) or melted butter. Dust with Parmesan.

Ossobuco alla milanese
Stewed Veal Shank, Milan Style (Lombardy)

Serves 6 to 8

6 to 8 thick pieces of veal shank
(each cut should include the
bone, about 6 pounds)
4 medium carrots
4 stalks celery, minced
2 pounds fresh, ripe plum
tomatoes
1 bunch fresh parsley
4 tablespoons butter
Enough all-purpose flour to dust
the shanks
6 tablespoons first-quality olive
oil
1 cup white wine
1 cup beef stock + enough to
periodically moisten the
shanks
3 medium onions, minced
3 cloves garlic, minced
1/2 teaspoon each of thyme and
oregano
2 bay leaves
Salt and black pepper

For the gremolata:
2 lemons
2 bunches fresh Italian parsley,
minced
5 cloves garlic, minced

Approximate preparation time:
50 minutes;
570 calories per serving.

Ossobuco, a veal shank, stewed
with the meat and bone, is a
typical example of the cuisine of
Lombardy. Only if the meat and
the vegetables are simmered
gently and with patience, does
the dish acquire the unique aroma that is enhanced by the flavor of the sautéed fat of the
bone marrow. The dish should
simmer for at least 2 hours to
produce a juicy and tender piece
of meat.

Important appliance: A heavy,
flat casserole or a Dutch oven
with a cover, which can hold all
the shanks.

An important part of this dish is
the *gremolata*, a flavorful mixture
made with parsley, garlic, and
grated lemon peel, which will
lend its unique aroma to the dish.

• Wine serving suggestion:
A young and fruity red wine,
such as a *Bardolino*.

1 Melt 4 tablespoons of butter in the casserole or Dutch oven. As soon as the fat is melted and still clear, sauté the vegetables until they are limp, glossy, and slightly golden brown. Remove the casserole from the heat.

2 Wrap and tie each meat and bone shank portion with kitchen string. Season with salt and pepper. Dip each shank into flour. In a frying pan, heat the olive oil and brown the shanks on both sides at moderate temperature. Remove the shanks from the pan and place them in the casserole or Dutch oven on top of the sautéed vegetables.

3 Remove the excess oil from the pan. Moisten the pan juices with the white wine and bring to a boil while whisking to dissolve all solids until the liquid has reduced to about 4 to 6 ta-blespoons. Preheat the oven to 350°F.

4 Scald the tomatoes with boiling water and peel them. Cut them in half and seed them. Chop the tomatoes and the parsley (including the stems).

5 Dilute the juices of the pan with the beef stock. Add the chopped parsley, thyme, oregano, bay leaves, and the chopped tomatoes. Bring to a simmer and season with salt and pepper.

6 Pour the sauce over the pieces of meat. Place the casserole on the heat, bring it to a boil, then cover it and place it in the preheated oven. Bake the shanks 2 to 3 hours and moisten them periodically as necessary with more beef stock.

7 For the gremolata: Grate the lemon peel on a fine grater. Mix the parsley, garlic, and lemon peel. When it is ready, place the stewed meat on a serving platter and ladle the vegetables and sauce over the meat. Top everything with the gremolata.

Brasato alla milanese
Braised Beef in Red Wine, Milan Style (Lombardy)

Serves 6

2 pounds beef shoulder, whole (either pot roast or chuck steak)
1 stalk celery
1 small kohlrabi with trimmed
   young top leaves
1 carrot
4 tomatoes
1 1/2 cup red wine
Approx. 1 cup beef stock
3 tablespoons oil
3 tablespoons butter
1 onion
2 cloves of garlic
2 whole cloves
Salt and freshly ground pepper
Nutmeg

Approximate preparation time:
   35 minutes
   (+ 3 hours cooking time);
   380 calories per serving.

1 With a sharp pointed knife, make several deep incisions, equally spaced, on both sides of the meat, and insert a small piece of garlic in each incision

(use 2 cloves of garlic).

2 In a heavy casserole or Dutch oven, heat the oil and melt the butter. Add the meat and brown well on all sides.

3 In the meantime, prepare the vegetables. Clean the celery and kohlrabi while setting aside the young trimmed top leaves for later use. Trim, peel, and mince the onion and carrot. Add them to the casserole and sauté them. Season with salt and pepper and add the cloves. Add the red wine, allowing it to cook down.

4 Bring the water to a boil in a large pot. Drop the tomatoes into the boiling water, remove them with a slotted spoon, and when they are cool enough to handle, peel them. Mince the peeled tomatoes and add them to the meat in the casserole.

5 As necessary, periodically moisten the stew with the beef stock, and simmer, covered, for 3 hours.

6 Before serving, pass the sauce through a strainer. Season with salt and freshly ground pepper, and, before serving, bring to a rapid boil. Thinly slice the kohlrabi leaves and sprinkle them over the sliced meat.

• People of Milan love to be generous with their cuisine; for example, they love large, flavorful stews. As a side dish, *polenta* is a perfect accompaniment; it can be served either as a yellow corn mush or as pan-fried slices as described in the recipe on page 102.

• Wine serving suggestion: A full-bodied red wine, such as a *Bardolino Classico Superiore.*

Milan or Vienna?

 In one place, it is a juicy veal rib cutlet with the bone; in the other, it is a boneless veal cutlet, pounded with a mallet, and cut either from the rump and sirloin or from the bottom, eye, or top round. Some like to fry it carefully in a lot of fresh butter; others prefer to deep – fry it in oil. Whether this is called *costoletta alla milanese* (breaded veal cutlet), or the true *Wiener Schnitzel* (Viennese breaded, boneless veal cutlet), the similarity here is no coincidence. Culinary historians still ponder today the cultural origins of the perfect breaded cutlet. The people of Milan stick to one version only: The prominent recipe wandered to Austria in the suitcase of Field Marshall Radetzky during the last century, but the acclaimed golden yellow specialty dish was

Involtini alla milanese
Stuffed Veal Rollups, Milan Style (Lombardy)

known in Italy much earlier. This is evidenced by its inclusion in a menu of the year 1134.

Costoletta alla Milanese

The quality of the meat is the main determining factor whether the cutlet is tender or hard and chewy. The preparation is easy: Slit a first-quality veal cutlet around the bone, pound it carefully with a mallet, and season it with salt. Dip it in beaten egg and unseasoned, freshly grated breadcrumbs. Press the breading onto the meat. In a frying pan, melt enough butter until it foams, add the cutlet, and fry on both sides until golden brown. Reduce the heat, and simmer the meat until it is done, or for 5 minutes. Garnish with slices of lemon.

Serves 4

4 thin, boneless veal cutlets
   (approx. 3 ½ ounces each)
2 small Italian sausages
2 chicken livers
2 ounces or about 4 very thin
   strips bacon
1 bunch fresh parsley, minced
8 to 10 fresh sage leaves
2 tablespoons Parmesan
   cheese, freshly grated
2 egg yolks
3 tablespoons butter
½ cup white wine
½ cup beef stock
2 cloves garlic, crushed
Enough all-purpose flour to dust
   the rollups
Salt and freshly ground pepper

Approximate preparation time:
   1 hour;
   620 calories per serving.

1 Pound each cutlet until it is very thin. Remove the casings from the sausages, mince the sausage filling, and put in a mixing bowl.

2 Mince the chicken livers for the stuffing. Add the Parmesan cheese and egg yolks to the sausage. Combine the garlic, onion, and sausage thoroughly and season with freshly ground pepper.

3 Spread the mixture evenly on the cutlets and roll them up. Around each piece wrap 1 sage leaf and 1 strip of bacon. Keep the rollups together with short skewers or toothpicks.

4 Dust the rollups with flour. In a large frying pan, heat the butter and sauté the rollups until golden brown on all sides. Season with salt and moisten with the wine, which should be cooked down by about half.

5 Add the beef stock and simmer for about 20 minutes. After simmering the rollups for 10 minutes, top them with more sage leaves (or add the sage leaves to the juice in the pan).

6 Remove the rollups and keep them warm. Bring the sauce to a rapid boil one last time. Season it as needed and serve it with the meat.

• Thin, pounded slices of meat can be filled with spicy stuffing and simmered in wine. Suitable side servings are potatoes and vegetables.

• Wine serving suggestion: A dry, full-bodied white wine, such as a *Riesling* from Oltrepò Pavese.

Fegato alla veneziana
Pan-fried Calf's Liver, Venetian Style (Veneto)

Serves 4

*About 1 pound calf's liver
2 medium onions
1 bunch fresh Italian parsley
4 tablespoons olive oil
2 tablespoons butter
1/3 cup beef stock (or ready-to-
   use veal demi-glace)
Salt and freshly ground pepper*

*Approximate preparation time:
   35 minutes;
   310 calories per serving.*

1 If necessary, remove the membranes, and cut the liver into thin slices. Slice the onions into thin rings and mince 1/2 bunch of fresh parsley.

2 In a large frying pan, heat the olive oil and melt the butter. Fry the minced parsley and the onion rings over medium heat for 10 minutes until glossy and limp.

3 Moisten the beef stock, raise the heat, and sauté the slices of liver for approximately 4 minutes. Chop the remaining parsley. Season the liver with salt, freshly ground pepper, and the remaining parsley.

• Suitable side dishes: Mashed potatoes, white bread, or polenta, prepared either as a mush or sliced and pan-fried according to the instructions on page 102.

• Variation: To enhance the flavor, drizzle with a dash of vinegar or substitute white wine for the stock.

• Wine serving suggestion: a full-bodied white wine, such as a *Soave Superiore*.

Scaloppine al limone
Veal Cutlets with Lemon Sauce (Lombardy)

Serves 4

*4 boneless veal cutlets
   (about 4 ounces each)
2 lemons
6 tablespoons olive oil
1 tablespoon butter
Salt and white pepper*

*Approximate preparation time:
   20 minutes;
   290 calories per serving.*

1 Butterfly the cutlets and pound them thin (1/4 inch) with a mallet. With a fine grater, grate the peel of 1 lemon and squeeze out the juice. Vigorously whisk together the lemon juice and 4 tablespoons of olive oil. Season with pepper and the grated lemon peel.

2 Pour the marinade over the cutlets and refrigerate, covered, for at least 1 hour. Turn once.

3 In a large frying pan, heat 2 tablespoons of olive oil. Remove the cutlets from the marinade and thoroughly drain. Place them in the frying pan and sauté 2 minutes on each side. Remove, cover, and set aside for later use.

4 Pour the lemon-oil marinade into the pan. Squeeze out the juice of the second lemon, add it to the marinade, and bring to a rapid boil. Whisk the butter into the sauce until it is melted and season with salt and pepper.

Vitello al latte
Roast Veal in Milk (Lombardy)

5 Place the cutlets back into the sauce and heat thoroughly. Place them on preheated plates, pour the sauce over them, and serve immediately.

• Before serving, you may garnish these cutlets with paper-thin slices of lemon and fresh herbs (for example, lemon balm).

Serves 6

2 pounds whole veal sirloin
4 cups milk
About $1/2$ pint or 1 cup whipping cream
2 cloves garlic, crushed
5 tablespoons butter
2 tablespoons all-purpose flour
1 bay leaf
1 sprig of thyme (fresh or dried)
Salt and pepper

Approximate preparation time: 2 hours; 480 calories per serving.

1 Sprinkle the veal with salt and pepper. Rub the meat with the crushed garlic.

2 In a Dutch oven, melt the butter. Add the veal and brown on all sides. Heat the milk in a separate saucepan.

3 Moisten the veal with the milk, and add the 1 bay leaf and thyme. Braise, covered, on moderate heat for about $1/2$ hour, and moisten with the milk as needed.

4 Remove the meat as soon as it is medium-rare and tender; set aside. Remove the bay leaf and thyme from the sauce, add the whipping cream, and simmer vigorously until you get a thick sauce.

5 Pass the sauce through a fine strainer, and season with salt and pepper. Thinly slice the veal, place it on a pre-heated platter, and serve topped with the milk sauce.

• Suitable side dishes are steamed vegetables such as broccoli, carrots, or young kohlrabi.

• Milk, a typical main ingredient of Lombardy's cuisine, is not only the basic source of butter and flavorful cheeses, but, as in this case, is used to marinate roasts. The smooth marinade wonderfully tenderizes the meat, and becomes, at the same time, a fine creamy sauce. Enhanced with whipping cream, the milk sauce will simmer down even better, gaining a special aroma.

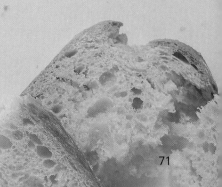

71

Radicchio rosso
Braised Radicchio with Bacon (Veneto)

Serves 4

4 ounces or about 8 very thin
*   slices bacon*
1 2/3 pound radicchio
4 small onions
2 cloves garlic, minced
5 tablespoons extra
*   virgin olive oil*
Salt and freshly ground pepper

Approximate preparation time:
*   30 minutes;*
*   290 calories per serving.*

1 Trim and clean the radicchio, removing the outer leaves. Quarter and core each head. Rinse and allow to drain thoroughly in a colander.

2 Cut the slices of bacon and cut onions into eighths. In a large frying pan, heat 3 tablespoons of olive oil and sauté the bacon and onions for 3 minutes. Add the minced garlic.

3 Add the drained radicchio to the pan and, at the lowest heat, braise for 5 minutes while turning each head over twice. Season with salt, freshly ground pepper, and 2 tablespoons of olive oil. Serve hot with braised or grilled meats.

• The radicchio from Treviso, with a smooth, elongated, pointed, rather then ball-shaped head is a unique specialty from Veneto. It is more delicate and more expensive than the common radicchio. It is especially suitable, brushed with olive oil and seasoned with salt and pepper, for grilling (*alla griglia*).

Asparagi alla parmigiana
Baked Asparagus, Parma Style (Emilia-Romagna)

Serves 4

2 pounds fresh green aspara-
*   gus*
2 ounces or 2/3 cup grated
*   Parmesan cheese*
3 ounces or 5 tablespoons
*   butter*
Salt and freshly ground pepper

Approximate preparation time:
*   50 minutes;*
*   210 calories per serving.*

1 Peel the asparagus and trim the woody lower parts of the stems. Wash the asparagus and tie them together in 4 equal bundles.

2 In a large pot, place the bundles standing vertically, and pour boiling water over them, making sure not to cover the tops. Add salt, cover, and cook, according to the thickness of the asparagus, 10 to 15 minutes, taking care not to overcook them.

3 Preheat the oven to 425 °F. Melt the butter. With a slotted spoon, remove the asparagus and drain in a colander. Brush a large baking dish with 1 tablespoon of melted butter.

4 Place the asparagus carefully in even layers in the baking dish, making sure that the tops remain as free as possible. Drizzle with the melted butter and top with the Parmesan cheese. Bake 3 minutes in the preheated oven. Season with freshly ground pepper and serve immediately.

• An asparagus specialty from the city of Parma: Cook the tops of the asparagus for 10 to 15 minutes, wrap them in *prosciutto*, and bake briefly, topped with Parmesan cheese and pats of butter.

• Another asparagus specialty, this one originally from Lom-

Melanzane marinate
Marinated Eggplants (Emilia-Romagna)

bardy: *Asparagi alla Milanese*. Prepare the asparagus as previously described and simmer until done but still firm. Sprinkle with freshly grated Parmesan cheese and serve topped with eggs over easy.

• These specialties can of course be prepared with white, green, purplish green, or pink asparagus. When developing the portions for asparagus, pay close attention to the variety you are using; when using white asparagus, for example, be generous with the portions, since these require more peeling and trimming than the green variety. The cooking time should be planned according to the thickness of the stems (ranging from 5 to 10 minutes).

Green asparagus have a stronger flavor than the white ones, and are often less expensive.

Serves 4

4 small eggplants (about 1 pound)
1/2 bunch fresh Italian parsley, minced
1/2 bunch fresh basil, minced
6 to 8 sage leaves, minced
3 cloves garlic, minced
2 to 3 tablespoons vegetable oil
5 tablespoons wine vinegar
Salt and freshly ground pepper

<u>Approximate preparation time:</u>
70 minutes;
100 calories per serving.

1 Wash, trim, and cut the eggplants into 1/4-inch-thick slices. Sprinkle the slices with salt, place them in horizontal layers on a large platter, and cover them with another large platter, which will need to be kept in place with a heavy object. Set aside at least 30 minutes to draw out the bitter juices with the salt.

2 Rinse the slices of eggplant and pat them dry with paper towels. In a large frying pan, heat 1 to 2 tablespoons of shortening. Add the eggplant gradually, and fry 2 minutes on each side; add more shortening as needed. Remove the fried eggplant slices from the pan and place them on paper towels to drain any excess fat.

3 Combine the parsley, basil, sage leaves, and garlic. Place the eggplant slices horizontally in a large flat dish. Season each layer with salt and pepper. Drizzle some wine vinegar on each layer and cover each layer with the herb-garlic mixture. Cover and refrigerate overnight to allow the marinade to seep into the slices. Serve with either boiled or grilled meats.

• When it comes to aroma and the use by themselves, raw eggplants don't have much to offer; however, their unique and surprising flavor comes through when they are roasted, grilled, marinated, and braised. They are absolutely recommendable with strong spices. They easily also soak up fat and oil; for this reason, prepare them only with the freshest ingredients and put the fried eggplant immediately on paper towels to soak up any undesirable fat excess.

Uova zuccate
Almond-flavored Pumpkin Casserole (Lombardy)

Serves 4 to 6

14 ounces peeled pumpkin
About ³/4 cup ground almonds
About 1 ²/3 cups grated Parme-
*   san cheese*
6 eggs
2 ounces or 4 tablespoons soft-
*   ened butter*
Salt and white pepper

<u>*Approximate preparation time:*</u>
*   1 hour;*
*   360 calories per serving.*

1 Dice the peeled ripe pumpkin. In a medium saucepan,
combine the pumpkin meat
with some salt and 2 to 3 tablespoons of water. Cover and
simmer until tender. With a
hand blender, puree, or press
through a fine strainer. Set
aside to cool. Preheat oven to
400°F.

2 Fold 6 tablespoons of
ground almonds and half of
the butter into the pumpkin

mixture. Beat the eggs and mix
them with ²/3 cup of freshly
grated Parmesan cheese. Gradually add the pumpkin mixture
and combine all the ingredients.

3 Brush a large baking dish
with 1 tablespoon of butter.
Pour the pumpkin-egg mixture
into the dish, sprinkle with the
remaining ground almonds and
Parmesan cheese, and dot with
butter. Bake in the preheated
oven until it has set (about 30
minutes). Serve immediately.

• The fresh pumpkin can also
be cut in slices and fried in aromatic olive oil until they are
crispy. Drain well, and season
either with salt, pepper, or red
cayenne pepper.

Verdure alla primavera
Braised Spring Vegetables (Emilia-Romagna)

Serves 4

11 ounces broccoli
3 stalks celery
9 ounces green asparagus
9 ounces snow peas
1 bunch scallions
About 1 pound fresh small or
*   cherry tomatoes*
Juice of 1 lemon
1 bunch fresh basil
2 tablespoons freshly grated
*   Parmesan cheese*
2 tablespoons balsamic vinegar
*   (original vinegar specialty of*
*   Modena; see page 51)*
3 tablespoons butter
Salt and freshly ground pepper

<u>*Approximate preparation time:*</u>
*   70 minutes;*
*   230 calories per serving.*

1 Clean the broccoli and cut into florets. Trim and peel the
stems, and slice them thin.
Clean and rinse the celery, and
cut into 1¹/4-inch-long pieces.
Clean and peel the asparagus,

and trim all woody stem parts.
Cut these into 1¹/4-inch-long
pieces. Trim, clean, and rinse
the snow peas and the scallions. Cut the bottom parts of
the scallions into ³/4-inch-long
pieces. Thinly slice the remaining green tops of scallions.
Rapidly scald the tomatoes;
peel them and slice them.

2 Bring enough salted water
to a rolling boil in a large pot,
and drizzle the lemon juice into
it. Gradually, one after another,
blanch first the pieces of asparagus (5 minutes), then the
celery (4 minutes), the broccoli
florets (3 minutes), and the
snow peas (2 minutes). Dip in
iced water and drain. Keep the
vegetable water.

3 In a large frying pan, melt 2
tablespoons of butter. Sauté
the bottom of the scallions and
the sliced broccoli stems for 3
minutes. Gradually add and
sauté the remaining blanched

Timballo verde
Baked Greens and Potato Casserole (Lombardy)

vegetables and, as needed, add a few tablespoons of vegetable broth. Add chunks of tomatoes.

4 Sauté the vegetables until they are done but still crunchy inside and firm to the bite. Season with the balsamic vinegar, salt, freshly ground pepper and a pinch of freshly ground nutmeg. Sprinkle with sliced scallion tops, freshly grated Parmesan cheese and pieces of basil leaves, and serve immediately.

• Both large farming areas of Northern Italy, Emilia-Romagna and Veneto are abundantly blessed with vegetables; there is therefore no shortage here of wonderful, vegetable-based recipes…

Serves 6

1 1/3 pounds potatoes (prefer-ably of a variety that is good for baking)
About 1 pound fresh spinach leaves
2 bunches fresh Italian parsley
3 1/2 ounces or 1 2/3 cups fresh-ly grated Parmesan cheese
4 eggs
4 tablespoons whipping cream
3 tablespoons butter
Salt and freshly ground pepper
Nutmeg

Approximate preparation time:
2 hours;
290 calories per serving.

1 Wash the potatoes and boil in salted water in a large saucepan until soft. Bring enough salted water to a boil in a large pot to cook the spinach. Clean, trim, rinse, and blanch the spinach for 2 minutes. Remove it from the wa-ter and drain thoroughly.

2 Tear the parsley leaves from the stems and, with a hand mixer, puree them together with the spinach. Season with salt, pepper, and freshly ground nutmeg.

3 Preheat the oven to 350°F. Drain the potatoes, peel while still hot, and press through a ricer into a large saucepan. Beat the eggs to-gether with the whipping cream, and fold this mixture in-to the riced potatoes. Add the spinach mixture and two thirds of the grated Parmesan cheese, and mix all ingredients thoroughly. Season again as necessary.

4 Grease a large baking dish with 1 tablespoon of butter. Pour the potato mixture into it and bake it in the preheated oven for 20 minutes. Sprinkle the remaining grated Parmesan cheese and 2 tablespoons of butter divided into small pieces

over the top of the baking dish. Bake until golden brown and crispy. Serve immediately.

• You may find peas or carrots used in other variations of this vegetable dish; sometimes vari-ous cheeses or a mixture of noodles and white béchamel sauce are also used.

• If you do not have a potato ricer, you can mince or chop the potatoes with a knife.

Semifreddo
Cold Trifle (Emilia-Romagna)

Serves 8 to 10

For the bottom:
9 ounces or 2 cups blanched
    and peeled almonds
2 egg whites
1 ³/₄ cups confectioners' sugar

For the filling:
3 eggs at room temperature
1 ¹/₂ sticks butter
¹/₃ cup confectioners' sugar
5 ounces bittersweet chocolate
    in a bar
1 to 2 tablespoons brandy (or
    rum)
1 ¹/₂ cups strong, cold espresso
3 tablespoons slivered almonds

Approximate preparation time:
    1 ¹/₂ hours;
    500 calories per serving.

An ice-cold dream made of
sweet foam and almonds—perfect for all occasions.

Another favorite version, easily
made, is prepared with
amaretti. These are small almond cookies, available in the
store, which can also be made
at home (recipe page 120).

• Crumble about 30 (about 7 to
8 ounces) amaretti and drizzle
with 1–2 tablespoons of rum.
Prepare a *zabaione* (recipe page
120); let it cool, and when cold,
fred the whipped cream into it.
In a loaf pan, alternate layers of
rum-flavored amaretti with
whipped cream mixture, and refrigerate for several hours. Turn
the pan over, remove trifle, and
slice. Both versions can be
served either cold or partly
frozen.

• This dough does not call for
flour. However, use flour when
you roll it out, in case it is too
sticky.

• If you use eggs that are too
cold, the egg cream will tend to
be runny. In this case, whisk all
ingredients in a double boiler
until the cream is thick and
smooth.

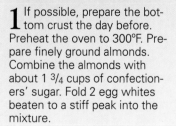

1 If possible, prepare the bottom crust the day before.
Preheat the oven to 300°F. Prepare finely ground almonds.
Combine the almonds with
about 1 ³/₄ cups of confectioners' sugar. Fold 2 egg whites
beaten to a stiff peak into the
mixture.

2 Divide the mixture into 3 portions. Between two sheets
of plastic wrap, roll out each
portion to the size of the bottom
of a spring form pan (8 to 9 inches in diameter). Bake the crusts
one at a time on the middle rack
of the oven for 10 to 15 minutes. Allow the crusts to cool
entirely before using them.

3 For the filling, separate the
eggs and beat the egg
whites to a stiff peak. Cream
the butter with the egg yolks
and about ¹/₃ cup of confectioners' sugar. With a spoon, gradually fold in the egg white mixture.

4 Mix the brandy with 2 cups of cold espresso. With one-third of the cold coffee-brandy mixture, moisten 1 cold almond crust.

5 Spread one-third of the cream filling evenly onto this moistened crust. With a four-sided grater, finely grate one-third of the chocolate bar over this layer of cream. Cover this layer with another almond crust, and moisten the crust with one-third of the cold coffee-brandy mixture. Repeat the layers of cream, chocolate, almond crust, brandy, and coffee, until you have no more ingredients.

6 Place the cake in a storage container and seal. Refrigerate for 4 to 5 hours (or freeze for less time) and allow to set. With a grater, grate the chocolate into flakes over the last layer of cream. Garnish with slivered almonds. Serve chilled.

Tiramisù
Mascarpone Trifle (Veneto)

Serves 8

1 lemon peel
About 1 pound mascarpone
(Italian fresh double-cream
cheese; or 12 ounces
whipped cream cheese
mixed with 8 ounces sour
cream)
4 egg yolks
4 tablespoons granulated sugar
1 cup strong, cold espresso
2 1/2 tablespoons brandy or rum
About 18 ladyfinger cookies
Unsweetened cocoa powder

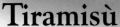
Approximate preparation time:
25 minutes
(+ 5 hours chilling time);
500 calories per serving.

1 Beat the egg yolks and sugar until fluffy.

2 Fold in the mascarpone. Flavor with the grated lemon peel.

3 Prepare a baking dish. Combine the cold espresso with the brandy or rum. Dip half of the ladyfingers into the coffee-brandy and line the bottom of the dish with them.

4 Spread one half of the cream over the bottom layer of cookies. Dip the remaining ladyfingers in the coffee-brandy. Place these over the cream in the baking dish, and repeat until you have no more ingredients.

5 Cover and refrigerate for 5 hours. Serve dusted with unsweetened cocoa powder.

• *Crema di mascarpone* is the name of an ancient recipe that originated in Lombardy. A second culinary connection seems to indicate possible origin of Tuscany.

Monte Bianco
White Mountain Chestnut Cream with Whipped Cream (Lombardy)

Serves 6

1 1/3 pounds edible chestnuts
2 cups or 1 pint milk
About 1 cup whipping cream
1 whole vanilla bean
1 cup confectioners' sugar
1 cup cocoa powder
About 1 1/4 tablespoons rum

Approximate preparation time:
1 1/2 hours;
480 calories per serving.

1 Preheat the oven to 475°F. Score the chestnuts with a paring knife, place them on a baking sheet, and bake in the oven for 20 minutes or until the cut portions pop open. Remove from the oven and peel while still hot.

2 In a saucepan, combine the peeled chestnuts, milk, and the vanilla bean cut open horizontally. Cook for 45 minutes or until the chestnuts are soft. Remove vanilla bean and, puree the milk-chestnut mixture.

3 Fold into the chestnut mixture the confectioners' sugar, cocoa powder, and rum. Beat until smooth. Distribute the mixture into cups and serve topped with whipping cream.

• You can use peeled canned chestnuts (14 ounces). In this case, shorten the cooking time and test after 30 minutes.

Panna cotta
Upside-down Whipped Cream Pudding (Emilia-Romagna)

Serves 4 to 6

2 cups whipping cream
1 whole vanilla bean
2 ounces granulated sugar
1 envelope Knox unflavored
    gelatin
Commercial caramel syrup (or
    fresh fruit)

Approximate preparation time:
    20 minutes
    (+3–4 hours to set);
    310 calories per serving.

1 Dissolve 1 envelope gelatin in 1/4 cup of cold water. Pour the whipping cream into a saucepan; add 1 vanilla bean, cut open, and its scrapings; combine with the sugar. Heat the mixture and simmer for about 15 minutes.

2 Remove the saucepan from the heat. Remove the vanilla bean. While stirring, dissolve the gelatin into the hot cream. Pour the cream into pudding cups that have been rinsed with cold water, and refrigerate for about 3 to 4 hours.

3 Turn the cream over into serving plates. Serve either with caramel syrup or with fresh fruits.

• If the flavor of the plain whipping cream seems too rich, soak the gelatin in 1/4 cup cold Marsala wine and add this mixture to the whipping cream.

• Wine serving suggestion: *Marsala* or a sweet fruity *Prosecco* labeled *amabile*.

Fragole all'aceto
Marinated Strawberries (Emilia-Romagna)

Serves 4

About 1 pound, or 1 pint small,
    sweet, fresh strawberries
2 tablespoons aceto balsamico
    (Italian vinegar specialty
    made with fermented grape
    juice)
1 to 2 tablespoons sugar

Approximate preparation time:
    10 minutes
    (+ 1 hour to marinate);
    60 calories per serving.

1 Clean, hull, and thoroughly rinse the strawberries; put them in a small mixing bowl.

2 Sprinkle the berries with the sugar, and drizzle the *aceto balsamico* vinegar over them. Mix thoroughly but carefully. Marinate at room temperature for at least 1 hour. If you wish, you may refrigerate them briefly before serving.

• Balsamic vinegar is anything but a simple vinegar; a few drops are enough to enhance the flavor of gourmet ingredients such as very delicate seafood, even to give a final special touch to a dessert. The magic basis of this product, which comes from Modena, is described in detail on page 51.

79

Cheese—Product of Milk and Rennet

It is difficult to mention any Italian specialty that does not include some cheese. Cheese is the ingredient that binds poor and rich from the North to the South. With only two ingredients, milk and rennet, a product is developed that has practically no equal in mastery and creativity. It remains historically undetermined just when the history of cheese may have begun; however, ancient Greeks were masters of cheese production and they brought this art to Sicily and southern Italy. The climate would not allow the preservation of milk, but with the invention of cheese, a safe, preservable, and nutritional product was created, allowing its storage for later use in case of famine. And, since goats and sheep were commonly kept as domesticated animals in the South, it was this milk that was in turn used in cheese production. A classic example is Pecorino, a hard cheese made with sheep's milk.

Northern cheese varieties are produced with cow's milk, since the lush foraging vegetation allows for a more intense cattle economy than in the South. It is possible that ancient Celts, who moved into this region around 400 B.C., developed the basis for the local production of cheese. Cheese making was undoubtedly heavily influenced by the presence and activities of cloisters and monastic communities, which, as early as 1200 A.D., had already developed several

Right: Parmesan cheese is allowed to age up to five years. With the increased years of aging comes an increased value in quality. Only 5 percent of the cheese drums leave the country; the rest is used in local cuisine.

varieties of cheese, including *grana, gorgonzola, pecorino,* and *taleggio.*

The most prominent Italian cheese, Parmesan, more accurately labeled Parmigiano Reggiano, comes from Northern Italy, from the city of Parma in Emilia-Romagna. The original name, branded into the golden brown crust, is the guarantee of authenticity. With the passing of years, it increases in pungency and value. It is mild and soft when it is young *(giovane)*, only one to two years old. It becomes perfect for grating after at least three years of aging *(vecchio)*. In addition, there is the Grana Padano from the Po Basin. Both types belong to the grana family,

Production stages for the making of Parmesan cheese.
Far left: A mixture of de-fatted evening milk and fresh fat whole morning milk is heated to 95ºF in a copper kettle and treated with veal rennet.

Left: After approximately 15 minutes, the curdling begins, and the resulting cheese mass separates into very small curds. This phase is followed by the most delicate and determining stage of all; the gradual heating process of the whole mass to about 130ºF with constant stirring.

with hard grainy cheeses that are cut with a pointed flat-bladed knife known as an *ago*. Cheeses of the *filata* type (spun curd cheese) are *mozzarella, provolone,* and *caciocavallo.* For these types of cheeses, curdling occurs in hot water, and the curds are kneaded to a doughy cheese mass. *Provolone* originates from the mountainous countryside of Naples. For the making of this cheese, preferably raw winter milk is combined with a special enzyme extract mixture, called rennet, that contains fat-curdling enzymes. Shaped into various forms, it is also often tied in ropes and smoked to impart a pungent flavor to the cheese. A mature provolone is also suitable for grating.

Above, left: With an almost sixth sense, the cheese master evaluates the consistency and size of the curds to determine exactly when the next step should begin.

Above, middle: The fine-grained mass is lifted in a cloth from the kettle and is hung up on rails (picture on the left). The drained whey feeds pigs throughout the Parma area—those that will provide meat for the famous prosciutto ham.

Above: A Consortium (Consorzio) *inspector taps the body of the mature cheese drum with a small metal hammer; he recognizes from the special sound of the tap if the cheese has attained the desired quality. Only after this stage is the king of cheeses, the Parmigiano Reggiano, awarded the much-sought-after sign of recognition: a branded quality mark.*

Left: In the Alpine area, where raclette *and* fondue *originated, flavorful cheese is still produced with raw milk according to traditional methods, as with fontina cheese from the Aosta Valley.*

Right: The fine multipurpose ricotta cheese is made from the remaining reheated whey of certain varieties of cheeses. The protein rises and curdles; it is scooped up and filled in small baskets.

Left: Tied in small pairs, the pear-shaped pieces of caciocavallo are hang up for aging in the storage room of a cheesemaker in Naples.

Right: Caciocavallo and its cousins of the filata *spun curd cheese family, with their different types of aging, shapes, forms, and cream and fat contents, vary from mild to pungent according to their aging time, and are available on the market for table consumption or for grating into recipes.*

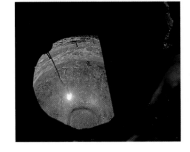

Right: Gorgonzola, a classic cheese, with over 1,000 years of tradition. In the past, this gourmet delicacy was stored in humid caves where the light blue mold began to form naturally.

Left: An unusual delicacy is the formaggio di fossa, *originally from Brisighella, located southeast of Bologna. The cheese is packed in bags and stored in a deep pit until it is brought forth the next year with cheering and celebration.*

Caciocavallo, with a lower fat content than the pear-shaped provolone, is produced almost identically to provolone. Mozzarella, first as a topping for pizza and latter as an ingredient served with tomatoes and basil, has become known worldwide. Truly original mozzarella is made with buffalo milk; however, since there are so few buffaloes today, cow's milk is usually used. Caciocavallo, on the other hand, has a higher water content and is more similar to a fresh cheese than provolone. Then let's talk about mascarpone, a fresh cheese product obtained from the curdling and heating of heavy cream, which is wonderfully delicate and creamy and tastes like butter. It originates from the area around Lodi, became prominent with the popularization of Tiramisù (recipe page 78), and is used in Italy for baking and to make sauces.

Last, but not least, are the Italian table cheeses used for slicing. The soft and creamy Fontina comes from the valley of Aosta. The original is made with raw milk and has the *Consorzio della Fontina Tipica* stamp on the rind. The Asiago, which was once a farmer's cheese but now is usually produced by cooperatives, comes from the southern foot of the Dolomites. It is available in various degrees of fat content and maturation stages—from the leanest *Asiago d'Allievo*, a hard cheese, to the medium type (four to six months of maturity), the *piccante* (one to two years of maturity), and the high fat content slicing cheese, *Asiago Grasso di Monte*, which has a mild but clearly detectable aroma.

Softer in consistency are the washed rind cheeses, like the *taleggio*, which was originally produced only in the area of Bergamo and is now made throughout the Alpine regions and the countryside of Lombardy. The drums are square, matured for only a short time, with an aromatic, slightly sweet-and-sour taste. Aftermeal cheeses are Lombardy's *robiola*, *crescenza*, and the *Bel Paese*, a brand cheese with a mild taste that is reminiscent of butter.

A fine hand for the production of pecorino is demonstrated by Sardinian shepherds, who developed their highly perfected skills throughout the island.

In Tuscany, handmade cheeses have precedence over industrially produced cheeses. The perfect aging of this particularly delicate and mild pecorino requires, besides good air, manual care, such as periodically washing the rind.

An assortment that can be displayed with pride—this seems to be the opinion of a Calabrian cheese dealer, who is especially glad to cut regional classics from his home area, like a pecorino pepato speckled with peppercorns. Even more popular are the sheep cheese varieties from Sardinia and Latium— the pecorino sardo and the pecorino romano.

Prosciutto Ham—Curing with Air and Salt

the origin of production of Prosciutto di Veneto—a very fine, air-dried, mild prosciutto that is produced throughout the area between Padova and Vicenza. The winged Venetian lion, which is used by the Consorzio to certify its controlled origin, is unfortunately rarely found outside the regional borders. Also available, together with this air-dried specialty, are other types of smoked ham, which usually keep longer and are somewhat stronger in flavor. South Tirolean ham, *Südtiroler Speck*, is among these, a raw ham made from the shank of the pig, rubbed with salt and Alpine herbs before the smoking process.

Ancient Romans, surrounded by the gentle rolling hills of Parma, were the first to appreciate the taste of prosciutto ham (or just *prosciutto*), and they swiftly came up with a way to transport the juicy pork shanks, which so far had been enjoyed only by local Gallic tribes. So much for the history of the origins of the air-dried ham; the actual truth may be hidden in the fog of legends.

Fresh air is surely among the most important factors required for the production of Parma's ham, Prosciutto di Parma: gentle winds blowing from the mountains to the valley and carrying the breeze of pine woods and chestnut groves in addition to moderate average temperatures and low humidity. In small Langhirano, the prosciutto capital, storage halls with high, long windows are built, facing west and east to take advantage of the southern airflow. Hams in Langhirano remain stored for at least one year before they are shipped worldwide, branded as originals with a five-pointed crown and the word PARMA. With the brand comes the guarantee that the shanks used for aging are only obtained from certain pigs that are raised in a specific area of production. A Parma pig needs to weigh at least 352 pounds, since the aroma is hidden in the fat. Before going through the salting process, the fresh shanks weigh about 24 pounds, and the hams ready for shipment after drying and aging weigh about 15 pounds. A natural, uninterrupted, months-long process, from a salty meat to an almost buttery mild and spicy delicacy that is renowned throughout the world, is carried out under perfect care and ideal climatic conditions.

Above: Approximately 14 million prosciutto hams are produced yearly by the 250 producers located in the province of Parma, each ham having an inimitable quality and a unique flavor.

Prosciutto di San Daniele Connoisseurs state that the flavor of this ham is especially *dolce* (sweet), even more delicate and mild than its cousin from Emilia-Romagna. The famous name is associated with a small town located along the border of the province of Friuli, near Yugoslavia, and with first-quality and stringent production requirements, which, as in Parma, are enforced by a controlling Consortium (*Consorzio*). From a purely superficial viewpoint, the San Daniele prosciutto is recognizable by its mandolin-shaped form, the attached pig foot, which is missing from the Parma prosciutto, and its branded shank-shaped mark and the initials S.D. Also nationally protected is the branding that certifies

Above: Only the best shanks make it as Parma prosciutto ham, with well-balanced grainy and white fat, healthy bones, and shiny red muscles.

Relatively lean, and with a somewhat grainy taste, is the *Sauris* from Friuli, and Tuscany's juniper-smoked *Cosentino* prosciutto ham. Wild boar hams are often available only regionally; those prepared in Friuli, Tuscany, Umbria, and Sardinia are famous.

Coppa, which is actually not a ham because it is not made with the shank, is similar to prosciutto ham in taste and production, and is loved throughout Italy—a lean, trimmed picnic ham rubbed with salt turns into a delicacy, while it is aged in a cloth that is moistened with white wine. Something similar happens with the

capocollo, which is produced in various regions following a great variety of recipes: pieces of picnic meat, the pig's head, or the pork loin are marinated, preserved in wine, smoked, or dried. The very fine and precious *culatello*, made from the center portion of Parma's prosciutto ham, matures in humid, rather than dry, air.

Bresaola, not made from pork, but from marinated and air-dried beef, is considered a specialty of the Alpine regions. Similar to the prosciutto hams, it is sliced paper thin, served as an appetizer, and sometimes seasoned with oil, lemon juice, and coarsely ground pepper.

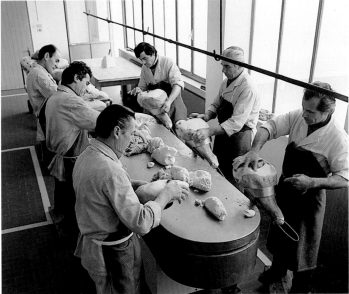

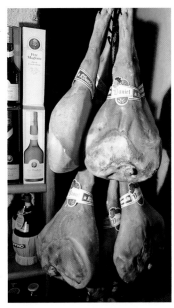

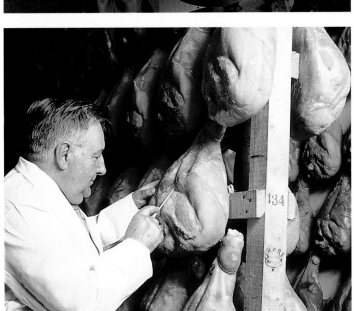

Top, left: After rubbing with salt and a limited curing time, each ham is carefully groomed with massage for the perfect shape and a fine clean trimming done to expose the bone.

Top, middle: All exposed crevices are rubbed with lard to prevent the meat from drying out.

Above, left: Since the very beginning, all hams are periodically monitored while they age, and the final products are stamped with seals of approval when they are ready.

Above, middle: A very sharp horse bone is used as the instrument for the final quality check; the expert punctures five points near the blood vessels in each ham, the aroma is evaluated, and the judging follows.

Top, right: San Daniele's prosciutto ham is left to mature to the bone.

Above: The best way to eat prosciutto is when it is freshly bought, expertly deboned, and sliced paper thin.

Sausages—Flavorful Variety Galore

dispensable for cooking. *Pancetta arrotolata* is air-dried bacon roll with less fat content that is often offered shaved as a cold cut. The wealthy North is not the only region that has a satisfying sausage cuisine.

Other regions are also famous for their sausages, such as Tuscany with its

They are recognizable as inch-long or foot-long foods, shaved paper thin off a huge loaf, in slices, as one piece, or as a pair, with mild, strong or fiery and spicy flavors—we are talking about sausages, indeed, an unending topic of conversation. Leaders in sausage production are the regions of Emilia Romagna and Lombardy, reflected also by many names of such sausage specialties as: *salami* from Milan, *mortadella* from Bologna, *zampone*, and *cotechino*, filled pork trotter, and smoked pork sausage made in Modena. Sausage varieties from Varzi, Verona, and Felino originate also in the northern regions of the Italian boot.

Italian sausage is often served as an appetizer, but it is also very important for cooking: finely ground for fillings, sliced in soups and one-pot meals, or served whole as a side dish as in *bollito misto* (recipe page 110). *Pancetta*, the striped pink-white, *marinated bacon* is in-

Top: Salumi, *the general term for sausages and hams, are served in Italy preferably shaved as* antipasti *(appetizers) on platters garnished with mixed pickled vegetables or with fruits like melons and figs.*

Above: No trace of mildew, as is often found in other air-dried raw sausages, is present in Naples' sausage spread, since it is smoked briefly before being hung in the air to age.

finocchiona, a variety of raw sausage that is flavored with fennel seeds. Since early times, the best butchers have been trained in Umbrian Norcia. In fact, until recently, skilled butchers would travel from Norcia throughout Italy to settle and open *norcinerias*, which in Central Italy was the name for ham and sausage specialty stores. Especially in the poorest southern regions, such as Basilicata, "butcher's day" was an opportunity to celebrate with family and friends. The pig was considered a gift from God; it provided the main ingredient for those rare meat meals, served as trail food for the shepherds and hunters, and filled the storage rooms before the winter months. In Calabria, the tasty pig was even assigned a patron saint, and Saint Anthony's day became in time the animal's day for its last hour.

Left: The fine, ice cold, seasoned mortadella mixture, made of lean pieces of beef and pork, passes through the meat grinder before being pressed into natural or artificial casings and being cooked under dry heat.

Left: The secrets of first-class sausages lie in well-kept recipes: the mixture of certain cuts of meat, the fine or coarse grinding of the meat, and the aging according to either traditional or modern methods.

Above: The weight of an original mortadella varies from 11 ounces to 330 pounds, and its diameter is also quite impressive.

Above, top: Sopressata sausages, well seasoned and pressed into shape, hang near air-dried salami.

Above, bottom: Zampone, filled with ground meat, hanging near coppa, made from pig's head and bacon.

The Alpine Regions

Aosta Valley, Piedmont, Northern Lombardy,
South Tirol, Trentino, and Friuli-Venezia Giulia

Peaks and Valleys:
High up on the pasture of Siusi in South Tirol.

The Regions and Their Products

It is not easy to treat as a uniform area the Alpine region of Italy, which includes the Aosta Valley, Piedmont, Northern Lombardy, South Tirol, Trentino, and Friuli-Venezia Giulia. The monumental natural catastrophe that caused this range of mountains to appear like a huge multidimensional tablecloth created an intricate system of mountain peaks with casually spread-out layers of rock formations. Later, during the Ice Age, U-shaped cross sections came into being with their wide valleys, their cradles of land, and

Pasture economy, as here in Friuli, is the most important source of income in the Alpine areas of Italy. The milk of the pasture cattle is mainly turned into cheese.

their high plateaus with escarpments located above the ancient ice line. Everything that was carried south by the enormous glaciers and the rivers caused by the melting of the ice is today the vast moraine landscape located above the Po Basin.

The more one proceeds from the south into the mountains, the scantier and harsher the landscape becomes, and the more rugged the climate, eventually reaching the eternal ice of world-famous peaks that surround the Aosta Valley: Mont Blanc, the Matterhorn, Monte Rosa, Gran Paradiso. The numerous glaciers supply water for a dense network of fish-

filled rivers. The pasture economy and, of course, the cheese industry, play important roles in the cuisine. In the Aosta Valley, it is frugal; bread chowder with cheese usually begins the meal. Smoked bacon, speck (a type of country ham), butter, and heavy cream are used in abundance, while pasta is not

used very often. In the old days, only a few houses in the villages had ovens for baking; bread was baked in advance for storage for all the village families, and baked goods were rarely prepared. Meat is boiled rather than roasted: *bollito misto*, mixed boiled meat, has its origins in Piedmont. Large and

Above, left: Apple harvest near Terlan (Terlano), in South Tirol. The climatically blessed slopes produce fruit in abundance. Here, a whole family harvests apples using wobbly ladders made from narrow poles.

Left: For South Tiroleans, you can never go wrong with a gift of flowers; flower women can be found in every farmer's market.

small dumplings made mostly from potato dough show that northern specialties did not stop at the Italian border.

On the other hand, the convenient climatic conditions in the northern Alps are advantageous for a well-developed fruit-related agriculture. Spring is greeted along the slopes by scented, brilliant, pale rose clouds of fruit trees in bloom. The climate is also suitable for vineyards. Throughout the interior planes, vegetables grow abundantly. Fish from the Mediterranean Sea are rarely used, but freshwater fish are common, such as trout and whitefish from clear mountain brooks and lakes that are also great tourist attractions: Lago Maggiore and Lago d'Aorta in Piedmont, Lombardy's lakes of Varese, Iseo, Como, and Garda.

Friuli-Venezia Giulia is a rather flat region surrounded, like an amphitheater, by moraines that originated during the Ice Age. As in neighboring Veneto, corn, beans, potatoes, lots of vegetables, pork, and venison are used here. Trieste, as the most important seaport of the Austria-Hungarian Empire, came in contact with many different cuisines that were incorporated into the local cuisine in a unique

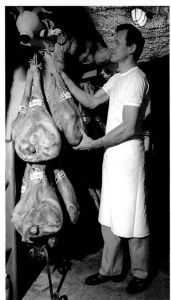

Above: Vegetable market in Bolzano (Bozen). Each town has its buzzing farmer's market where people come, find, choose, buy, and leave.

Left: Original San Daniele prosciutto hams from Friuli are as famous as Parma's prosciutto hams. While they are fresh, they are pressed between two boards to give them their typical violin shape. Mildly marinated and air-dried, they are especially delicate with a superb flavor.

Top: Autumnal still life in Tolmezzo with fresh edible chestnuts, wild porcini mushrooms, air-dried sausages, and cheese.

Above: Edible chestnuts and freshly picked walnuts displayed in the market of Bozen (Bolzano) signal that it is time to taste the new wine.

Above, right: Farmers' dried flat bread, stored in open air, can last to eternity. The stone-hard and very thin bread is a typical specialty of South Tirol.

way. Favorite flavorings and spices are poppy seeds, caraway, and anise, as well as paprika and horseradish. Desserts play an important role here, as in all other mountain areas where sugar is highly valued; on one hand, it provides a good energy source for hard laborers; on the other hand, it is easily stored.

Greatly valued for their high quality are pork products from Friuli, especially hams. Not only is the royal and delicate San Daniele prominent, but also the smoked Sauris, the Carso, and Trieste's baked ham.

People, Events, Sightseeing

can range from a small *Stiebr* (a push) to a *Reiberle* (a rub) or a heavy *Klosterrausch* (a cloister's inebriation).

Piedmont, on the other hand, with the Fiat city of Turin as its most productive hub, represents modern Italy. Piedmont's people are open and hate pretenses; opinions are outspokenly ex-

pressed. However, this good disposition also has its opposites: Turin is known as the city of black magic and occultism, as well as a place where people are known for having a sweet tooth.

Interesting sightseeing possibilities: In Turin, the Porta Palazzo market with its unique culinary offerings. In Piazza Castello, the

In the thirteenth century, German-speaking settlers arrived to Aosta from Switzerland. Ancient Bohemian-Danubian tribes that had entered through the Brenner Pass (Brennero) around the sixth century showered South Tirol with dumplings, culinary arts, and culture, while the Franks followed with pasta pockets. Local cuisine was more or less well entrenched when Longobards and Italians took over in the region.

Friuli-Venezia Giulia is not among the wealthiest regions. The hazards of local earthquakes, the worst of which occurred in 1976, do not help, either. Behind the Adriatic coast there are still areas untouched by tourism. The tradition of the *tajut*, a cheering and drinking ritual among friends, is also still to be found—when a Friuli local meets a friend, one can be sure that both will wind up in a cafè for a glass of white wine. Not accepting this first invitation without extending in return an invitation for another glass of wine would seem rude. A somewhat lengthy drinking and cheering session is

part of this custom, but you will rarely find anyone drunk, since the tradition is long-standing and the wine is served in small glasses.

Something a little bit different happens in South Tirol during Törggelen time, the traditional fall hiking season enjoyed by old and young, when the grape cider turns into new wine. People go in colorful groups, from farm to farm, where green branches are hung outside the doors as a sign that the new wine is available. During this occasion, roasted chestnuts and fresh walnuts are served. With this young wine, of course, more than one intoxicated incident can occur, which, according to South Tirolean dialect,

This old pub sign in Pordenone, Friuli, announces a place for food and good wine from the barrel.

Above: An enoteca *in Friuli is a place where old and very fine wines can be found like treasures. It also offers an opportunity for the tajut, the ritual of friendly drinking if one happens to meet a friend on the road.*

Left: A peddler of roasted chestnuts in Bolzano (Bozen). The chestnuts are at their best when eaten freshly roasted and still hot out of the bag.

Left: A regional aspect of Piedmont, where the large family system still exists.

Middle, left: A hearty South Tirolean snack in the castle tavern of Leonburg is just the right way to take a break after a good hike.

Above: In the area of Langhe, especially around Alba, you can find the most expensive and valuable mushroom: the truffle. Around the last week of November, a truffle festival and market are held here, during which the precious mushrooms are auctioned and sold for staggering prices. Piedmont's truffle is considered a unique specialty; it is white inside and usually used raw for its aroma, for example shaved on pasta dishes.

Left: In the valley of Gresonney in Aosta, regional costumes are still seen today on Sundays and during holidays.

Café Baratti with its pastry specialties prepared right there. Before entering Alba, the Castle of Grinzane Cavour, today's headquarters of the Enoteca Regionale. In Barolo, the Barolo Museum in the Falletti Castle. In Bolzano, the farmer's market in Piazza delle Erbe and on Saturday morning in Piazza della Vittoria. The Wine Road that goes from Firmiano to Ora. In Trieste, the Café Tommaseo, a favorite place for taking an aperitif.

The events: The grape festival in Chambave, in the Valley of Aosta at the end of September; a chestnut festival in Perloz during the end of October. In Piedmont, in Castiglione d'Asti and in Bellinzago Novarese, at the beginning of January, a bean festival, during which beans previously collected in the neighborhood from house to house are cooked for everyone in the town's central square. In Monastero Bormida on March 7, the *polentonissimo* festival: in the middle of the town square polenta is cooked for everyone. A similar festival is held in Ponti at the end of April. Teglio, in northern Lombardy, celebrates at the end of July the *pizoccheri* festival, a culinary event during which pizzoccheri, noodles made with potatoes and cabbage, are the main attraction. During the fall, in South Tirol and throughout Trentino, the *Törggelen*, a grape festival, is held in Merano in early October.

The Wines

Excellent wines are produced in the Aosta Valley protected by Alpine peaks. A light red wine, the *Enfer d'Arvier*, is produced in the county of the same name. It goes well with appetizers and pasta. An abundance of Nebbiolo grapes is found throughout the hills of Donnaz; the wine with the same name is brilliant red, mild, and with a delicate aroma of almonds. It is best served with meat dishes.

Best suited for Piedmont's hearty peasant cuisine are the local vigorous wines, such as wines made from Barbera grapes from the Province of Asti and Cuneo and from the hills of the Monferrato. The *Barolo*, among the first-quality Italian wines, originates from the calcium-rich soil of the Langhe mountains and is produced from Nebbiolo grapes. A delicate violet aroma is typical of this wine. The *Barbaresco*, lighter and milder and also made from Nebbiolo, is, like the *Barolo*, a good wine suitable for roasts. Named for its grape variety, the *Nebbiolo d'Alba* is, among these types of wines, the one that has the strongest aroma of violets.

The straw yellow, sweet sparkling wine, *Moscato d'Asti Spumante*, a suitable accompaniment for desserts, with its light-bodied muscat grape aroma, originates in Asti and Cuneo. In Franciacorta, a wine area located in northern Lombardy near Lago d'Iseo, dry spumante wines such as *Cà del Bosco* are produced, bottled, and treated according to classic sparkling wine methods. In addition, mild red and white wines should also be mentioned. Originally from the Valtellina valley (Veltlin) are the most popular Swiss consumer wines and some very remarkable wines of superior quality, such as the *Sassella, Grumello, Valgella,* and *Inferno*.

South Tirolean and Trentino's wine growers are exemplary role models of dedication to wine production, since their areas suitable for growing grapes are very limited in size. More than half of their wines are DOC wines and a large part of their production is exported. To be found here are notable fruity white wines with clearly detectable acidity, and delicate red wines that should be consumed while still young. Many white wine grape varieties here are world famous, such as *Riesling, Müller Thurgau, Silvaner, Traminer,* and *Sauvignon*. For the red wines, the favorite grape variety is the *Vernaccia* with the addition of a local grape variety like the Teroldego and the *Merzemino*, which, especially in Trentino, produces very interesting wines, as well as the *Lagrein* grape. Wines for fish and appetizers, as well as for venison and hearty roasts, can be found in this area.

Although more red wines are produced in Friuli, the best wines of this region are white. The To-cai grape, which has nothing in common with the Hungarian *Tokai*, is very popular. DOC wine areas are Collio Goriziano, Colli Orientali del Friuli, Grave del Friuli, and Isonzo, the small area near the river Isonzo. An extraordinary part is played by the *Picolit*, a sweet dessert wine high in alcohol content, made from the grape of the same name, which is unfairly compared to the Chateau d'Yquem.

Top: The pergola *grape-growing method, a way to train vines to grow along arbors among foliage and bunches of grapes, making work easier and increasing the yield, is popular in South Tirol.*

Middle: Artistically decorated barrels of wine owned by the wine-growing cooperative in Cormons, located in the center of the Collio Goriziano area in Friuli.

Left: The best wines of Piedmont, Barolo, Barbera, Barbaresco, and Dolcetto, ready for wine sampling are kept in a wooden barrel five or even seven years.

Regional Recipes

Bagna cauda

Raw Vegetable Fondue with Hot Anchovy Dip (Piedmont)

Serves 6 to 8

For the dip:
35 canned, drained anchovy fillets (or the contents of one and a half 2-ounce tubes of anchovy paste)
4 to 6 cloves garlic
3 tablespoons butter
3/4 cup olive oil

Vegetables:
1/2 young cauliflower
9 ounces broccoli
1 small fresh fennel bulb
1 bunch of celery
3 small peppers
    (red, green, yellow)
10 to 12 young carrots
7 ounces mushrooms

Approximate preparation time:
    1 1/4 hours;
    330 calories per serving.

This is indeed a fondue with the Italian touch—crunchy vegetables are dipped in a tangy sauce prepared with butter, oil, garlic, and anchovies, which needs to remain hot during the meal—this is very important!

There are innumerable possibilities to enhance the flavor of the dipping sauce. Each Alpine valley has its own variation: from a splash of red wine, to light shavings of white truffle, or the addition of walnut oil.

Bagna cauda is served as an appetizer but can also be a full-course meal if flanked by boiled potatoes, red beets, slices of cabbage, kohlrabi, and julienned zucchini.

The vegetables can be served either raw or blanched.

Tip: Keep the raw vegetables in iced water to keep them cold and have them retain their crunchiness until serving time. Drain them and place decoratively on a platter.

To enhance this dish prepare plenty of fresh bread to pair the powerful dip with a pleasantly plain and mild side accompaniment.

1 For the dipping sauce: Rinse the anchovies under running water, pat dry with a paper towel, and mince. Mince the garlic (or press the cloves through a garlic press).

2 In a small frying pan, melt the butter. Lightly sauté the minced garlic, but do not allow it to get too brown. Gradually add the olive oil and stir constantly over low heat, making sure not to burn the garlic.

3 Prepare the vegetables: Trim the cauliflower and the broccoli and divide in florets; blanch in salted boiling water (4 minutes for the cauliflower, 2 minutes for the broccoli). With a slotted spoon, drop the cauliflower and the broccoli into iced water to stop the cooking process, and drain. Cut the fennel into 1/4-inch-thick slices. Cut the celery into 1 1/3-inch-long pieces. Cut in half, seed, and slice the peppers. Peel the carrots and slice lengthwise into thin, long strips. Thoroughly clean the mushrooms but leave them whole.

4 Remove the frying pan with the hot dipping sauce from the heat. Add the minced anchovies to the hot liquid, making sure to press down all the ingredients with a fork to reduce the mixture to a paste. Return the frying pan to the heat, and heat the mixture until it becomes a creamy dipping sauce.

5 To serve: Prepare a food warmer in the middle of your table. Place your vegetables decoratively on a serving platter. Place the frying pan on the food warmer, or put the hot dipping sauce in smaller saucepans on individual food warmers for each guest. According to taste, dip each piece of vegetable in the hot dipping sauce and serve with *grissini* (thin Italian breadsticks) and fresh white bread.

Prosciutto e fichi
Prosciutto Ham and Fresh Figs (Friuli)

Carpaccio
Raw, Shaved, Marinated Beef (Piedmont)

Serves 4

5 ounces San Daniele prosciutto ham, sliced paper thin
(you may substitute import-
ed prosciutto ham)
8 fresh, fully ripe figs
Freshly ground coarse pepper

Approximate preparation time:
10 minutes (+ 15 minutes
refrigeration time);
180 calories per serving.

1 Place the fresh figs in iced
water to thoroughly cool.

2 Separate the thin and delicate slices of prosciutto ham
and place them on a serving
platter. Drain the figs, quarter or
cut them in cross sections, and
place them near the prosciutto.

3 At the table everyone will
take some of the prosciutto
and several sections of figs.
Prepare a pepper mill for the
prosciutto. Only those figs cut

in cross sections will be easy to
peel.

• Serve freshly baked white
bread with this dish.

• Variation: You may substitute
a spicy variety of salami
sausage for the prosciutto or
serve the prosciutto with a fully
ripe cantaloupe sliced into fairly
thin, seedless pieces.

Serves 4 to 6

7 ounces beef tenderloin,
whole (the center portion,
should be without connec-
tive tissue and fat)
5 ounces fresh, small, brown
or white mushrooms (you
may substitute fresh, delicate porcini, if available)
1 to 2 lemons
1/2 bunch of fresh basil
2 ounces Parmesan cheese,
whole
8 tablespoons extra virgin olive
oil + enough olive oil to
serve at the table
Freshly ground coarse pepper

Approximate preparation time:
30 minutes
(+ 1 hour for refrigeration);
210 calories per serving.

1 Wrap the piece of tenderloin in either plastic wrap or
aluminum foil; freeze until firm
(about 1 hour).

2 Brush four serving plates
with 1 tablespoon of olive
oil. With a sharp knife or with
an electric slicer, slice the tenderloin paper thin. Remove the
foil or the plastic wrap from
the meat slices and, if necessary, pound the meat with a
meat mallet to make the slices
much thinner. Place the slices
of meat in a layer on the plates
and drizzle with the remaining
olive oil.

3 Clean and thoroughly brush
the mushrooms. Slice them
paper thin. Thinly shave the
Parmesan cheese and distribute the shavings over the
meat. Season with freshly
ground coarse pepper and garnish with fresh basil leaves.
Cut the lemon into halves and
serve with the carpaccio, together with salt and olive oil.
Season to individual taste at
the table.

Vitello tonnato
Boiled Sliced Veal with Tuna Sauce (Piedmont)

• Serve with fresh, crispy bread on the side.

• This dish prepared with raw meat is also called *carne cruda*. It is a classic appetizer from Piedmont and has become a great favorite even outside the borders of the region. It is hard to find a fine eating establishment that would have the courage to leave this gourmet delicacy off the menu. For creative chefs using other ingredients, such as raw salmon, tuna, breast of duck, or for a vegetarian touch, sliced raw cepes mushrooms, carpaccio has become an interesting culinary challenge. Mandatory for every carpaccio recipe: absolutely fresh and first – quality raw main ingredients!

Serves 4 to 6

1 1/3 pound veal sirloin tip
1 stalk celery, coarsely chopped
1 carrot, coarsely chopped
2 lemons
3 cups dry white wine
2 tablespoons white wine
    vinegar
1 6-ounce can of light chunk
    tuna in spring water
3 canned anchovy fillets,
    drained
2 egg yolks
3/4 cup olive oil
3 tablespoons pickled capers,
    drained
1 onion, coarsely chopped
1 bay leaf
2 cloves
Salt and freshly ground pepper

Approximate preparation time:
  2 hours (+ 24 hours for marinating + 3 to 4 hours refrigeration);
  550 calories per serving.

1 Put the veal sirloin tip in a large pot and pour the white wine over it. Add the celery, carrot, and onion to the meat along with the bay leaf and cloves. Cover and set aside to marinate for 24 hours. Periodically turn the meat in the marinade.

2 Pour in enough water to cover the meat and bring to a boil. Add 1 teaspoon of salt. Simmer for 1 hour, then remove from heat. Allow the meat to cool in the broth.

3 Drain the tuna. Rinse the anchovies, pat dry with a paper towel, and mince. In a food processor, process the tuna, anchovies, egg yolks, and 2 tablespoons of capers with the juice of 1/2 lemon and the wine vinegar until you get a smooth puree. While pureeing, gradually add 2 or 3 tablespoons of broth and the olive oil. Puree to a smooth sauce. Season with salt and pepper.

4 Slice the meat into thin slices and place on a large platter. Cover everything evenly with the tuna sauce. Cover and refrigerate for 3 to 4 hours.

5 Before serving the meat, thinly slice 1 1/2 lemons. Garnish the meat with the slices of lemons and 1 tablespoon of capers distributed evenly over the sauce.

• Very important: Serve chilled with a lot of white bread.

• The sauce should be smooth, creamy, and not too dense. If necessary, add more broth until you get the right fluid consistency.

Antipasto di peperoni
Appetizer of Roasted Peppers (Piedmont)

Serves 4 to 6

4 large peppers (red, green, and yellow)
Juice from 1 small lemon (about 2 tablespoons)
2 cloves garlic
6 tablespoons olive oil
Salt and freshly ground pepper

Approximate preparation time:
20 minutes (+ approximately 1 hour for cooling off and marinating);
120 calories per serving.

1 Wash, cut in halves, trim the inside, and seed the peppers. Place the pepper halves, with the skin facing up, on a baking sheet, and broil until blisters appear on the skin. Remove from the oven and cover with a damp, clean dishcloth. Set the peppers aside to cool off. When they are cool, peel off the skins with a paring knife.

2 If possible, keep the juice of the roasted peppers and mix this with the lemon juice. Peel the garlic, slice into very thin slices, and add to the lemon juice.

3 Cut the pepper halves vertically into 1 1/4-inch-wide slices. Place on a serving platter and season with salt and pepper. Drizzle with the lemon-garlic marinade and olive oil. Cover and set aside to allow the juice to flavor the peppers.

• Peeling can also be done in the microwave: Prepare the peppers as described above, lay them on a large microwave-proof platter, and microwave on high for 3 minutes. The skin will peel off very rapidly and easily.

Carote in agro
Sweet-and-Sour Carrots (Piedmont)

Serves 4

1 pound small, young carrots
1 bunch of fresh mixed herbs including rosemary, parsley, peppermint, and bay leaf
1 bunch fresh basil
1/2 cup dry white wine
1/2 cup white wine vinegar
2 cloves garlic
1 tablespoon granulated sugar
4 tablespoons olive oil
Salt and pepper

Approximate preparation time:
25 minutes (+ 1 to 2 days for marinating);
160 calories per serving.

1 Clean the carrots and cut them into 1/2-inch-thick diagonal slices. Bring the carrots to a boil in a large saucepan with 1/2 cup water, the wine, and the vinegar.

2 Peel and cut the cloves of garlic in halves. Add the garlic to the carrots, with the granulated sugar and olive oil. Add the mixed fresh herbs, cover, and simmer all the ingredients for 10 to 15 minutes.

3 Remove from the heat and allow to cool off. Remove the garlic and herbs and place the carrots in a separate bowl. Pass the cooking liquid through a fine strainer and drizzle the carrots with the liquid. Cover and refrigerate for 1 to 2 days until the flavors have seeped into the carrots. Serve topped with fresh basil.

• Preserved vegetables not only have a very delicate and good flavor, but they are also very easy to prepare. They are a wonderful menu item when you plan a multicolored appetizer buffet for numerous guests, or when you have plans for a simple and easy appetizer meal. You can use this recipe for many other vegetables, such as strips of zucchini or small white carrots.

Fagioli con cotechino
Beans with Cotechino Sausage (Friuli)

Serves 4

7 ounces cotechino sausage
   (you may substitute kielbasa)
1/2 cup dried white beans
2 small onions
1/2 teaspoon chopped fresh
marjoram leaves (or 1/4 teaspoon dried marjoram)
1 ounce or 2 tablespoons butter
2 tablespoons extra virgin olive
   oil
1 to 2 tablespoons red wine
   vinegar
Salt and freshly ground pepper

Approximate preparation time:
   40 minutes (+ 12 hours for
   soaking beans);
   290 calories per serving.

1 Soak the beans overnight in
water; the next day cook
them in the soaking water for
about 30 minutes.

2 In the meantime, trim, peel,
and cut the onions into
eighths. In a large saucepan,
heat the butter and sauté the

onions until glossy. Add the
marjoram and season with salt
and pepper.

3 Slice the sausage, add to
the onions, and brown on
both sides. When the beans are
cooked, drain them, and add
them to the sausage-onion mixture. Drizzle with the olive oil
and, if you wish, with more red
wine vinegar. Season again
with salt and pepper, and serve
immediately.

Sedani al formaggio
Raw Celery with Cheese Dip (Lombardy)

Serves 6

1 large bunch celery
3 1/2 ounces Gorgonzola
   cheese (or blue cheese)
4 tablespoons whipping cream
3 1/2 ounces mascarpone
   cheese
Freshly ground pepper

Approximate preparation time:
   15 minutes;
   130 calories per serving.

1 Thoroughly clean and rinse
each celery stalk and keep
the green tops. Cut each stalk
into 3 to 4 pieces and pat dry.

2 Crush and press the Gorgonzola cheese with a fork,
and cream together with the
whipping cream. Gradually add
the mascarpone cheese and
mix until you get a smooth
cream.

3 Fill a bowl with the cheese
mixture and season with
freshly ground pepper. Garnish
with the remaining green celery

tops and serve with the pieces
of celery.

• Celery stalks are a favorite in
Italian vegetable cuisine. The
leader in celery production is
Piedmont, followed by Latium
and Apulia.

101

Polenta pasticciata

Polenta Casserole (Piedmont)

Serves 6

12 ounces ground beef
5 ounces mild Italian sausage
1 2/3 cups freshly grated
   Parmesan cheese
9 ounces or 1 3/4 cups
   + 2 tablespoons cornmeal
1 onion, minced
2 tablespoons tomato paste
6 tablespoons butter
Salt and freshly ground pepper

<u>Approximate preparation time:</u>
   1 1/2 hours;
   580 calories per serving.

Considering how important corn flour is in regional Northern Italian peasant cuisine, it is hard to remember that corn was brought to Europe by Christopher Columbus not so long ago. A duke from the mountains south of Rimini, who was a friend and companion of the explorer, seems to have been the one who recognized the value of the golden kernels, bringing them back from the New World wrapped in velvet. It is because of traditional cooks and peasants that the popular corn mush is still prepared in the regions of Lombardy and Veneto, Friuli, South Tirol, Piedmont and

Trentino according to old regional culinary rules. As in the past, polenta is stirred today with great care and patience until the mush is poured out of the pot and the delicious crusty borders can be removed.

Important: The pot should be made of copper, cast iron, or aluminum, and should be high enough to prevent the polenta from spilling over the rim. The classic implement for stirring the mush is the *bastone*, a long, flat, wooden spatula. For home use, a simple long wooden stirring spoon will do fine.

1 In a suitable pot, bring 4 cups of salted water to a boil. While stirring constantly with a long spoon, gradually pour the cornmeal into the water. To prevent lumps, reduce the water temperature and be careful, since the bubbles could burst and splatter.

2 Reduce the heat and let the polenta simmer for 30 minutes, stirring vigorously as often as possible. A crusty layer will gradually appear as the cornmeal begins to pull away from the bottom and the walls of the pot. Should the polenta be too firm and dry, add more boiling water; should it be too runny, very carefully add a bit more cornmeal. Pour the finished polenta onto either a large wooden board or a clean dishcloth dusted with semolina, and shape evenly into a 2-inch-thick cake. Set aside to cool off.

3 In a large frying pan, heat 2 tablespoons of butter. Gradually add the ground beef and sausage meat without the casing, and brown. Season with salt and pepper. Stir in the tomato paste and 2 tablespoons of water. Simmer for 5 minutes. Preheat the oven to 300°F.

4 On the side, melt the remaining butter. Brush a large baking dish with 2 tablespoons of the melted butter. Cut the cold polenta into 1/2-inch-thick slices (the best way to do this is to cut the slices with a kitchen thread).

5 Place a layer of polenta slices on the bottom of the baking dish. Drizzle with butter, dust with Parmesan cheese, add a layer of the meat mixture (Note: keep 2 to 3 tablespoons of grated Parmesan cheese for final use before serving). Place another layer of polenta slices, drizzle with melted butter, sprinkle with grated Parmesan cheese and more ground meat. Repeat until no more ingredients are left. Finish with a layer of polenta drizzled with the remaining butter.

6 Bake in the preheated oven for about 30 minutes. Sprinkle with the remaining grated Parmesan cheese and serve in the baking dish.

Polenta smalzada trentina
Polenta Casserole with Anchovies (Trentino)

Canederli in brodo
Bread and Ham Dumpling Soup (South Tirol)

Polenta smalzada trentina

Serves 4

1 ¼ cups freshly grated
    Parmesan cheese
1 ¾ cups + 2 tablespoons
    cornmeal
10 canned anchovy fillets,
    drained
6 tablespoons butter
Salt

Approximate preparation time:
    1 hour;
    550 calories per serving.

1 In a large, heavy pot (made of cast iron or copper), bring 4 cups of salted water to a rolling boil, and gradually pour the cornmeal into the water. Simmer for 40 minutes, stirring as often as possible.

2 Preheat the oven to 425°F. Melt the butter, but do not burn. Brush a large baking dish with the butter.

3 As soon as the polenta has reached the proper consistency, and when it pulls away from the sides of the pot, pour the mixture into the buttered baking dish and spread it evenly with a spatula.

4 Rinse the anchovies and pat dry. Mince them and distribute them evenly over the polenta. Drizzle with half of the melted butter and sprinkle with half of the grated Parmesan cheese.

Canederli in brodo

Serves 4

4 ounces or 4 slices Speck (you
    may substitute country ham
    or double smoked bacon),
    finely chopped
2 ounces or 2 slices Italian
    salami, sliced thick
1 bunch fresh Italian parsley,
    minced
1 bunch fresh chives
9 ounces stale white bread
3 eggs
1 cup milk
6 cups clear beef broth
1 onion, finely chopped
6 tablespoons all-purpose flour
Salt and freshly ground pepper
Nutmeg

Approximate preparation time:
    1 ½ hours;
    620 calories per serving.

1 Dice the white bread and place in a medium mixing bowl. Whisk together the eggs and milk and pour the mixture over the bread. Set aside to soak for 20 minutes. Stir periodically.

2 In a small frying pan, sauté the Speck (or country ham), onion, and half of the parsley for 2 minutes.

3 Dice the salami and fold it into the Speck mixture, with the remaining parsley. Add this to the soaked bread, with the flour. Season with salt, pepper, and freshly grated nutmeg.

4 Bring the clear beef broth to a boil in a medium saucepan. With wet hands, form 10 small dumplings of approximately equal shape and size, and simmer these in the broth until they float to the surface. Snip the chives, sprinkle them over the soup, and serve.

• For this dish, you are probably better off preparing the beef broth the day before. Prepare lots of fresh vegetables (car-

Strangolapreti
Spinach Dumplings (Trentino)

rots, celery, onions, and leeks) in advance. Wash, trim, and slice them. Combine with 8 cups of salted water and a few marrow bones. Add a bay leaf, clove, and peppercorns, and bring to a boil. In the boiling water, you may add a piece of beef at this point. Reduce the temperature and simmer for 1 to 2 hours, making sure that the temperature remains below boiling point.

Serves 4 to 6

1 pound fresh spinach leaves
Several fresh sage leaves
2/3 cup freshly grated Parmesan cheese
9 ounces stale white bread
2 eggs
1/2 cup + 1 tablespoon milk
3 tablespoons butter
4 to 5 tablespoons all-purpose flour (the amount will vary according to the moistness of the mixture)
Salt and freshly ground pepper
Nutmeg

Approximate preparation time: 1 hour (+ 2 hours refrigeration); 330 calories per serving.

1 Dice the bread. Drizzle the bread with the milk and combine thoroughly. Cover and set aside for at least 2 hours to allow the bread to absorb the milk.

2 Trim and clean the spinach leaves. Bring salted water to a rolling boil in a pot. Blanch the spinach for 2 minutes. Remove the spinach and drop it into iced water. Drain thoroughly and set it aside to cool off. When the spinach is cold, squeeze the remaining moisture out of it, and chop it as finely as possible.

3 Mix and knead together the chopped spinach, soaked bread, eggs, and flour. Season with salt, pepper, and grated nutmeg.

4 In a pot, bring salted water to a boil. With two tablespoons, form a test dumpling and let the dumpling simmer for 5 minutes. According to the dumpling's consistency, either add more flour or more milk. When the dough is of the proper consistency, form the dumplings and simmer them in the water.

5 Drain the dumplings with a slotted spoon and place them on preheated plates. Melt the butter with the sage leaves, allowing the butter to soak up the flavor. Add the dumplings and mix them in the flavored butter. Sprinkle with the Parmesan cheese and serve.

• An accompaniment for a dish such as a meat stew or sauce!

Gnocchi di patate alla piemontese
Small Potato Dumplings, Piedmont Style (Piedmont)

Serves 4 to 6

<u>*For the dough:*</u>
2 pounds potatoes (preferably
  of a variety used for baking)
1 ³/₄ cups all-purpose flour
Salt

<u>*For the sauce:*</u>
1 ²/₃ pounds fresh ripe
  tomatoes
Fresh sage leaves
1 onion, minced
3 tablespoons butter
Salt and freshly ground pepper

<u>*Topping:*</u>
²/₃ cup freshly grated
  Parmesan cheese

<u>*Approximate preparation time:*</u>
  1 hour;
  360 calories per serving.

Not only in Piedmont will gourmets encounter these small humble-looking dough dumplings made of boiled, riced potatoes, flour, and salt. Throughout other regions they are sometimes also prepared with 1 to 2 eggs added to the dough in order to make them smoother. The most important factor here is the variety of the potatoes.

The easy-to-prepare tomato sauce is only one of many serving suggestions for this dish. The easiest way: is to simply top the dumplings with melted butter, and season them with freshly ground pepper and lots of freshly grated Parmesan cheese. These dumplings can also be served with any type of rich gravy, made of rabbit meat, stewed vegetables, beef, or stewed mushrooms with fresh herbs.

An interesting variation of this specialty is made in Trentino: Small potato and red beet dumplings are topped with butter and poppy seeds.

• Wine serving suggestion: A smooth and mild red wine, such as a *Barbaresco* or a *Barbera*.

1 For the dough, wash the potatoes and boil them in salted water in a large saucepan until they are soft. Remove the potatoes and peel; while they are still warm, press the potatoes through a ricer onto a well-floured work surface. Prepare the tomato sauce while the potatoes are boiling (see picture 3).

2 Sprinkle a little salt over the dough and knead enough flour into it to make a smooth, silky dough. The amount of flour will vary according to the type of potatoes used; the dough should not be sticky.

3 For the sauce: Blanch the tomatoes, and with a slotted spoon drop them into iced water, and peel them. Seed and chop them. Sauté the minced onion in 1 tablespoon of butter in a medium saucepan until glossy. Stir the tomatoes into the onions. Season with salt and pepper and simmer until you get a smooth sauce.

4 To make the dumplings, divide the dough into portions and roll each portion of dough into sausage-shaped finger-thick ropes. Cut each rope into smaller pieces that are $3/4$ to $1 1/4$ inches long. Press each small piece of dough onto a four-sided grater or onto a fork. Set the shaped gnocchi aside onto the floured work surface. In the meantime, bring 8 cups of salted water to a rolling boil in a large pot.

5 Gradually drop the gnocchi into the boiling water, reduce the heat, and simmer for 4 minutes. Periodically stir to prevent the gnocchi from sticking to the bottom of the pot. With a slotted spoon, remove the gnocchi from the water as soon as they float to the water's surface. Drain them thoroughly.

6 Sauté the fresh sage leaves in 1 tablespoon of butter in a large frying pan. Add the cooked gnocchi, making sure that all the dumplings are coated with the flavored butter. Serve topped with tomato sauce and freshly grated Parmesan cheese.

Minestra d'orzo

Barley Soup (Alto Adige/South Tirol)

Serves 4

*3 ounces or 2 thick slices
    Speck (you may substitute
    double-smoked bacon)
1 small fresh leek
2 stalks celery
2 medium carrots
2 medium potatoes
1 bunch fresh parsley
1 cup + 3 tablespoons pearled
    barley
1 onion
2 cloves garlic
1 bay leaf
8 cups beef or bone broth
2 tablespoons olive oil
Salt and freshly grated pepper*

*Approximate preparation time:
    80 minutes;
    430 calories per serving.*

1 Cut the Speck into thin strips. Thoroughly clean the leek and celery and slice thin. Slice the carrots, and dice the potatoes. Mince the onion and garlic cloves.

2 In a large pot, sauté the Speck, adding 2 tablespoons of oil. Add the vegetables and sauté for 5 minutes. Add the barley, bay leaf, and broth. Bring everything to a boil.

3 Reduce the heat and let the soup simmer for about 1 hour or until the barley is done. Remove the bay leaf and season with salt and pepper. Sprinkle with parsley leaves.

• Pearled barley is hulled and polished kernels of barley; in the market it is also labeled either rolled or hulled barley.

Fonduta

*Cheese Fondue
(Warm Cheese Dip) (Piedmont)*

Serves 4 to 6

*11 ounces Fontina cheese (you
    may substitute Provolone or
    Italian mountain cheese that
    has at least a 40 percent fat
    content)
1/3 cup + 2 tablespoons milk
1 tablespoon butter
Yolks of 3 small eggs
Freshly ground pepper
8 small slices of bread*

*Approximately preparation time:
    30 minutes (+ 12 hours for
    soaking the cheese);
    520 calories per serving.*

1 Dice the Fontina cheese, place it in a bowl, and pour the milk over it. Cover and refrigerate for at least several hours, or overnight, to allow the milk to be absorbed by the cheese.

2 For this next step, use either a double boiler or a suitable fondue pot. Melt the butter in the container that will be placed in the hot water bath.

3 Add the cheese and milk mixture, and gradually, on a very low heat, melt the cheese, whisking constantly with a heat-resistant whisk.

4 Raise the temperature of the water bath as soon as the cheese makes threads and is melted. One after another, gradually add the eggs, whisking them vigorously with a whisk or a wooden spoon. Whisk and stir until the cheese fondue is evenly colored and smooth, and the cheese threads are no longer visible.

5 Divide the cheese mixture into smaller individual bowls and season with freshly ground pepper. Serve with toasted bread.

• A splendid example of a simple but refined cuisine, with its

Zuppa di Valpelline

Cabbage, Ham, and Cheese Soup (Aosta Valley)

special culinary secrets. The whole thing begins with the maturity of the cheese, then goes to the material from which the bowl used to prepare this dish is made, to the size of the eggs, and to the degree of the cook's patience. Vigorous whisking and stirring are also essential for this dish, as well as the proper overall temperature of the ingredients.

• A small detail for beginners: First, very lightly brown 1 tablespoon of flour together with the melted butter, and later add the cheese with the milk.

• If you can afford it, crown this special effort with a thin layer of freshly shaved truffle, preferably from Piedmont.

Serves 4

5 ounces or 10 to 12 slices bacon, sliced very thin
1 fresh cabbage (1 ¹/₃ pound)
5 ounces Fontina cheese, sliced
8 small slices of Italian semolina bread (you may substitute slices of whole grain bread)
About 4 cups meat stock
2 tablespoons butter
Salt and freshly ground pepper

Approximate preparation time:
1 ¹/₄ hours;
690 calories per serving.

1 Remove the outer leaves and thoroughly clean and core the cabbage. Blanch the remaining leaves in salted water in a large pot for 8 minutes. With a slotted spoon, remove the cabbage and drop it into iced water to stop the cooking process. Cut into thin strips.

2 Cut the bacon into thin strips, sauté in a small frying pan, and remove when the fat has been rendered. Brush a deep baking dish with the bacon fat. Preheat the oven to 350°F.

3 Lightly toast the bread slices and place 4 of them on the bottom of the baking dish. Top the bread with several strips of bacon and cabbage. Top this layer with slices of cheese. Alternate layers of bacon and cabbage and cheese until no more ingredients remain. Top the last layer with bread and slices of cheese and dot with 2 tablespoons of butter.

4 Pour enough meat stock into the baking dish to cover all the ingredients (about 4 cups of stock). Bake the soup in the preheated oven for 45 minutes. Season with salt and pepper before serving very hot.

Bollito misto con salsa verde

Mixed Boiled Meat with Green Sauce (Piedmont/Aosta Valley)

Serves 8 to 10

1 fresh calf's tongue
(about 1 1/3 pounds)
2 pounds beef (either brisket or
chuck steak)
1 young chicken
(about 3 pounds)
1 pound veal (preferably sirloin
tip)
1 pork garlic-flavored sausage,
about 11 ounces (try kielbasa)
4 stalks of celery
3 carrots
1 small leek
2 onions
Salt
1/2 teaspoon peppercorns

For the green sauce:
4 bunches fresh Italian parsley
6 canned anchovy fillets, drained
1 clove garlic
1 to 2 tablespoons pickled
capers, drained
2 egg yolks
5 tablespoons olive oil
2 teaspoons wine vinegar
Salt

Approximate preparation time:
2 1/2 hours;
740 calories per serving.

A traditional substantial family
meal that can feed many people
gathered around a large table
without too much work.

All considered, several more
meat varieties and sausages
would be required for the authentic bollito misto, for example, *zampone*, a stuffed pork
trotter, which is rarely found on
the American market (in Italian
specialty stores it is sometimes
available precooked, and
prepackaged; if you find one,
just follow the cooking instructions on the package, heating
the zampone for several hours in
hot water). More simply, you
could complete the dish with oxtail (cooking time about 1 1/2
hours) and marrowbones (simmer only for 15 minutes).

Tangy fruits pickled in sweet-
spicy mustard sauce (Mostarda
di Cremona), a northern Italian
specialty, are preferably served
with this meat dish.

1 In a large pot, cover the calf's tongue with water and bring to a boil. Reduce the heat and simmer the tongue for about 1 1/2 hours.

2 In another large pot, bring about 3 quarts of salted wa-ter to a rolling boil and add the beef and the peppercorns. Re-duce the heat, and simmer the meat approximately 30 min-utes. Add the chicken.

3 Thoroughly clean the celery, carrots, and leek. Cut them in smaller pieces, together with the onions, and add them to a third large pot, along with the veal. Simmer all ingredients for approximately 1 hour.

4 Green sauce: Trim the stemless leaves of parsley and process together with the anchovies, garlic, capers, and egg yolks until you get a smooth puree. Gradually add the oil in a very thin stream until you get a smooth sauce. Season with salt and pepper.

5 Prick the pork sausage, cover with water in a medium saucepan, and bring to a gentle boil. When the calf's tongue is tender, remove it from the water, drop it into iced water, and, with a pointed sharp paring knife, begin to peel it from the tip inward. Before serving all the meats, heat them thoroughly, once more, in one of the large pots. Slice all the meats, including the sausage, and divide the chicken in suitable portions, placing everything on a large preheated platter. Serve with the green sauce, and boiled vegetables. As a side dish, you may also serve steamed potatoes.

Spezzatino d'agnello
Lamb Stew (Friuli)

Serves 4

1 1/3 pound boneless lamb
  (either shoulder or leg)
2 ounces or two thin slices
  bacon
1 onion, minced
2 cloves garlic, minced
5 tablespoons oil
1 tablespoon flour
1/2 cup beef stock
1/2 cup red wine
2 tablespoons tomato paste
1 pinch powdered cinnamon
Salt and freshly ground pepper

<u>Approximate preparation time:</u>
  1 1/4 hours;
  570 calories per serving.

1 Cut the lamb into 1- to 1 1/4-inch cubes. Cut the bacon in thin strips. In a large pot, heat the oil. Add first the bacon, then the onion and the garlic, and brown until golden.

2 Gradually add the lamb cubes, and brown evenly on all sides. Season with salt and pepper, and dust with the flour, allowing the mixture to brown thoroughly. Add the beef stock, stir and simmer, covered, for 1 hour.

3 After 30 minutes of cooking, add the red wine and season with the powdered cinnamon. Stir in the tomato paste, and finish cooking. Toward the end of the cooking stage, you can remove the cover of the pot to allow the juices to cook down further. Season once more with salt and pepper.

• Suitable side dish for this specialty: steamed potatoes or soft polenta, sliced and pan-fried as described in the recipe on page 102.

Coniglio in peperonata
*Stewed Rabbit with Peppers
(Piedmont/Aosta Valley)*

Serves 4

1 ready-to-use rabbit (about 2
  pounds)
3 ounces or 2 thick slices of
  fatty bacon
3 large green peppers
1 fresh sprig of rosemary (or 1
  tablespoon of stemless dried
  rosemary)
2 to 3 cloves garlic, crushed
5 canned anchovy fillets,
  drained
4 tablespoons olive oil
4 tablespoons white wine
  vinegar
1 cup beef stock
Salt and freshly ground pepper

<u>Approximate preparation time:</u>
  70 minutes;
  620 calories per serving.

1 Rinse and pat the rabbit dry. Divide into 8 to 10 pieces. Rub on all sides with salt, pepper, and a halved clove of garlic.

2 Dice the bacon and, in a large casserole or Dutch oven; sauté until the fat has melted. Remove the bacon bits and set them aside for later use. Add and heat 2 tablespoons of olive oil. Add the pieces of rabbit and brown on all sides. Add the rosemary and pour the beef stock over the meat. Cover and simmer for about 40 minutes.

3 Thoroughly clean the peppers. Cut them in halves, seed, and slice in 1/2-inch-wide strips. Rinse the anchovies, pat them dry with paper towels, and mince.

4 In a large frying pan, heat 2 tablespoons of olive oil. Add the peppers and sauté together with 2 crushed garlic cloves. Pour the white wine vinegar, bring to a rolling boil, and cook down to a half. Stir in the minced anchovies.

5 Add the pepper-garlic mixture to the rabbit and cook

Lingua in salsa piccante
Calf's Tongue with Spicy Sauce (Piedmont/Aosta Valley)

for 15 more minutes. Remove the rosemary, and season the sauce with salt and pepper. Add the bacon pieces to the rabbit and serve while still hot.

• For stewing, you can substitute the beef stock with white wine.

• Wine serving suggestion: A dry mild red wine, such as a *Donnaz*.

Serves 4 to 6

1 fresh calf's tongue (2 pounds)
1 carrot
3 stalks celery
1 small leek
1/2 lemon
11 ounces fresh, ripe tomatoes
1 bunch fresh Italian parsley
3/4 cup dried mushrooms (porcini or mixed mushrooms)
2 onions
3 cloves garlic
2 cups dry white wine
2 tablespoons butter
1 bay leaf
1 clove
1/2 teaspoon peppercorns
Salt and freshly ground pepper

Approximate preparation time:
1 3/4 hours (+ 2 hours for soaking the mushrooms); 330 calories per serving.

1 Soak the dried mushrooms in 1/2 cup of water. Rinse the calf's tongue. In a pot, simmer the tongue, together with 4 cups of water and 1 cup of white wine. Clean the carrot, 2 celery stalks, and leek, and cut in small pieces. Cut 1 onion in half. Slice the lemon. Add these ingredients to the tongue together with the clove, bay leaf, and peppercorns. Add salt. Partially cover and simmer 1 1/4 hours.

2 After 1/2 hour of simmering, prepare the sauce. Mince the onion, garlic, 1 celery stalk, and 1/2 bunch of parsley. In a saucepan, melt 2 tablespoons of butter and sauté the mixture for 10 minutes. Drain the soaked mushrooms, and set the water aside. Finely chop the mushrooms, add them to the vegetables, and sauté.

3 Blanch the tomatoes, drop them into iced water, and peel them. Chop them coarsely, strain them, and add them to the other ingredients in the pot. Pour in the wine and the mushroom water. Season with salt and pepper. Cook on a high heat for 20 minutes. If necessary, add some tongue broth.

4 After 1 1/4 hours cooking, remove the tongue from the water, drop it into iced water, and, when it is cold, begin to peel it from the tip inward. Cut the tongue in 1/4-inch-thick diagonal slices. Place the slices in the tomato sauce and finish simmering for 10 more minutes. Season the sauce, chop the remaining parsley, and sprinkle it over all the ingredients.

• Wine serving suggestion: A white wine, such as a *Pinot Grigio* from the Trentino region.

Pollo alla Marengo

*Stewed Chicken with Tomato Sauce and Scrambled Eggs
(Piedmont/Aosta Valley)*

Serves 4 to 6

1 young chicken (2 pounds)
4 to 6 unpeeled large shrimps
   (at least one shrimp per
   serving)
1 pound fresh, ripe tomatoes
9 ounces fresh mushrooms
   (white or baby portobello)
7 ounces fresh pearl onions
   (you may substitute tiny
   onions)
1 bunch fresh Italian parsley
1/2 bunch fresh basil
2 cloves garlic, crushed
Juice of 1 lemon (2 to 3 tablespoons)
4 eggs
1/2 cup dry white wine
1/2 cup chicken stock
5 tablespoons olive oil
2 tablespoons butter
Slices of white bread
Salt and freshly ground pepper

<u>Approximate preparation time:</u>
  1 1/4 hours;
  450 calories per serving.

This dish, richly garnished, has been a favorite for the past 200 years, served with a mixture of legends and culinary stories. The seafood, tomatoes, and scrambled eggs were added to the recipe much later, making this chicken dish as substantial as it is.

Around 1800 no less a personality than Napoleon Bonaparte asked for this specialty after the battle of Marengo—was this dish a culinary coincidence created by an overwhelmed farmer woman in Piedmont? Or was it indeed a creation of the Frenchman's field cook who did not want to miss an opportunity to celebrate the victory over the Austrians with his culinary wooden spoon? Whatever might have happened, this unusual recipe, still a favorite today in France, became a gift to the world of gourmets.

Tip: Enhance the recipe with more vegetables, such as celery and scallions. The shrimp will also be delicious if sautéed in garlic-flavored olive oil instead of being braised.

1 With a sharp butcher's knife, cut the chicken into 6 to 8 sections. Rub with salt and pepper. In a large frying pan or Dutch oven, heat the olive oil and brown the chicken pieces on all sides for about 10 minutes. Remove only the breasts and set them aside.

2 In the meantime, blanch the tomatoes, drop them with a slotted spoon into iced water, and peel them. Remove the seeds and chop them coarsely, adding them gradually to the chicken. Moisten with the white wine and chicken stock. Add the crushed garlic. Cover and simmer for 45 minutes.

3 Thoroughly clean the mushrooms. You can cut the larger ones in halves. Peel the pearl onions. In a medium frying pan heat 1 tablespoon of butter. Add the onions and mushrooms, and sauté about 10 minutes. Moisten with 2 tablespoons of lemon juice and season with salt and pepper.

4 Bring ½ cup of water and the remaining 1 tablespoon of lemon juice to a boil in a medium saucepan. Add the shrimp and simmer for about 6 minutes, or until they become a reddish color (for a flavoring juice, you can also sauté 1 crushed clove of garlic in 2 tablespoons of olive oil and moisten with lemon juice).

5 Remove the pieces of cooked chicken, season the pan sauce, and allow it to cook down further until it has reached the desired consistency. Return the chicken pieces, together with the breasts, to the sauce, and heat everything once more. Add the onions and mushrooms.

6 Melt 1 tablespoon of butter in the mushroom pan and add the eggs, lightly beaten. Cook the egg mixture over low heat and scramble it with a fork. Season with salt and pepper.

7 Mince the parsley. Toast the bread slices. Place the chicken pieces with the shrimp, scrambled eggs, and toasted bread on a platter. Garnish with stemless basil leaves and minced parsley.

Cavolo rosso
Stewed Red Cabbage (Alto Adige/South Tirol)

Serves 4 to 6

2 ounces or two slices Speck
 (you may substitute country
 ham or double smoked
 bacon)
1 small head of red cabbage
 (1 ²/₃ pounds)
³/₄ cup red wine
1 onion, minced
2 tablespoons butter
1 pinch of granulated sugar
Salt and freshly ground pepper

<u>Approximate preparation time:</u>
 1 hour;
 140 calories per serving.

1 Remove the outer leaves of
the red cabbage; cut the
head into quarters and core.
Cut each quarter of cabbage into very thin strips. Thoroughly
wash and drain.

2 Mince the Speck (or the
country ham or bacon). In a
large frying pan, add the Speck
with the butter and sauté until
glossy and the fat is rendered.

Remove the crispy pieces of
Speck and set them aside for
later use. Sauté the onion in the
butter until golden and glossy.

3 Add the sliced cabbage and
season with salt, pepper,
and a pinch of sugar. Stir periodically. Moisten with the red
wine and cook, covered, for 30
minutes. Top with the crispy
bits of Speck.

• Alpine regional flavors are not
limited to bacon and cabbage.
For connoisseurs, there are
variations: Cabbage can be
stewed in olive oil or enhanced
at the end with 2 tablespoons
of red currant jelly. This side
dish is absolutely wonderful
when served with venison and
wild bird specialties.

Cipolle ripiene
Stuffed Baked Onions (Piedmont)

Serves 4 to 6

9 ounces ground beef
4 large, Vidalia-type onions
1 bunch fresh Italian parsley
Several small sage leaves
²/₃ cup grated Parmesan
 cheese
About 2 ¹/₂ tablespoons grappa
1 egg
3 to 4 tablespoons butter
3 tablespoons unseasoned
 breadcrumbs
Salt and freshly ground pepper

<u>Approximate preparation time:</u>
 1 ³/₄ hours;
 260 calories per serving.

1 Peel the onions and cook
them for 15 minutes in salted boiling water. With a slotted
spoon, remove them from the
water, drain, and set them aside
to cool. Cut the onions horizontally in halves and scoop out the
centers to form "onion bowls."
Mince half of the removed
onion pulp and set aside the
leftover onion for other culinary

uses. You can also stew the
leftover pulp with the stuffed
onions.

2 Melt 1 tablespoon of butter.
Sauté the minced onions
and brown the ground beef.
Season with salt and pepper.
Add 1 tablespoon of grappa and
bring to a rapid boil. Allow the
mixture to cool. Preheat the
oven to 400°F.

3 Whisk the egg with the
cheese and fold into the
ground meat. Mince parsley
and add half of it to the meat
mixture. Season the stuffing
with salt and pepper. Use the
mixture to fill the onions.

4 Brush a large baking dish
with 1 tablespoon of butter.
Place the onions in the baking
dish. Melt 2 tablespoons of butter in the frying pan and brown
the breadcrumbs until golden.
Evenly distribute the breadcrumbs and the sage leaves

Insalata di funghi

Raw Mushroom Salad (Aosta Valley)

over the onions, and drizzle them with 1 2/3 tablespoons of grappa. Bake in a preheated oven for about 45 minutes. Top with the remaining strips of parsley.

• The grappa gives a special touch to this dish; you can also use either wine or stock as a substitute.

• Another variation for this dish is a stuffing mixture prepared with pureed pumpkin, minced sweet-and-sour pickled fruits, eggs, and crumbled amaretti cookies (see recipe page 120).

Serves 4

11 ounces fresh, raw, mixed mushrooms (farm-raised white button, chanterelles, or brown baby portobello mushrooms)
Juice of 1 lemon (2 to 3 table-spoons)
1 bunch fresh Italian parsley, minced
1 egg yolk
1 clove garlic, crushed
About 1/3 cup olive oil
Salt and freshly ground pepper

<u>Approximate preparation time:</u>
35 minutes;
330 calories per serving.

1 Thoroughly clean the raw mushrooms; slice them thin and drizzle with the juice of 1/2 lemon (briefly sauté the chanterelles in butter).

2 Whisk the egg yolk with the lemon juice; season the mixture with salt and pepper. Add the crushed garlic. Gradually

add the olive oil, stirring constantly. Fold the parsley into the sauce. Season the sauce and pour it evenly over the sliced mushrooms.

• Variation: Prepare a sauce with lemon juice, olive oil, minced anchovies, and 1 finely chopped hard-boiled egg yolk.

• Or: Slice mushrooms very thin, sauté in olive oil or nut oil, season, and serve as a luke-warm salad.

117

Strudel di mele
Pastry Roll Filled with Apples

Serves 6 to 8

For the dough:
1 3/4 cup all-purpose flour +
    more flour to roll out the
    dough
2 tablespoons butter
1 egg
1 pinch salt
1 tablespoon oil to brush

For the filling:
2 pounds or 4 large, firm, and
    not too sweet apples
1 lemon (juice and peel)
3/4 cup raisins
3 tablespoons pine nuts
About 1/3 cup granulated sugar
1/2 teaspoon powdered cinna-
    mon
2 to 3 tablespoons unseasoned
    breadcrumbs

Additional ingredients:
Nonstick baking spray oil for
    the baking sheet
Butter to brush the dough
Confectioners' sugar to dust
    the strudel

Approximate preparation time:
    1 1/2 hours;
    330 calories per serving.

Strudel—a magic word for
many skilled bakers and for
people who are tempted just by
looking at it in a picture.

Making nearly transparent
strudel dough that is so thin
that one can read the newspa-
per through it has become almost a part of everyday life
throughout southern Germany
and Austria, but making strudel
in Italy has also come to be a
general matter of culinary good
sense, as shown by this one
from Alto Adige (or South Tirol),
which is delicate and flaky.

Aside from tart apples, other ingredients are also suitable for
the filling, such as pears and
apricots. And, in case you prefer to bake your strudel in a
rimmed baking pan, you can
pour over the strudel and periodically brush up to 1 cup of
whipping cream.

1 For the dough: Make a well on a work surface with the flour,
and add 2 tablespoons of softened butter, the egg, and a pinch
of salt. Mix the ingredients from the outside inward, and knead to a
smooth and springy dough while gradually adding about 1/3 cup of
water. Brush the dough with oil and set it aside to rest for 20 minutes in a sealed plastic bag.

2 For the filling: Soak the raisins in water. Cut the apples into
quarters. Core, peel, and slice the apple quarters, and place
them in a mixing bowl. Add and combine the grated lemon peel,
the lemon juice, the pine nuts, powdered cinnamon, and sugar. Set
aside to allow all the flavors to blend. Drain the raisins and combine
them with the filling before using it for the strudel. Preheat the
oven to 400°F and spray the baking sheet with the nonstick baking
spray.

3 Use a floured dishcloth to
roll out a thin strudel dough.
First, roll out the ball of dough
with a rolling pin, and then,
with both hands made into
loose fists, pull the dough outward in all directions until you
get a very thin sheet of dough.
Place the sheet onto the dishcloth.

4 Drizzle the thin sheet of dough with butter and sprinkle with the breadcrumbs. Distribute the apple mixture evenly on the dough, leaving a 1-inch-wide edge around the border of the dough sheet. Brush these edges with butter and roll inward over the filling.

5 Holding and pulling the dishcloth upward, roll up the strudel. Still using the dishcloth, place the strudel in the middle of the baking sheet. Brush the surface generously with butter. Bake for 1 hour. Allow the strudel to cool off and dust with confectioners' sugar.

caffè
Bei & Nannini
LUCCA
CONFEZIONATO DA
FIGLI DI PININ Pero & C.
NIZZA MONFERRATO (AT)

119

Zabaione con bacche
Egg Wine Cream with Berries (Piedmont)

Serves 4

*About 1 cup fresh mixed
  berries*
1/2 lemon (juice and peel)
4 egg yolks
*4 tablespoons Marsala wine
  (sweet Sicilian wine)*
4 tablespoons granulated sugar

<u>*Approximate preparation time:*</u>
  35 minutes;
  430 calories per serving.

1 Thoroughly wash the
berries. Drain and hull them.
If you wish, cut strawberries in
half. Place the berries in a mixing bowl and drizzle with the
lemon juice. Refrigerate.

2 Heat water in a large pot.
Place a smaller stainless
steel bowl in the middle of the
pot. In the smaller bowl, put
the egg yolks together with the
sugar and the lemon peel.
Whisk the mixture vigorously.
Continue whisking and gradually add the Marsala wine.

3 Beat to a foamy cream over
low heat. Remove from the
heat, distribute the cream into
4 serving bowls, and garnish
with the mixed berries.

• An even simpler way: Prepare
this cream in a double boiler.

• Variations: Prepare zabaione
with wine, champagne, or
brandy.

• Easy to make: Cream of
zabaione—allow the warm
cream to cool off in an iced
bath, fold in 7 ounces of
whipped cream, and chill very
well before serving.

Amaretti
Almond Cookies (Piedmont)

Yield: Approximately 30 pieces

*2 cups almonds, blanched and
  peeled*
*1 teaspoon bitter almond flavor-
  ing (optional)*
*3/4 cup + 2 tablespoons granu-
  lated sugar*
4 egg whites
1 tablespoon butter
1 tablespoon flour
*Enough confectioners' sugar to
  dust the cookies*

<u>*Approximate preparation time:*</u>
  80 minutes;
  80 calories per cookie.

1 Grind the almonds, and combine them in a mixing bowl
with 3/4 cup of granulated sugar
and 1 teaspoon of bitter almond
flavoring.

2 Beat the egg whites to a stiff
peak and add the remaining
2 tablespoons of granulated
sugar. Fold the ground nuts into
the egg whites by hand and stir
until it becomes smooth.

3 Spray the baking sheet with
a nonstick baking spray, and
dust with 1 tablespoon of flour.
Fill a pastry bag that has a
round tip with the almond mixture and squeeze small nut-size
portions onto the greased baking sheet, setting them aside to
rest for 2 hours (you can also
drop these small pieces by
hand).

4 Preheat the oven to 300°F.
The almond cookies should
be dried rather than baked for 1
hour in the hot oven air. Remove the cookies from the
oven and dust them with confectioners' sugar.

• Crumbled amaretti are used
in many dishes, either in
desserts or in tangy vegetable
dishes.

• You may also serve amaretti
dipped in *Vin Santo*, or simply
eat them with espresso after a
meal.

Cappuccini affogati
Drunken Capuchins (Fried Red Wine-soaked Bread Slices) (Alto Adige/South Tirol)

Serves 6

1 small stale loaf of white bread (about 9 ounces)
1 cup good red wine
1/2 lemon
4 eggs
3 tablespoons ground almonds
3/4 cup raisins
3 1/2 ounces or 1 cup or 10 envelopes vanilla sugar
1 cinnamon stick
2 cloves
Enough oil to deep-fry and to brush the baking pan

Approximate preparation time:
45 minutes;
400 calories per serving.

1 In a small saucepan, heat the red wine with 1/2 cup or 5 envelopes of vanilla sugar, the cinnamon stick, and cloves. Cut the lemon peel into a ribbon and add to the wine.

2 Cut the white bread into 1-inch-thick slices. Whisk together the eggs with the ground almonds. Heat enough oil in a large frying pan to deep-fry.

3 Dip both sides of each slice of white bread in the egg mixture and fry in the hot oil until golden brown. Remove the deep-fried bread slices and place them on paper towels to drain excess fat.

4 Preheat the oven to 350°F. Brush a large baking dish with 2 tablespoons of oil. Pour the red wine through a fine strainer into the saucepan, and place the saucepan back on the heat. Briefly simmer the raisins in the wine.

5 Place the bread slices in layers in the baking dish and sprinkle them lightly with the remaining vanilla sugar. Drizzle with 1 to 2 tablespoons of red wine and sprinkle them with raisins. Bake in the preheated oven for 10 minutes. Serve hot.

Crostoli
Fried Dough (Friuli/Trentino)

Serves 6 to 8

Peel of 1 lemon
2 eggs
3 tablespoons butter
3 tablespoons rum or grappa
About 1/3 cup + 2 tablespoons or 7 envelopes vanilla sugar
2 1/2 cups all-purpose flour + enough flour to roll out the dough
Shortening or oil for deep frying (about 2 pounds)
Confectioners' sugar to dust the fried dough
Salt

Approximate preparation time:
45 minutes;
360 calories per serving.

1 Cream the eggs with the vanilla sugar. Add the lemon peel, the rum or grappa, and 1 pinch of salt.

2 Soften the butter. Make a well with 2 1/2 cups of flour. Pour the softened butter and the egg cream into the center of the well, and knead until you get a smooth, silky dough.

3 In a frying pan, heat the shortening or the oil. Dust the work surface with flour. Roll out the dough as thin as possible. With a pastry cutter, keeping the sides approximately 1 1/2 to 2 inches long, cut the dough in uneven squares or diamonds. Cut a cross in the middle of each piece of dough.

4 Fry the crostoli in the hot shortening or oil. With a slotted spoon, remove them from the oil, and place them on paper towels to drain the excess fat. Dust with confectioners' sugar. Serve either warm or cold.

• Wine serving suggestion: a fizzy refreshing sparkling wine, such as a *Trento Classico*.

Grappa—The Good Witches' Brew

It was not long ago that people used to talk about "that grappa," including it among those Italian "moonshine type of drinks" made from grape skins that could help prevent the feeling of heaviness and bloating after a heavy meal. How fast certain images can be turned into trends! Today, as it should be, "grappa" is spoken about with a somewhat gentle quality description: mild, full of body, well-rounded, preferably not too old. Only during recent years has this Northern Italian farmers' spirit acquired the status of a fine brandy. In the past, the distilled product of grape *marc*—pressed skins of grapes—was used to comfort the souls and bodies of alpine

In the beginning, the marc, the leftover from the pressed grapes used for winemaking, is set aside. It must be processed right away; otherwise, undesirable chemical reactions occur.

winemakers when it was cold and gloomy outside their doors. More and more people became familiar with the unusual flavor, and the industry picked up the know-how of producing it, creating various types of fairly uniform good quality.

Some rare and quality-obsessed distillers try to focus their efforts on producing a grappa that indeed has turned out to be among the finest distilled products. Usually, these distillers are stubborn wizards who, during distilling, rely on their own common sense, their own sense of smell, and on the position of the sun and moon during the distilling operation. Indeed, an almost sixth sense is required for producing an extraordinary product from left over grape skins. The marc can be left over from the production of white wine, in which case the berries are pressed immediately after the harvest. They can also be left over from red wine production; here, the grapes are squeezed and mixed, allowed to ferment, then the skins are removed from the dark mixture. The marc of white wine usually has a very low alcohol content but it still must ferment. On the other hand, the red wine marc has a high alcohol content. And of course, as in every fermentation process, microorganisms here can become active and spoil the marc. It can turn into vinegar or become moldy; therefore, everything must be processed right away. Fortunately, grape varieties ripen at different speeds and the marc is not all ready at the same time. For example, especially in the Trentino region, it has become a tradition to produce grappe (Italian plural of grappa) using pure single-grape varieties. Usually, large distilleries purchase the marc leftovers

Grappa should traditionally be consumed young and clear as water. In addition, there are other aromatic types like grappa alla ruta (flavored with rue, a strong bitter herb), grappa flavored with peppermint, or even with radicchio (a red type of chicory). In the past, grappa was used in the Alpine regions as a medicinal drink. As to its origin, important regions are Trentino, Friuli, Piedmont, Lombardy, and Veneto.

from various winemakers, store them in silos (various varieties eventually bring forth one unique flavor), and process these according to the distillery's own time schedule. The strength of the pressure on the grapes plays an important role in the quality of the grappa. If the grapes are squeezed very heavily, not only will the wine be thin, but so will the distilled product. It is for this reason that press leftovers of winemakers that produce the best wines are also suited for the best grappe. However, "moist" marc can produce only a little alcohol. The mixture must first be reduced to brandy. For this purpose, the different boiling points of water and alcohol are

A simple method for testing and selecting a good grappa from one that is mediocre is to pour a few drops onto the palm of your hand...

...and rub the hands together. The drops of grappa will be partially absorbed into the skin of the hands and will dissolve with the heat. During this process, the aromatic essences are released.

used—a process of distillation. The mixture is heated in a closed container until the alcohol boils at about 175°F and evaporates. The alcohol vapor is then separated and cooled until it becomes fluid again.

Basically, this is a simple idea and method, at least in theory. In practicality, the process of producing a grappa requires knowledge and experience. Making grappa begins with the heating process: If a fire were placed under the mush of the marc, what would happen is what usually happens when a thick soup is cooked in a pot— the brew would get dense, stick to the bottom of the pot, and begin to give off a burned

smell. The strong smell would evaporate with the alcohol, giving the grappa that smell and flavor. To prevent this from happening, two methods have been developed over time. The first method is to heat the marc in a *bagno maria*, a double bath. In this way the container filled with marc is placed in a second container with water that is never allowed to heat beyond 212°F, because otherwise it would begin to boil off. With the second method, the marc is heated by water vapor in order to prevent any heat from directly touching the marc itself.

The distillation method used by small grappa producers is an "intermittent" one; that is, the

distillation container is filled with marc, heated, and, after the distillation process, it is emptied and reused. This method is uneconomical for high-volume production, which uses a continuous method that provides the distillation process with fresh marc that is heated to evaporate the alcohol, and is continuously moved automatically until the extracted remainders are finally ejected on the other side.

During both methods, not only does the alcohol leave the equipment, but also the additional elements that give the typical character to a grappa. There are both desirable and undesirable substances in the

By immediately smelling the aroma, any unsuitable perfume would become clearly noticeable. Another method is the caffè corretto, an espresso spiked with grappa that signals the quality of the grappa from the first smell and taste of the coffee.

marc. Some, like the toxic methyl alcohol, begin to dissolve at lower temperatures. It boils at 150°F, and is part of the liquid that drips out of the cooling equipment. It is called *testa*, the head that needs to be cut off. The expertise in distillation can also be evaluated by exactly how the toxic substance is removed from the first product of distillation while retaining the aromatic elements. After this, the alcohol is combined with other aromatic substances until the water finally begins to boil. This step is called *coda*, the tail that also is not desirable because it dilutes the product. What comes between the head and the tail is called *cuore*, the heart. This is what gives the quality to a good grappa with aroma and flavor. The so-called sixth sense is what indicates to the grappa maker when it is time to collect the distilled substance, as the head and the tail also contain important flavoring elements. So it is easy to understand why an industrially produced grappa will never reach the refined quality and aromatic fullness of a grappa produced by a small artisan's distillery, since, as with high volume, safety comes first. For mass-produced grappa, it is obviously not possible to attach a special nose to the grappa spigot.

With both methods, the final product is a concentrated spirit that has a content of 60 to 80 percent pure alcohol. Only after dilution to 43 to 50 percent will the liquid become a drinkable grappa. Modern grappe are water clear and should not be kept too long.

The brandmarks issued by the cooperatives (*consorzi*) signify the quality of the grappa. These marks have been used since 1969 in Trentino, and since 1975 in Friuli. The main purpose of the brandmarks is to serve as indicators of first-quality grappe and also—or maybe especially—to support the small individualist grappa makers who sometimes have a production of only 200 bottles and who have the goal of producing only first-quality products.

Right: The small grappa makers still work with old distillation equipment, consisting of a copper kettle that has a dome-shaped lid that can be completely sealed. Attached to the kettle is a tube shaped like a gooseneck that leads to a serpentine bend, which is immersed in a water-filled basin for condensing the grappa.

Far right: The grape marc mixture needs to be heated; the job is indeed an arduous one.

Right: The kettle is emptied after each distillation and the leftover marc mixture is dumped into a cake mold. It will dry until next year and serve as a firing source for the next process. The ash is used to fertilize the vineyards, a closed recycling process.

Right: In addition to the young grappe, *there are also varieties labeled* riserva, *which implies that they are left to age in barrels for a longer time. This aging gives the product a definite aging flavor and brownish color. To round out the final aroma, barrels made of various woods are used. A relatively new specialty is the* Uva *(grape)* distillate *made from grape mush.*

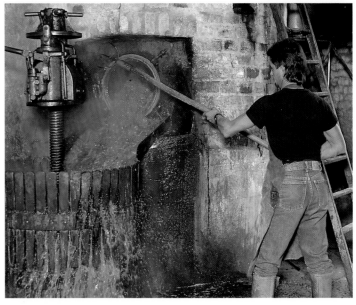

Left: For high-volume grappa production, the product boils and bubbles in stainless steel kettles and columns, steaming throughout tubes and multilevel divided containers in which the various components separate from each other.

Left: Filling the typically clear bottles is done automatically. Usually, large distilleries mix together various marc mixtures from different regions in order to produce a grappa that has generally the same flavor.

Left: Grappe acquire early, after about half a year, their typical aromas and characters. The terms vecchia *(old) or even* stravecchia *(very old) may look good on a label and indicate a state-monitored aging, but they are not guarantors of extraordinarily good quality, since a grappa must be good from the beginning in order to improve during aging.*

Above: Grappa has become an elegant digestive after-meal treat. Specially shaped glasses have even been blown for it: Young grappe should be served in thin glasses or rounded chimney-type glasses in order to better retain the aroma. Older grappe can be served in typical round cognac glasses.

Tuscany, Umbria, and Le Marche

Hills and Cypresses:
A solitary farm in the Elsa Valley.

The Regions and Their Products

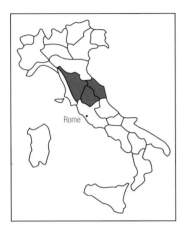

In a fairy tale landscape with hill after hill flanked by slender and dark lines of cypress trees, lies Tuscany, if not the most classic Italian region, at least one of the most renowned. But this is only one aspect of the central Italian region's multifaceted personalities. Wide valleys with fertile land can alternate with dark woods, with gently rolling hills filled with olive groves, or with the rugged mountain peaks of the Apennine range. The cuisine is a mixture of sophisticated simplicity and country-type cooking. Here, cooking is done with olive oil; for example, instead of the many appetizers as they are served in Piedmont, sausages and hams are served, as well as the famous crostini. Legumes—lentils and beans—play an important role, as do tomatoes, which found their way from Naples very early in the history of Italian cooking.

Meat is mainly cooked either on a grill or on a spit. Birds are favorites, and, of course, so is the *bistecca alla Fiorentina*, a large piece of meat from the white Chianina beef from the Chiana Valley, grilled over charcoal and seasoned at the end with only salt, pepper, and a few drops of the finest olive oil. Vegetables are fried preferably in olive oil, as are poultry and fish. An additionally indispensable side dish is the Tuscan unsalted farmers' bread with a hard crust and firm crumbs, which takes the place of noodles.

Gentle hills, fertile land, the black spires of the cypresses, and old farmhouses—the postcard image of Tuscany.

Top: The white Chianina cattle provide the meat used in bistecca alla Fiorentina *that is grilled (picture of the steak in the middle) over wood charcoal.*

Right: Legumes, especially beans, are indispensable in Tuscany's cuisine.

Umbria is the only Italian region that does not border on the sea. The region is mainly mountainous and rich in woods, especially in the eastern part, where there are the highest peaks and the narrowest valleys. The Mediterranean Sea does not influence the climate here. Summers are hot but not always dry; winters are rough. Rainfalls occur especially around November and December. In the west are fertile hills, which resemble very much those of Tuscany, especially the areas surrounding Perugia and Orvieto, with gentle hills and valleys and fertile land. Crossed by the Tiber River, this region is among the most water – rich areas and thrives on its agriculture. Products are wheat and wine as well as sunflowers, vegetables, olives, and fruits. Pigs, cattle, and sheep are also important to this region. Umbria is also rich in delicate freshwater fish from rivers and lakes. One local specialty is *tegamaccio*, a fish soup that is made with only freshwater fish. The Transimeno Lake is the largest lake in Central Italy. It has huge, delicious carp.

A hidden gourmet center in Umbria is Norcia, a small town in the mountains. It is famous for its ham made from small black pigs fed with chestnuts, and also for its top-quality sheep's milk cheese and its black truffles, which are roasted here in paper on an open fire.

Le Marche, the region between the Adriatic Sea and the Apennines, is marked by hills that reach to the shores of the sea. Wide valleys stretching from the sea to the mountains turn into steep formations and ravines. Topping the summits are castles, fortresses from the Middle Ages, and many small towns that are wonderful for those who wish to discover them, where the old crafts are still alive. Contrary to what happened in many other regions, buildings that were passed on generation after generation have been preserved and restored to fit to modern requirements.

A typical dish of this region is *vincisgrassi*, a specialty made with pasta layers, alternated with layers of chicken livers, mushroom sauce, and white sauce, and baked in the oven. The name apparently originated with the name distortion of Austrian Field Marshal Windisch-Grätz, who loved this dish. Typical of the coastal regions are the fish soups and chowders that are especially abundant here. Two basic specialties that need to be outlined: in the northern region bordering Ancona are robust fish soups flavored with tomatoes, and in the southern part of the region, fish that is first rolled in flour and fried, then simmered in a saffron-based gravy.

Top: Fresh fish is important; fish soups of these regions call for many different varieties of fish.

Above: Sheep's cheese milk comes in various shapes and sizes. The oval Marzolino, very popular in Tuscany, comes as fresh cheese with a light rind, and as a more seasoned grating cheese with a reddish rind.

Left: Lilies, which grow in abundance throughout the region, are the flowers of Tuscany.

Top: Onions, set to dry on walls for the winter, are, along with garlic, very important seasoning ingredients.

Above: It is hard to imagine the cuisine of this region without tomatoes.

People, Events, Sightseeing

While Emilia-Romagna's cuisine uses great amounts of butter, Tuscany's people use olive oil. And, instead of meat roasts and stews, a lot of vegetables are included here. This way of cooking clearly stresses a frugal approach to dishes that call for only a few ingredients. It is therefore easy to conclude that Tuscany's people are stingy; however, the cuisine is reflection of the region, which can be perceived as basic and almost geometric. It is not always wealthy, and in many areas, it is poor, scanty, and solitary, as in Garfagna and Lunigiana.

Umbria's culture has deep-rooted rites and superstitions. Even

the cooking and baking is influenced by some magic rules: Dishes are required to have a certain amount of ingredients; baked goods are shaped like ghost-cursing fetishes, often snakes, with reference to the old myth of the sibyls. According to legend, sibyls were prophetesses who lived in the caves of the Monte Vettore mountain.

Farmers of Le Marche's countryside also take legends and tall tales very seriously. For work in the fields, careful attention is paid to the position of the moon. The waxing moon is considered undesirable, while the waning moon favors the sprouting of newly sown wheat and clean wine fermentation. There are strict rules even for fishing and for the butchering of pigs.

Florence was once a city of power and wealth. The other side of the Arno River throughout the artisans' district of San Frediano is for those who are looking for less tourism and more of the personality of Florence.

However, standing in front of the leaning tower of Pisa in the Piazza dei Miracoli, one is forced to distance oneself from black magic. The same is true when standing in the crowd that feeds the early morning farmers' market throughout the narrow side streets of the Borgo Stretto.

Florence, the city of the Medici, is overshadowed today by Rome, Naples, or Milan, but it is still the city of arts and science. In the Piazza Santo Spirito, one finds the weekly farmers' market, to which producers bring their fruits and vegetables with carts and small cars. Tourists should visit San Gimignano, with its medieval towers. Among the rooms of the Fortezza Medicea is the Enoteca Permanente, a national wine museum.

In Umbria, one should visit Norcia and taste the ham made from young black pigs, the

Top: An osteria *(tavern) and snack bar is ready for the lunch guests.*

Middle: Tradition is still kept in high esteem, as shown here during a wedding performed in the Cathedral of Lucca.

Left: Meetings for a chat outside the stores can turn into serious discussions. Tuscany's people have the image of sharp interest-driven individuals, who, at the same time, are creative and artistic.

cheese, and the black truffles. Delicatessens here are an experience worth trying out. Near Perugia, in Spello, an olive and bruschetta festival takes place around the beginning of February. Here, bread is toasted over an open fire, drizzled with olive oil from Spello, seasoned with garlic, and eaten. In November, in Sigillo, the festival of San Martino is celebrated with chestnuts and new wine.

Ascoli Piceno, located in Le Marche with its medieval district, is among the most historic cities dating from the Italian Middle Ages. A meeting place for the residents is the Piazza del Popolo. On the first Sunday

Top, left: Siena, among the most interesting cities in Tuscany, was built on three hills that are visible from a distance before entering it. The heart of the city is Piazza del Campo, located on the slope between the hills. The Palio, the big horseriding competition, is held here every July and August. It is sponsored by all 17 city districts, the contrade. And, obviously, there is a celebration at the end of the event.

Top right: Street vendors offer porchetta, *a whole, stuffed, roasted suckling pig seasoned with fennel.*

Top: Eating is often done under the open sky, as shown here at this pizza stand.

of August a knight's tournament, the Torneo della Quintana, is held, with costumes from the fifteenth century. In Frontino near Urbino, there is, at the beginning of September, a bean festival during which guests sample delicious dishes prepared with beans.

The Wines

Possibly among the oldest, and surely among the most popular, red wines of Tuscany is the *Chianti*. Its growing area is practically located in the province of Florence and Siena and includes approximately 100 counties. The center of focus is the 270-square-mile area of the Chianti Classico. Only those wines that come from this area are allowed to be labeled as "Classico." These wines carry the red seal with the black rooster, the Gallo Nero. Located around the old classic area are six additional zones: Colli Aretini (around Arezzo), Colli Fiorentini (around Florence), Colline Pisane (Pisa), Colli Senesi (Siena), Montalbano, and Rufina. Chianti wines are dry, of a ruby red color that turns dark red when aged, with a scent reminiscent of violets. Young wines are full – bodied, slightly tannic, and suitable for many dishes. Aged wines are mellow, smooth, and velvety, and are at their best when served with dark meat, roasts, and venison.

A superb wine of Tuscany is the *Brunello di Montalcino*, full-bodied and strong, dry and rough while young, and smooth and mellow after aging. It should be served with dark meats and venison, and should be opened and poured into a decanter a few hours before being served. The *Vino Nobile di Montepulciano* is a relative of the Chianti. It is slightly bitter and goes well with roasts. Additional red wines are the *Montescudaio* (also available as a white wine) and the *Carmignano*. Among the best white wines is the *Vernaccia di San Gimignano*. It is golden yellow, dry, and slightly bitter, and goes well with appetizers and fish. Also suitable for fish dishes are the *Bianco Vergine della Valdichiana* and *Galestro*, a new white Chianti.

In Tuscany, a dry, almost sweet wine, the *Vin Santo*, is made from very ripe, almost dried, grapes. It is dark yellow with an intense bouquet and is preferably used to dip the local flaky cookies.

Among the most famous wines in Umbria is the *Orvieto* that originates from the hills located west of the Tiber River. It is mainly produced from grapes of the Trebbiano Toscano variety, straw yellow in color, usually slightly bitter and refreshing, and it goes very well with fish. Among the most precious wines is the *Torgiano*, which is available either as red or white. The *Colli di Trasimeno*, which is available as red and white wine, good but fairly unknown, comes from Lake Trasimeno.

The Chianti region in the heart of Tuscany: A wine rich in tradition is produced throughout picturesque hill landscapes that reach up to 1,600 feet above sea level.

Popular among the wines of Le Marche is the white *Verdicchio dei Castelli di Jesi*. It is typified by its amphora-shaped bottles, pale yellow color, delicate scent reminiscent of unripe fruit, and its dry, refreshing, slightly bitter aroma, which persists beyond the acidity of some salads. Naturally, this wine goes well with appetizers and fish dishes. Another delicate white wine is the *Bianchello del Metauro*, straw yellow, dry, refreshing, and at its best if consumed while young.

Rosso Piceno and *Rosso Conero*, which reach their quality peak after three years of aging, are dry and well-balanced red wines.

Wines of this region: from left Chianti Classico *(Castello di Uzzano),* Solatio Basilica *(Villa Cafaggio),* Vino Nobile di Montepulciano, Orvieto Classico *(Castagnolo), and* Verdicchio di Matelica.

Regional Recipes

Crostini alla toscana

Toasted Bread Slices, Tuscany Style (with Chicken Livers and Olive Paste) (Tuscany/Umbria)

Yield: 30 Pieces

7 ounces raw chicken livers
1/2 lemon (juice and peel)
1 stalk celery, minced
1 carrot, minced
1/2 bunch fresh Italian parsley, minced
1/2 cup red wine
2 tablespoons tomato paste
1 tablespoon pickled capers
1 small onion, minced
2 tablespoons olive oil
2 tablespoons butter
1 bay leaf
1/2 teaspoon juniper berries
Salt and freshly ground pepper

For the olive paste:
5 ounces black olives, pitted
2 canned anchovy fillets, drained
1 dried chili pepper
1 teaspoon lemon juice
4 cloves garlic
1 teaspoon each of fresh stemless rosemary and thyme leaves (or 1/2 teaspoon each of dried)

6 sage leaves
1 tablespoon pickled capers
About 1/2 cup olive oil
Salt and freshly ground pepper

To serve:
30 small toasted slices of white bread

Approximate preparation time:
1 hour (+ 12 hours of marinating); 60 calories per piece (chicken livers) 120 calories per piece (olives).

1 For the chicken liver pâté: rinse, trim, and mince the chicken livers. Put them in a medium mixing bowl with the bay leaf and juniper berries. Pour in the red wine and soak the chicken livers overnight.

2 In a medium saucepan, heat the olive oil and butter. Sauté the onion, celery, and carrot. Drain the chicken livers (keep the juice), and pat dry. Pour the marinade through a strainer.

3 Add the chicken livers to the sautéed vegetables and brown quickly. Stir in the marinade juice and tomato paste. Simmer for 10 minutes and season with salt, pepper, lemon juice, and grated lemon peel. Add the minced parsley to the mixture. Cool, and puree in a food processor with the capers. Stir in 1 tablespoon of softened butter and finish to season with salt and pepper.

4 For the olive paste: Rinse, pat dry, and mince the anchovies. Seed the chili peppers. Puree all the ingredients together with the olives, the herbs, garlic, and capers. In a thin stream, add the olive oil and stir until you get a smooth paste. Season with 1 teaspoon of lemon juice, salt, and freshly ground pepper.

5 Toast the small slices of white bread in an oven or a toaster. Spread each slice with either chicken liver pâtè or olive paste.

• If you are lucky enough to find in your favorite supermarket or Italian bakery an authentic Tuscan bread that has a firm crust, dense crumbs, and is almost unseasoned, simply cut the large slices into smaller decoratively shaped crostini pieces. It is, of course, up to you if you wish to spread both pastes as thick as we have done in our photograph. After tasting the spread, regulate the thickness according to your own palate.

Panzanella
Cold Bread Salad (Tuscany)

Serves 6 to 8

11 ounces white bread (slice the bread one day before)
11 ounces or 3 fresh, ripe, plum tomatoes
1 small yellow and 1 small red pepper
2 scallions, trimmed
1 bunch fresh Italian parsley, minced
1 bunch fresh basil
Optional: fresh stemless mint leaves
3 cloves garlic
2 tablespoons capers
6 to 8 tablespoons red wine vinegar
8 tablespoons extra virgin olive oil
1 bay leaf
Salt and freshly ground pepper

Approximate preparation time:
45 minutes
(+ 1 hour refrigeration);
190 calories per serving.

1 Slice the bread ahead of time. Cut off the crust of the bread and set the bread aside to dry. The next day, in a small saucepan, bring to a rapid boil 1/2 cup of water with 6 tablespoons of red wine vinegar and the bay leaf. Allow the liquid to cool off and pour it over the slices of bread. Soak for about 30 minutes.

2 Blanch, peel, seed, and cube the tomatoes. Seed and cube the peppers. Slice the scallions very thin.

3 Drain and shred the soaked bread. Remove the bay leaf. Combine with the tomatoes, peppers, onions, and capers. Whisk the garlic with the olive oil, minced parsley, salt, and freshly ground pepper. Pour this dressing over the bread salad and toss. Refrigerate for about 1 hour. Before serving the bread salad, season with salt, pepper, and vinegar. Top with the remaining stemless herbs.

Acquacotta
"Cooked Water" Soup
with Mushrooms and Bread (Tuscany)

Serves 4

9 ounces fresh cepes mushrooms or brown baby portobello mushrooms
2 fully ripe, fresh tomatoes
2 stalks celery, chopped
1 tablespoon fresh stemless leaves of thyme (or 1 teaspoon dried)
1 bunch fresh chives
2/3 cup freshly grated Parmesan cheese
8 small slices white bread
1 onion, chopped
1 garlic clove, crushed
4 cups beef stock
4 tablespoons olive oil
Salt and freshly ground pepper

Approximate preparation time:
45 minutes;
360 calories per serving.

1 Thoroughly clean the mushrooms and slice thin. Blanch, peel, seed, and mince the tomatoes.

2 Heat the olive oil in a large pot. Sauté the onion and celery. Add the crushed garlic, beef stock and minced tomatoes. Season with 1/2 tablespoon of thyme, salt, and pepper. Simmer uncovered for 20 minutes.

3 Stir the slices of mushrooms into the soup and let simmer for an additional 10 minutes. Thinly snip the chives. Toast the white bread slices and distribute them in 4 soup bowls. Season the soup and ladle it over the bread slices. Top with thyme, chives, and freshly grated Parmesan cheese, and serve.

• This is the rich version of an originally very frugal meal; in the old days this soup was made of nothing more than bread, oil, cheese, and water!

Vincisgrassi
Pasta Casserole with Meat Sauce (Le Marche)

Serves 8

For the dough:
2 ½ cups + 2 tablespoons all-pur-
    pose flour + flour to roll out
    the dough
¾ cup + 3 tablespoons
    semolina flour
4 eggs
Salt
2 tablespoons Vin Santo or
    Marsala (Italian sweet wine;
    you may substitute a fruity
    white wine)

For the meat sauce:
9 ounces either calf's brain or
    calf's sweetbreads
14 ounces ground lamb
7 ounces chicken livers
3 ½ to 4 ounces or 4 slices bacon
1 ounce or ¾ cup dried mush-
    rooms (either porcini or mixed
    mushrooms)
1 carrot, chopped
1 onion, chopped
1 cup dry white wine
½ cup beef stock
⅓ cup + 2 tablespoons milk
2 tablespoons tomato paste
1 tablespoon butter
Salt and freshly ground pepper
1 pinch of powdered cinnamon

For the white sauce:
2 tablespoons butter
2 tablespoons flour
2 cups milk
Salt and freshly ground pepper
Nutmeg

Additionally:
3 ½ ounces or 1 ⅔ cups freshly
    grated Parmesan cheese
3 tablespoons butter
Enough oil to spray a baking pan

Approximate preparation time:
    3 hours (+ 12 hours setting
    time);
    770 calories per serving.

This dish was named after Austrian Field Marshal Windisch-Grätz,
whose field cook was the creator
of the recipe during the Napoleon-
ic wars.

The especially delicate dough is
moistened with sweet wine, and
the flavor of the sauce is enhanced by a pinch of cinnamon.

For this dish, to save some time,
you may use ready-made sheets
of lasagna.

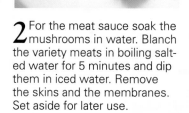

1 For the dough: Mix 2 ½ cups + 2 tablespoons of all-purpose flour with ¾ cup + 3 tablespoons of semolina flour and make a well. In the middle of the well, add the eggs, ½ teaspoon salt, and wine. Knead to a smooth, springy dough. Cover with a clean dishcloth and set aside.

2 For the meat sauce soak the mushrooms in water. Blanch the variety meats in boiling salted water for 5 minutes and dip them in iced water. Remove the skins and the membranes. Set aside for later use.

3 Chop the bacon. In a large saucepan, sauté the bacon in 1 tablespoon of butter. Briefly sauté the carrots and onions. Add the ground lamb and brown. Add 1 cup of wine and cook down until reduced to about half. Stir in the beef stock with tomato paste, salt, and freshly ground pepper. Simmer covered for about 30 minutes.

4 On a well-floured work surface, roll out the dough to thin sheets. Prepare a large baking pan and cut sheets of dough to fit the baking pan. Place the sheets on a clean dishcloth and let them dry a little. In a large pot, bring 1 gallon of salted water to a rolling boil. Cook the pasta sheets for 3 minutes, rinse them with cold water, and place them to dry on a clean dishcloth.

5 Chop the chicken livers and variety meats. Drain the mushrooms (keep the juice) and chop. Sauté for 30 minutes and add to the meat sauce. Add the mushroom water and $1/3$ cup + 2 tablespoons of milk, season with a pinch of powdered cinnamon. Simmer for an additional 10 to 15 minutes and season to taste.

6 White sauce: In a small saucepan, melt the butter and stir the flour to make a very light roux. When all the ingredients are combined and smooth, remove from the heat, and, while stirring constantly, pour in 2 cups of milk. Put back on the heat and let simmer for 10 minutes, stirring constantly. Season with salt, pepper, and freshly grated nutmeg.

7 Spray the baking pan with oil and line the pan with the sheets of pasta. Cover the pasta sheets with a portion of meat sauce and a portion of white sauce. Top these layers with Parmesan cheese. Place another layer of pasta sheets and repeat the layering process until there are no more ingredients. Top with a final layer of pasta. Cover, and evenly distribute a lot of Parmesan cheese and 3 tablespoons of butter over the last layer. Cover and refrigerate for several hours (preferably overnight). Preheat oven to 400°F. Bake 30 minutes until a golden crust has formed. Cut in portions and serve hot.

Pappardelle alla lepre
Pasta with Rabbit Sauce (Tuscany/Umbria)

Serves 4 to 6

1 ²/₃ pounds ready-to-use rabbit
3 stalks celery, chopped
14 ounces fresh, ripe tomatoes
1 bunch fresh Italian parsley
1 tablespoon fresh thyme (or 1
*   teaspoon dried)*
14 ounces pappardelle (wide
*   ribbon pasta)*
2 cups strong red wine
2 onions, chopped
3 cloves garlic, chopped
1 teaspoon fennel seeds
1 bay leaf
2 cloves
6 peppercorns
2 tablespoons tomato paste
7 tablespoons olive oil
Salt and freshly ground pepper

<u>*Approximate preparation time:*</u>
*   3 hours (+ 24 hours marinat-*
*   ing time);*
*   570 calories per serving.*

1 For the sauce: Cut the rabbit into small pieces, place the meat in a large bowl, pour the red wine over it, add the celery, onions, garlic, fennel seeds, bay leaf, cloves, and peppercorns. Cover and marinate in the refrigerator for 24 hours. From time to time, turn the meat over in its marinating juice.

2 Remove the meat from the marinade and pat dry with paper towels. Pass the marinade through a fine strainer and remove the cloves and peppercorns. Drain the vegetables and keep any liquid.

3 In a Dutch oven, heat 5 tablespoons of olive oil. Thoroughly brown the rabbit pieces on all sides. Add the vegetables and simmer, stirring constantly. Add the marinating juice. Season with salt, pepper, and thyme. Cover and cook about 2 hours.

4 Blanch, peel, seed, and cube the tomatoes. Remove the rabbit pieces from the Dutch oven. When cool enough to handle, debone the rabbit meat, and cut it in small bite-size pieces. Remove the bay leaf and puree the sauce in a food processor.

5 Combine the tomatoes, tomato paste, rabbit meat, and ¹/₂ bunch of minced fresh parsley. Simmer the sauce until ready to serve.

6 In the meantime, in a large pot, bring 4 quarts of salted water to a rolling boil and cook the noodles for 8 to 10 minutes or until *al dente* (still firm to the bite). Drain and combine with 2 tablespoons of olive oil. Season the sauce to taste and fold it into the noodles. Serve topped with minced parsley leaves.

• Above all, this specialty is remarkable for its lengthy and carefully orchestrated method of preparation and for its deliciously unique flavor. For this reason, we have chosen ready-to-use pappardelle. For those who have a pasta machine or for those who are inclined to do so, pappardelle can also be made at home. Just make a dough with 3 cups + 3 tablespoons of all-purpose flour, 4 eggs, 1 tablespoon of olive oil, and ¹/₂ teaspoon of salt. If necessary, you may add some water to moisten the dough. Cover with a clean, moist dishcloth; set aside to rest for 20 minutes. Divide the dough into three portions, roll out to thin sheets, and dry. Very gently fold together the sheets of pasta and cut them in 1-inch-wide ribbons. For later use, keep the noodles on a well-floured clean dishcloth.

Paglia e fieno

"Straw and Hay" (Egg and Spinach Flat Pasta with Creamy Mushroom Sauce) (Tuscany)

Serves 4 to 6

For the dough:
3 ¹/₂ ounces fresh spinach
   leaves
3 cups + 3 tablespoons all-purpose flour + enough flour to
   roll out the dough
4 eggs
1 tablespoon olive oil
Salt

For the sauce:
3 ¹/₂ ounces mild raw prosciutto (or raw country ham)
11 ounces fresh mushrooms
   (baby portobello, oyster,
   chanterelles, or cepes mushrooms)
Juice of ¹/₂ lemon
¹/₂ bunch fresh Italian parsley
¹/₂ bunch fresh basil
¹/₂ pint or 1 cup whipping
   cream
¹/₂ cup + 1 tablespoon diluted
   beef stock
1 clove garlic, crushed
1 ¹/₂ tablespoon butter
Salt and freshly ground pepper

To serve:
²/₃ cup freshly grated Parmesan
cheese

Approximate preparation time:
   2 hours;
   620 calories per serving.

1 For the green pasta: Trim and clean the spinach leaves. In a pot, bring salted water to a boil and blanch the spinach for 2 minutes. Drain the spinach and drop it into iced water. Squeeze to remove excess moisture and puree in a food processor.

2 For both pasta varieties: make a well with the flour and place the eggs, olive oil, and ¹/₂ teaspoon of salt in the center. Gradually work the ingredients until you get a smooth and springy dough. Separate one-third of the dough and knead the pureed spinach into it. Cover the dough.

3 On a floured work surface, roll out the dough into thin sheets and let these dry on a floured dishcloth.

4 For the sauce: Cut the ham into thin strips. Clean the mushrooms, slice them thin, and drizzle with lemon juice.

5 In a saucepan, melt ¹/₂ tablespoon of butter and add the crushed garlic. Simmer until soft. Pour in the whipping cream and beef stock and allow to cook down until smooth and dense.

6 Roll up each sheet of pasta. Cut each roll into ¹/₄-inch-thick strips and place the noodles on a well-floured dishcloth. In a pot, bring salted water to a rolling boil.

7 In a frying pan melt 1 tablespoon of butter. Add the mushrooms and sauté until limp. Mince the parsley and stir

it into the mushrooms with the strips of ham. Simmer until ready to serve, and season with salt and pepper.

8 Cook the pasta 7 to 8 minutes or until al dente. Drain well and place in a preheated serving bowl.

9 Season the cream sauce with salt, pepper, and more lemon juice, and pour over the hot noodles. Top the pasta with the ham-mushroom mixture and fresh, shredded basil leaves. Add freshly ground pepper and serve with freshly grated Parmesan cheese.

• This green and yellow pasta is called straw and hay, but has no flavor in common with dried grass!

Minestra di riso
Rice Soup with Lentils (Umbria)

Serves 6

3 ½ ounces or ½ cup lentils
3 ½ ounces or 4 slices bacon
¾ cup rice
1 bunch fresh Italian parsley
3 large, peeled tomatoes (from the can)
1 small onion
2 cloves garlic
2 tablespoons olive oil
4 cups strong beef stock
6 peppercorns
Salt and freshly ground pepper

<u>*Approximate preparation time:*</u>
35 minutes (+ 12 hours to soak the lentils);
290 calories per serving.

1 In a large pot, cover the ½ cup of lentils with water and soak overnight. Bring the same water to a boil and simmer lentils for 15 minutes.

2 Mince the bacon, ½ bunch of fresh parsley, and onion. Mash the peppercorns and gar-

lic to make a paste. Mix everything with the bacon. In a large saucepan, heat the oil and sauté the bacon mixture until soft.

3 Drain and cube the peeled tomatoes. Add the tomatoes, tomato juice, and stock to the contents of the saucepan. Bring to a rapid boil, add the rice, and cook. Season with salt and pepper.

4 Stir the cooked lentils with their water into the soup. Simmer 2 more minutes and season to taste. Mince the remaining parsley, add it to the soup, and serve.

Ginestrata
Yellow Soup (Creamed Egg Soup) (Tuscany)

Serves 4

4 fresh egg yolks
2 cups cold chicken stock
1 tablespoon + 1 teaspoon Marsala or Vin Santo (sweet Italian wine)
2 ounces or 3 tablespoons butter
¼ teaspoon powdered cinnamon
1 pinch sugar
Nutmeg
Salt

<u>*Approximate preparation time:*</u>
20 minutes;
190 calories per serving.

1 In a medium bowl, gradually combine and whisk the egg yolks, chicken stock, and Marsala wine. Season with the powdered cinnamon and a pinch of salt. Pass through a fine strainer and drop into a large pot (either continue to cook the soup in a double boiler or make the soup in an electric crockpot at very low temperature).

2 Heat up the soup, whisking constantly. Still whisking constantly, add the butter. To prevent the egg cream from curdling, do not allow the soup to boil.

3 As soon as the soup is hot and has reached a creamy stage, season it with a pinch of sugar and freshly grated nutmeg. Ladle the soup into preheated serving bowls and serve immediately.

• A fairly unknown favorite from the Chianti region. The interesting name of this soup owes its original definition to the spiny and brilliantly yellow-flowering gorse shrub *(ginestra)*. This soup is especially pleasant and unique because of its contrasting sweet and tangy flavor.

Cipollata
Onion Soup (Tuscany)

Serves 6

About 1 pound fresh pork ribs
2 ounces or 2 slices bacon
2 ounces garlic-flavored
    sausage (or kielbasa)
2 pounds Vidalia type onions
2 carrots, chopped
2 stalks celery, chopped
2 garlic cloves
6 slices of semolina bread (or
    whole wheat bread)
5 tablespoons olive oil
Salt and freshly ground pepper

Approximate preparation time:
    1 3/4 hours;
    520 calories per serving.

1 In a large pot, combine the carrots, celery, and 1 chopped onion with the pork ribs. Add 6 cups of water, season with salt, and bring to a boil. Cook for 15 minutes.

2 Thinly slice the remaining onions, and briefly place them in iced water. Dice the bacon and the sausage.

3 Heat the olive oil in a saucepan and brown the sausage and bacon. Drain and add the onions and sauté them until they are soft.

4 Pour the water of the pork ribs through a strainer, add it to the onions, and simmer everything for 1 hour. Set aside the ribs. When the meat is cool, debone and dice it. Return the meat to the soup and simmer again. Season with salt and pepper.

5 Toast the slices of bread and rub them with garlic. Serve them with the soup.

• This recipe could also be used to make a *ribollita*, which is actually a general term for a chowder that is absolutely at its best when reheated.

Ribollita
Vegetable Chowder (Tuscany)

Serves 6

4 ounces or 4 slices bacon
1 ham bone (you can order it
    from your butcher)
1 1/4 cups dried white Great
    Northern beans (you may
    substitute baby lima beans)
1/2 fresh cabbage
1 small leek
2 carrots
2 stalks celery
1 to 2 sprigs fresh thyme
1 onion
2 cloves garlic
11 ounces one-day-old bread
8 cups beef stock or demi-glace
6 tablespoons olive oil
Salt and freshly ground pepper

Approximate preparation time:
    2 hours (+ 12 hours to soak
    the beans + 12 hours to set
    aside and refrigerate);
    550 calories per serving.

1 Soak the beans in water for at least 12 hours, then in the same water, simmer the beans for 1 1/2 hours.

2 Finely chop the leek, carrots, celery, onion, and garlic. In a large pot, heat 3 tablespoons of oil and sauté the bacon and vegetables. Add the stock, thyme, and ham bone. Cover and simmer for 30 minutes.

3 Thoroughly clean the cabbage and cut it into chunks and thick slices. Add to the other ingredients in the pot and cook for an additional 30 minutes. With a food processor, puree half of the cooked beans. Add the bean puree and the whole cooked beans to the pot and bring to a boil once more before serving. Drizzle with extra virgin olive oil and season with thyme, salt, and pepper.

Sogliola alla fiorentina
Sole, Florentine Style (Tuscany)

Serves 4

2 fresh sole (about 1 pound
    each)
1 2/3 pounds fresh spinach
    leaves
Juice of 1/2 lemon (1 to 2
    tablespoons of juice)
2 cloves garlic
2 tablespoons dry white wine
2 tablespoon butter
Freshly grated Parmesan
    cheese (optional)
Salt and freshly ground
    pepper

For the sauce:
1 small onion, minced
1 teaspoon fresh leaves of
    thyme (or 1/2 teaspoon
    dried thyme)
2 tablespoons butter
1 cup milk
1/2 pint or 1 cup whipping
cream
2 egg yolks
3 tablespoons freshly grated
    Parmesan cheese
1 tablespoon flour
Salt and freshly ground
    pepper

Approximate preparation time:
    1 hour;
    740 calories per serving.

Even fish beginners need not
fear when preparing this fine
fish; the flat fish is very easy
to fillet since skin and bones
come off without difficulties.

More care should be given to
purchasing the fish, since
freshness and top quality are
essential factors for this dish;
with a good sense of smell,
certain rules can help in selecting fresh fish:
• The eyes are bright, shiny,
and not flat.
• The skin surface is not
scratched or damaged, and
the color looks unblemished.
• Gills and fins are noticeably
undamaged and intact, almost
brilliant and not spotted or
faded.

• Wine serving suggestion:
Galestro, a white Chianti.

1 Either purchase ready-to-
cook fish fillets, or fillet the
fresh fish at home. If you do
the work yourself, place the
dark side of the fish facing up
on the working surface. Cut off
the fins with kitchen scissors.

2 Score the upper part of the
tail of the fish with a small,
sharp paring knife, and firmly
rip the skin from the tail toward
the head of the fish. Turn the
sole over and repeat the same
operation with the white skin of
the fish.

3 With a very sharp knife, cut the flesh of the fish on the right and
left side of the middle bone and along the outside borders. De-
tach and remove the fillets from the head and remove all larger
bones from the fish. Season the fish with salt and pepper, and drizzle with lemon juice.

4 Trim, thoroughly clean, and
wash the spinach leaves.
Drain them well. Heat them in a
large frying pan with 2 tablespoons of white wine, salt, and
pepper. Add the pressed garlic.
Cover and allow the spinach to
wilt.

5 For the sauce: Sauté the minced onion in 1 tablespoon of butter in a small saucepan. Add the thyme and milk, and season with salt and pepper. Bring rapidly to a boil and simmer for about 5 minutes.

6 Melt 1 tablespoon of butter in a second saucepan and stir in the flour. Make a pale roux. Add the thyme-milk mixture and whipping cream. Stirring constantly, simmer until creamy and dense. Remove the sauce from the heat. Fold the 2 egg yolks and grated Parmesan cheese into the sauce. Season with salt and pepper.

7 Brush a large baking dish with ½ tablespoon of softened butter. Place 4 fish fillets on the bottom of the pan. Cover the fish with a layer of spinach and top the spinach with the 4 remaining fish fillets. Pour the white sauce over the layers of fish and dot everything with butter. Preheat the oven to 400°F and bake 12 minutes. Place on preheated serving plates. Top if you wish with freshly grated Parmesan cheese, and serve.

Triglie al forno
Baked Mullets (Le Marche)

Serves 4

4 mullets (or any suitably sized white flaky mullet-type fish—about 7 ounces each)
4 thin slices mild raw ham or prosciutto
1 to 2 lemons (4 to 6 tablespoons of juice)
12 sage leaves
1/2 bunch fresh Italian parsley
2 to 3 tablespoons unseasoned breadcrumbs
5 tablespoons olive oil
Salt and freshly ground pepper

<u>*Approximate preparation time:*</u>
1 1/2 hours
(+ 2 hours to marinate);
360 calories per serving.

1 Scale, scrub, and clean the mullets and cut off their heads. Slice open each fish lengthwise and remove the middle bone structure. Rub the inside of the fish with salt and pepper, and drizzle with lemon juice. Line each of the fish insides with 2 sage leaves. Place the fish in a large flat baking dish.

2 Mix 4 tablespoons of olive oil, 2 tablespoons of lemon juice, salt, and pepper. Pour the marinade over the mullets, cover, and refrigerate for 2 hours. Turn the fish over once.

3 Brush a baking dish with 1 tablespoon of olive oil. Preheat the oven to 400°F. Cut the prosciutto into 1-inch-wide strips.

4 Remove the fish from the marinade and drain thoroughly. Sprinkle the fish on all sides with the breadcrumbs. Wrap each fish with a long, thin, strip of ham, and place them side by side in the greased baking dish. Top the layer of fish with the remaining sage leaves and drizzle with the marinade.

5 Bake in the oven for 15 minutes. Sprinkle with shredded parsley leaves and serve with lemon wedges.

Trote affogate
"Drowned Trout" (Herbed Trout in White Wine Sauce) (Tuscany)

Serves 4

4 fresh trout (7 ounces each)
1 bunch fresh Italian parsley
1 sprig fresh lemon balm
1 cup dry white wine
1 small onion
4 garlic cloves
6 tablespoon olive oil
2 tablespoons flour
Salt and freshly ground pepper

<u>*Approximate preparation time:*</u>
1 hour;
380 calories per serving.

1 Clean the trout and cut off the fins. Thoroughly rinse the fish under running water. Pat dry with paper towels and season with salt and pepper inside and outside. Dust on all sides with flour.

2 Mince and mix the parsley, lemon balm, onion, and garlic. In a large frying pan, heat the olive oil. Sauté the herb mixture.

3 Place all the trout in the frying pan and fry for 2 minutes on each side. Gradually drizzle with the white wine, and make sure that the wine you pour evaporates before adding more. Cook the trout this way for 15 to 20 minutes. Serve on a large serving plate drizzled with the pan juices.

• Wine serving suggestion: A dry white wine, such as *Vernaccia di San Gimignano.*

Merluzzo alla marchigiana
Fried Cod, Le Marche Style (Le Marche/Umbria)

Serves 4

1 ⅓ pounds cod fillets
1 pound or about 4 large, fresh, ripe tomatoes
1 stalk celery
1 bunch fresh Italian parsley
1 lemon
1 small onion
2 cloves garlic
3 tablespoons olive oil + enough oil to deep fry
1 tablespoon flour
3 tablespoons unseasoned breadcrumbs
Salt and freshly ground pepper

Approximate preparation time:
1 hour;
430 calories per serving.

1 Cut the fish into 1-inch cubes. Season with salt, pepper, and 2 tablespoons of lemon juice. Cover and allow the marinade to seep into the fish while refrigerated.

2 Blanch, peel, seed, and chop the tomatoes. Mince and mix the parsley, onion, and garlic.

3 In a large saucepan, heat the olive oil. Sauté the onion mixture and add the chopped tomatoes. Simmer uncovered. Season with salt, pepper, and lemon juice.

4 Dust the cubes of fish with the flour on all sides. Roll the cubes in the breadcrumbs. In a large frying pan, heat enough oil to deep-fry. Fry all the fish cubes until they are golden brown and crispy. Place the fried cubes on paper towels to allow the excess fat to drain. Serve with the tomato sauce and slices of lemon.

• This recipe is also often applied to dried codfish; however, the version prepared with fresh codfish is less laborious and juicier.

Anguilla in umido
Stewed Eel (Umbria)

Serves 4

About 1 ¾ to 2 pounds fresh eel, ready to use
1 bunch fresh Italian parsley
1 tablespoon fresh rosemary leaves (or 1 teaspoon dried rosemary)
About 28 ounces or 1 ¾ pound peeled tomatoes (or the contents of a 28-ounce can)
½ cup dry white wine
3 tablespoons white wine vinegar
1 onion, minced
3 cloves garlic, minced
4 tablespoons olive oil
Salt and freshly ground pepper

Approximate preparation time:
1 hour;
710 calories per serving.

1 Have the eel skinned at the fish market and cut it into 2 ½-inch-long chunks. Rinse briefly and pat dry with paper towels.

2 In a large saucepan or Dutch oven, heat 4 tablespoons of olive oil, and sauté the onions and garlic. Drain the canned tomatoes, setting aside the juice. Chop the tomatoes and mince the rosemary.

3 Add the eel pieces to the onion and garlic, and brown thoroughly on all sides. Sprinkle with salt, pepper, and rosemary. Drizzle with wine vinegar and cook until the vinegar has evaporated.

4 Add the wine and the tomatoes. Simmer the eel, uncovered, for about 30 minutes. Gradually add the remaining tomato juice.

5 Chop the parsley. When the fish is cooked, season the tomato sauce with salt and pepper. Sprinkle the chopped parsley over it and serve.

Coniglio in porchetta
Stuffed Rabbit with Fennel (Le Marche)

Serves 4

1 ready-to-use rabbit (about 2 1/2 pounds and preferably with an intact liver)
2 ounces raw country ham, in slices
2 ounces or 3 thick slices salami
2 ounces or 2 slices bacon
2 whole fennel bulbs (about 1 pound)
1/2 lemon
4 cloves garlic
1 teaspoon fresh rosemary leaves (or 1/2 teaspoon dried rosemary)
1 one-day-old roll (without any crust)
1 cup dry white wine
2/3 cup or about 1/4 pint whipping cream
6 tablespoons olive oil
6 peppercorns
Salt and freshly ground pepper

<u>*Approximate preparation time:*</u>
1 1/4 hours;
880 calories per serving.

When it comes to preparing rabbit, Italians do not have many competitors who know to do a better job, either in stuffed roasts, savory meat sauces, or grilled kebabs.

Whether from the wild or out of the cage, the meat of the rabbit is not only lean and rich in protein, but also mild in flavor. As for taste, one could almost use this meat to replace chicken.

A tangy or spicy marinade always enhances the flavor of this meat—tender and flavorful meat can be created overnight as if by magic; the marinade can be prepared, for example, with buttermilk, vinegary mixtures flavored with herbs, or refreshing white or velvety red wines. The remarkable thing is that everything seems to go well with this meat!

• Wine serving suggestion: A light, refreshing white wine, such as *Verdicchio dei Castelli di Jesi.*

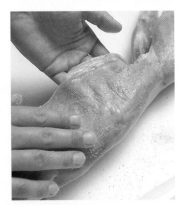

1 Rinse and thoroughly wash the rabbit. Pat dry with paper towels. Rub inside and out with salt and pepper. (Keep the liver for the stuffing). Dice the roll and soak in 1/2 cup of white wine.

2 Clean and thoroughly rinse the fennel. Trim the upper ends of the stems and set aside the fluffy greens. In a large pot, bring 3 cups of salted water to a boil. Slice 1/2 lemon, peel the garlic cloves, and add to the boiling water, with the peppercorns. Simmer the fennel and the trimmed stems for 15 minutes in the boiling water, and remove the vegetables from the water. Pass the vegetable stock through a fine strainer and set aside for later use. Cover and let the fennel cool. Mince the fluffy fennel greens with the cooked trimmed fennel stems.

3 Dice the ham and salami. Mince the rabbit liver, garlic, and 1 teaspoon of rosemary. Drain and squeeze the soaked roll. Mix all these ingredients with the minced fennel greens. Season this stuffing with salt and pepper.

4 Preheat the oven to 350°F. Stuff the rabbit with the prepared stuffing. With a trussing needle and string, sew the rabbit together to keep the stuffing inside. Heat the olive oil in a Dutch oven. Brown the rabbit on all sides.

5 Moisten the rabbit in the Dutch oven with ¹/₂ of the fennel stock you had reserved, cover, and bake for about 1 hour. Periodically turn the rabbit over and, if necessary, moisten with more fennel stock.

6 Slice the fennel 10 minutes before serving the rabbit. Mince the bacon and, sauté in a frying pan until golden and crispy. Remove the bacon bits. In the bacon fat, stir-fry the fennel slices, moisten with fennel stock, if necessary, and season with salt and pepper.

7 Remove the rabbit from the Dutch oven and keep the meat warm in the oven. To the gravy, add ¹/₂ cup of wine and the whipping cream. Simmer the gravy on top of the stove in a small saucepan. Slice the rabbit and garnish with fennel. Mince the remaining fennel greens, and sprinkle the greens with the bacon bits over the rabbit.

Fegatelli alla toscana
Liver Kebabs, Tuscany Style (Tuscany)

Serves 4

About 1 pound fresh pork liver
5 ounces pork caul (order it at the butcher's shop ahead of time)
2 tablespoons lard
8 slices of white bread
1 tablespoon fennel seeds
8 dried sage leaves
8 small bay leaves
1 clove garlic
4 tablespoons unseasoned breadcrumbs
1 tablespoon oil for the pan
6 peppercorns
Salt and freshly ground pepper

Approximate preparation time:
50 minutes;
500 calories per serving.

1 Blanch the pork caul for 2 minutes, and drop it into iced water. Carefully spread it out on a clean dishcloth. Cut it in squares about 3 inches wide.

2 Cube the pork liver (make as many pieces of liver as pieces of pork caul). In a mortar with a pestle, crush the fennel seeds, crumbled dried sage leaves, garlic, salt, and peppercorns. Combine the breadcrumbs with the crushed spices.

3 Rub the pieces of liver with the spice mixture and wrap each piece of liver in pork caul. Spread the lard evenly over the slices of bread and cut the slices into halves. On a kebab skewer, alternate pieces of liver with pieces of bread, separating each of them with bay leaves. Season with salt and pepper.

4 Spray a griddle with oil and grill the kebabs for about 10 minutes on all sides.

• Caul is a fatty, almost transparent membrane that lines the abdominal cavity of animals and that melts during cooking.

Arista alla fiorentina
Herbed Pork Roast, Florentine Style (Tuscany)

Serves 6

About 2 pounds boneless pork cutlets
1 lemon (or 1 to 2 teaspoons of dried granulated lemon peel)
2 to 3 fresh sprigs of rosemary
3 cloves garlic
1 teaspoon fennel seeds
1 pinch powdered cloves
Salt and freshly ground pepper

Approximate preparation time:
2 1/2 hours;
330 calories per serving.

1 If you cannot roast the piece of meat on a spit over a grill fire, preheat the oven to 400°F.

2 Mince 1 teaspoon of fresh rosemary leaves and the garlic and place both ingredients in a small mixing bowl. Grate the lemon peel, add to the previous ingredients in the bowl, and mix with the fennel seeds, powdered cloves, salt, and pepper.

3 With a sharp pointed knife, make several 1/2-inch-deep incisions at equal intervals on both sides of the meat. Fill each incision with a small portion of the spice mixture. Season the meat with salt and pepper, evenly distribute the rosemary over the meat, and, with a kitchen string, tie the whole piece of meat together like a rolled roast.

4 Bake the roast in a deep roasting pan in the oven (or push a skewer through it). To collect the meat juice, place a broiler pan under the meat.

5 Roast in a preheated oven for about 2 hours while periodically turning the meat over and drizzling with the meat juice. (Roasting the meat on the skewer will also require about 2 hours.)

Trippa alla fiorentina
Tripe with Vegetables, Florentine Style (Tuscany)

• A delicious side dish that will not require much work: Cook, together with the meat, cut-up vegetables and potatoes. The meat juice will contribute to the flavorful aroma.

• Wine serving suggestion: a wine that is not too heavy, such as a young *Chianti Classico* or a *Vino Nobile di Montepulciano*.

Serves 6

About 2 pounds precooked tripe
About 2 pounds fresh, ripe tomatoes (or peeled tomatoes from a 28-ounce can)
2 carrots
4 stalks celery
4 scallions
1 bunch fresh Italian parsley
1/2 bunch fresh basil
1 fresh sprig of rosemary (or 1/2 teaspoon dried rosemary)
1 cup dry white wine (or beef stock)
1 1/2 ounces or 2/3 cup grated Parmesan cheese
3 cloves garlic
2 tablespoon tomato paste
About 1/2 cup olive oil
2 tablespoons butter
1/4 teaspoon cayenne pepper
1/2 teaspoon peppercorns
Salt and freshly ground pepper

<u>Approximately preparation time</u>:
  2 3/4 hours;
  330 calories per serving.

1 Under running water, thoroughly wash the precooked tripe. Slice it thin with a very sharp kitchen knife.

2 Finely chop the carrots, celery, and scallions. Mince 1/2 bunch of parsley, rosemary, and garlic.

3 Heat 3 tablespoons of olive oil in a large saucepan. Melt the butter in it and sauté the vegetables. Stir in and sauté the parsley, rosemary, and garlic. Season with salt and pepper.

4 Heat 2 tablespoons of olive oil in a large frying pan. Add one portion of tripe and brown thoroughly. Add the browned tripe to the vegetables in the large saucepan. Pour more oil in the frying pan and brown a second portion of tripe. Continue the same procedure until no more tripe is left. Add each portion of browned tripe to the vegetables. Moisten with the white wine or stock and season with salt and pepper.

5 Blanch, peel, seed, and chop the tomatoes. Stir the tomatoes into the tripe, together with the tomato paste and cayenne pepper. Cover the saucepan only partially and simmer for about 1 hour. Shortly before serving, preheat the oven to 425°F.

6 In a mortar with a pestle, crush the peppercorns. Mince the remaining parsley. Season the tripe with salt and pepper, pour it into a large baking dish, top it with the crushed pepper, the minced parsley, and grated Parmesan cheese. Briefly bake in the preheated oven. Serve very hot with lots of white bread.

• The special touch to this recipe is in the baking of the stewed tripe. You can serve the dish in the Dutch oven with grated Parmesan cheese.

Lepre alla cacciatora
Hunter's Rabbit (Umbria)

Serves 4

1 young rabbit (about 2 ¹/₂
    pounds, ready to use and cut
    into pieces)
1 carrot, coarsely chopped
2 stalks, coarsely chopped
2 cloves garlic
1 sprig of rosemary
2 bay leaves
2 cups good-quality red wine
1 cup stock of venison (or, even
    better, venison demi-glace)
6 tablespoon olive oil
2 tablespoons flour
Salt and freshly ground pepper

Approximate preparation time:
    3 hours (+ 24 hours of mari-
    nating);
    570 calories per serving.

1 Thoroughly wash the rabbit
pieces and pat dry, making
sure to trim off the connective
tissue.

2 Cut the garlic cloves into
halves. Tie the sprig of rosemary and bay leaves together.

Place the herbs and meat in a
large mixing bowl and pour the
red wine over the mixture. Cover, refrigerate, and marinate for
24 hours.

3 Remove the meat from the
marinade, pat it dry, and dust
it with the flour. Pass the marinade through a fine strainer. Set
the wine and vegetables aside.
Heat the olive oil in a Dutch
oven.

4 Brown the rabbit pieces evenly on all sides in the Dutch
oven, season them with salt and
pepper, and lower the cooking
temperature. Add and cook the
vegetables, garlic, and herbs
with the meat, and moisten with
the stock. Cover the Dutch oven
and simmer on low heat for
about 2 ¹/₂ hours.

5 Remove the cooked pieces of
rabbit and the herbs. Puree
the gravy in a food processor and
season with salt and pepper.
Serve the meat in the sauce.

Quaglie al risotto
Quails with Risotto (Le Marche)

Serves 4

8 ready-to-use quails
8 slices of bacon (about 4
    ounces)
1 ¹/₃ to 1 ¹/₂ cups rice
1 tablespoon fresh thyme (or
    ¹/₂ tablespoon dried thyme)
2 bay leaves
¹/₂ cup dry white wine
1 cup chicken stock
3 tablespoon butter
4 tablespoons freshly grated
    Parmesan cheese
Salt and freshly ground pepper

Approximate preparation time:
    2 hours;
    760 calories per serving

1 Thoroughly rinse the quails
and pat dry; if necessary, remove the innards. You may
need to remove the remaining
pinfeathers with tweezers. Rub
the inside and the outside of
the quails with salt and pepper.

2 Fry the slices of bacon in a
large pot until crispy. Remove them and keep them
warm in a small saucepan. Melt
1 tablespoon of butter in the
large pot.

3 Gradually brown the quails
on all sides. Add the thyme
and 2 bay leaves, and moisten
with the white wine and stock.
Simmer covered for about 1
hour.

4 In a second large pot, bring
4 cups of salted water to a
boil, gradually add 1 ¹/₃ cups of
rice in a stream, and cook until
done. Drain the rice and fold 2
tablespoons of butter and 4 tablespoons of Parmesan cheese
into it. On a preheated platter,
serve the quails on a bed of rice
garnished with the crispy bacon. Season the pan juices and
serve with the quails.

Pollo alla cacciatora

Chicken, Hunter's Style (with Capers and Olives) (Umbria)

Serves 4

1 young chicken
   (about 2 pounds)
1 large lemon
1 bunch fresh Italian parsley,
   minced
1 teaspoon fresh stemless rosemary leaves (or ¹/₂ teaspoon
   dried rosemary)
2 canned anchovy fillets, drained
2 ounces black pitted olives
   (about 20 small)
2 tablespoons capers
2 tablespoons tomato paste
¹/₂ cup dry white wine (or
   chicken stock)
2 cloves garlic
6 tablespoons olive oil
6 peppercorns
Salt and freshly ground pepper

Approximate preparation time:
   1 hour (+ 30 minutes for marinating);
   520 calories per serving.

1 Cut the chicken into 6 pieces. In a mortar with a pestle, crush and reduce to a coarse paste the rosemary, garlic, and peppercorns. Fold into it 2 table-spoons of olive oil, salt, and the finely grated lemon peel. Rub the pieces of chicken with this mixture and set aside for 30 minutes to al-low the rub to seep into the meat.

2 Heat 4 tablespoons of oil in a large frying pan. Brown the chicken pieces evenly on all sides.

3 Whisk together 3 tablespoons of lemon juice with the tomato paste and white wine. Gradually moisten the chicken with it and simmer for about 15 to 20 min-utes.

4 Rinse and mince the anchovies. Cut the olives into halves. Add and mix the capers and let every-thing simmer for 5 minutes. Sea-son the gravy with salt and pepper and sprinkle with the parsley.

• Wine serving suggestion: a re-freshing white wine, such as an *Orvieto* wine.

Pollo alla diavola

Devil's Chicken (Hot and Spicy) (Tuscany)

Serves 2

1 chicken (about 2 pounds)
2 lemons
3 to 4 dried chili peppers
10 sage leaves
¹/₃ cup + 2 tablespoon olive oil
Salt and freshly ground pepper

Approximate preparation time:
   2 hours
   (+ 2 hours for marinating);
   670 calories per serving.

1 Cut open the bird with chick-en shears. Press the bird flat and place it on aluminum foil.

2 Mix the juice of 1 lemon olive oil, salt, and pepper. Seed and mince the chili pep-pers (make sure to wash your hands afterwards!). Slice the sage leaves and add to the marinade with the chili pep-pers.

3 Brush this marinade over the chicken on all sides. Wrap the chicken in foil and set aside for about 2 hours. Preheat the oven to 400°F.

4 Place the chicken wrapped in foil on a broiler pan. Open and fold the foil like a plate. Roast the chicken in the pre-heated oven for about 1 ¹/₂ hours or until golden brown and crispy. Garnish with lemon wedges.

• The reason why this chicken is called Devil's Chicken will be self-evident as soon as you taste it. For those who prefer a milder version, simply use less chili pepper!

Fagiano arrosto
Roasted Pheasant with Sage (Tuscany)

Serves 2

1 young pheasant (about 2 pounds), preferably with the liver intact
4 ounces raw country ham
3 large, thin slices of bacon
$1/2$ ounce or up to $1/2$ cup mixed, dried, wild mushrooms
6 to 8 sage leaves (fresh or dried)
1 tablespoon fresh rosemary leaves (or $1/2$ tablespoon dried rosemary), minced
$1/2$ pint or 1 cup whipping cream (or heavy cream)
1 tablespoon + 1 teaspoon brandy
$1/2$ cup venison demi-glace (or chicken stock)
2 cloves garlic
3 tablespoons oil
$1/2$ teaspoon juniper berries
Salt and freshly ground pepper

Approximate preparation time:
  $1 \ 3/4$ hours;
  1300 calories per serving.

If you are a hunter, these birds are available when hunting season is open. For those who are not into hunting, first-quality domesticated varieties (fresh or frozen) are available on the market.

The most visible differences between a wild and a domesticated pheasant mainly lie in the size and the weight of the bird. Domesticated birds are lighter and weigh between $1 \ 3/4$ pounds and 2 pounds, while the wild cousins weigh about 2 pounds. Only young pheasants are suitable for roasting; the old birds (about 1 year old) should only be braised or used to prepare pâtés, terrines, and fillings.

Three recipe variations from Tuscany and Umbria:

• Easy to prepare:
Braise the pheasant in a Dutch oven, together with red wine, sliced potatoes, and fresh rosemary.

• Hearty Country Style:
Fill the pheasant with sausage and herbs, wrap it in pork caul (see page 148) and heavy baking parchment paper, and cook in the oven.

• Festive gourmet dish:
Season the pheasant lightly with salt and pepper, fill with bacon and black truffles, and braise in whipping cream.

• Wine serving suggestion: a hearty red wine, such as *Brunello di Montalcino*.

1 In a small bowl, soak the dried mushrooms in the brandy. Thoroughly rinse the pheasant, inside and out, under running water, and pat dry. Remove the liver and set aside.

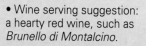

2 In a mortar, crush the garlic, juniper berries, and 1 pinch of salt into a paste. Mince the ham. Drain the mushrooms (keep the brandied mushroom water) and mince them. Combine minced mushrooms, crushed juniper berries, garlic, rosemary, and sage.

3 Rub the inside of the pheasant with pepper and fill it with the prepared mixture. With a trussing needle and string, sew up the bird. Season the outside of the bird lightly with salt and pepper. Preheat the oven to 425°F.

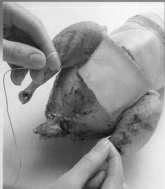

4 Wrap the bird's breast with thin slices of bacon and tie the bird and the bacon slices with a string.

5 Heat the oil in a roasting pan. Add the pheasant and brown thoroughly and evenly on all sides. Moisten with the brandied mushroom water and allow the mushroom juice to cook down. Place the pan with the bird in the oven. Roast the pheasant for 20 minutes, turning the bird once during the cooking process.

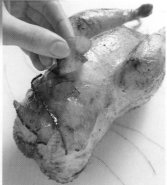

6 Remove the roasting pan from the oven, untie, and re-move the bacon slices around the bird. Return the bird in the roasting pan and moisten it with the venison demi-glace or stock. Finish roasting the bird for an additional 20 minutes, basting frequently.

7 Remove the bird and keep it warm. Place the roasting pan on top of the stove, add whip-ping cream, and bring to a rapid rolling boil. While the cream simmers, cube the liver, add it to the gravy, and simmer until the liver is cooked. Puree the gravy. Season with salt and pepper.

Frittata con le zucchine
Zucchini Omelet (Umbria)

Serves 2 to 4

*9 ounces or about 2 small, firm
   zucchini*
1 bunch fresh chives
*1/2 teaspoon fresh rosemary (or
   1/2 teaspoon dried rosemary)*
5 eggs
5 tablespoons milk
1 small onion, minced
2 cloves garlic, minced
4 tablespoon olive oil
Salt and freshly ground pepper

<u>*Approximate preparation time:*</u>
   30 minutes;
   310 calories per serving.

1 Wash and trim the zucchini.
Cut it first into thin slices
and then into thin strips.

2 Heat the olive oil in a medium frying pan. Add the zucchini strips, onion, garlic, and
rosemary, and sauté for about 5
minutes or until limp. Season
with salt and pepper. Thinly
snip the chives.

3 Whisk together the eggs,
milk, salt, and pepper. Fold
the chives into the egg mixture.
Pour the eggs over the zucchini
and distribute evenly. On low
heat, allow the mixture to set
and solidify. Turn the frittata
over and fry the other side.
Sprinkle with the remaining
chives and serve lukewarm.

• An easy way to turn over the
frittata: Slide the frittata from
the frying pan over onto a larger
plate, or a large lid, hold the frittata with the uncooked side up
parallel to the frying pan and,
with a decisive movement, turn
the uncooked side over and allow it to fall into the frying pan.

Frittata al formaggio
Cheese Omelet (Tuscany)

Serves 2 to 4

*2/3 cup freshly grated Parmesan
   cheese*
5 eggs
5 tablespoons whipping cream
10 fresh sage leaves
*14 ounces or about 8 peeled
   Italian-type tomatoes (or
   plum tomatoes from a can)*
1 small onion
1 clove garlic
3 tablespoons olive oil
1 tablespoon butter
Salt and freshly ground pepper

<u>*Approximate preparation time:*</u>
   30 minutes;
   380 calories per serving.

1 For the sauce: Mince the
onion and garlic. Drain and
cube the canned tomatoes
(keep the juice).

2 Heat 1 tablespoon of oil in a
small frying pan. Sauté the
onion and garlic. Stir in the
tomatoes. Season with salt and

pepper and simmer on low
heat. Gradually, in small portions, add the juice of the tomatoes.

3 For the frittata: Beat together the eggs with the whipping cream. Fold in 1 ounce or
about 1/2 cup of freshly grated
Parmesan cheese and season
with salt and pepper.

4 Heat 2 tablespoons of olive
oil and melt 1 tablespoon of
butter in a medium frying pan.
Add the sage leaves and sauté
them until they are lightly gold-
en and limp. Pour the egg mixture into the pan and immediately distribute everything
evenly. On low heat, allow the
mixture to set and solidify. Turn
over and fry on the other side
until golden brown.

5 Cut the pancake into slices
and serve with the tomato
sauce. Top with the remaining
Parmesan cheese.

Frittata ai funghi
Mushroom Omelet (Umbria)

Frittata in zoccoli
Bacon Frittata, Peasant Style (Tuscany)

Serves 2 to 4

*9 ounces or 15 small to medi-
um-sized fresh brown button
mushrooms (or baby porto-
bello mushrooms)*
1 bunch fresh Italian parsley
5 eggs
3 tablespoons olive oil
1 tablespoon butter
Salt and freshly ground pepper

<u>Approximate preparation time:</u>
30 minutes;
290 calories per serving.

1 Clean the mushrooms thoroughly and slice thin. Mince
the parsley.

2 Beat together the eggs, salt,
and pepper. Fold in three-
quarters of the mushrooms and
three-quarters of the minced
parsley.

3 Heat the olive oil and melt
the butter in a medium frying
pan. Pour in the egg mixture
and allow to set and to solidify.

4 Season with salt and pepper. Evenly distribute the remaining sliced mushrooms in
the center of the frittata and
fold the frittata halves together.
Sprinkle with the remaining
parsley.

• Instead of turning over the
pancake as in the previous
recipe, simply fold the frittata
together like an omelet and
serve it with a soft and creamy
inside.

• A specialty of Umbria prepared late in the fall: an omelet
filled with very thin truffle shavings.

Serves 2 to 4

*4 ounces or 4 slices bacon (or
raw country ham)*
1/2 bunch fresh basil
5 eggs
1 tablespoon olive oil
Salt and freshly ground pepper

<u>Approximate preparation time:</u>
30 minutes;
380 calories per serving.

1 Slice the bacon into thin
strips. Heat them in a medium frying pan with the olive oil;
stir-fry until the fat has rendered, and the bacon bits are
crispy.

2 Beat the eggs together with
salt and pepper (be careful
in seasoning because the bacon is already salty). Pour the
egg mixture into the frying pan
and immediately distribute
evenly. On low heat, allow the
egg mixture to set and solidify,
then turn the frittata over and

fry on the other side until gold-
en brown. Serve topped with
shredded basil leaves.

• Frittata is usually served lukewarm and cut in slices or
wedges; it is also used in small
pieces as an appetizer.

155

Fagioli all'uccelletto
White Beans with Sage (Tuscany)

Serves 6

About 2 cups white dried Italian
  beans (or white Great Northern or baby lima beans)
17 1/2 ounces or about 5 large or
  10 fresh, ripe plum tomatoes
10 fresh sage leaves
2 cloves garlic, minced
5 tablespoons olive oil
Salt and freshly ground pepper

<u>Approximate preparation time:</u>
  2 hours
  (+ 12 hours to soak the beans);
  300 calories per serving.

1 Soak the beans overnight. The
next day, add enough water to
the soaking liquid to make 8
cups, add 1/2 teaspoon of salt,
and simmer the covered beans at
least 1 1/2 hours (or until soft) in a
large pot.

2 After about 1 hour, blanch,
peel, seed, and cube the
tomatoes. Cut 10 sage leaves into thin strips.

3 Heat 4 tablespoons of olive oil
in a large saucepan. Simmer
the garlic and 1/2 of the sage
leaves in the oil.

4 Drain the beans. Put them in
the saucepan with the tomatoes, and season well with salt
and pepper. Cook covered for
about 20 minutes.

5 Heat 1 tablespoon of olive oil
in a small frying pan, and add
the remaining sage leaves. Drizzle the beans with this sage-
flavored oil and serve topped
with the sage leaves.

• Tuscany is famous for its
beans, and it has no equal when
it comes to extraordinary recipes.
The origins of the round-bellied
bottle that is used as a cooking
implement remains a mystery.
Filled with fresh white beans, flavorful olive oil, sage, water, and
spices, and left to cook overnight
on hot, smoldering wood charcoal, it turns into *fagioli al fiasco*
(beans in the bottle).

Spinaci gratinati
Baked Spinach (Tuscany)

Serves 4

2 pounds fresh spinach leaves
1/3 cup grated Parmesan
  cheese
2 tablespoons butter
1 tablespoon olive oil
1 clove garlic, crushed
Salt and freshly ground pepper

<u>For the sauce:</u>
1/3 cup grated Parmesan cheese
1 tablespoon butter
1 tablespoon flour
1 cup milk
1/2 lemon (juice)
Nutmeg
Salt and freshly ground pepper

<u>Approximate preparation time:</u>
  70 minutes;
  240 calories per serving.

1 Trim and wash the spinach
leaves. Place in a pot and let
wilt at high temperature. Remove the spinach and drain it
thoroughly.

2 Heat the oil in a frying pan.
Add the spinach and the
crushed garlic. Season with salt
and pepper while you melt 1 tablespoon of butter into the
spinach. Remove from the
heat. Preheat oven to 400°F.

3 For the sauce, melt 1 tablespoon of butter in a
saucepan, stir in the flour, and
lightly brown. Pour in the milk,
and while stirring constantly,
simmer until creamy. Remove
from heat, stir in the Parmesan
cheese, and season with a
pinch of grated nutmeg, salt,
pepper, and 1 to 2 tablespoons
of lemon juice.

4 Place the spinach into a baking dish, pour the sauce
over the spinach, and top with
another 1/3 cup of grated
Parmesan cheese. Bake in the
oven approximately 5 minutes.

Funghi alla toscana
Stewed Mushrooms, Tuscany Style (Tuscany)

Serves 4

17 1/2 ounces or about 30 small
   to medium fresh, mixed
   mushrooms (brown button
   mushrooms, horse mush-
   rooms, oyster mushrooms,
   chanterelles)
1 sprig fresh mint (or parsley)
1 lemon (juice)
3 to 4 cloves garlic
2 tablespoons tomato paste
5 tablespoons olive oil
1 teaspoon butter
Salt and freshly ground pepper

Approximate preparation time:
   45 minutes;
   130 calories per serving.

1 Clean the mushrooms thoroughly and slice them thin.
Drizzle with 1 tablespoon of
lemon juice. Thinly slice 3 to 4
cloves of garlic.

2 Heat 5 tablespoon olive oil in
a small frying pan. Gradually
add the mushrooms, sauté, remove from the pan, and set

aside for later use. Preheat
oven to 400°F.

3 Melt 1 tablespoon of butter
in a small saucepan. Stir in
the garlic and sauté until gold-
en. Add the remaining lemon
juice and tomato paste, and
season with salt and pepper.
Add the mushrooms, fold in the
other ingredients, and season
with salt and pepper.

4 Place the mushrooms in a
small stoneware baking
dish, and cook for 10 minutes
in the preheated oven. Top the
mushrooms with shredded
mint leaves or parsley, and
serve piping hot in the same
stoneware baking dish.

• To intensify the flavor of this
dish: simmer 1/2 bunch of fresh
minced Italian parsley with the
garlic slices.

Finocchi al forno
Baked Fennel (Tuscany)

Serves 4

4 small fennel bulbs
1/2 lemon (juice and peel)
1 bunch fresh Italian parsley
3 tablespoons fresh grated
   Parmesan cheese
1 small can of peeled tomatoes
   (about 14 ounces or about 8
   plum tomatoes)
4 tablespoons unseasoned
   breadcrumbs
1 small onion
2 cloves garlic
6 Tablespoons olive oil
Salt and freshly ground pepper

Approximate preparation time:
   90 minutes;
   260 calories per serving.

1 Cut each fennel vertically in
half, trim, and remove the
woody outer leaves. Keep the
fluffy fennel greens.

2 In a large pot, bring 4 cups
of salted water and the juice
of 1/2 lemon to a rolling boil.
Add the fennel halves and cook

for 20 minutes. Drain the fennel
and keep the fennel broth for
later use.

3 Preheat the oven to 400°F.
Brush a large baking dish
with 2 tablespoon of olive oil.
Drain the canned tomatoes
(keep the juice for another
dish), cube them, and place in
the baking dish. Add the fennel
halves. Drizzle with 1/2 cup of
fennel broth. Season with salt
and pepper.

4 Mince the parsley, fennel
greens, onion, and garlic.
Heat the 4 tablespoons of olive
oil in a medium frying pan.
Sauté the onion and garlic. Stir
in the breadcrumbs and stir-fry
until golden. Remove from the
heat. Fold the Parmesan
cheese and herbs into the
breadcrumbs, and sprinkle the
mixture over the fennel. Bake
in the preheated oven for 20
minutes.

Cavolfiore fritto
Fried Cauliflower (Le Marche)

Serves 4 to 6

1 whole cauliflower (about 2 pounds)
1 egg
1/2 cup dry white wine
About 1 tablespoon anise-flavored liqueur (anisette, Sambuca, or Ouzo)
3/4 cup flour
Enough olive oil to deep-fry
Salt and freshly ground pepper

<u>*Approximate preparation time:*</u>
1 hour;
240 calories per serving.

1 Combine the flour, salt, and pepper in a medium mixing bowl and make a well. Pour 1 egg, the white wine, and the anise-flavored liqueur into the center of the well's indentation and vigorously whisk everything together until you get a smooth mixture. Cover and set aside to rest for 30 minutes.

2 Clean, trim, divide and thoroughly rinse the cauliflower florets. Bring 8 cups of salted water to a boil in a large pot. Gradually drop the florets in the boiling water and blanch for 2 minutes. With a slotted spoon, remove the florets from the hot water, drop them in iced water to stop them from cooking further, and drain.

3 Heat enough oil for deep-frying in a large frying pan. With a fork, dip each floret into the anise mixture, and add each floret to the hot oil to fry until golden and crispy. Drain the excess oil from the cauliflower pieces on paper towels, and season with salt and pepper.

• The most attractive way to serve these cauliflower florets is to place them on a bed of green lettuce. You can use this recipe also for other types of vegetables; simply blanch the vegetables according to their texture before using them with the batter.

Zucchine ripiene
Stuffed Zucchini (Le Marche)

Serves 6 to 8

11 ounces ground beef
8 small and firm zucchini or any small summer squash
17 1/2 ounces or 5 medium large fresh ripe tomatoes
1 bunch of fresh Italian parsley
4 tablespoon freshly grated Parmesan cheese
1/2 of a day-old roll
1 onion, minced
1 clove garlic, crushed
2 tablespoons olive oil
1 tablespoon butter
Salt and freshly ground pepper

<u>*Approximate preparation time:*</u>
1 1/2 hours;
180 calories per serving.

1 Wash the zucchini and trim the flowers and stems. In a medium saucepan, blanch the zucchini in boiling salted water for 5 minutes. With a slotted spoon, dip the zucchini in iced water, leaving them to drain in a colander.

2 Grate the stale 1/2 roll with a four-sided grater. If necessary, chop the chunks of bread, then soak them in some water. Blanch, peel, seed, and chop the tomatoes.

3 In a large saucepan with cover, where 16 zucchini halves should fit snugly, heat the olive oil. Brown the minced onion, then add the chopped tomatoes. Season with salt and pepper, and add the crushed garlic. Simmer these ingredients until they have visibly cooked down.

4 Cut the zucchini in halves vertically, and scoop out some of the zucchini pulp. Mince it for later use. Melt 1 tablespoon of butter in a large pan, and brown the ground beef thoroughly on all sides. When the meat is done, set it aside in a mixing bowl until it is cool enough to handle.

Pinzimonio
Raw Vegetables with Dip (Tuscany)

5 Drain the bread and squeeze all the excess moisture from the soaked bread by hand. Mince the parsley. Add both ingredients to the ground meat. Fold the minced zucchini pulp and Parmesan cheese into this mixture. Mix all the ingredients thoroughly and season with salt and pepper. Fill the zucchini halves with this mixture.

6 Place the filled zucchini, one next to the other, on top of the tomato sauce in a large baking dish. Cover and simmer 30 minutes. The zucchini should still be relatively firm. Serve the zucchini on plates with some tomato sauce around each portion.

• For a lighter meal without a first course, these zucchini can also serve 4.

Serves 6

2 fresh fennel bulbs
2 medium peppers, one red and one yellow
2 small, firm zucchini
2 large, fresh, fully ripe plum tomatoes
1 head of radicchio (Italian red chicory-type salad green)
Romaine lettuce
4 scallions, trimmed

For the dip:
6 tablespoons wine vinegar
12 tablespoons of the best olive oil
Salt and freshly ground pepper

Approximate preparation time:
40 minutes;
200 calories.

1 Remove the outer leaves of each fennel bulb and trim the stems. Vertically slice each fennel into either four or eight wedges.

2 Cut each pepper in half, seed, and remove the internal membranes. Rinse the peppers and cut them in long 1/2 - inch-wide strips.

3 Rinse and trim the zucchini. Slice them 1/4 inch wide. Rinse the tomatoes and cut them in long, narrow strips, removing the stem.

4 Tear open and rinse the radicchio and Romaine lettuce. Drain the salad leaves. Rinse the scallions and cut the stems vertically in halves.

5 On a serving platter, place the lettuce and all the vegetables. For the dip, mix the wine vinegar, salt, and pepper, then add to the olive oil. Pour the dip into individual bowls and place these on the table. Each guest can choose his or her favorite vegetable, briefly dip a piece of vegetable in the dip, and eat the vegetable raw

together with fresh Italian white bread.

• Wonderful as an appetizer, as a snack, or as a summer meal.

• It is difficult to say exactly how much dressing should be prepared for this dish—better more than not enough. You can always keep it for the next salad meal.

Zuccotto
Iced Dome-shaped Trifle (Tuscany)

Serves 8 to 10

<u>For the sponge cake bottom</u>
<u>(Bake ahead of time):</u>
5 eggs
1 cup confectioners' sugar
1 tablespoon vanilla sugar
$1/3$ cup cornstarch (or arrowroot
    powder)
$1/3$ cup cake flour

<u>For the filling:</u>
7 ounces bittersweet chocolate
$1/3$ cup blanched almonds
$1/3$ cup blanched hazelnuts
2 ounces ready-to-use
    meringue
4 cups whipping cream
$1/2$ cup confectioners' sugar

<u>Other ingredients:</u>
About 1 tablespoon brandy
About 1 tablespoon Amaretto
    (almond flavored liqueur)
Butter for greasing
$3 1/2$ ounces chocolate glaze
Enough confectioners' sugar to
    dust

<u>Approximate preparation time:</u>
    $1 3/4$ hours (+ at least 6
    hours refrigeration);
    740 calories per serving.

This is a rich and tempting
dessert —it has a liqueur-
soaked sponge cake bottom,
lots of whipped cream,
meringue, chocolate, and nuts.
There are several recipe variations as rich as this version:
• Instead of Amaretto, a mixture of Maraschino, rum, and
orange-flavored liqueur is often
used to drizzle over the cake
bottom.
• Small pieces of candied fruit,
such as brilliantly red, sweet
cherry pieces, can also be hidden in the whipped cream.
• Coffee beans, slivered almonds, chocolate sprinkles, or
candied fruit can be used to
garnish.
• The sponge cake for the bottom can also be cut in large circles and placed one on top of
the other.

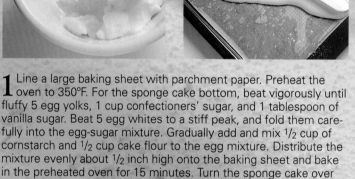

1 Line a large baking sheet with parchment paper. Preheat the oven to 350°F. For the sponge cake bottom, beat vigorously until fluffy 5 egg yolks, 1 cup confectioners' sugar, and 1 tablespoon of vanilla sugar. Beat 5 egg whites to a stiff peak, and fold them care-fully into the egg-sugar mixture. Gradually add and mix $1/2$ cup of cornstarch and $1/2$ cup cake flour to the egg mixture. Distribute the mixture evenly about $1/2$ inch high onto the baking sheet and bake in the preheated oven for 15 minutes. Turn the sponge cake over on a flat work surface, gradually remove the parchment paper, and allow the cake to cool off entirely.

2 Line a deep dome-shaped bowl—the diameter of the bowl should be about 4 inches—with either butter-greased baking parchment paper or aluminum foil. Cut a thin sponge cake round from the sponge cake for the bottom of the dome-shaped bowl, and cut suitable pieces to line the bowl entirely. Line the bowl up to the rim with pieces of the cake like a bowl-shaped puzzle. Mix the brandy with the Amaretto. Brush the liquid on the sponge cake lining.

3 Filling: Grate half of the chocolate, and melt the oth-er half in $1/2$ cup whipping cream. Chop the almonds and hazelnuts and roast them. Crush the meringue. Whip to a stiff peak the remaining whip-ping cream and confectioners' sugar. Fold the nuts and the chocolate into the cream.

4 Divide the whipped cream into two portions. Fold the meringue into one portion and the cooled (almost liquid) chocolate into the second portion. Line the dome-shaped cake bowl with the whipped cream mixed with the crumbled meringue, and refrigerate for 20 minutes. Then fill the remaining space in the sponge cake bowl with the chocolate and distribute the cream evenly in the cake bowl. Finally, cover the cream with the remaining pieces of sponge cake. Refrigerate at least 6 hours or overnight.

5 To decorate the dome, cut paper wedges: On paper draw a circle about 8 to 10 inches in diameter, mark rays from the center toward the rim of the circle, and cut out these rays to make several sharply pointed triangles.

6 Melt the chocolate. Turn the cake over and remove the parchment paper. Cover with chocolate and allow the glaze to dry. Place the paper triangles over the cake. Dust the cake with confectioners' sugar in a ray-shaped pattern. Remove the paper triangles. Cut in triangle-shaped portions and serve.

Frittelle di riso
Rice Fritters (Tuscany)

Serves 4 to 6

1 medium orange (peel)
1 medium lemon (peel)
About 1 tablespoon Vin Santo
   (Italian sweet wine) or rum
1 1/3 cups short-grain rice
1/2 cup raisins
3 cups milk
2 eggs
2 tablespoons butter
3 ounces or 1/3 cup + 1 tablespoon granulated sugar
1 tablespoon flour
Enough oil to deep-fry
Salt
Enough confectioners' sugar to
   dust the fritters

Approximate preparation time:
   80 minutes;
   480 calories per serving.

1 Soak the raisins in the wine
or rum. Bring 3 cups of milk
to a boil in a medium saucepan
with 1 pinch of salt, and in a
stream, gradually pour in and
stir the rice, and cook, stirring
constantly until done.

2 Remove the rice from the
heat and set aside to cool.
Rinse, scrub clean, and dry the
orange and lemon. With a fine
grater, grate the lemon and orange peels. Stir the grated peels
into the rice with 2 egg yolks, 2
tablespoons of butter, 1/3 cup of
granulated sugar, and the raisins
with their juice.

3 Heat enough oil in a large frying pan to deep-fry. Beat 2
egg whites to a stiff peak and
fold the egg whites, remaining
sugar, and 1 tablespoon of flour
into the cooked rice mixture.

4 With a tablespoon, spoon out
small dumpling-shaped portions of rice and fry in the hot oil,
periodically turning the fritters
over with a fork. Place the fritters
on paper towels to allow the excess fat to drain, and keep warm
until all the fritters are fried.
Place on a large serving platter,
dust with confectioners' sugar,
and serve while still warm.

Panforte di Siena
Siena's Honey Fruit Nut Cake (Tuscany)

Serves 10 to 12

2/3 cup blanched almonds
2/3 cup blanched hazelnuts
2/3 cup walnuts
5 ounces dried figs
5 ounces mixed candied fruits
1 3/4 cups confectioners' sugar
About 1/2 cup honey
Enough rice paper to line the
   bottom and top of the cake
1/2 teaspoon powdered
   cinnamon
1 pinch each of powdered
   cloves, powdered coriander,
   powdered ginger, nutmeg
   (or powdered mace)
1 to 2 tablespoon flour
Butter to brush a baking pan
Enough confectioners' sugar
   and powdered cinnamon to
   dust the cake

Approximate preparation time:
   1 1/4 hours;
   310 calories per serving.

1 In a small frying pan, quickly
roast the almonds, the hazelnuts, and the walnuts, stirring
constantly. Allow the nuts to
cool off, chop, and put in a mixing bowl.

2 Chop the dried figs and candied fruits, add to the nuts,
and mix. Add and mix the cinnamon, powdered cloves, powdered coriander, powdered ginger, and freshly grated nutmeg
(or powdered mace).

3 In the top part of a double
boiler, mix the confectioners' sugar and honey and place
the double boiler pot on the
bottom of the pot filled with
water. On low temperature,
heat the water and the sugar-
honey mixture, stirring constantly until it melts and
threads can be pulled. Remove
from the heat and allow to cool
off.

4 Preheat the oven to 300ºF.
Fold the sugar-honey mix-
ture into the nut mixture and
add the flour. With butter

Biscotti di Prato

Almond Biscotti (Hard Cookies), Prato Style (Tuscany)

grease either a round (about 8" x 2") or a square baking pan (about 8" x 8" x 2"), line it with rice paper, pour the dough and spread it out evenly 1 inch high.

5 Bake in preheated oven for about 30 minutes. Cool off and dust with a thin layer of a mixture of confectioners' sugar and powdered cinnamon. You can cut the cake in wedges, or long strips, and store in a sealed container.

• No visitor leaves Siena without this sweet souvenir; many have someone at home who is impatiently waiting for this specialty. This well-known honey spiced cake, even centuries ago, was considered a fine, sought-after delicacy.

Yield: 70 cookies

7 ounces or 1 ²/₃ cup slivered almonds
1 lemon (peel)
3 eggs
1 ¹/₄ cup granulated sugar
3 tablespoons vanilla sugar
About 14 ounces or 3 cups + 3 tablespoons all-purpose flour
¹/₂ package baking powder (1 ¹/₄ tablespoons)
1 teaspoon butter + butter to brush a baking sheet
1 pinch salt

Approximate preparation time:
50 minutes;
60 calories per piece.

1 Briefly stir and roast the slivered almonds in a pan and set them aside for later use.

2 Preheat the oven to 350°F and brush a large baking sheet with butter. In a large mixing bowl, cream 3 egg yolks, the granulated sugar, and the vanilla sugar. Beat 3 egg whites with 1

pinch of salt to a stiff peak. Gradually fold into egg-sugar mixture.

3 Add and mix the grated peel of 1 lemon and the roasted slivered almonds. Mix the all-purpose flour with the baking powder and sift. Combine all the ingredients and knead until you get a smooth dough.

4 Divide the dough into portions, and with each portion make 1-inch-thick sausages of dough. Place the dough sausages on the buttered baking sheet. Bake in the preheated oven for about 35 minutes or until the surface is golden brown. Remove the cookie sausages from the oven and, with a sharp knife, immediately slice them diagonally ¹/₂ inch thick. Cool the slices off entirely before storing them in a sealed cookie jar.

• For those who unknowingly taste one of these slices, it may not be love at first bite, since

these biscotti are hard and made especially to dip in the deliciously sweet *Vin Santo*. For those who have no Vin Santo ready, try dipping the cookies in espresso.

Chianti Classico— A Living Legend

The "Gallo Nero" (the black rooster), the traditional symbol of the Consorzio Vino Chianti Classico.

In order for a wine to gain in worldwide popularity, it needs a market—a place where demand meets suppliers to make this wine available everywhere. Once the wine is indeed world-renowned, and has, of course, a suitable price, the problems of mass production and low-quality imitations begin to appear.

This is the dilemma that has plagued the history of *Chianti* wine as no other wine in the world. Due to its closeness to a Renaissance world trade center, wine produced in regions located between Florence and Siena found their way very early into England and France. A Rosso di Firenze (red wine of Florence) is mentioned in London in the early sixteenth century as rough and full-bodied, which basically meant that the wine was considered to be aged and dry in comparison to the existing popular sweet wines of the time.

Such wines were listed in Florence under the category of vermiglia (dark red) and were produced in the areas of Castelli Uzzano, Vignamaggio, and Montefioralle—still important names today in the region of the *Chianti Classico*. For its fur-

ther worldwide popularization, especially in England and France, an old "Chianti" denomination of origin (DOC), which had been established in 1398, gradually became known during the seventeenth century. In 1716 Cosimo III, Granduke of Tuscany, mandated a protection law intended to prevent illegal competition. It established that only those red wines produced in a certain limited region surrounding the counties of Greve, Radda, Gaiole, and Castellina could be called *Chianti*. This is the same region that today is the production area of the *Chianti Classico*.

From that time, the development of Chianti continued. Chianti red wines are the result of mixed grapes that are typical of the region. In general, *Chianti* red wines are made from Sangiovese grapes and a wide variety of Sangiovese substrains, and from red Canaiolo Nero as well as from white Trebbiano Toscano and Malvasia del Chianti grapes. An additional categorization occurred when Bettino Ricasoli, Baron at the Castello Brolio located near Gaiole, introduced an official recipe. In 1834, after many years of experimentation, the nobleman recommended a recipe for Chianti that used 70 percent Sangiovese, 15 percent Canaiolo, 10 percent Trebbiano and Malvasia mixed together, as well as 5 percent of other grapes. At the same time, as a typical characteristic of Chianti production, he also established the basic rule of a second fermentation. This stage is implemented with the addition of unfermented new wine made from dried grapes or grape concentrate to the first fermentation.

These fundamentals formed the basis for all further developments of Chianti up to the pres-

ent. The Consorzio Vino Chianti Classico, established in 1924, and known today as the Consorzio del Gallo Nero, is, above all, based on the guidelines established by the Baron Ricasoli. Today, the Consorzio requires that the wine produced by its members be marketed with a *symbol* displaying the black rooster (Gallo Nero).

The image and quality of this wine are still not firmly secured. Over and over again, the pendulum that swings between balancing the interests of the producers' community, with its quality control and production limits, and the individual production interests, with their desire to increase profit and quantity in favor of mass production, produce unavoidable consequences that impact wine quality.

The most recent stages of this voyage on the path of quality warranty were the Italian wine laws of 1963 and the gradual application of these laws in various wine production regions. In 1967 an origin denomination sign with attached production-related requirement—*Denominazione di origine controllata, DOC* (controlled origin label)— was introduced for the Chianti Classico. The controlled and warranted production sign—*Denominazione di origine controllata e garantita, DOCG* (controlled and warranted origin la-

bel)—became binding in 1984. Each of these certifications also attached various modifications to the requirements related to the production of the wine.

According to current DOCG requirements, Chianti Classico wine is made from 75 percent to 90 percent Sangiovese, 5 to 10 percent Canaiolo, and 2 to 5 percent Trebbiano and Malvasia grapes. It can include up to 10 percent of other grapes, which today is mainly Cabernet Sauvignon, a grape that is not originally from Tuscany, but has gained the favor of the local wine producers. The DOCG mandates also limit the wine production to 6,500 pounds per acre. A second fermentation is permitted but is not required. For this phase, only new wines or concentrates from the region that have been pressure-produced and concentrated at temperatures not exceeding 86°F are used. It also makes a distinction between one-year-old aged wine *Annata* and three-year-old aged wine *Riserva*. The old category of the two-year-old aged wine *Vecchia* has been eliminated.

This new regulation also tries to balance the need for accurate quality standards with the individual creativity of the various wine producers. The new regulation maintains, within reasonable limits, the historical traditions of the grape mixtures of this large wine region, where each wine producer has its own blends of grapes, which can be mixed as early as during the harvesting. However, since the regulation only applies to some wines, it does not completely cover the large variety of wines produced in this region.

*Above: Traditional wine production in a mixed grape – growing culture (*Vigneto promiscuo – *mixed vineyard). Here, the harvest is way below the allowed 6 700 pounds per acre – a luxury that can be afforded only by a few. The size of land reserved for mixed grape growing remains a typical characteristic of vineyards in Chianti. The change to a monoculture is made more difficult by the wine regulation, but it is not totally impossible.*

The classic grapes for the Chianti Classico. From left: Sangiovese, Canaiolo Nero, Trebbiano Toscano, Malvasia del Chianti.

From a desire to increase the Sangiovese portion in the Chianti wine, a new white wine production has developed, mainly on Trebbiano. The *Bianco della Lega*, produced exclusively by the members of the Consorzio del Gallo Nero, aims to gain the recognition of a fine-quality wine according to the local stringent wine regulations. The *Galestro* is a brand wine that is also made by producers located outside the region.

Many wine producers here also make their own white table wines. They are all refreshing, should be consumed while young, and are not suitable for long periods of storage.

Many new wine varieties have been developed from the Chianti area's white wine production. They have arisen from the need to use the white grapes that are not needed for the Chianti Classico and from the wine producers' desires to expand their recognition and profile. The most recent trend has resulted in relatively expensive fine – quality wines that do not fit into the mold of the Chianti region's typical wine production. And, since all these wines fail to fit the wine specifications of the typical regional wines, producers are usually forced to offer wines labeled simply as table wine, or *vino da tavola*.

A good example of this type of wine is the red *Solatio Basilica* from Villa Cafaggio, which is produced mainly with Sangiovese grapes, following the successful model of the Brunello di Montalcino. Even if this *vino da tavola di Panzano* does not fit the requirements of the Chianti Classico, its fruitiness and acidity bouquet are comparable to the ideal regional wine.

A totally different approach seems to be taken by wines like the Brunesco di San Lorenzo produced by Giovanni Capelli, which are made with *barriques*, small barrels, usually of French oak, that are used only once more after the first use. This method, originally developed in France, allows winemakers to take advantage of a balanced dose of tannin present in the new oak wood. In this case, the final result is a very strong wine, which has nothing in common with Chianti Classico.

Many similar trends that depart from the Chianti Classico tradition of the Chianti Classico seem to have increased in frequency over recent years. Atypical red Cabernet Sauvignon and white Chardonnay grapes have gradually became part of the region's wine production. The increased demand for

wines that are not yet mature, such as the *Beaujolais Primeur*, has also found an audience among Chianti wine-makers who began producing table wines that are young and almost fizzy. This type of production has evolved into an interesting kaleidoscope of wine products, which has brought forth not only the traditional Chianti Classico and the familiar white wines produced with Trebbiano and Malvasia grapes, but a whole array of rosés *primeurs* chardonnays, cabernets, and other wines. Like the more ambitious wine creations from the classic region of the Chianti grape, whether made with or without the use of barriques, these wines also are offered as vino da tavola.

In the background of this restless wine development lies a deep-rooted economic change in the region's wine culture. This change began during the middle of the 1960s with a remarkable investment effort from outside, which was undoubtedly related to the profit expectations for the classic wine production of the region. The 1963 wine law had especially stressed quality control and limited wine production.

Above right and near right: The bulk of the wine harvest in Chianti is grown today in monoculture (vigneto specializzato)*; however, the distances between the rows are still remarkable here. The space between vines is still larger than vineyards where specially built narrow row machines work.*

The first two weeks in October are harvest weeks throughout Chianti (above, left and near left). After the harvest, the grapes are gathered first (above) and then set aside, since a good wine requires not only the acidity but also the yeast from the berries and the skins to begin fermentation, while the undesirable stems are to be removed.

Left: The mark of a classic Chianti still rests on the principle that the wine gains in quality with aging. Barrels like these made from oak, and less frequently from chestnut wood, are a big investment. This investment is worthwhile mainly for the best part of the harvest, which is destined for a Riserva quality (three years of aging before being filled in bottles).

The new large wine cellars such as Le Bocce, Villa Cafaggio, and Rocca della Macie, although equipped with the latest enological technology, were able to produce wines according to the classic Chianti wine requirements.

In addition to similar new wine companies, often financed by shareholders, there were many changes in proprietorship. The traditional and well-established Castello Brolio changed hands more than once, even being briefly owned by a whiskey company. Finally, several successful businesspeople, such as designer Emilio Pucci and Florentine jeweler Aldo Torrini, who, with a mixture of good business sense and personal involvement aimed to challenge their personal winemaking talent, entered the wine industry through partly inherited and partly purchased Chianti Classico wineries.

When it became evident during the 1970s that, contrary to the case of the Brunello di Montalcino, the high expectations in price and profit would not pan out, there were several economic failures, such as the new winery Le Bocce and the old, established winery Vignamaggio.

The new economic changes were followed by measures that required refining the methods used in the cellars. This stage of modernization took place with automatically cooled pump equipment, with sanitary stainless steel piping, and the latest in bottle-filling technology. Throughout the wineries, traditional mixed growing methods for wine, olives, and other produce have been largely replaced by monocultures.

What is occurring today in the region of Chianti is exciting and interesting. It invites us to pay close attention and promises to feed our sense of curiosity. A good sign of the present situation is offered throughout the wine shops in Florence, Siena, Panzano, and especially in the Enoteca del Gallo Nero, in Greve in Chianti.

Hermann Rademacker

Latium and Sardinia

City and Suburbs:
View toward St. Peter's Square and Rome.

The Regions and Their Products

R ome, the Eternal City. The flow of history glides from antiquity to modern times; it has filled the city with monuments and famous works of

art. Over centuries of Roman dominion, the city grew into an economic, cultural, and scientific center of a vast empire. In the meantime, the surrounding country suburbs around Rome not only served to supply the metropolis, but were also sought after as land for luxury country estates for high government employees, and for magnificent villas owned by wealthy citizens. Therefore, Romans, rather than farmers, molded the surrounding countryside, and this influence is still found in today's cuisine.

The region of Latium is economically connected with the capital. Industrial neighborhoods are rare and the volcanic range of the Apennines, with mountain peaks and high plateaus, numerous lakes, and thermal spas, invites relaxation.

Dishes have been kept in Rome more than in other cities of central Italy, due to the pride of Romans who approach with skepticism everything that comes from the outside. On the other hand, Roman cuisine has absorbed, without any apologies, many specialties that originally come from the surrounding regions. This cuisine does not favor complicated dishes that are difficult to prepare, and seems

Above, top: Bizzare rock formations on the coast of Sardinia.

Above, bottom: One of the many bridges over the Tiber River towards the city district of Trastevere, a typical, and now very expensive, residential area.

Top, right: Livestock breeding, especially sheep, mark Sardinia's landscapes.

Middle: Pigs are also favorites here. The meat is especially flavorful because acorns are fed to the animals.

Right: Butcher shop in Rocca di Papa.

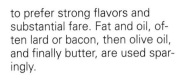

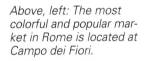

Above, left: The most colorful and popular market in Rome is located at Campo dei Fiori.

Left: Worldly and Christian Rome gathers around the chestnut vendor.

Above, top: Even if Sardinians are not known as famous navigators, there is always fresh fish here.

Above: A very important ingredient in Sardinian cuisine is pecorino, the sheep's milk cheese that is also a favorite in Latium.

to prefer strong flavors and substantial fare. Fat and oil, often lard or bacon, then olive oil, and finally butter, are used sparingly.

Favorites are beef, lamb—above all the young suckling lamb called *abbacchio*—and poultry, innards and sweetbreads, legumes, and of course, such vegetables as artichokes, celery, and peppers. In Roman cuisine there are few typical seafood dishes apart from Tevere's (Tiber's) eel and squid. Latium has in common with Sardinia the love for products made from sheep's milk: pecorino and ricotta.

Sardinia also has preserved its traditional cuisine fairly well. The residents of this sparsely populated island have always lived on the outskirts of Italy's history. They still speak their own language, and the ancient original dishes have kept their old names. The typical Sardinian is not a navigator nor a fisherman, but, rather, a shepherd. The internal part of the island is still more populated than the coast, and its main economy stems from agriculture and animal breeding rather than from fishing activities. The cuisine is mainly based on a few ingredients: milk, sheep cheese, meat, and, above all, bread. Together with several regional breads, one plays an especially important role here: a flat and paper-thin bread, *carta da musica*, or sheet of music. Shepherds take it with them while tending their flocks and make soup with it; fine restaurants serve it as crispy bread.

Pigs that often run free and feed on acorns are especially enjoyed; firm hams and spiced sausages flavored with fennel are prepared from their meat. Sardinian dishes are usually flavorful and simple, often prepared in only one pot and seasoned with local herbs.

An important product made in Sardinia is sheep's milk cheese, the pecorino. It is available in various grades of texture and at different maturation stages, from fresh, soft, and mild, to hard, aged, and pungent.

People, Events, Sightseeing

Rome is a capital in two ways: the capital of Italy and the capital of Christianity. Over and over, Romans managed to survive in spite of the city's many involvements in historical wars, the chaos of the ancient Barbarian migrations during the fall of the Roman empire, and the increasing cultural influence of the papacy. With the constant flow of pilgrims to the Eternal City came also the money and the wealth that allowed art-loving citizens to build more imposing palaces and villas and to construct monuments or even churches for their own family use. Today, Rome is still a must visit for anyone who travels throughout Italy, even if Romans themselves believe that one should admire art in art books. Those Romans! A typical characteristic seems to be their feeling of superiority toward everything that does not originate in Rome. They are not intimidated by anything or by anybody. Social status or titles do not impress them.

Weekend outing destinations for the city's residents are the Albani mountains near Frascati (the Pope also has a summer residence here), especially with its open restaurants, lined up one after the other along the street. A culinary treasure is the

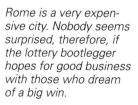

Rome is a very expensive city. Nobody seems surprised, therefore, if the lottery bootlegger hopes for good business with those who dream of a big win.

Above, top, right: All roads lead to Rome, but in the city, follow a map.

Above: Cornetto, the flaky and crispy crescent that is part of breakfast.

Top and bottom right: The Spanish Staircase and a trattoria on the Piazza Navona in Rome.

small city of Rocca di Papa, above Lake Albano, where there is a market every morning.

Right around the corner, one finds a *norcineria*, a pork butcher shop, where tempting sausages and hams hang from the ceiling and *porchetta*, a whole suckling pig seasoned with fennel, rosemary, salt, and pepper, is being roasted on the spit. A paradise of mushrooms is what one finds next if one goes from there through the narrow streets to the Belvedere restaurant. Fresh wild mushrooms are available here 12 months a year. They are served baked in the oven, preserved in oil and vinegar, and stewed with herbs.

Sardinia is made up of mountains, woods, wide planes, swampy landscapes, sand, rocky beaches, and cliffs with bizarre rock formations on the coasts. In spite of all this, tourism is concentrated mainly throughout the northern coast; along the Costa Smeralda with the newly built villages of Porto Cervo and Porto Rotondo, life equals luxury, at least for those who are rich and those who travel.

In the background are the stubborn, goal-oriented, and persevering Sardinians, who not only know good food, but good wine as well. An interesting destination from the culinary point of view is Macomer, the Cheese City with many regional variations of sheep cheese.

Culture buffs can learn a lot here. The Nuraghes, enormous piles of stones from a prehis-

toric culture, prove that the island has been inhabited since prehistory. These constructions, which sometimes rise higher than one floor, could be graves, fortresses, or temples. Bronze works from a prehistoric era are on display at the Museums of Cagliari and Sassari.

Events: Rome has a celebration with dance and food every July and August on the Tiber Island. In the middle of July, an ancient popular celebration, the Festa de Noantri, is held in Trastevere. Latium holds a festival at the beginning of February on Monte San Biagio. Connected with this event is a market featuring crafts and agricultural products. At Montefiascone, a wine festival with comedy and folk skits that refer to the famous local wine is held at the beginning of August.

In Sardinia, a popular chestnut and hazelnut festival with folk songs and dances is held in Aritzo at the end of October. In Sedilo, S'ardia, a wild horseracing show that commemorates the victory of Constantine over Maxentius on the Milvian Bridge is held at the beginning of July.

Above, left: Peace and lack of stress mark Sardinia's daily life—there are still many beautiful little spots that remain undiscovered by tourists.

Middle, left: Jovial informality is part of a program for a festival.

Left: The ancient Nuraghes, throughout Sardinia, look like mysterious stone bowling pins made of huge blocks without mortar.

Above: Fresh cepes (mushrooms) are always available at the Belvedere restaurant in Rocca di Papa. They are kept all year in cool caves at high humidity.

The Wines

Rome has been a travelers' destination since antiquity, and, as recorded in many legends that tell about the famous *"Est! Est! Est!"* from Montefiascone on the Bolsena Lake, traveling makes one thirsty. One legend tells of a bishop who had sent his servant ahead to explore suitable overnight places where good wine would also be available. The servant was to mark the doors of those inns that were suitable with an Est! sign. Along the old Cassia road toward Montefiascone, in the best inn in town, he found a wine that was so good that he wrote three times on the door of the place: Est! Est! Est!

This white wine is made from Trebbiano and Malvasia grapes; it is available as dry, slightly fruity, or Asciutto, with a delicate almond flavor that is recommended for fish dishes, and as a semisweet dessert wine, *Abboccato*, which goes best with cheeses. For a while it seemed that the wine would live more by its reputation than by its own merit, but in the meantime, several winemakers have been in the process of producing a much better quality.

The *Colli Albani* and the *Castelli Romani*, both white wines, have an interesting history. During the time when Rome extended over only three hills, the best wine came from the foothills of the Albani Mountains, but, this area was owned by the Latinians. In order to be able to enjoy the wines, the Romans were left with no other option but to take over the area around 4 B.C. Both wines are usually dry, straw yellow in color, with a typically fruity flavor.

The vineyards that produce *Frascati* are also located in the Castelli Romani. Known in the past as sweet *Cannellino*, it is now usually produced dry. Today, Romans still like to visit Frascati's wineries to enjoy the mild, smooth, and straw yellow wine directly out of the barrels. It can be served during all courses of a menu, with pasta, fish, poultry, and desserts. The *Marino, Colli Lanuvini*, and *Montecompatri Colonna* can also be included in the group of Frascati wines.

In addition to the white wines, there are the ruby red wines made from Cesanese grapes from the area east of Rome: the *Cesanese del Piglio, Cesanese di Affile*, and *Cesanese di Olevano Romano.* The dry versions are delicately scented and slightly tannic with a touch of bitterness that is very well suited for stewed meat dishes.

Sardinia's wines suit the island's hearty cuisine. Some develop their true characters only after several years of aging, such as the white *Vernaccia di Oristano*, originally from one of the most picturesque areas of the island, which is drinkable after three years but is often stored for up to thirty years. The wine is similar to sherry; it is strong, but not fortified with pure alcohol. It has a delicate scent of almonds, is full-bodied, fruity, with a lighter bitter aftertaste, since it is made from grapes normally grown for dry wines. It goes well with fish dishes. Old wines of this kind are also served chilled.

Sardinia's wines tend to be rather light and dry, such as the *Nuragus di Cagliari*. It is light in color, greenish yellow, dry, and rather neutral in flavor, with a delicate hint of bitterness. It is a typical fish wine. The red *Monica di Sardegna* that is produced throughout the island, is always dry, of a light ruby red color, smooth, and with a long, lingering flavor that increases with aging. It is a wine that goes well with roasted meats and grilled fish. *Cannonau di Sardegna* is a strong and full-bodied wine that is produced in many areas of the island. It has a bright red color, is sold after one year of aging in either oak or chestnut wood barrels, and is generally consumed while still relatively young. After at least three years of aging, it is labeled *Riserva*. If it has a high alcohol content, it is recognized as *superiore* with a gradation that goes from dry to sweet. As a *secco*, this wine goes best with dark meats and venison, as does the *Carignano del Sulcis*, originally from the extreme southwestern portion of Sardinia and from the tiny islands of San Pietro and Sant' Antioco.

Additionally, there are several dessert wines like the *Malvasia di Cagliari*, which is available *dolce* (sweet) and *secco* (dry) as well as *liquoroso* (liqueur like) with high alcohol content. Others are the *Moscato di Cagliari* with a typical fortified moscato flavor, and the *Moscato di Sorso-Sennori* from the regions of the same name north of Sassari.

Above: Vineyards in the Frascati area.

Far left: Grape harvest in Sardinia.

Left: A sample of new-style Sardinia wines is the Calaluna—dry and refreshing, and to be consumed while young.

Regional Recipes

Pane carasau
Crispy Bread Flats (Sardinia)

Yield: 8 Pieces

For the dough:
1 ¾ cups bread flour
1 ½ cups + 2 tablespoons
    semolina flour
About ½ cube of compressed
    fresh yeast or 1 envelope of
    active dry yeast
2 tablespoons lukewarm water
1 cup lukewarm water
1 pinch sugar
Salt

Other ingredients:
Flour to roll out the dough
Oil spray for the baking sheets
Olive oil
Salt and freshly ground pepper
Rosemary (fresh or dried)

Ingredients for Pane Fratau:
Crispy bread flats (as described
    here—see step 6)
4 Pane carasau
2 ¼ cups pureed tomatoes
⅔ cup freshly grated pecorino
or Parmesan cheese
4 eggs
1 cup hot beef stock
2 tablespoons butter
Salt and freshly ground pepper
Fresh parsley and basil to garnish

Approximate preparation time:
    2 ½ hours
    (+ 2 hours resting time);
    380 calories per each Pane
    fratau.

Sardinians lovingly call this
bread flat destined for storage
Carta da Musica, or sheet of
music. The preparation requires
some patience, since the flats
need to be baked twice. (In this
case, a convection oven would
be preferable, since you can
bake more than one sheet at a
time).

In the old days, shepherds took
the bread with them to the
fields; today it is found in restaurants as a crispy delicacy that is
served with appetizers. For this
purpose, the "sheets of music"
are baked quickly, drizzled with
aromatic olive oil, and sprinkled
with salt and minced rosemary.

Pane carasau can also be the basis for a small meal—see step 6.

1 Dough: In a large mixing bowl, combine the bread flour and
semolina flour. Crumble about ½ cube of compressed fresh
yeast (or 1 envelope of active dry yeast) in a cup together with a
pinch of sugar and 2 tablespoons of lukewarm water. Pour the
yeast mixture in the middle of the flour, and combine all the ingredients. Cover with a clean dishcloth, and set aside to rest in a
warm place for 1 hour. After 1 hour, gradually add 1 cup lukewarm
water and 1 teaspoon of salt, and knead until you obtain a smooth,
silky dough. Return the dough to the bowl and set aside again to
rest, covered, for 1 hour.

 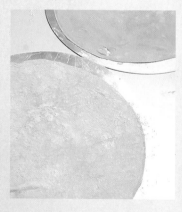 

2 Preheat the oven to 475°F.
Spray 2 flat round baking
sheets (you may use flat, round
10- to 12-inch-diameter pizza baking pans). Vigorously knead the
dough once more. Divide the
dough into 8 round portions, and
on a well-floured work surface,
roll out each piece of dough to
the size of the baking rounds.

3 Put the large, round, thin
bread flats on the oiled baking sheets. Bake each in the
preheated oven for 5 minutes,
or until the dough blisters but is
not yet brown.

4 Remove the freshly baked
bread flats from the oven
and stack them up one on top
of the other. Cover the pile with
a large platter or a suitable
board, and set them firmly in
place. Let the stacked bread
flats cool.

5 Return each bread flat to the oven and bake again for 8 to 10 minutes or until lightly crispy. Let cool, then store in parchment paper. Before serving the bread flats (with appetizers), rebake them quickly, brush them with olive oil, and sprinkle with salt, coarsely ground pepper, and rosemary.

6 *Pane fratau:* A kind of layered *pane carasau.* On a large plate, place 4 bread flats one on top of another, and drizzle with the hot beef stock. Heat the pureed tomatoes and season with salt and pepper. In a small frying pan, melt 2 tablespoons butter and fry 4 eggs sunny-side up. Line the bread flats with the pureed tomatoes, and top them with the fried eggs. Season with salt, pepper, and grated cheese. Garnish with shredded leaves of parsley and basil.

Pandorato

Pan-fried Bread Pockets (Latium)

Serves 6

3 thin slices Italian prosciutto
   ham (or raw country ham)
5 ounces mozzarella cheese
12 fresh leaves of basil
6 canned anchovy fillets,
   drained
one-day-old loaf of white toast
   bread, toasted
1/2 cup milk
2 eggs
2 tablespoon flour
Enough oil to fry
Salt and freshly ground pepper

Approximate preparation time:
  45 minutes;
  400 calories per serving.

1 Cut off the crust from the loaf of bread. Slice the loaf in 1/2-inch-thick slices. Cut through the bottom crust only every second slice to make 6 double slices connected at the bottom.

2 Cut the mozzarella into 6 slices. Place cheese in each pocket. Fill half of the bread pockets with ham. Rinse the anchovies and pat them dry. Fill the bread pockets with the anchovies.

3 Press together and dip the bread pockets in milk. Dust them on both sides with flour and place them on a rimmed baking pan. In a mixing bowl, whisk 2 eggs and season with salt and pepper. Pour the egg mixture over the bread pockets, and allow the egg mixture to seep into the bread for 15 minutes. Turn the bread pockets over once.

4 In a frying pan, heat oil to fry. Fry the bread pockets until golden brown on both sides, and drain them on paper towels. Cut pockets diagonally in half. Serve two with different fillings, garnished with basil leaves.

Focaccia sarda

Potato Dough Pizza with Sheep's Milk Cheese, Sardinian Style (Sardinia)

Serves 4 to 6

1 large baking potato
12 fresh, ripe, plum tomatoes
7 ounces or 2 small blocks fresh
   goat cheese
1/2 to 1 cup milk
1/2 to 1 cube fresh compressed
   yeast (or 1 1/2 1/4-ounce envelopes active dry yeast)
1 onion, minced
2 cloves garlic, minced
1 3/4 to 2 cups bread flour
4 tablespoons olive oil
1 pinch sugar
Salt and freshly ground pepper

Approximate preparation time:
  1 3/4 hours;
  380 calories per serving.

1 Wash and cook the potato in salted water. Peel while still hot and press through a ricer onto a work surface. Add and combine 1 3/4 cups of flour and 1/2 cup milk. Make a well in the middle.

2 In a bowl, combine the yeast with 1 pinch of sugar and 2 tablespoons of lukewarm milk, and mix until all ingredients are dissolved. Add the mixture to the well you had made on the work surface and dust with additional flour. Cover with a dishcloth and let rise in a warm room for 30 minutes. Knead with 1/2 teaspoon salt (and, if necessary, with more flour and milk) until you get a smooth dough. Set aside to rise for an additional 30 minutes.

3 In the meantime, blanch, peel, seed, and chop the tomatoes. In a saucepan, heat 2 tablespoons of olive oil and sauté the onion and garlic. Add the tomatoes and season with salt and pepper. Simmer on low heat until you get a smooth sauce.

4 Preheat the oven to 400°F. Brush a large rimmed baking

Supplì alla romana
Stuffed Rice Balls, Roman Style (Latium)

sheet with 2 tablespoons of oil and dust with flour.

Roll out and shape the dough to fit the baking pan. Top the dough with evenly distributed tomato sauce. Crumble the goat cheese and distribute it evenly over the tomato sauce. Season with freshly ground pepper and bake in the preheated oven for 30 minutes.

• How much more flour and milk you will need for this dough will be mainly determined by the quality of the potato. Knead into the dough only small portions of potato until you obtain the right consistency: it should be smooth, and absolutely not sticky.

• Wine serving suggestion: a refreshing white wine, such as *Vermentino di Gallura.*

Yield: 30 Pieces

7 ounces ground beef
2 ounces raw Italian prosciutto
   ham, chopped
2/3 cup grated Parmesan cheese
5 ounces mozzarella (or provolone cheese)
3/4 cup dried mushrooms
2 eggs
4 tablespoons butter
1 2/3 cups short/round-grain
   Vialone, Avorio, or Arborio
   risotto rice
2 cups beef stock or demi-glace
14 ounces or 1 2/3 cups
   chopped tomatoes
2 tablespoons tomato paste
1 onion, chopped
3/4 cup unseasoned bread-
   crumbs
Oil or shortening to deep-fry
Salt and freshly ground pepper

Approximate preparation time:
   1 1/2 hours (+ 2 hours for
   soaking mushrooms)
   130 calories per piece.

1 Filling: Soak the mushrooms in 1/2 cup of water for 2 hours.

2 In a saucepan, mix and boil the beef stock, chopped tomatoes, and 3 tablespoons of butter. Add the rice and simmer until the rice is done, stirring periodically. Spoon out the rice and put it in a mixing bowl. Gradually add the eggs and the grated Parmesan cheese. Set aside to cool off.

3 Filling: Melt 1 tablespoon of butter in a saucepan. Sauté the onion and ham, then add the ground beef and brown. Drain, chop, and add mushrooms (keep the water). Dissolve the tomato paste in the mushroom water and add these to the other ingredients. Simmer.

4 Dice the cheese. Season the sauce with salt and pepper. With a spoon, make bite-size egg-shaped portions of the rice mixture. Press them down in the center to make a small indentation. Put 1 teaspoon of sauce and a couple of pieces of cheese in this indentation. Wrap the rice around the filling to form small balls. Roll in unseasoned breadcrumbs and set aside on a plate. Shape 30 rice balls.

5 Heat oil or shortening in a frying pan. Fry the rice balls until golden brown. Place them on paper towels to allow the excess fat to drain. Serve while still warm. You can serve the balls with leftover meat sauce or with spicy tomato sauce.

• Appetizer for 10 to 12 servings; main course for 6 servings when served with a large salad.

Spaghetti alla carbonara
Spaghetti with Eggs and Bacon (Latium)

Serves 4 to 6

4 ounces or 4 thick slices of bacon
1 2/3 cups freshly grated Parmesan cheese (or 2/3 cup Parmesan cheese and 2/3 cup pecorino cheese)
3 tablespoons whipping cream
3 eggs
About 1 pound spaghetti
2 tablespoons oil
2 cloves garlic
Salt and freshly ground pepper

Approximate preparation time:
25 minutes;
530 calories per serving.

1 Dice the bacon. In a large frying pan on medium heat, sauté the bacon in 2 tablespoons of oil.

2 In a large pot, bring about 1 gallon of salted water to a boil. Add the spaghetti and cook 8 to 10 minutes or until al dente.

3 Vigorously beat the eggs, whipping cream, salt, and pepper together until you get an almost foamy and creamy mixture. Fold in 2/3 cup of grated cheese.

4 Remove the crispy bacon bits and keep them warm. Mince the garlic and sauté in the bacon fat until glossy.

5 Drain the spaghetti and place it in the frying pan. Toss it in the bacon fat, making sure that all sides are well coated, then remove from the heat. Pour the egg mixture into the spaghetti and very quickly fold in the cream, making sure that the eggs do not solidify in the pan. The sauce should remain creamy.

6 Sprinkle with the crispy bacon bits and season with a lot of freshly ground pepper. Serve with the remaining grated cheese.

Bucatini all'amatriciana
Bucatini with Spicy Bacon Sauce (Latium)

Serves 4 to 6

5 ounces smoked pork or smoked bacon
2 medium fresh ripe tomatoes
2/3 cup freshly grated romano (or Parmesan) cheese
About 1 pound bucatini noodles (thick spaghetti)
1 onion, minced
2 tablespoons oil
1/2 dried hot chili pepper (or chili pepper flakes or cayenne pepper)
Salt and freshly ground pepper

Approximate preparation time:
20 minutes;
460 calories per serving.

1 Cube the smoked pork or bacon. In a large frying pan with 2 tablespoons of oil, fry the meat on medium heat on all sides until golden brown. Add the onion and sauté until glossy.

2 Blanch, peel, seed, and chop the tomatoes. Add the tomatoes to the bacon and onions in the pan and stir-fry. Season with salt and crushed chili pepper (or chili pepper flakes or cayenne pepper).

3 In the meantime, bring about 1 gallon of salted water to a rapid boil in a large pot. Add the bucatini and cook 10 minutes or until al dente.

4 Thoroughly drain the bucatini. Add them to the contents of the pan and fold them into the mixture, making sure that all the noodles are coated with the sauce. Add half of the grated cheese and season again with salt and pepper. Put the pasta in a preheated serving bowl. Serve with the remaining grated cheese.

• This fiery and hearty pasta specialty originated in the border town of Amatrice located between the regions of Latium and Abruzzi.

Fettuccine alla romana
Linguine with Chicken Liver Sauce (Latium)

Serves 4 to 6

For the basic sauce:
9 ounces chicken giblets
1 1/2 ounces or 2 slices bacon
1 carrot, chopped
1 onion, chopped
1 cup dry white wine
1 clove garlic, crushed
2 cloves
1 bay leaf
2 tablespoons olive oil
2 tablespoons tomato paste
Salt and freshly ground pepper

Other ingredients:
9 ounces chicken livers
1 1/2 ounces raw Italian pro-
    sciutto ham (or raw country
    ham)
2 scallions
2 small, fresh, ripe plum toma-
    toes
1 ounce or 3/4 cup dried mush-
    rooms (preferably porcini
    mushrooms)
2/3 cup freshly grated Parmesan
    or romano cheese

About 1 pound green fettuccine
    pasta (flat, green pasta)
2 tablespoons butter
Salt and freshly ground pepper

Approximate preparation time:
    1 hour;
    570 calories per serving.

1 First soak the dried mushrooms in water, then prepare
the basic sauce. Dice the bacon
and render it in a large
saucepan in 2 tablespoons of
olive oil. Brown the chicken
giblets in the fat.

2 Add the chopped carrot and
onion to the chicken giblets,
and sauté briefly. Add the
crushed garlic, and season with
salt and pepper. Add the cloves
and bay leaf. Moisten with the
wine. Simmer at least 30 minutes. Pass everything through a
fine strainer, return the sauce
to the saucepan, and stir in the
tomato paste.

3 Trim and thoroughly clean
the scallions, and mince.
Blanch, peel, seed, and chop
the tomatoes. Thinly slice the
prosciutto or country ham.

4 Melt 1 tablespoon of butter
in a large frying pan. Sauté
the scallions and the ham in the
butter. Drain the mushrooms,
chop, and add, with the mushroom water, to the onion and
ham mixture. Bring the sauce
to a rapid boil and simmer for
10 minutes. Add the chopped
tomatoes and season with salt
and pepper.

5 In the meantime, bring
about 1 gallon of salted water to a rolling boil in a large
pot. Add the flat green pasta
and cook for about 10 minutes
or until al dente.

6 Chop the chicken livers.
Melt 1 tablespoon of butter
in a small frying pan. Brown the
chicken livers in the butter for 3

minutes. Season with salt and
pepper and add to the tomato
sauce.

7 Drain the fettuccine. Place in
a preheated serving bowl,
top with the prepared sauce,
and serve with grated cheese.

• You can, of course, make the
fettuccine at home: prepare a
dough according to the instructions on page 139. Roll it out,
and cut it into long, flat, narrow
strips of pasta. Let the pasta
dry before using it.

181

Penne all'arrabbiata
Penne with Spicy Chili Pepper Sauce (Latium)

Serves 4 to 6

4 ounces or 4 slices bacon
17 1/2 ounces or 5 large medium or 10 fresh, ripe, plum tomatoes
1 bunch fresh Italian parsley
2 small, whole, red hot chili peppers
2/3 cup freshly grated pecorino (or romano or Parmesan) cheese
About 1 pound penne (diagonally cut noodles)
1 onion
2 cloves garlic
2 tablespoons butter
Salt and freshly ground pepper

Approximate preparation time:
45 minutes;
450 calories per serving.

1 Slice the bacon into thin strips. Blanch, peel, seed, and chop the tomatoes, then pass them through a fine strainer. Mince the onion and thinly slice the garlic.

2 Bring about 1 gallon of salted water to a rolling boil in a large pot. Add the penne and cook for 5 minutes.

3 In the meantime, melt the butter in a large frying pan. Add the bacon and onion and sauté, stirring constantly. Stir in the garlic, the strained tomatoes, and the chili peppers. Season with salt and pepper and allow the sauce to simmer.

4 Drain the penne and fold them into the sauce. Keep a few spoonfuls of pasta water and, if necessary, moisten the sauce with the water. Continue to cook until the pasta is done.

5 Mince and add the parsley. Remove the chili peppers. Serve with the freshly grated cheese.

Culingionis
Ravioli (Pasta Pockets) with Sheep's Milk Cheese (Sardinia)

Serves 4 to 6

For the dough:
1 1/2 cups all-purpose flour + flour to roll out the dough
1 1/4 cups + 1 tablespoon semolina flour
3 eggs
Salt

For the filling:
11 ounces fresh trimmed leaves of spinach
7 ounces or about 1 cup fresh sheep or goat cheese (or a mixture of grated romano and ricotta)
2 tablespoons butter
Nutmeg
Salt and freshly ground pepper

Other ingredients:
5 large or 10 small fresh, ripe, plum tomatoes
2 tablespoons olive oil
2/3 cup grated romano or Parmesan cheese
Salt and freshly ground pepper

Approximate preparation time:
80 minutes;
550 calories per serving.

1 Make a dough with the flour, eggs, and 1 pinch of salt. Make a ball, cover, and set aside to rest for 30 minutes.

2 For the filling: Trim and clean the spinach and, while still wet, cook them. When the spinach is cool, squeeze and chop. Briefly sauté the spinach with 2 tablespoons of melted butter. Season with salt, pepper, and grated nutmeg.

3 Crumble the cheese. In a bowl, mix the cheese with the spinach.

4 Blanch, peel, seed, and chop the tomatoes. Heat the oil, add the tomatoes, and simmer. Season with salt and pepper.

Malloreddus
Saffron-flavored Dumplings (Sardinia)

5 Divide the dough into two portions and roll out each portion as thin as possible. On one sheet of pasta, place 1 teaspoon of filling at distances of 1 1/2 inches. Top this first sheet with the other. With a pastry cutter, cut out the ravioli. Allow to dry.

6 Bring salted water to a boil. Drop the ravioli into the boiling water and cook until they float to the surface. Remove and drain. Fold in the tomato sauce and grated cheese.

• A similar dish is prepared in Latium.

Serves 4 to 6

For the dough:
(If possible, prepare the dumplings a day ahead.)
2 cups semolina flour
3/4 cup all-purpose flour + enough flour to roll out and dust the dumplings
1 envelope of powdered saffron (or 1 teaspoon of dried saffron threads)
Salt

Other ingredients:
5 ounces smoked garlic-flavored sausage
14 ounces or 3 large or 8 fresh, ripe, plum tomatoes
1 bunch fresh basil
2/3 cup freshly grated romano or Parmesan cheese
1 onion, chopped
3 cloves garlic
3 tablespoons olive oil
Salt and freshly ground pepper

Approximate preparation time: 2 hours (+ 30 minutes resting time + 24 hours drying time); 430 calories per serving.

1 Dough: Dissolve the saffron in 1/2 cup of lukewarm water. Mix the semolina flour with the all-purpose flour. Add 1 pinch of salt, the saffron and its water, and enough water (about 3 to 4 tablespoons), and knead until you get a firm, smooth dough. Cover with a moist, clean dishcloth and set aside to rest for 30 minutes.

2 Tear off small portions of the dough and, on a well-floured work surface, shape these portions into 1/2-inch-thick sausages. Cut off 1/2-inch-long dumplings and lightly roll them in flour. With your finger, press each dumpling on a grater. Each dumpling should be curved lengthwise and almost shell-shaped. Put all the dumplings on a clean, floured dishcloth, cover, and set aside to dry for 24 hours.

3 For the sauce, blanch, peel, seed, and chop the tomatoes. Thinly slice the sausage and garlic.

4 Heat the olive oil in a large saucepan. Sauté the sausage, garlic, and onion until the onions are glossy. Add the tomatoes and season with salt and pepper. Simmer briefly.

5 In the meantime, bring about 1 gallon of salted water to a rolling boil in a large pot. With the slotted spoon, drop the saffron dumplings into the water and cook for 13 to 15 minutes, or until they float to the surface and are done. Remove the dumplings from the water and drain thoroughly. Distribute the dumplings on preheated plates, top with the sauce, sprinkle with the grated cheese, and garnish with fresh shredded basil leaves.

Minestra di broccoli
Broccoli Soup (Latium)

Stracciatella alla romana
Eggdrop Soup, Roman Style (Latium)

Serves 4 to 6

4 ounces or 4 slices bacon
About 1 pound broccoli
1 large, fresh, ripe plum tomato
1 bunch fresh Italian parsley
2/3 cup freshly grated Parmesan cheese
6 cups beef stock
5 ounces spaghetti noodles
2 cloves garlic
1 to 2 teaspoons lemon juice
1 tablespoon vegetable oil
Salt and freshly ground pepper

<u>*Approximate preparation time:*</u>
30 minutes;
290 calories per serving.

1 Clean the broccoli, divide into florets, and wash thoroughly. Trim and thinly slice the stems. Cut the bacon into thin strips. Blanch, peel, seed, and chop the tomatoes. Thinly slice the garlic.

2 Bring the beef stock to a boil in a large pot. Sauté the bacon strips in the vegetable oil in a large saucepan. Add the garlic and briefly sauté. Add the broccoli florets and sliced stems and sauté 2 minutes. Add the tomatoes and season with salt and freshly ground pepper.

3 Gradually add the hot stock and bring to a rolling boil. Break the spaghetti into 1 1/4-inch-long pieces, drop them into the soup, and let simmer. As soon as the spaghetti and broccoli are done, season the soup with the salt, pepper, and lemon juice. Mince the parsley and stir into the soup. Serve with the freshly grated Parmesan cheese.

Serves 4

4 cups strong beef stock (preferably defatted, that has been homemade and refrigerated)
4 eggs
4 tablespoons freshly grated Parmesan cheese
Nutmeg
Salt and freshly ground pepper

<u>*Approximate preparation time:*</u>
15 minutes;
210 calories per serving.

1 In a mixing bowl, vigorously beat the eggs to a fluffy consistency. Add and stir in the freshly grated Parmesan cheese, cold beef stock, grated nutmeg, and a pinch of salt.

2 Heat the remaining beef stock in a large pot. Remove from the heat and with a heat-resistant whisk, stir the egg mixture into the stock. Replace the pot on the heat, and on low,

simmer for 5 minutes, whisking constantly until you get small, shredded pieces of egg.

Serve immediately in preheated soup bowls, making sure that the shredded egg is still evenly floating in the soup.

• A suitable accompaniment for this soup is freshly toasted, crispy slices of bread.

• This recipe is a classic that can be prepared easily and rapidly. You will find this soup served in all restaurants throughout Rome.

Minestrone di ceci

Garbanzo Bean Soup (Chick-pea Soup) (Sardinia)

Serves 4 to 6

2 ounces or 2 thin slices bacon
4 stalks celery
2 carrots
1 bunch fresh Italian parsley
1 2/3 cups dried garbanzo beans
  (also called chick-peas),
  soaked overnight
4 cups beef stock
1 onion
2 garlic cloves
2 tablespoons tomato paste
3 tablespoons olive oil
8 small slices of white bread
Salt and freshly ground pepper

<u>*Approximate preparation time:*</u>
  2 1/4 hours
  (+ 12 hours soaking time);
  360 calories per serving.

1 Soak the garbanzo beans in 3 cups of water overnight. The next day heat the beef stock in a medium saucepan, add the garbanzo beans with the soaking water, and simmer for 2 hours or until the garbanzo beans are soft.

2 In the meantime, prepare the other ingredients. Cut thin and mince the bacon, celery, and carrots. Mince 1 onion and 2 cloves of garlic.

3 In a large frying pan, heat and sauté the bacon strips in the olive oil. Add the onion, garlic, carrots, and celery, and sauté on low heat for 5 minutes. Dissolve the tomato paste in a few spoonfuls of garbanzo bean broth and stir this mixture into the soup.

4 As soon as the garbanzo beans are soft, add the contents of the frying pan to the soup, mix everything thoroughly, and season with salt and pepper. Garnish with stemless parsley leaves. Toast 8 slices of white bread and serve these with the soup.

• If you are in a hurry, substitute the dried beans with canned garbanzo beans.

Favata

Lima Beans with Fennel (Sardinia)

Serves 4 to 6

4 raw Italian sausages (about
  14 ounces)
1 thick slice bacon, preferably
  with a rind (about 3 1/2
  ounces)
2/3 cup freshly grated pecorino
  or Parmesan cheese
1/2 head of fresh cabbage (14
  ounces)
2 fennel bulbs (14 ounces)
1 bunch fresh Italian parsley
1 1/2 cups dried baby lima
  beans (soaked overnight)
1 large onion, sliced
2 cloves garlic, crushed
3 cups hot beef stock
4 tablespoons oil
Salt and freshly ground pepper

<u>*Approximate preparation time:*</u>
  2 1/4 hours
  (+ 24 hours soaking time);
  570 calories per serving.

1 Soak the dried baby lima beans in 4 cups of water overnight. Simmer for 1 hour in the soaking water. Drain the lima beans and keep the bean water warm.

2 Pierce the casings of the Italian sausages with a fork. In a large saucepan, heat the oil and sauté the sausage and onion on low heat. Add the crushed garlic. Add the bacon, drained beans, and warm lima bean water. Simmer on low heat for 30 minutes.

3 Thinly slice the cabbage. Cut the fennel in halves. Trim the stems. Cut the lower bulb-like part into thin slices.

4 Combine the beef stock, cabbage, and fennel in the pot. Simmer for an additional 30 minutes. Season with salt and pepper. Mince the parsley and stir into the soup. Serve the lima bean soup sprinkled with the freshly grated cheese.

Calamari ripieni
Stuffed Squid (Sardinia)

Serves 4

About 2 ¹/₂ pounds fresh
   medium-sized squids
2 lemons
2 teaspoons fresh rosemary
   leaves (or dried rosemary)
1 bunch fresh Italian parsley
1 egg
3 to 4 canned anchovy fillets,
   drained
2 cloves garlic, crushed
3 tablespoons unseasoned
   breadcrumbs
Salt and freshly ground pepper
Enough olive oil to brush the
   squid

Approximate preparation time:
   1 ³/₄ hours;
   380 calories per serving.

For this recipe, of course, you
may also use frozen squid that
is often sold in packages.

When you buy the squid, pay
careful attention to the type
you select; not all squid is suitable for filling as the larger
types, like the East Coast long-
finned "winter squid" (*Loligo
pealei*) and the short-finned
"summer squid" (*Illex illecebro-
sus*). The octopus, for example,
has long, strong tentacles, a
small body, and requires especially long cooking before it is
chewable. The cuttlefish, the
common mollusk also called
sepia, is the smallest of all and
is mainly used together with its
ink sac.

A delicious filling for squid can
also be made with fillet of
fish—pureed and flavored with
lemon juice, herbs, and garlic.
Another stuffing variation can
be made with a mixture of unseasoned breadcrumbs
browned in olive oil, minced anchovies, and lots of fresh
minced parsley.

• Wine serving suggestion: a
dry white wine, such as *Vernaccia di Oristano*.

1 Thoroughly wash and rinse
the squid under running water. Peel off the membranes
from the mantle; the squid
should be white after this
process.

2 Pull out the innards from the
whole squid, with the cuttlebone and the tentacles. With a
sharp knife, cut off the head
and discard. Keep the tentacles
for the filling.

3 Turn the mantles inside out
and thoroughly wash the insides of the squid. If necessary,
peel off any remaining membranes. Pat everything dry with
paper towels. Turn the mantles
rightside out, drizzle with the
juice of ¹/₂ lemon, and set aside
for later use.

4 For the filling, with a sharp
knife, mince the tentacles
and any suitable part of the
body that is available (about 7
ounces of squid meat), and put
everything in a mixing bowl.
Mince and mix 1 teaspoon of
rosemary and the parsley.

5 Rinse the anchovies and pat
them dry with paper towels.
Mince and add to the mixture in
the bowl. Add the crushed garlic, unseasoned breadcrumbs,
grated peel of ¹/₂ lemon, and 1
egg.

6 Mix everything well and season with salt and pepper (pay attention to the amount of salt because the anchovies can be pretty salty!). Preheat the oven to 400ºF (or use a griddle). Stuff the squid with the prepared mixture.

7 With a trussing needle and cotton thread, sew the ends of the squid bodies. Place the stuffed squid in a large baking dish that has been brushed with oil, or on the oiled griddle. Brush thoroughly on all sides with more olive oil, season with salt and pepper, and sprinkle with rosemary. Bake in the preheated oven or broil. Bake for about 40 minutes (or grill for about 20 minutes), turning the squids over at least once. Serve very hot; you can garnish the squid with herbs and lemon wedges.

Tonno con i piselli
Tuna with Peas (Latium)

Serves 4

4 tuna fillets (1 ¹/₃ pound)
About 2 pounds fresh young
*   peas (or about 4 cups frozen*
*   peas)*
1 bunch fresh Italian parsley
¹/₂ bunch fresh basil
1 medium-large onion, chopped
2 tablespoons tomato paste
1 cup dry white wine
3 tablespoons butter
Salt and freshly ground pepper

<u>*Approximate preparation time:*</u>
*   70 minutes;*
*   600 calories per serving.*

1 Shell the fresh peas. Mince ¹/₂ bunch of fresh Italian parsley. Melt the butter in a large frying pan and sauté the onion and parsley.

2 Stir in the peas and season with salt and pepper. Moisten with the white wine, cover, and simmer on low heat for about 15 minutes. Stir in the tomato paste.

3 Quickly rinse the tuna fillets under running water and pat them dry with paper towels. Sprinkle both sides with salt and place the tuna over the peas. Cover again and simmer the fish for about 10 minutes. Turn the fish over and simmer 5 more minutes. Season with salt and fresh, coarsely ground pepper, and garnish with fresh, shredded parsley and basil leaves.

• A similar dish can also be prepared with Mako shark. Variation: Lightly dust the fish pieces with flour and pan-fry in olive oil, and place them on the peas.

Sarde arrosto
Grilled Sardines with Fennel (Sardinia)

Serves 4

8 small, fresh sardines (or fresh
*   smelts or small whitefish)*
3 fennel bulbs
1 lemon (juice)
¹/₂ cup dry white wine
1 tablespoon fennel seeds
3 cloves garlic, minced
About ¹/₄ cup olive oil
Salt and freshly ground pepper

<u>*Approximate preparation time:*</u>
*   35 minutes*
*   (+ 2 hours marinating time);*
*   410 calories per serving.*

1 Thoroughly clean and rinse the sardines (or smelts or whitefish), and pat dry with paper towels. Rub them inside and out with salt and place them on a shallow platter. Whisk the minced garlic with the olive oil. Stir 1 tablespoon of fennel seeds into the oil-garlic mixture. Drizzle over the fish. Pour the wine over the fish and marinate, covered, in the refrigerator for at least 2 hours.

2 In a large pot, bring 4 cups salted water to a boil. Trim and clean the fennel and blanch for 5 minutes in the boiling salted water. Remove the fennel with the slotted spoon, drop it into iced water, and drain well. Cut each fennel vertically in 1-inch-wide pieces. Season on both sides with salt and pepper.

3 Remove the fish from the marinade, drain, and pat dry with paper towels. Keep the marinade. Place the fish and fennel on a griddle and, with a pastry brush, brush them with half of the marinade.

4 Cook slowly on the griddle for 10 to 15 minutes (or, in a frying pan, pan-fry the fish and fennel for about 10 minutes). Periodically brush the fish and the fennel with the marinade. Turn the fish and fennel over at least once. Before serving, drizzle everything with lemon juice and season with salt and pepper.

Sarde ripiene
Stuffed Sardines (Sardinia)

Serves 4 to 6

16 small fresh sardines (about
2 1/4 pounds) (or fresh
smelts or small white fish)
2 lemons
1 bunch fresh Italian parsley
3 1/2 ounces or 1/2 cup or 1
small block fresh sheep or
goat cheese
1 1/2 ounces or 2/3 cup freshly
grated romano or Parmesan
cheese
8 canned anchovy fillets,
drained
2 large cans peeled tomatoes
(about 26 to 28 ounces each)
3 cloves garlic, minced
8 tablespoons unseasoned
breadcrumbs
1/2 cup olive oil
3 tablespoons flour
Salt and freshly ground pepper

Approximate preparation time:
1 hour;
620 calories per serving.

1 Cut off the heads of the sardines (or smelts or whitefish); remove their central spiny
bone and the tail. Rinse the fish
thoroughly under running water
and pat dry with paper towels.
Rub the insides with salt and
drizzle the fish with the juice of
1/2 lemon.

2 Crumble the cheese. Rinse
the anchovies, pat dry, and
cut in halves. Mince 1/2 bunch
of fresh parsley. Stuff the sardines with the fresh cheese,
the minced parsley, and with 1/2
anchovy fillet each.

3 Drain the canned tomatoes
and chop them coarsely. Set
aside the tomato juice for later
use (for example, for tomato
soup). In a large baking dish,
distribute the tomatoes evenly,
and season with salt and pepper. Preheat the oven to 425°F.

4 Very lightly dust the fish on
all sides with the flour. Heat
5 tablespoons of olive oil in a
medium frying pan. Fry the

stuffed sardines on both sides
for 2 minutes. Place them on
the tomatoes in the baking
dish.

5 Mince the remaining parsley
and garlic and mix it with
the grated cheese, minced garlic, and breadcrumbs. Sprinkle
the mixture over the stuffed
sardines, drizzle all ingredients
with the remaining olive oil, and
bake in the preheated oven for
10 minutes. Serve with lemon
wedges.

• Variation without tomatoes:
Rub the fish with salt and pepper, dust lightly with flour, dip in
beaten egg, then roll in a mixture of breadcrumbs and grated
cheese. Pan-fry in olive oil or
bake in a baking dish, and drizzle with oil and white wine.

• Wine serving suggestion:
a young white wine, such as
Nuragus di Cagliari.

189

Coda alla vaccinara
Stewed Oxtail (Latium)

Serves 6

About 3 pounds oxtail
4 ounces or 4 slices bacon
2 tablespoons vegetable oil
2 carrots
4 to 5 stalks celery
2 bunches fresh Italian parsley
1 cup dry white wine
3 tablespoons tomato paste
1 large onion
2 cloves garlic
Paprika or red chili pepper
    powder
1 pinch cinnamon
Salt and freshly ground pepper

<u>Approximate preparation time:</u>
    3 hours;
    640 calories per serving.

The original version of this very old Roman favorite, which is still popular today, does not fit the mold of other regional dishes because of its spiciness: raisins and pine nuts, bitter chocolate, and aromatic herbs simmer in the sauce merging with the celery to explode into a strong and unique flavor.

Our modernized version has kept the emphasis on celery and the patient stewing (at least 1 hour, if not longer) that is the best method for attaining fine culinary results.

• Instead of browning the meat in bacon and oil, you may also use the olive oil variation: Thoroughly brown the oxtail, season with minced garlic and crushed dried chili peppers, and later add pureed tomatoes and white wine. As a side dish, no other choice would be better than white bread, especially for the wonderful gravy!

• Wine serving suggestion: a dry white wine, such as *Frascati secco*.

1 Ask the butcher to cut the oxtail into chunks. Rinse the pieces under running water, bring 6 cups of salted water to a boil and drop in the chunks of oxtail. Simmer 10 minutes. With a slotted spoon, remove the oxtail from the broth and drain thoroughly. Keep 2 cups of the oxtail broth.

2 Cut the bacon into thin strips. Mince 1 bunch of parsley and 2 cloves of garlic. Chop 2 carrots and 1 onion. Put into a mixing bowl with the minced garlic and parsley.

3 Heat the oil in a Dutch oven, add the bacon strips, and sauté until golden brown and glossy. Gradually add the oxtail and brown thoroughly on all sides.

4 Add the prepared vegetables and sauté. Moisten with 1/2 cup of white wine and simmer uncovered until the liquid has reduced to half of its original amount. Moisten again, with 1/2 cup of wine and season with salt and pepper.

5 Dissolve the tomato paste in the remaining 2 cups of oxtail broth (see picture 1) and pour the liquid over the meat. Cover the Dutch oven and stew on low heat for at least 2 1/2 hours.

6 After 2 hours, trim and clean the celery. Set aside the tender greens of the tops of the stalks for later use. Slice the celery and add to the meat after 2 1/4 hours. Simmer for 15 more minutes.

7 Rinse the celery greens and the rest of the parsley, and mince. As soon as the meat is done, season the gravy with salt, pepper, paprika (or red chili pepper powder), and 1 pinch of cinnamon. Sprinkle the celery greens and the parsley over the meat and serve this stew in a preheated serving bowl.

Abbacchio alla romana
Braised Suckling Lamb with Garlic Gravy, Roman Style (Latium)

Serves 6

2 pounds lamb meat, preferably from the shoulder (for the sake of authenticity, select suckling lamb, if it is available)
1 tablespoon fresh rosemary leaves (or 1/2 tablespoon dried rosemary)
3 canned anchovy fillets, drained
5 cloves garlic
6 tablespoons olive oil
3 to 4 tablespoons white wine vinegar
Salt and freshly ground pepper

Approximate preparation time:
 70 minutes;
 500 calories per serving.

1 Prepare the ingredients for the gravy. Mince the rosemary leaves. Rinse the anchovies, pat them dry, and mince. Mince 3 cloves of garlic. Put these ingredients in a mortar and crush to a paste with a pestle. Mix the wine vinegar

and cream until smooth.

2 Cut the garlic in halves. Rub the lamb meat with them. Cube the meat (pieces should not weigh more than 2 ounces each) and season with pepper.

3 In a Dutch oven, heat the oil. Add the meat and brown well on all sides. Reduce the heat and simmer for 5 more minutes.

4 When the meat is done, stir in the garlic paste. Heat up everything, season with pepper, and, if necessary, with salt, and serve on a preheated serving platter.

• Suckling lamb is found usually in the early spring and throughout the season that precedes Easter. If the meat seems tough, cook it longer.

Saltimbocca alla romana
Veal Cutlets with Sage, Roman Style (Latium)

Serves 4

8 thin veal cutlets (about 1 pound)
8 thin slices Italian prosciutto ham (preferably Parma ham)
8 fully grown sage leaves
3 to 4 tablespoons butter
1/2 cup dry white wine
Salt and freshly ground pepper

Approximate preparation time:
 25 minutes;
 400 calories per serving.

1 Carefully flatten the slices of meat with the smooth side of a meat mallet.

2 Place 1 leaf of sage on each veal cutlet and spear the leaf onto the slice of meat with a wooden toothpick.

3 Melt 2 tablespoons of butter in a large frying pan. Add the cutlets and pan-fry 2 to 3 minutes on each side. Lightly season the meat with salt and pep-

per, remove the cutlets from the pan, and keep warm.

4 Dilute the pan juices with 1/2 cup of white wine and bring to a rapid boil. With a heat-resistant whisk, dissolve 1 to 2 tablespoons of butter into the sauce. Season with salt and pepper, return the cutlets to the pan, and heat them up quickly. Serve on a preheated platter and drizzle with the pan juices.

• "Jump into the mouth!"— The literal translation of the name of this very delicious dish is an indication of its value as a culinary favorite.

• Wonderful side dishes: white bread and freshly picked peas.

• Wine serving suggestion: a white wine with a grand personality, such as an *Est! Est! Est!* from Monte Fiascone.

Vitello alla sarda
Veal Roast with Green Capers, Sardinian Style (Sardinia)

Serves 4

1 ⅓ pounds whole boneless
   veal, either loin chop, rump,
   or sirloin tip
2 carrots
3 scallions
1 bunch fresh Italian parsley
½ lemon
½ cup dry white wine
½ cup beef stock
2 tablespoons capers
2 cloves garlic
1 to 2 tablespoons flour
5 tablespoons olive oil
Salt and freshly ground pepper

Approximate preparation time:
   1 ½ hours;
   330 calories per serving.

1 Rub the boneless piece of veal with pepper and dust very lightly with the flour. Mince 1 carrot, the white portions of 3 scallions (keep the green tops), ½ bunch of parsley, and 2 cloves of garlic.

2 Heat the olive oil in a Dutch oven. Add the meat and brown evenly on all sides. Add the minced vegetables, parsley, and garlic, and sauté briefly. Season with salt and pepper. Moisten gradually with ½ cup of dry white wine and with ½ cup of beef stock. Brush and rinse the lemons in hot water, grate the peel, slice thin, and add to the meat.

3 Cover the Dutch oven and stew for 50 minutes. After about 40 minutes, cut the second carrot into thin strips (or julienne), and thinly slice the scallions.

4 After 50 minutes, remove the meat and discard the lemon slices. Pass the gravy through a fine strainer and return it again to the Dutch oven. Also return the roast of veal and stir the minced vegetables and 2 tablespoons of capers into the gravy. Finish cooking

covered, for 10 to 15 minutes more.

5 Mince the remaining parsley. Remove the veal roast, slice thin, and place on a large, preheated serving platter. Stir the parsley into the sauce, season with salt and pepper, and distribute the sauce evenly over the slices of meat.

• Green capers are delicate gray-green buds that acquire their snappy piquant flavor only after pickling. Only a few spoonfuls of these are enough to turn either a sauce, stew, or stuffing into a refined culinary specialty with a slightly pungent touch. The quality of these buds is easily detectable from the size; the tiniest are the finest!

Pollo in padella
Pan-fried Chicken with Tomato Sauce (Latium)

Cinghiale in agrodolce
Sweet-and-Sour Boar with Plums (Latium)

Serves 4

1 young chicken (about 2 1/2 pounds)
3 ounces or 3 slices bacon
About 2 pounds or about 20 fresh, ripe, plum tomatoes
2 tablespoon fresh marjoram (or 1 teaspoon dried)
1 cup dry white wine
2 cloves garlic, crushed
2 tablespoons vegetable oil
Salt and freshly ground pepper

Approximate preparation time:
70 minutes;
670 calories per serving.

1 Cut the chicken into 10 pieces and rub with salt and pepper. Thinly slice the bacon. Blanch in boiling water, peel, seed, and chop the tomatoes.

2 In a Dutch oven or a large frying pan, heat the vegetable oil, sauté the bacon strips, and brown the pieces of chicken evenly on all sides.

Sprinkle half of the marjoram over the chicken pieces and stir in the chopped tomatoes. Add the crushed garlic.

3 Simmer on low heat for 40 minutes, and gradually moisten with the wine. The stew's gravy should ultimately be thick and dense.

4 When the meat begins to fall off the bones, season with salt and pepper. Serve sprinkled with fresh marjoram leaves.

• If you have only dried marjoram, serve the chicken pieces sprinkled with fresh minced parsley or fresh snipped chives.

Serves 4

1 2/3 pounds boar (from the shank or from the butt)
3 1/2 ounces or 3/4 cup pitted prunes
1 ounce or 1/4 cup candied orange peel
1 ounce or 1/4 cup raisins
Optional—2 tablespoons pine nuts
1 teaspoon fresh rosemary (or 1/2 teaspoon dried)
1 large onion
5 tablespoons olive oil
2 tablespoons butter
Salt and freshly ground pepper

For the marinade:
2 cups strong red wine
1/2 cup mild red wine vinegar
1 onion
1 carrot
1 stalk celery
1 bay leaf
1 teaspoon dried thyme
1/2 teaspoon peppercorns
2 cloves
1 teaspoon sugar

1/4 teaspoon salt

Approximate preparation time:
2 1/2 hours
(+ 12 hours for marinating);
690 calories per serving.

1 For the marinade: In a medium saucepan, bring the red wine and red wine vinegar to a rolling boil. Trim, clean or peel, and chop 1 onion, 1 carrot, and 1 stalk of celery, and add these with the herbs and spices, to the marinade in the saucepan. Cover and simmer the marinade for 5 minutes, then remove from the heat and set aside to cool off.

2 Cut the boar meat into 1- to 1 1/4-inch large cubes and put into a large mixing bowl. Pour the cold marinade over the meat, cover, and refrigerate overnight.

3 Remove the meat from the marinade, drain, and pat dry

Pernici con lenticchie
Partridges with Lentils (Sardinia)

with paper towels. Keep the marinade, pour it through a fine strainer, and set aside for later use.

4 Heat the olive oil in a Dutch oven. Gradually add the meat and, on medium heat, brown evenly on all sides. Season with salt and pepper, moisten with half of the marinade, and simmer covered for 1 1/2 hours.

5 Soak the prunes in the remaining marinade. Soak the raisins in water.

6 After about 1 hour of stewing the meat, chop the candied orange peel into tiny pieces. Drain the raisins and soaked prunes. Mince 1 onion and 1 teaspoon rosemary.

7 Melt the butter in a medium frying pan. Sauté the onion until glossy. Stir in the prunes, orange peel, raisins, and rose-

mary. Mix thoroughly and season with freshly ground pepper. Moisten gradually with the remaining marinade and simmer for several minutes.

8 Add the fruit mixture to the boar's stew and simmer 10 more minutes. As soon as the meat is tender, season the gravy with salt and pepper. You can sprinkle the dish with 2 tablespoons of pine nuts and serve piping hot.

• Based on the main ingredient, this dish is definitively of Roman origin; however, a modern landscape of free-ranging, only half-domesticated boars fits more with Sardinia's village lifestyle than with a modern city's tempo. In Sardinia, the inhibited squealing of the local black-spotted house pigs is a common sound—a reality that impacts the flavor of their meat rather favorably!

Serves 2

2 ready-to-use partridges (about 8 ounces each) (you may substitute Cornish hens)
2 ounces or 2 slices bacon
1 tablespoon vegetable oil
1 cup lentils
1 bunch fresh Italian parsley
1 onion, minced
1 tablespoon tomato paste
Salt and freshly ground pepper

Approximate preparation time:
1 3/4 hours
(+ 12 hours soaking);
860 calories per serving.

1 Cover the lentils with water and soak overnight in a large saucepan. The next day, bring the lentils to a rapid boil in their soaking water and cook 30 minutes. In the meantime, using tweezers, remove any leftover pinfeathers from the birds. Drain the lentils and keep the cooking water.

2 Dice the bacon. Sauté in a large frying pan with the vegetable oil.

3 Season the partridges with salt and pepper. Brown them in the fat and bacon mixture on all sides. Add the minced onion, and sauté on low heat until glossy.

4 Add the lentils, moisten with about 1 cup of lentil broth, and stir in the tomato paste. Season with salt and pepper and simmer, partially covered, for about 50 minutes or until most of the liquid has evaporated.

5 Chop the parsley. Season the lentils with salt and pepper. If you wish, cut the partridges into smaller pieces and sprinkle with parsley.

• Wine serving suggestion: an aromatic red wine, such as *Monica di Sardegna*.

Piselli al prosciutto
Peas with Ham (Latium)

Serves 6

About 2 pounds or 35 ounces fresh young peas (or 24 ounces or about 4 cups frozen peas)
4 ounces or 4 slices Italian prosciutto (or raw country ham)
1/2 cup strong beef stock or demi-glace
2 small onions, thinly sliced
2 tablespoons butter
Thin slices of white bread
1 pinch sugar
Salt and freshly ground pepper

<u>*Approximate preparation time:*</u>
45 minutes;
330 calories per serving.

1 Shell the peas. Remove the white fat from the ham and slice it thin. In a small saucepan, heat the beef stock and set aside for later use.

2 In a large frying pan, melt 1 1/2 tablespoons of butter and the white fatty part of the

ham. Stir in the slices of onion and fry until glossy. Stir in the peas. Season with a pinch of sugar, salt, and pepper. Moisten with the beef stock and simmer for 10 to 20 minutes, according to the variety of peas.

3 In the meantime, cut the lean red part of the ham into thin slices. Toast the thin slices of white bread. Add the lean ham and 1 1/2 tablespoons of butter to the peas while they are still firm to the bite. Season again with salt and pepper and serve with the white bread.

• This is a small and delicious vegetable dish that is also suited for a light dinner menu (in this case, use the same amount for 4 servings). Without the white toasted bread slices, it is suitable as a side dish for pan – fried liver or for a lean meat dish.

Carciofi alla giudia
Artichokes, Jewish Style (Latium)

Serves 4

8 young fresh artichokes
2 to 3 lemons
About 2 cups olive oil
Salt and freshly ground pepper

<u>*Approximate preparation time:*</u>
30 minutes;
400 calories per serving.

1 Fill a large mixing bowl with iced water, and add the juice of 1 to 2 lemons.

2 Trim and cut the wooden parts of the artichoke stems. Remove the harder external leaves and trim the points of the remaining leaves with scissors. Immediately place the trimmed artichokes in the cold lemony water.

3 Remove the artichokes from the water, drain well, and thoroughly pat dry. Loosen the leaves as you would to open a flower. Season with salt and pepper.

4 Put the artichokes in a large saucepan, pour enough olive oil over them to cover them up to half of their standing height. Heat gradually. Fry the artichokes on medium heat for 10 minutes, then turn them over and fry them for 10 more minutes. The oil should not be too hot in order to prevent the outer leaves from burning before the artichoke heart is done inside.

5 Shortly before removing the artichokes from the oil, drizzle them very carefully with cold water. Remove the crispy vegetables and place them on paper towels to allow the excess fat to drain. Serve garnished with lemon wedges.

• This very famous recipe was created in the Jewish ghetto of ancient Rome. Serve with bread.

Spinaci alla romana
Spinach with Raisins, Roman Style (Latium)

Fagiolini al tonno
Green Beans and Tuna (Latium)

Serves 4 to 6

About 2 pounds fresh spinach
    leaves
$1/2$ cup raisins
2 tablespoons pine nuts
2 cloves garlic
3 to 4 tablespoons olive oil
2 tablespoons butter
Salt and freshly ground pepper

<u>Approximate preparation time:</u>
    35 minutes;
    140 calories per serving.

1 Soak the raisins in water. Trim, clean, and thoroughly wash the spinach leaves and put them in a large pot while still wet. Heat and rapidly cook, allowing the leaves to wilt. Thoroughly drain the cooked spinach.

2 In a large frying pan, heat the olive oil. Add and melt the butter. Cut the garlic cloves in halves, and, on low heat, sauté lightly and later remove from the pan (if you wish, keep the garlic to sprinkle over the spinach when you serve).

3 Put the spinach into the pan, stir, and turn it over in the hot fat. Drain the raisins, add them to the spinach, and sauté them for about 10 minutes. Season with salt and pepper. Finally, add the pine nuts and, if you wish, distribute the fried garlic over the spinach.

Serves 4

1 $1/3$ pounds fresh, young, green
    beans
14 ounces or 8 fresh, ripe plum
    tomatoes
2 scallions
1 bunch fresh Italian parsley,
    minced
1 can of tuna without oil or
    water (about 6 oz.)
3 to 4 tablespoons white wine
    vinegar
5 tablespoons extra virgin olive oil
Salt and freshly ground pepper

<u>Approximate preparation time:</u>
    45 minutes;
    260 calories per serving.

1 Trim and clean the green beans; if necessary, peel off any bean strings. Wash and drain. In a large pot, bring enough salted water to a boil to cook the green beans. Drop the green beans into the boiling water and cook for 10 to 12 minutes or until still firm to the bite.

2 In the meantime, wash, core and cube the tomatoes. Wash the scallions; mince the white parts, and slice the green tops. Remove the tuna from the can, drain, and break open into large flakes.

3 In a medium mixing bowl, whisk together 3 tablespoons of wine vinegar with salt, pepper, and the olive oil. Stir in the minced green onions and half of the minced parsley. Drain the cooked green beans, drop into iced water, and drain again thoroughly. Put the beans in the mixing bowl and toss well with the dressing.

4 Finally, add and mix the tomato cubes, the sliced scallion tops, and the tuna. You can season with more vinegar, salt, and pepper. Sprinkle the remaining parsley over the beans and tuna. Serve still warm.

197

Crostata di visciole
Tart Cherry Pie (Latium)

Serves 12

Cherry filling:

1 ²/₃ pounds of fresh tart or
   fresh sweet red cherries (or
   the drained contents of two
   16-ounce cans of tart red
   cherries)
1 lemon (use the peel for the
   filling and the juice for the
   pastry crust)
²/₃ cup granulated sugar
2 cloves
1 cinnamon stick

For the crust:

2 cups all-purpose flour + flour
   to roll out the crust and for
   the pan
²/₃ cup granulated sugar
3 ¹/₂ ounces or 6 tablespoons
   softened butter + 1 tablespoon for the springform pan
2 tablespoons vegetable shortening
Enough milk to moisten the
   dough if necessary
1 egg
2 egg yolks
1 pinch salt
Confectioners' sugar to dust
   the pie

Approximate preparation time:
   1 ¹/₂ hours
   (+ 1 hour refrigeration);
   400 calories per serving.

Crostata is a general term used
to describe a flaky type of filled
cake made with pastry dough.
Filled with red tart cherry filling
or jam, this Italian specialty is
very similar to the famous Linzer
Torte originally from the city of
Linz, located in neighboring Austria.

The Italian crostata, however, is
often also made with other
fruits—plums, peaches, apricots,
grapes, or strawberries. The lattice of dough is only mandatory
when used with fillings of jam
and compote; for pie-type cakes,
the dough is baked first and later
filled with fresh fruits.

If the crostata is a two-crust pastry cake, it usually hides a juicy
filling of ricotta and mixed candied fruits underneath the top
crust.

1 For the filling: First prepare the fruit compote. Pit the tart cherries. Brush and thoroughly wash the lemon and slice the peel in
a long spiral-shaped ribbon (keep the juice of the lemon for the
dough). In a large saucepan, combine the cherries with the sugar,
cloves, and cinnamon stick. In the uncovered saucepan, cook for
about 15 minutes or until the juice has visibly reduced (you can also flavor the filling with some red wine or with any suitable
brandy). Set aside to cool, and later remove the lemon peel, the
cloves, and the cinnamon stick.

2 For the dough: Mix the all-purpose flour with the granulated
sugar. With a pastry mixer, cut the softened butter and vegetable oil into the flour-sugar mixture until the particles of dough
are like large peas. Knead the egg, 1 egg yolk, and the juice of 1
lemon into the mixture. Season with a pinch of salt. Knead until
you get a smooth, silky dough; if the dough seems too firm and
crumbly, knead a few spoonfuls of milk into it. In a mixing bowl,
set the dough aside, cover, and refrigerate for 1 hour.

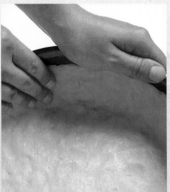

3 With 1 tablespoon of softened
butter brush a 8 to 9 inch
springform pan (or pie pan). Dust
lightly with flour. Remove the
dough from the refrigerator, and
on a floured work surface, take
two-thirds of it, and roll it out thinly
and shape it into a wheel. Line the
bottom of the pan with the dough
and build up a 2-inch-high rim.

4 Preheat the oven to 350°F. Evenly spread the tart cherries over the bottom of the dough. Fold the dough around the edge of the pan inward.

5 Roll out the remaining dough, and with a pastry wheel, cut the dough into 1/2-inch strips. Place the pastry strips across the filling at about 1-inch intervals to make a lattice pattern. Whisk 1 egg yolk with 1 tablespoon of milk. With a pastry brush, brush the mixture over the dough lattice. Bake in the preheated oven for 30 to 40 minutes. Remove the pie and set aside to cool. Preferably serve the next day. Dust lightly with confectioners' sugar.

Gelato di ricotta
Rum-flavored Ricotta Ice Cream (Latium)

Serves 6 to 8

*About 1 pound or 2 cups fresh
ricotta or fresh well-drained
cottage cheese
1 1/2 cup whipping cream
1/2 lemon (peel)
4 egg yolks
2 tablespoons + 2 teaspoons
rum or Maraschino
1/2 cup granulated sugar*

<u>*Approximate preparation time:*</u>
*30 minutes
(+ 2–3 hours freezing);
500 calories per serving.*

1 In a mixing bowl, combine
the egg yolks and sugar and
cream until fluffy. In a trickle,
gradually pour in the rum or
Maraschino and beat vigorously.

2 Press the ricotta through a
fine strainer and gradually
fold into the egg cream. Flavor
with the finely grated lemon
peel. Whip the whipping cream
to a stiff peak, and gradually

fold this into the ricotta mixture.

3 Line an 8- or 9-inch round
cake pan with baking paper.
Pour in the mixture and spread
out evenly. Cover with another
layer of baking paper. Set in the
freezer to chill for 2 to 3 hours.

4 Remove the ice cream from
the freezer 30 minutes before serving it and set it aside
to thaw for a few minutes. Turn
the ice cream over on a fancy
serving platter. Slice and serve.

• Best if served with fresh
berries and fresh fruits; for example, balls of honeydew melon and cantaloupe, apricot
slices, and blackberries.

Torta di mandorle
Almond Cake (Sardinia)

Serves 6

<u>*For the batter:*</u>
*1/2 lemon (peel and juice)
4 eggs
3 1/2 ounces or 2/3 cup blanched
almonds
1/2 cup granulated sugar
1/4 cup vanilla sugar
About 1/2 cup or 10 tablespoons
all-purpose flour + 1 tablespoon for dusting the baking
pan
1 teaspoon baking powder*

<u>*Other ingredients:*</u>
*2 tablespoons lemon juice
1 3/4 cup confectioners' sugar
Optional: 2 tablespoons almond
liqueur
1/3 cup blanched almonds
Enough baking spray oil for the
pan*

<u>*Approximate preparation time:*</u>
*1 hour;
500 calories per serving.*

1 For the batter: With a sharp
knife or a food processor,

coarsely chop the blanched almonds.

2 Separate the eggs. In a mixing bowl, mix the egg yolks
with the granulated sugar and
vanilla sugar and whisk vigorously until fluffy and almost
foamy.

3 Add the chopped almonds,
all-purpose flour, and 1 teaspoon baking powder to the
mixture. Add the finely grated
lemon peel. Preheat the oven
to 350°F.

4 Beat the egg whites and 1
splash of lemon juice to a
very stiff peak. Gradually (in 2
to 3 portions) fold into the batter and combine carefully.

5 Spray a round, 10-inch cake
pan with baking oil and dust
with flour. Pour in the batter
and distribute evenly. Bake in
the preheated oven for about
40 minutes. Turn the cake over

Pàrdulas
Cheese Cookies (Sardinia)

onto a wire rack and set aside to cool.

6 For the glaze: Mix the confectioners' sugar with 2 tablespoons of lemon juice until smooth. You can also stir in 2 tablespoons of almond liqueur (or, to taste, more lemon juice).

7 Coarsely chop the blanched almonds. Roast them in a small frying pan, stirring constantly. Spread the lemon glaze over the cooled cake and distribute it smoothly and evenly with a cake knife or spatula. Before the glaze hardens, sprinkle the chopped blanched almonds over the top of the cake.

• Wine serving suggestion: a dessert wine, such as a *Malvasia* or a *Moscato* from Sardinia.

Yield: 10 Pieces

For the dough:
1 1/2 cup all-purpose flour +
    flour to roll out the dough
1 1/4 cup semolina flour
3 tablespoons butter
Salt

For the filling:
1 2/3 cups well-drained cottage
    cheese
1 egg
Peel of 1 lemon
Peel of 1 orange
5 tablespoons granulated sugar
1 envelope of saffron
1 pinch of salt

Other ingredients:
Oil to spray the baking sheet
1 egg
Enough confectioners' sugar to
    dust the cookies

Approximate preparation time:
    70 minutes;
    360 calories per cookie.

1 For the dough: Mix the all-purpose flour with the semolina flour. Knead the flour to a smooth dough, gradually adding about 1 cup of water. Season with a pinch of salt and, while still kneading add the softened butter. Set the dough aside under a moist dishcloth until the filling is ready.

2 For the filling: Beat the egg with the granulated sugar until fluffy. Stir in the saffron until dissolved, and season with 1 pinch of salt. Add the cottage cheese and mix. Rinse and brush the lemon and orange. Pat them dry and grate the peels with a fine meshed grater. Fold the peel gratings into the cheese mixture.

3 Preheat the oven to 350°F. Spray a baking sheet with oil. On a floured work surface, roll out the dough to a 1/16-inch thin sheet. With a glass, cut out rounds. Gather the leftover

dough, roll out again, and cut out more rounds.

4 Separate the egg, and beat the egg white. In the centers of half of the dough rounds, place 1 teaspoon of cheese filling. Brush the rounds' borders with egg whites and cover each with an empty round of dough. Using a fork, press indentations around the borders of the doubled dough rounds.

5 Place the cheese-filled rounds on the baking sheet. Beat the egg yolk and brush each cookie. Bake in the oven for about 25 minutes. Set aside to cool and serve dusted with confectioners' sugar.

• You can also use a nut filling for the cookies.

Coffee—Culture Experienced in Small Sips

As soon as it is put under pressure, it is ready to be served, with a delicate creamy top and giving off its voluptuous aroma—seduction *all'-italiana* (Italian style). It is the *espresso*, the "fast one," also called by those familiar with it, very simply, *Caffè, per favore!* ("Coffee, please!"). If taken in small sips, it has more flavor, a tactic that is especially rewarding when consuming the *espresso lungo* (long espresso), the diluted, less concentrated variation. Connoisseurs let the small, black, hot beverage glide past their throats with one guzzle and only a few hand movements, especially when drinking the *espresso corto*, which is the undiluted and strong coffee, or the *ristretto*, which is the double concentrated, strong, and extremely bitter espresso.

Whatever it was that motivated Mr. Achille Gaggia about five decades ago to pressurize a few thimbles full of water through seven grams of powdered coffee, he undoubtedly set in motion gourmet and steam-related social history. The raw material for this culinary experiment appeared for the first time in Italy about 300 years ago, as a marvelous cure for gout and headache. In time, however, the health conscious discovered that coffee also had other properties: Freshly brewed it is an exciting wake-up call, sweetens the hours of the gloomy, unties tongues, and sets the spirit in motion. Throughout large European cities, cult places for the exotic drink suddenly sprang up; the hour of coffeehouses arrived. Venice is considered one of its first showplaces; Caffe' Florian still exists today, almost unchanged since the middle of the eighteenth century. Outside Europe, coffeeshops existed long before artists and freethinkers gathered in Paris, Rome, Florence, or Vienna and talked incessantly over steaming cups of coffee. Coffee had already been served publicly during the middle of the fifteenth century in Mecca near the Red Sea. And, a little bit further south, in Ethiopia, lay the roots of the coffee culture: Throughout the woods in the province of Kaffa, since ancient times, people had gathered the red berries of the wild-growing tree for their mesmerizing and exciting properties. Even today, the areas with the best growing conditions are located where there are subtropical and tropical climates. Colonial powers recognized very early the economic value of this new taste, and they secured rapidly and (sometimes) unscrupulously the terrain suitable for coffee production. Gigantic coffee plantations were built to cultivate this luxury product. For the local populations, this development brought forth exploitation and misery, a bitter flavor of the pure enjoyment that still has lingering effects today. Coffee is now, after petroleum, and before coal and wheat, the second most important commercial commodity worldwide.

Two types of coffee plants are economically valued: the high-altitude Arabica and the disease-resistant Robusta. Arabica coffee has a fine, lower toned acidity, relatively less caffeine, and is more expensive. Robusta is easy to grow and does not have the same refined flavor as Arabica. Both types have in common that the trees carry both flowers and berries at the same time, with the harvest being protracted over several months.

Above: Oasis for enjoyment, magnet for culture seekers, monument to coffee history, the honorable Caffè Greco in Rome, in which today only a few artists, poets, and revolutionaries find warm refuge.

Left: For 400 years now in Italy, the dark magic art of brewing coffee has been mastered, a tradition whose origins are rooted in Africa and in the Arab world.

Above: It does not matter how the espresso is consumed, pure or with its foamy milk as cappuccino, it is always beneficial, since much of the caffeine disappears with the intensive roasting of the coffee beans.

The cherry-like berries are ideally harvested by hand, or are "sucked" from the branches and gathered in sheets. What finally turns into the precious coffee powder is hidden in the hearts of the fleshy fruits, the oblong seed pits that are extracted with more or less careful processing and then roasted. Roasting, done in the old days by shops that carried colonial goods, remains a unique and almost artful skill. First, however, a coffee expert mixes coffees for the individual coffee brands, since the secret of quality and aroma lies not in the purity of the coffee, but in the flavor harmony created by the mixture of beans. The type and time of the roasting process depend also on the intended use of the beans; espresso mixtures, for example, are roasted more than beans for filtered coffee.

The crushing of the roasted beans is the next important step. The wonderful scent of freshly ground coffee should confirm that leaving the coffee powder open for a long time will not improve the coffee. Ideally, single portions should be ground before using them; for espresso fans, this is a common tradition. One of these huge, shiny, and steaming machines is visible in every Italian bar, in every street coffeeshop, and in every restaurant—the beans are freshly ground and the hot boiling water is pressurized through the finely ground powder for every small cup. To allow the release of only the finest and most pleasant flavors, everything happens in only a few seconds while the bitter taste is left in the coffee residue. In the small manual coffee machines for stovetop and gas that are used at home, the heated water rises with steam pressure, permeates the filter filled with coffee powder, passes through a thin tube, and is collected in the upper part of the equipment. With this method, however, one detail is missing that otherwise would be part of the authentic Italian espresso made with a coffee machine: the delicate, foamy, and creamy froth, *la crema*.

Coffee pleasure—a daily enjoyment experienced with celebrated tradition throughout Italy. To be worthy of such culture, one should master one important aspect of it: the proper way to order coffee at the right time. *Cappuccino*, an espresso mixed with foamed milk is, for example, the beverage for a late morning breakfast, and is never taken as the final hot drink for a rich meal. In this case, a plain coffee is called for—deep, black, sweet, and steaming hot.

Right: Maragogipe, a fine Arabica variety from Mexi-co, in a bag near unroasted green coffee beans, both raw materials for exquisite coffee mixtures.

Pictures below and right, center: According to gen-uine old tradition, a type of locust tree wood instead of oil or gas fuels this roasting equipment. The coffee beans roast gently, sparing-ly, and below 300°F. For generations, the same fami-ly has owned this small cof-fee roasting shop in the vicinity of Florence, which is among the last manually op-erated businesses in Italy.

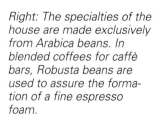

Right: The specialties of the house are made exclusively from Arabica beans. In blended coffees for caffè bars, Robusta beans are used to assure the forma-tion of a fine espresso foam.

Middle: This special skill for working with coffee goes beyond brewing the beverage behind the counter for only lucrative purposes; Italians are masters with their huge machines that dominate the entire coffee-making process, from grinding the beans for perfect granulation, to measuring, and to the steaming operation.

Left: Leftovers are not used here; the machine is activated for each small cup.

Left: Hot steam turns hot milk into fluffy foam, the crowning of a genuine cappuccino. Other specialties with milk are, for example, Caffè con latte (a diluted espresso with cold milk), Caffè e latte (half coffee and half milk), Caffè macchiato (coffee with a splash of milk).

Left: Fully enjoying coffee creates a good mood, whether or not the espresso is "corrected" with a shot of grappa as Caffè corretto.

Abruzzi, Molise, and Apulia

Tradition and Trulli:
Typical stonehouses in Alberobello.

The Regions and Their Products

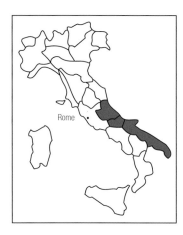

The Abruzzi region not only offers golden beaches, pine groves that reach to the sea, and gentle hills, but also about a 115-square mile national park and the massive Gran Sasso that is almost 9,750 feet high. The small region of Molise, reaching from rocky limestone peaks over high plateaus interspersed with woods, also gradually slopes to the sea. Apulia, by comparison, has a more even landscape. Excluding the extension of the Apennines and the mountainous Gargano, the region is a large plane on which olives, grapes, and wheat grow. Almost half of Italy's olive oil originates here. All three regions are connected culinarily through the sheep. The traditional economy, was, at least until the past century, based on livestock, in which animals were driven in the spring to higher pastures, where they stayed over the summer until they were returned to the milder planes of the lower valleys in late fall. Abruzzi's livestock spent the winter mainly on the Tavoliere, Southern Italy's largest plane. With their sheep meat, the shepherds not only delivered an important culinary ingredient, but they also developed recipes that influenced the

local cuisine of the pasture regions in which they moved. Out of their culinary arts sprang forth the *a cutturo*. A cutturo is a kettle that is hung with chains over an open fire and in which bubbles a stew of lamb meat, onions, herbs and, above all, *peperoncini*, fiery hot chili peppers. Here we come across another vital ingredient that is central in this cuisine: peperoncini, which are important for Spaghetti all'Amatriciana and many other typical dishes. The cuisine of this region is simple, without complicated methods and without unnecessary fluff.

Above: Apulia—entrenched in chains of hills and in fruitful valleys with farmland and olive and almond trees.

Far left: Pulo Valley looks like a garden landscape with beds of vegetables on which you can find multicolored peppers, for example.

Left: Beans, either fresh from the fields or dried for the winter, are used abundantly in many dishes.

Culinary favorites include pasta dishes, like Maccheroni alla chitarra, which is not made with long pasta tubes, but with pasta ribbons. Rolled dough is pressed out with a metal device that looks like a musical sitar. Classic additions are sheep or mutton ragù. The sheep industry also developed an intensive cheese production; *caciocavallo*, *scamorza*, and *pecorino sott'olio* (sheep cheese preserved in olive oil) are regional specialties, along with *quagliata*, also called *giuncata*, which is a fresh cheese hung to dry in a small rush basket (*giunca*). Apulia can also be called Italy's breadbasket. Gigantic fields of wheat, together with vegetables like tomatoes, eggplants, peppers, zucchini, potatoes, and spinach, overwhelm the regional picture, while legumes, like lentils and beans, also abound. Dried legumes remain a very important staple; in the spring, seven varieties are cooked in the traditional minestrone. The popular fish soup is served over toasted bread to remind us that its "poor people" origin should not be forgotten.

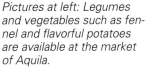

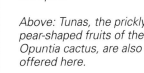

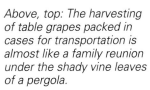

Pictures at left: Legumes and vegetables such as fennel and flavorful potatoes are available at the market of Aquila.

Above: Tunas, the prickly pear-shaped fruits of the Opuntia cactus, are also offered here.

Above, top: The harvesting of table grapes packed in cases for transportation is almost like a family reunion under the shady vine leaves of a pergola.

Above, left: Peperoncini (fiery chili peppers) hung up to dry are indispensable ingredients for many dishes.

Above, right: Cabbages are presented proudly, while the money is also counted carefully by the farmer.

People, Events, Sightseeing

tal of the region is Campobasso with its characteristic hill and Castle of Monforte. The city is renowned for its scissors and knife industry. From here, past the village of Vinchiatura, one can reach the ruins of the Roman settlement of Saepinum, which was once a market and midway stop for shepherds

moving from the mountains of Abruzzi to the coastal regions of Apulia and back.

Restaurants, where one can eat Apulia's fish soup, *zuppa di pesce*, are plentiful in the loud port city of Taranto, in the district of the old fish market. Oysters and mussels are farmed in

Pescara is located exactly in the middle of Abruzzi. From there, the high region of Abruzzi begins; however, before leaving, one should taste the *brodetto*, a delicious and spicy fish chowder. The Gran Sasso, the highest peak of the Apennine range where snow is almost perennial, can also be reached from Teramo. Beautiful villages in the national park are Barrea and Civitella Alfedena on the shores of Lake Barrea. Here, one can find not only wolves but also, in Civitella Alfadena, the famous baker Antonio with his baked creations shaped like a bear and called *U Dulcit*. The market in Aquila's Piazza del Duomo square is the place for those looking for a wooden working surface for *maccheroni alla chitarra* and where to find the best sheep cheese.

Molise's small coastal land tongue has only one town: Termoli. The old town surrounded by picturesque walls is located on a peninsula that stretches into the sea and is marked by an overlooking cathedral and a thirteenth-century castle. The capi-

Above: Orange trees grow very well under the southern sun. Many desserts are flavored with the peels of the fruits.

Above: The small town of Martina Franca appears to be dusted with confectioners' sugar, especially during the early hours of dusk.

Far left: A public fountain in the city of Bari. In the old city center with its narrow streets, the road becomes an extention of the home.

Near left: A smiling fisherman in the port city Taranto, which is well known to lovers of oysters and mussels.

two bays that are supplied with fresh water from springs located under the sea.

Trulli liven up the countryside between Alberobello and Martina Franca. The houses, shaped like half a Chianti bottle, cool and ventilated inside, are built from natural stone without mortar. Martina Franca is a small and quaint town that looks as if it were made of candied sugar. As is common throughout the Tavoliere area, where lamb meat is roasted on stone griddles by many village butchers, grilled meat, sausages, white bread, and salads are served on simple tables set up in the backyard by the butcher Ricci.

The festivities: Around the middle of January, Collelongo, near l'Aquila, celebrates the feast of Saint Anthony, during which cooking pots are blessed and the most attractive copper pots receive awards. In Rocca Pia, the festival of Saint Joseph is held with beans and ham around the middle of March. Pollutri (near Chieti) celebrates a grape and wine festival around the beginning of August, and a potato festival around the beginning of December. In Capracotta, near Isernia, the Pezzata, a gastronomical event with lamb dishes from the pastures of Campo Gentile, is held in the middle of August. Huge fireworks highlight the fish festival held in the old port of Termoli around the end of August.

Above: Billiards is a favorite hobby for the men in the Abruzzi.

Left: Apulia's renowned fish chowder is made with seafood and is enhanced, of course, with spicy peperoncini.

Far left: Antonio, the creator of the U Dulcit *cake in Civitella Alfedena, one of the most picturesque villages in the National Park.*

Left: In his backyard, the butcher Ricci offers grilled meat and sausages with bread and wine.

Above, top: Caffe' Tripoli in Martina Franca. In spite of the neon light, time seems to have stopped here.

Middle, left: Not only children's eyes sparkle at the sight of the selection of sweet treats available in Apulia.

211

The Wines

Abruzzi is usually associated with images of mountains and of the Gran Paradiso. However, the region that carries this name includes multifaceted and attractive landscapes that range from the coastal Adriatic strip to the hilly backcountry that turns mountainous after about 30 miles. This area has many different conditions for wine production, since the climate can vary greatly among various individual locations. It ranges from a balanced Mediterranean type of climate to a rugged alpine climate with marked temperature changes between day and night, summer and winter. With selective acumen, one could actually find in this region a suitable condition for every type of grape; however, only a few winemakers have tried to do this so far. Traditionally, there are only two types of grapes: the red Montepulciano and the white Trebbiano.

The *Montepulciano d'Abruzzo* is deep red, dry, and full-bodied, with a light tannic content that lessens with the age of the wine. The bouquet is reminiscent of flowering pasture meadows. It is among Italy's best wines, and for this reason, it is also a favorite abroad.

It is especially suitable for the regional lamb dishes and for maccheroni alla chitarra, if served with a meaty sauce. Also made from the same grape is a rosé wine, the *Cerasuolo d' Abruzzo*, which is made after briefly pressing the peels. It has a definite light red color, is dry with a very slight sweetness, and should not be older than three years. It is recommended for lamb in light sauces and for pasta dishes with tomato sauce.

The white *Trebbiano d'Abruzzo*, made essentially from the grape variety of the same name, is light yellow, almost straw-colored,

very dry, with a mild, almost neutral, flavor. It is served young and chilled with fish and seafood dishes.

Molise, the small region with mountains and a narrow tongue of land, has only recently developed its two DOC's: *Biferno*, available as white (made from Trebbiano grapes), and the *Pentro di Isernia*, which uses the same amounts of Montepulciano and Sangiovese grapes for the red and the rosé. There is also the *Ramitello*, a fine and smooth red wine, and a *Montepulciano del Molise*.

The grape harvest in Apulia, the relatively flat southern coastal region, is abundant. For quite

some time, especially from throughout the peninsula of Salento, came regional wines that were heavy and suitable for mixing with others. However, with new methodologies and techniques, regional table wines gradually became lighter and more refined. Examples of this type of wine are the *Squinzano* and the *Copertino* from the area around Lecce. The main variety of grape for both these wines is the Negroamaro. Red wines are especially outstanding—deep red, velvety, dry, and full of aroma and flavor, improving even further if kept for more than four years. The rosato (rosé) wines are bright red, refreshing, and aromatic, and should be consumed while young. The Primiti-

vo grape, once used mainly to cut other wines, now gives its blackberry-like aroma to the *Primitivo di Manduria*, a wine that is heavy and full-bodied. These wines are available in a spectrum of varieties ranging from dry to sweet. All the red wines are especially recommended for dishes prepared with lamb and innards, and the rosato wines for dishes with tomato sauce and pecorino cheese. Further north, together with red wines, one can also find fruity white wines, like the *Locorotondo* from the town of the same name located in the Itria Valley, and the *Martina* or *Martina Franca*. All of them have a straw yellow-greenish color and are refreshing and delicate in flavor. While young and chilled, these wines are particularly suitable with fish and seafood dishes.

The *Castel del Monte*, named after Emperor Frederick II's octagonal fortress, is among Apulia's most renowned wines. The *Rosato*, dry with a fine aroma and flavor, is a special favorite and is suitable for many dishes. The *Rosso* (red) is also remarkable, deep red, slightly tannic, and recommended especially for longer aging and marketed as *Riserva* (aged) with a minimum alcohol content of 12.5 percent.

Top: Red Montepulciano and white Trebbiano are the predominant grape varieties of Abruzzi's regional vineyards, although the climate here would allow the growth of many different varieties.

Left: Cerasuolo d'Abruzzo, a rosé made from Montepulciano grapes, in which the marc of grapes is briefly fermented together with grape peels, is also available in addition to both of these other wine varieties.

Regional Recipes

Bruschetta
Toasted Garlic Bread (Abruzzi)

Serves 4

4 fresh, ripe tomatoes
4 large slices of country bread
(preferably sourdough)
4 cloves garlic
8 tablespoons aromatic extra
virgin olive oil
Salt and freshly ground pepper

Approximate preparation time:
24 minutes;
260 calories per serving.

1 Blanch, peel, seed, cube, and drain the tomatoes.

2 Cut the slices of bread in halves, and toast them on both sides (or toast the slices on both sides in a frying pan with some olive oil) until golden brown and crispy.

3 Peel the garlic and cut in halves. Rub the toasted slices of bread with them and drizzle each with 1 tablespoon of olive oil.

4 Top the slices with crushed tomato pulp. Season with salt and freshly ground pepper. Serve immediately.

• Bread and olive oil, two rich ingredients of a hearty country cuisine that presents gourmet items of great simplicity. This dish is a masterpiece created by field workers and discovered in time by those who know how to enjoy a food that shows the triumph of wholesomeness. In Italy, you may find Bruschetta just about everywhere: sometimes with thin slices of garlic and garnished with olive oil and fresh basil, another entirely without tomatoes, or topped with thin slices of anchovies. For the preparation at home it is important to use good country bread with firm and preferably large crumbs and the purest and most aromatic olive oil available.

Pizza di patate
Potato Pizza (Apulia)

Serves 6

1 2/3 pounds or about 5 medium
potatoes (baking type)
1 2/3 pounds or about 6 to 7
medium large, fresh, ripe
tomatoes
1 bunch fresh Italian parsley
1 tablespoon stemless fresh
oregano (or 1 teaspoon dried)
3 1/2 ounces or 40 small black
pitted olives
11 ounces mozzarella cheese
10 to 12 canned anchovy fillets,
drained
2 garlic cloves, peeled
5 tablespoons olive oil
1/3 cup + 2 tablespoons all-pur-
pose flour
Salt and freshly ground pepper

Approximate preparation time:
1 1/2 hours;
450 calories per serving.

1 Thoroughly wash the potatoes and boil them in their jackets in a medium saucepan. Peel them and press them through a ricer while they are still hot. Add and mix 1 teaspoon salt and 2 tablespoons of olive oil. Set aside to cool.

2 Blanch, peel, seed, and cube the tomatoes. Sprinkle them with salt and let them drain thoroughly in a colander.

3 Briefly rinse the anchovies with water, pat them dry with paper towels, and, if necessary, cut in halves. Combine the crushed garlic with the well-drained tomatoes. Dice the mozzarella.

4 Preheat the oven to 400°F. Brush a round pizza pan (about 8 inches in diameter) with 1 tablespoon of olive oil. Combine the flour with the riced potatoes, knead, and place the dough in the pizza pan. Line the bottom of the pan with dough and build up a dough rim along the walls of the pan.

Pizza pugliese

Onion Pizza, Apulia Style (Apulia)

5 Top the potato dough with the tomatoes and season with freshly ground pepper. Evenly distribute the diced mozzarella, anchovies, and black olives over the tomatoes. Sprinkle with oregano and drizzle with the remaining olive oil.

6 Bake in the preheated oven for about 40 minutes. Mince the parsley and sprinkle over the potato pizza. Cut in slices and serve hot.

• For a more substantial meal, this pizza provides 2 to 3 servings accompanied by a large mixed green salad.

• To make sure the dough does not turn out sticky, add more flour during kneading if the potatoes are not starchy enough.

Serves 4

For the dough:
1/4 package fresh compressed or 1 1/4-ounce envelope active dry yeast
1 1/2 cup all-purpose flour + flour to roll out the dough
2 tablespoons olive oil + oil for the pizza pan
1 pinch of sugar
Salt

For the topping:
3 small onions
Optional: 1 teaspoon fresh stemless oregano (or 1/2 teaspoon dried)
2/3 cup freshly grated pecorino or romano cheese
4 tablespoons olive oil
Salt and freshly ground pepper

Approximate preparation time:
45 minutes;
480 calories per serving.

1 For the dough: Mix the yeast with 1 pinch of sugar and 2

---

tablespoons of lukewarm water, and add 2 tablespoons of flour to it. Put the remaining flour in a large mixing bowl. Make a well and add the yeast mixture. Cover the yeast with some flour and set aside in a warm place to rest for 30 minutes.

2 Add to the flour 1/2 teaspoon of salt and 2 tablespoons of olive oil and, together with 1/2 cup lukewarm water, knead to a smooth dough. On the well-floured work surface, finish kneading vigorously and return the dough to the mixing bowl. Cover with a dishcloth, set aside in a warm place for 1 hour, and allow the dough to rise until it has doubled in size.

3 For the topping: Thinly slice the onions (or mince them). Preheat the oven to 425°F. Brush a round, small pizza pan (about 9 inches in diameter) with oil.

---

4 Punch down the dough and briefly knead again. Stretch the dough by hand and evenly line the bottom of the pizza pan with it. Brush the surface of the dough with 1 tablespoon of olive oil.

5 Evenly distribute the onions, the freshly grated cheese, and the oregano on the dough. Drizzle with the remaining 3 tablespoons of olive oil. Bake the pizza in the preheated oven for about 25 minutes.

6 Season the crispy, freshly baked pizza with salt and freshly ground pepper and serve immediately.

• A fine pizza does not necessarily need to be topped with many ingredients; the best way to enjoy it is if it is prepared simply and with first-quality toppings.

Orecchiette alla pugliese
"Little Ears" Pasta with Broccoli, Apulia Style (Apulia)

Serves 4 to 6

For the dough:
(Prepare the orecchiette ahead
    of time.)
$\frac{1}{2}$ cup + 2 tablespoons
    semolina flour
1 $\frac{1}{2}$ cups all-purpose flour +
    enough flour to roll out the
    dough
2 tablespoons olive oil
Salt

Other ingredients:
1 $\frac{1}{3}$ pounds fresh broccoli
4 tablespoons olive oil
3 cloves garlic, minced
1 red, either dried or pickled
    peperoncino (you may sub-
    stitute chili pepper)
Salt and freshly ground pepper

Approximate preparation time:
    1 $\frac{1}{2}$ hours;
    310 calories per serving.

Apulia's housewives are role
models for the pleasure of making *orecchiette* from scratch at
home. These unique pasta creations, which look like either little ears or little hats, are a daily
pasta specialty in Italy's South.
Orecchiette are also available in
stores, a great time saver.

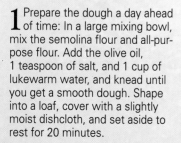

1 Prepare the dough a day ahead
of time: In a large mixing bowl,
mix the semolina flour and all-purpose flour. Add the olive oil,
1 teaspoon of salt, and 1 cup of
lukewarm water, and knead until
you get a smooth dough. Shape
into a loaf, cover with a slightly
moist dishcloth, and set aside to
rest for 20 minutes.

2 Divide the dough into smaller pieces and, on a well-floured work
surface, roll the dough into finger-thick sausages about 1 inch
thick in diameter. Slice each dough sausage into $\frac{1}{2}$-inch-thick
slices and, using your thumb, press a deep indentation into each
small dough slice. Cover the orecchiette with a dishcloth and set
aside to dry overnight.

3 The next day, trim and thoroughly clean the broccoli and
divide them into florets. You can
peel and cut the very thick broccoli stems. Bring 3 quarts of salted water to a rolling boil in a
large pot. Drop the broccoli
stems into the water and, after 5
minutes, add the broccoli florets.
Blanch everything for 5 minutes.

4 Remove the vegetables with a slotted spoon, drop them into iced water, and drain them thoroughly. Bring the remaining vegetable water to a rolling boil. Drop the orecchiette into the boiling water and cook until still firm or al dente.

5 In the meantime, chop the broccoli stems. Thinly slice the peperoncino. Heat 4 tablespoons of olive oil in a large frying pan. Sauté the broccoli and minced garlic, and add the peperoncino. Season with salt and pepper. Moisten with a few spoonfuls of vegetable water.

6 As soon as the orecchiette are cooked, remove them from the water and drain them well. Add them to the frying pan and fold them into the vegetables. If necessary, season again with salt and pepper, and serve.

Riso ai carciofi
Artichoke Rice (Apulia)

Serves 4 to 6

8 small fresh artichokes
1 bunch fresh Italian parsley, minced
Some fresh mint leaves
1 lemon (juice + peel)
1 ounce or 1/2 cup freshly grated pecorino or romano cheese
1 1/3 cups long-grain rice
3 cups hot chicken stock
2 garlic cloves, minced
4 tablespoons olive oil
Salt and freshly ground pepper

<u>*Approximate preparation time:*</u>
50 minutes;
230 calories per serving.

1 Trim the artichokes, remove the woody outer leaves, and cut off the harder points. Immediately place the trimmed artichokes in a bowl filled with iced water mixed with the lemon juice.

2 Preheat the oven to 400°F. Cut the fresh mint leaves into strips. Mix the parsley, garlic, and mint with the grated lemon peel.

3 Put the long-grain rice in a wide baking dish. Drain the artichokes and place them on top of the rice. Sprinkle with the herb mixture and season with salt and pepper. Drizzle the olive oil over everything.

4 Pour the hot chicken stock over the mixture, cover, and place in the preheated oven. Cook approximately 25 minutes or until the rice is done. If necessary, gradually add more hot stock or hot water. Sprinkle the finished dish with freshly grated cheese and serve at once.

Orecchiette con la rucola
"Little Ears" Pasta with Arugula (Apulia)

Serves 4 to 6

2 ounces or 2 slices prosciutto (or raw country ham)
12 ounces fresh arugula (you may substitute either young dandelion, watercress, or spinach leaves)
About 1 pound fresh, ripe tomatoes
2/3 cup freshly grated romano or Parmesan cheese
11 ounces orecchiette pasta (see recipe on page 216 or use store-bought pasta)
6 tablespoons aromatic olive oil
1 small onion, minced
2 cloves garlic, minced
Salt and freshly ground pepper

<u>*Approximate preparation time:*</u>
1 hour;
360 calories per serving.

1 Thoroughly clean and trim the arugula. In a large pot, bring 2 quarts of salted water to a rolling boil, and blanch the leaves of arugula. Remove the leaves, drop them into iced water, and drain thoroughly. In the same pot, bring 3 quarts of salted water to a rolling boil for cooking the pasta.

2 Blanch, peel, seed, and mince or finely chop the tomatoes with a knife. Put the tomatoes in a medium saucepan and add 2 tablespoons of olive oil. Season with salt and pepper, and simmer.

3 Drop the orecchiette pasta into the salted boiling water and cook for 10 to 15 minutes or until still firm to the bite or al dente.

4 In the meantime, thinly slice the prosciutto. In a large saucepan, add and sauté the onion and ham until the onion is limp and glossy. Add and stir in the arugula and garlic and moisten with a few spoonfuls of hot pasta water. Season with salt and pepper.

Minestra maritata

One-pot Vegetable Soup (Apulia)

5 Remove the orecchiette, drain thoroughly, and add the arugula-vegetable mixture. Top with the tomato sauce and serve with freshly grated cheese.

• Arugula, relatively new on the market, is a green longish variety of slightly bitter lettuce that has an almost nutty flavor. Other suitable substitutes for arugula could be young dandelion leaves, watercress, or fresh spinach leaves.

Serves 6 to 8

4 ounces or 4 slices bacon
1 fresh fennel bulb
3 bunches of fresh dandelion (or 3 heads of Belgian endive)
About 11 ounces or 4 medium carrots
3 celery stalks
1 leek
1/2 small green cabbage (about 11 ounces)
2/3 cup freshly grated romano or Parmesan cheese
About 2 quarts concentrated hot beef stock (best if homemade)
2 cloves garlic, crushed
6 tablespoons olive oil
Salt and freshly ground pepper

Approximate preparation time:
80 minutes;
230 calories per serving.

1 Trim and thoroughly clean the vegetables. Cut the fennel into sections, slice it thin, and keep the green fluffy tops.

Chop the dandelion (or Belgian endive), and slice the carrots, celery, and leeks. Slice the 1/2 cabbage into very thin strips.

2 In a large pot, heat enough salted water for blanching. Blanch all the vegetables for 2 minutes. With a slotted spoon, remove the vegetables, drop into iced water, and allow them to drain thoroughly. Rinse the large pot and pat dry.

3 Thinly slice the bacon. Brush the pot with 2 tablespoons of olive oil and heat the oil in the pot. Sauté the bacon in the oil until crispy. Add the garlic, and lightly sauté. Remove the bacon bits and set them aside for later use.

4 In another large pot, heat the beef stock. In the meantime, make layers of vegetables in the first pot. Sprinkle each layer of vegetables with bacon bits and grated cheese, and

drizzle each layer with olive oil. Season well with freshly ground pepper.

5 Pour the hot beef stock over the layered vegetables and sprinkle the mixture with more grated cheese. Cover and simmer the *minestra* for about 45 minutes.

• This layered vegetable soup is often baked in the oven; sometimes it is topped with cheese toward the end of baking to form a golden crispy top layer.

219

Fettuccine all'abruzzese
Saffron-flavored Flat Pasta, Abruzzi Style (Abruzzi)

Serves 4

8 fresh zucchini blossoms with attached young zucchini
1/2 bunch fresh basil
1/2 bunch fresh Italian parsley, minced
4 tablespoons freshly grated romano or Parmesan cheese
1 envelope powdered saffron (or 1 teaspoon dried saffron threads)
1/2 cup beef stock
About 1 pound flat pasta
1 onion, minced
4 tablespoons olive oil
Salt and freshly ground pepper

<u>Approximate preparation time:</u>
40 minutes;
450 calories per serving.

1 Separate the flowers from the zucchini. Julienne 4 flowers, the zucchini, and the basil leaves.

2 For the noodles, bring 3 quarts of salted water to a boil in a large pot.

3 Heat the olive oil in a large saucepan. Sauté the onions. Soak the saffron in 2 tablespoons of lukewarm water and add to the onions. Stir in the strips of flowers, zucchini, and herbs. Add the beef stock and simmer. Season with salt and pepper.

4 Drop the pasta into the boiling water and cook 8 to 10 minutes or until still firm to the bite. If necessary, moisten the vegetable sauce with a few spoonfuls of pasta water. Top the sauce with the remaining zucchini flowers, cover, and allow the flowers to briefly wilt and cook in the saucepan.

5 Drain the cooked pasta. Fold the pasta into the sauce and season with salt and pepper. Garnish with the wilted zucchini flowers. Serve with additional cheese.

Pasta e lenticchie
Pasta with Lentils (Apulia)

Serves 6

4 ounces or 4 slices bacon
4 stalks celery with tops
1 cup lentils
1/2 pound spaghetti
1/2 cup dry white wine
1 onion
2 cloves garlic, crushed
4 tablespoon olive oil
Salt and freshly ground pepper

<u>Approximate preparation time:</u>
70 minutes
(+ 12 hours soaking);
400 calories per serving.

1 Soak the lentils overnight.

2 The next day, dice the bacon and the onion. Thoroughly rinse 2 celery stalks and slice thin. Set aside the remaining celery and the green celery tops for later use.

3 Sauté the bacon in a large pot brushed with 1 tablespoon of olive oil. Add the onion and celery and stir-fry until limp. Add the soaked lentils with their water, and the crushed garlic.

4 Simmer the lentils for 30 to 40 minutes and gradually add the white wine and, if necessary, some water—the lentils should have a final soup consistency.

5 Season the lentils with salt and pepper. Thinly slice the remaining celery. Break the spaghetti into 1 1/4-inch-long pieces. Add both ingredients to the lentils and simmer for 8 to 10 minutes. Season again with more salt and pepper. Drizzle with 3 tablespoons of olive oil and sprinkle over the green celery tops.

• *Pasta e fagioli*, a delicious combination of pasta and beans, is also typical of these regions. For this dish, dried white beans are soaked

Spaghetti con aglio, olio, e peperoncino
Spaghetti with Garlic, Oil, and Peperoncino (Abruzzi/Molise)

overnight and cooked the next day in their soaking water. In a second pot, pork ribs are simmered with leeks and onions until the meat falls off the bones; these are cooked to the very end with the beans. The broth, from which the leeks and the onions are removed, is used to cook the noodles, preferably elbow or shell pasta. The noodles are cooked to the al dente stage, drizzled with olive oil, and folded into the beans. They are seasoned with salt, pepper, and minced parsley. The variation prepared with bacon bits is even heartier.

Serves 4 to 6

1 bunch fresh Italian parsley, minced
1 peperoncino (Italian hot chili pepper), (either dried or fresh as available)
3 cloves garlic
About 1 pound spaghetti
$1/4$ cup olive oil
Salt and freshly ground pepper

Approximate preparation time: 35 minutes; 400 calories per serving.

1 Bring 4 quarts of salted water to a boil in a large pot. Cook the spaghetti for about 8 to 10 minutes or until still firm to the bite or *al dente*.

2 Heat the olive oil in a large frying pan. Peel the garlic cloves, add them to the hot oil together with the dried peperoncino, and simmer.

3 Remove the pasta from the water and drain thoroughly. Remove the garlic and the peperoncino from the oil and add the spaghetti and parsley to the oil. Season with salt and freshly ground pepper. Serve the spaghetti garnished with the peperoncino.

• Sauté the peperoncino only to the degree of hotness you wish the oil to absorb according to your personal taste. It is probably safe to assume that you will reach your perfect and favorite chili heat only after having tried this at least twice—therefore, use some caution at first! For the lover of fiery foods, the peperoncino can be left in the oil and tossed together with the pasta.

• A milder variation of this pasta dish is called *Spaghetti aglio e olio*. You might be surprised how flavorful the noodles can taste with nothing more than garlic and oil.

• Wine serving suggestion: a full-bodied red wine, such as *Montepulciano d'Abruzzo*.

Cozze ripiene
Stuffed Mussels (Apulia)

Serves 4

2 pounds fresh mussels
1 cup dry white wine
About 1 pound or 2 cups
   chopped tomatoes (can be
   canned)
1 bunch fresh Italian parsley
1 bunch fresh basil
2 eggs
3 tablespoons grated romano or
   Parmesan cheese
2 tablespoons butter
1 onion, minced
3 cloves garlic, minced
4 tablespoons unseasoned
   breadcrumbs (preferably
   grated fresh)
3 tablespoons olive oil
Salt and freshly ground pepper
1 pinch cayenne pepper

Approximate preparation time:
   70 minutes;
   450 calories per serving.

In other regions of Italy, these
mussels are also called cozze
alla tarantina. The stuffing
comes in many variations; main

ingredients, however, are usually cheese, herbs, and breadcrumbs. In Tuscany, a very unusual mixture with sausage is a
favorite.

1 Under running water, remove the "beards" of the
mussels and thoroughly rinse,
brush, and clean the mussels.
Discard those mussels that are
already open and don't close
when tapped lightly.

2 Put the mussels in a large
pot, moisten with the white
wine, heat and simmer for
about 5 minutes or until the
mussels open. Remove and
discard those mussels that are
closed. Remove the mussels
with a slotted spoon and set
them aside to cool.

3 Pour the mussel liquid through a very fine strainer and set
aside. Heat 3 tablespoons of olive oil in the pot and sauté the
minced onion and garlic. Chop the tomatoes, add, and stir into the
onion-garlic mixture. Add the mussel liquid and season with salt
and pepper. Allow the sauce to simmer until it has reduced and become denser. Line a large baking dish or casserole with the sauce.
Preheat the oven to 425ºF.

4 Carefully break the cold mussels' shells apart and discard the empty halves. Set aside those shells that have the mussel meat for later use.

5 For the stuffing: Vigorously beat the eggs. Mince the parsley and basil, and add these and 2 minced garlic cloves to the eggs. Add and mix the breadcrumbs and season this mixture with salt, pepper, and 1 pinch of cayenne pepper.

6 On each half of the mussels place 1 teaspoon of the herbed stuffing. Gradually put each stuffed mussel on the tomato sauce in the baking dish (the sauce should not cover the mussels). Sprinkle the mussels with the grated cheese. Distribute 2 tablespoons of butter, divided in small pieces, among the mussels. Bake the mussels in the preheated oven for approximately 10 minutes (or broil them for 5 minutes). Serve with fresh crusty bread.

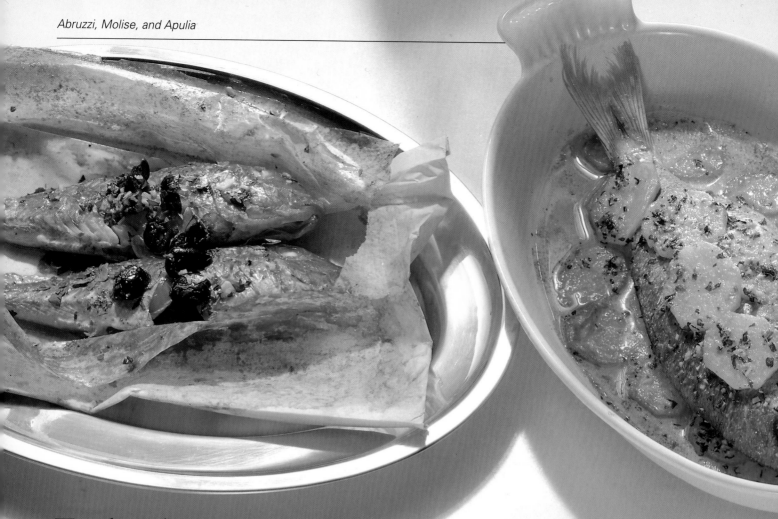

Triglie al cartoccio
Red Mullets Wrapped in Paper (Abruzzi/Apulia)

Serves 2

4 medium large red mullets (or American red goatfish, or any suitably sized white flaky mullet-type fish)
1/2 lemon (juice)
10 to 15 small, unpitted black olives
2 cloves garlic, crushed
8 tablespoons olive oil
3 bay leaves
1/2 teaspoon peppercorns
Salt and freshly ground pepper

Approximate preparation time:
30 minutes
(+ 2 hours marinating);
550 calories per serving.

1 Scale and rinse the mullets and set them aside in a bowl. Whisk the crushed garlic with the lemon juice and 4 tablespoons of olive oil. Crush or finely shred the bay leaves with the peppercorns. Stir both into the marinade.

2 Drizzle the marinade over the fish. Allow the marinade to seep into the flesh for at least 2 hours in the refrigerator. Turn the fish over once.

3 Preheat the oven to 400°F. Brush each of 4 sheets of parchment paper with 1 tablespoon of oil (you may substitute aluminum foil or a roasting bag).

4 Remove the fish from the marinade, place them on the papers brushed with oil, season them with salt and pepper, and drizzle with the marinade. Remove the pits, mince the olives, and sprinkle them over the fish. Wrap the fish in the paper, making sure to fold and firmly close the wrappers.

5 Bake in the preheated oven for about 8 minutes. Serve the mullets in their paper wrappers and unwrap only at the table.

Orata alla pugliese
Baked Bass, Apulia Style (Apulia)

Serves 4

1 golden bass (or croaker or other suitably sized flaky white fish—no more than 2 pounds)
1 pound potatoes (red or waxy)
1 large bunch fresh Italian parsley, minced
2/3 cup freshly grated romano or Parmesan cheese
3 cloves garlic, crushed
10 tablespoons olive oil
Salt and freshly ground pepper

Approximate preparation time:
80 minutes;
550 calories per serving.

1 Scale, gut, and rinse the fish, and pat dry. Bring 4 cups of salted water to a boil in a large pot. Clean, rinse, and peel the potatoes, and slice them 1/2-inch thick. Blanch the potato slices for 5 minutes in the boiling salted water. Drain the potato slices.

2 In a mortar with a pestle, make a paste of the parsley and garlic. Stir 8 tablespoons of olive oil into the paste and cream to a smooth mixture. Preheat the oven to 425°F. Brush a large baking dish with 2 tablespoons of olive oil.

3 Line the bottom of the baking dish with one half of the potato slices. Season with salt and pepper, drizzle some of the herbed oil garlic paste over the potatoes, and evenly sprinkle half of the grated cheese over this layer.

4 Put the fish on the layer of potatoes, season with salt and pepper, and drizzle with more herbed garlic oil. Top this layer with the remaining slices of potato, season again with salt, pepper, herbed oil, and the remaining grated cheese.

5 Bake in the oven for 30 minutes. Serve the bass hot.

Zuppa di pesce
Fish Chowder (Apulia)

• Bass is among Italy's favorite culinary fish varieties; it has a flavorful, delicate, flaky, and relatively lean meat. Several bass-like types of fish are available; you can also prepare this dish with halibut, hake, or haddock. You can use this recipe to prepare fillets of fish; in this case, use potatoes cooked in their jackets and sliced, season with the herbed oil, and don't bake as long.

• Bass, as well as mullets, are white fish varieties that are available on both sides of the Atlantic Ocean; however, their sizes, textures, and colors may differ greatly as a result of the waters from which they come.

• Wine serving suggestion: a dry white wine, such as *Martina Franca*.

Serves 4

About 2 pounds mixed fillets of fish (Atlantic ocean perch, haddock, cod)
9 ounces shelled shrimp
4 celery stalks
1 bunch fresh Italian parsley
1 1/2 cup dry white wine (or fish stock)
1 28-ounce can of peeled tomatoes
2 onions, chopped
4 cloves garlic
6 tablespoons olive oil
1/2 teaspoon peppercorns
Salt and freshly ground pepper

<u>Approximate preparation time:</u>
1 hour;
520 calories per serving.

1 Cut the fish fillets into bite-size pieces, season them with salt, and refrigerate for later use.

2 Thoroughly rinse celery and cut into 1-inch-long slices.

Set aside the leafy tops for later use. Coarsely chop the garlic and, together with the peppercorns, crush everything into a paste. Stir 2 tablespoons of olive oil into the paste. Drain the canned tomatoes, chop them, and keep the tomato juice.

3 Heat 4 tablespoons of olive oil in a large saucepan. Stir in and sauté the chopped onions and the celery. Add the tomatoes, moisten with the white wine, and bring to a rapid boil. Stir in the garlic paste and season with salt. Gradually add the tomato juice and cook for 5 minutes.

4 Put the pieces of fish in the pot. Cover and cook for 10 minutes. After 5 minutes of cooking, add the shrimp and finish cooking. Season with salt and pepper. Chop the parsley and the celery tops and sprinkle over the chowder.

• A little bit more complicated variation would mean using whole fish instead of fillets; gutting, rinsing, and portioning the fish at home, preparing a fish stock with the fish bones, and using this stock for the chowder.

• Wine serving suggestion: a strong full-bodied white wine or a rosé, such as white or rosé *Castel del Monte*.

Agnello alle olive
Roasted Lamb with Olives (Abruzzi/Molise)

Agnello brodettato
Stewed Lamb with Lemon Gravy (Abruzzi)

Serves 6

About 2 pounds boneless lamb
   from the leg
5 ounces or 30 to 40 small,
   black unpitted olives
1 to 2 lemons (juice)
1 bouquet of fresh oregano (or
   1 tablespoon dried)
1 cup beef stock
1 dried chili pepper
1 tablespoon flour
6 tablespoons olive oil
Salt and freshly ground pepper

Approximate preparation time:
   2 1/2 hours;
   550 calories per serving.

1 Dust the meat with the flour.
In a Dutch oven, heat the
olive oil, add the meat, and
brown evenly on all sides. Season with salt and pepper and
moisten with the juice of 1
lemon and with 1/2 cup of
stock. Cover and simmer on
low heat for 30 minutes.

2 Remove the pits from 20 to
30 olives, seed the chili pepper, and mince. After 30 minutes cooking time, add these
to the lamb. Sprinkle half of the
oregano over the lamb, then
moisten with the remaining 1/2
cup of beef stock. Cover and finish cooking for about 1 1/2 hours
or until the meat is soft and flaky.
Add the remaining whole olives.

3 Season the gravy with salt,
pepper, and lemon juice.
Thinly slice the meat and place
on a preheated platter. Pour the
gravy over the meat and sprinkle it with oregano. Serve hot.

• Should the gravy be too wa-
tery, thicken it with whipping
cream whisked and cooked into
the pan juices.

• A very fine version is prepared
with fresh wild mushrooms
added to the gravy approximately 30 minutes before the
roast is done.

Serves 4 to 6

1 2/3 pounds lamb from the
   shoulder
2 ounces or 2 slices bacon
2 tablespoons vegetable oil
1 lemon (juice and peel)
1/2 to 1 cup dry white wine
1/2 cup beef stock
3 egg yolks
1 onion, coarsely chopped
1 clove garlic, crushed
1 to 2 tablespoons flour
Nutmeg
Salt and freshly ground pepper

Approximate preparation time:
   2 hours;
   600 calories per serving.

1 Peel the membranes and remove all sinews from the
meat. Cube the meat and dust
the cubes lightly with the flour.
Dice the bacon. Heat the vegetable oil in a large Dutch oven.
Stir in and sauté the diced bacon. Gradually add the cubes of
meat and brown evenly on all
sides, stirring occasionally. Add
the onion and sauté until
glossy.

2 Moisten with 1/2 cup of
white wine and season with
salt, pepper, and 1 pinch of
freshly ground nutmeg. Cook,
stirring occasionally until the
wine has evaporated.

3 Add more wine and some
stock. Simmer the meat for
about 1 hour on low heat. If
necessary, moisten occasionally with wine and stock.

4 Remove the meat with a
slotted spoon, as soon as it
is soft and done. Place it on a
preheated plate, and cover it to
keep it warm.

5 In a small bowl, whisk together 3 to 4 tablespoons
lemon juice, the egg yolks, and
crushed garlic. Remove the
Dutch oven from the heat, and
gradually, while whisking vigor-

Agnello alla pugliese
Roasted Lamb, Apulia Style (Apulia)

ously, pour the egg mixture in a thin stream into the Dutch oven, and stir into the lamb stock. Return the Dutch oven with the beaten egg mixture gravy to the heat and heat one last time without allowing the gravy to boil.

6 Cut the lemon peel into very thin strips. Season the egg-lemon gravy once more with salt, pepper, and nutmeg. Pour the gravy over the chunks of meat, sprinkle with lemon strips, and serve immediately.

• This is a traditional Abruzzi Easter recipe.

• Wine serving suggestion for lamb's meat: a hearty red wine, such as *Montepulciano d'Abruzzo* or a *Rosso di Cerignola* from Apulia.

Serves 4 to 6

About 2 pounds leg of lamb
1 1/3 pounds small new potatoes (preferably red or waxy)
1 1/3 pounds fresh ripe tomatoes
1 large bunch of fresh Italian parsley, minced
1 lemon (juice and peel)
2/3 cup freshly grated romano or Parmesan cheese
3 tablespoons vegetable oil
4 tablespoons unseasoned breadcrumbs (preferably freshly grated)
4 cloves garlic, minced
6 tablespoons olive oil
Salt and freshly ground pepper

<u>Approximate preparation time:</u>
  2 1/2 hours;
  650 calories per serving.

1 Brush the leg of lamb with the juice of 1 lemon (keep the lemon halves). Wash and peel the potatoes, and slice them 1/4 inch thick. Blanch, peel, and seed the tomatoes.

2 Brush a large Dutch oven with olive oil. Add the slices of potatoes in layers, season with salt and pepper, and drizzle with 2 tablespoons of vegetable oil. Distribute the tomatoes among the slices of potatoes. Preheat the oven to 350°F.

3 Mix the parsley and garlic with the breadcrumbs and the grated lemon peel. Mix two-thirds of the herbed crumb mixture with 4 tablespoons of olive oil until you get a paste. Mix the remaining crumbs with the freshly grated cheese and set aside for later use.

4 Season the leg of lamb with salt and pepper. Evenly brush all sides of the lamb with the herbed oil paste. In the Dutch oven, top the potato layers with the meat and bake in the preheated oven for approximately 1 1/2 hours.

5 About 15 minutes before removing the meat from the oven, increase the oven temperature to 425°F and sprinkle the herbed cheese-crumb mixture over the lamb and the potatoes. Drizzle everything with 1 tablespoon of vegetable oil. Bake until golden brown and crispy.

• In Italy, this recipe is often used to prepare very young goats, hardly available in this market.

Peperoni ripieni
Stuffed Peppers (Apulia)

Serves 4

4 yellow sweet peppers
1 bunch fresh Italian parsley,
  minced
4 tablespoons freshly grated
  romano or Parmesan cheese
2 fresh rolls
4 canned anchovy fillets,
  drained
2 tablespoons pickled green
  capers
2 cloves garlic
1/2 cup olive oil
Salt and freshly ground pepper

Approximate preparation time:
  50 minutes;
  330 calories per serving.

Many Italian side dishes can also be served as small appetizers, like these tangy flavorful
peppers. In other Italian regions, this style of peppers is
sometimes called *involtini di
peperoni*, with stuffings based
on a great variety of ingredients
that range from tuna with black
olives or cheese with herbs, to
an almost oriental style filled
with aromatic bread and raisins.

Of course, you can use red and
green peppers instead of yellow (the color is only an indication of the pepper's stage of
maturation and does not reflect
another variety). Green peppers
have a rougher, almost grassy
taste, and require a little longer
cooking time compared to the
flavorful reds and the delicate
yellows.

1 Clean, rinse, and pat dry the
peppers. On the side of the
stem, cut the top from each
pepper and set this aside. Remove the internal white membranes and seeds.

2 Stuffing: Grate off the rolls'
outer crusts and use only
the insides. Shred the bread into small flakes, put in a small
bowl, and drizzle with 2 to 3
tablespoons of olive oil.

3 Briefly rinse and mince the
anchovies. Crush or mince
the garlic.

4 Add the minced parsley, anchovies, garlic, 2 table-spoons of grated cheese and 2 tablespoons of green capers to the breadcrumbs. Mix all the ingredients thoroughly. Preheat the oven to 350°F.

5 Season with salt (remember that the anchovies are salted!) and pepper. Gradually add 4 to 5 tablespoons of olive oil in a thin stream to allow the mixture to combine and become fairly soft. Brush a large baking dish with 1 tablespoon of oil.

6 Spoon the stuffing into the prepared peppers and top each portion of stuffing with ½ tablespoon of cheese. Put the tops back on the peppers and brush them on the outside with oil.

7 Place all the peppers straight up next to each other in the baking dish and bake in the pre-heated oven for 20 minutes. Serve hot and, if you wish, as a side course for a meat dish (or serve cold as an appetizer).

Tortiera di patate e funghi
Potato and Mushroom Casserole (Apulia)

Patate al forno
Oven-roasted Potatoes (Abruzzi/Apulia)

Serves 4

*1 3/4 pounds potatoes (prefer-
ably red or waxy)*
*About 1 pound fresh button
mushrooms, baby portobel-
lo, or fresh, wild, edible
mushrooms*
1 lemon (juice)
1 bunch fresh Italian parsley
*2/3 cup fresh grated romano or
Parmesan cheese*
*2 ounces or 6 tablespoons un-
seasoned breadcrumbs
(preferably freshly grated
from white bread)*
6 to 8 tablespoons olive oil
Salt and freshly ground pepper

*Approximate preparation time:
1 1/2 hours;
380 calories per serving.*

1 Wash and peel the potatoes,
and slice them 1/4 inch thick.
Thoroughly clean the mushrooms and trim the stems.
Slice the mushrooms and immediately drizzle them with the
lemon juice.

2 Cut the leaves of parsley into thin strips, mix with the
breadcrumbs and grated
cheese.

3 Preheat the oven to 350°F.
Brush a large baking dish
with 2 tablespoons of olive oil.
Line the baking dish with potato and mushroom slices in alternating layers. Season each
layer with salt, pepper, and the
herbed cheese-breadcrumb
mixture, and drizzle with a generous amount of olive oil.

4 Bake in the preheated oven
for 1 hour or until the potatoes are soft. Serve immediately.

• This is delicious served with
stewed meats.

Serves 4 to 6

*About 2 pounds medium pota-
toes (preferably red or waxy)*
*1 1/3 pounds fresh, ripe plum
tomatoes*
3 medium onions, sliced thin
*2 sprigs fresh oregano (or 1
tablespoon dried)*
*3 1/3 cups freshly grated
romano or Parmesan cheese*
1/2 cup dry white wine
2 tablespoons butter
6 tablespoons olive oil
Salt and freshly ground pepper

*Approximate preparation time:
1 1/2 hours;
380 calories per serving.*

1 Wash and peel the potatoes,
and slice them 1/4 inch thick.
Blanch and peel the tomatoes
and cut them in slices.

2 Preheat the oven to 350°F.
Brush a large baking dish
with 2 tablespoons of olive oil.

3 Line the baking dish with
layers of potatoes, toma-
toes, and onions, placed together like shingles on a roof.
Season each layer with salt,
pepper, oregano leaves, and
some grated cheese, and drizzle each layer with olive oil
(keep 2 tablespoons of grated
cheese aside for later use).

4 Top the final layer with 2 tablespoons of butter. Bake in
the preheated oven for about 1
hour. As soon as the potatoes
are soft (test with the point of a
knife), top with the remaining 2
tablespoons of cheese, and let
bake in the oven for 2 more
minutes. Serve very hot. Garnish with fresh oregano.

• This can be a side dish for
lamb and poultry. It can also be
a whole meal for 3 to 4 servings, plenty to eat when served
with a large mixed salad.

Cipolle fritte
Fried Onions (Abruzzi/Apulia)

• Wine serving suggestion: an aromatic wine, such as *Trebbiano d'Abruzzo* or a white *San Severo* from Apulia.

Serves 4 to 6

About 1 pound pearl onions or tiny onions
1 bunch fresh Italian parsley
3 tablespoons grated romano or Parmesan cheese
2 eggs
About 1/2 cup milk
2 cloves garlic, crushed
3/4 cup flour
Enough oil to fry
Salt and freshly ground pepper

<u>Approximate preparation time:</u>
45 minutes;
310 calories per serving.

1 Prepare the batter: In a large mixing bowl, beat together 2 egg yolks (keep the whites for later use), salt, pepper, and flour, and to this mixture add the milk by spoonfuls until you get a smooth batter. Fold the cheese and crushed garlic into the batter. Set the batter aside to rest for 30 minutes.

2 Peel the onions. Bring 2 quarts of salted water to a boil in a large pot, and blanch the onions for 2 minutes. Drop them in iced water, drain well, and pat dry with paper towels.

3 Mince the parsley and fold it into the batter. Beat the egg whites to a stiff peak and fold into the batter.

4 In a large frying pan (or a deep-fryer), heat enough oil to fry the onions. With metal tongs, dip each onion in the batter, drop into the hot oil, and fry until golden crispy on all sides. Gather up the onions with a slotted spoon and drain well on paper towels. Serve hot as soon as possible.

• *Lampasciuoli*—the bulbs of a variety of hyacinths that are considered an Apulian regional specialty. With their slightly bitter flavor, they are either prepared according to this recipe, or pickled, grilled, or baked in the oven.

Parozzo
Chocolate Cake (Abruzzi)

Serves 6

*3 ¹/₂ ounces or ²/₃ cup blanched
   almonds
7 ounces semisweet chocolate
   morsels or chocolate melting
   wafers
5 eggs
3 ounces or 5 tablespoons
   butter + 1 tablespoon for
   the cake pan
¹/₂ cup granulated sugar
³/₄ cup all-purpose flour
2 tablespoons cornstarch*

*Approximate preparation time:
   70 minutes (+ about 1 hour
   for cooling off);
   600 calories per serving.*

1 Grind the blanched almonds
(if you are in a hurry, you
may use pre-ground almonds).

2 Separate the eggs. In a
medium mixing bowl, cream
the egg yolks with the granulated sugar. In the meantime, in a
small saucepan, melt 3 ounces
or 5 tablespoons of butter.

3 Mix the flour and cornstarch. Spoon by spoon,
gradually stir the ground almonds and flour mixture into
the egg-sugar cream. Remove
the butter from the heat, let it
cool off, then mix it into the
cake batter.

4 Preheat the oven to 400°F.
Brush a springform pan
(about 8 inches in diameter)
with 1 tablespoon of melted
butter.

5 Beat the egg whites to a
stiff peak and carefully and
evenly fold into the cake batter.
Pour the batter into the prepared springform pan and
spread evenly. Bake the cake in
the preheated oven for 25 minutes, then cover the cake surface with aluminum foil and
bake the cake for 10 more minutes. Remove from the oven
and turn the cake over on a
rack to cool (about 45 minutes).

6 Melt the chocolate and cover the cake with it evenly.
For decoration, trace ridges on
the chocolate covered cake
with a fork. Let the melted
chocolate dry entirely. Cut the
cake into portions and serve.

• *Pane rozzo* is actually the
term used to describe a simple
rough farmers' bread. This
chocolate cake, *parozzo*, originally shaped like a loaf of farmers' bread, has the shape of the
farmers' bread, but nothing
else in common, especially the
flavor. Maybe it is the nonsensi-
cal connection with the Italian
culinary lingo that makes this
cake so attractive; it expresses
with loving humor what is being experienced both directly
and figuratively.

Torrone
Almond-honey Nougat (Abruzzi)

Serves 10 to 12

9 ounces or 2 cups blanched
   almonds
9 ounces or 1 2/3 cups
   hazelnuts
5 ounces or about 17 to 18
   dried mission figs
2/3 cup honey
7 ounces semisweet chocolate
7 tablespoons granulated sugar
3 egg whites
8 square sheets of rice paper
   (about 4 to 5 inches x about
   8 inches)

<u>Approximate preparation time:</u>
  1 3/4 hours
  (+ 12 hours cooling);
  530 calories per serving.

1 In a heat-resistant bowl in a water bath, bring the honey to a simmer, stirring frequently. The test that will determine the right consistency of the honey (after about 1 hour): Drop a bit of hot honey into a glass filled with cold water—if a soft or a semifirm, pliable, small ball is formed, the honey is ready to be used.

2 Preheat the oven to 425°F. Briefly roast the hazelnuts on a rimmed baking sheet. Rub off the skins of the nuts. Coarsely chop the blanched almonds and the hazelnuts, and dice the dried figs.

3 Break the semisweet chocolate into small pieces. In a saucepan, combine and, while stirring constantly, heat the 5 tablespoons sugar and 5 tablespoons of water until the sugar has dissolved. Add the pieces of chocolate and melt them in the sugar water. Stir frequently.

4 In a second saucepan, melt the remaining sugar with 3 tablespoons of water until you get a thick syrup. Beat the egg whites to stiff peaks.

5 As soon as the honey has reached the right consistency (see step 1), reduce the temperature of the water bath, and fold the egg white mixture into the honey.

6 Gradually fold the melted chocolate, sugar syrup, chopped nuts, and diced figs into the warm honey.

7 Prepare a (marble) working surface lined with half of the sheets of rice paper. Pour the nougat mixture 1 to 1 1/2 inches thick onto the rice paper and cover with the remaining rice paper. Allow to cool thoroughly. When the nougat is cold, cut it in small squares.

• During the cooling process, cover the nougat with a dishcloth and something to prevent the surface and the rice paper that top the nougat from bending or curving upward.

• Variation: Instead of distributing the *torrone* evenly on the rice paper, spoon the nougat out in small portions into small *petit four*-size paper cups.

• In Sicily, *torrone* is prepared with the addition of roasted sesame seeds.

233

Fish—The Daily Luxury

When we were in school, we learned that Italy is shaped like a boot. More precisely, it is a water boot surrounded as it is by the Mediterranean Sea. Therefore it comes as rather a surprise when we learn—according to statistics, that Italians don't eat as much fish as we would assume considering their coastal location; in fact, they eat only about as much as we do. However, there is a great difference between the coastal and the interior regions, with the agriculture-oriented wealthier North more interested in meat than the South, where fish remains a daily staple that is taken for granted.

Fishing methods here have hardly changed since the old days; in essence, fishing is done with fishing lines or rods and nets. With lines and rods, hooks are patiently baited with a piece of fish or bread, according to the type of fish that is sought after, and cast out. A hobby fisherman uses the rod and a professional fisherman ties numerous strings on long lines that he leaves floating in the sea. This method, of course, does not result in a great yield but, rather, a catch of great quality, because the fish are not squeezed together and damaged. Because of this intense labor and small output, fish market prices are consequently very high.

Fish that are caught with nets are less expensive. An especially popular method is to use a circular enclosing net that is cast by boats positioned in a circle, and that shows very clearly where the fish are, since the borders of the net are held above the water surface. The skill here is to pull the net in such way that it can enclose as many living fish as possible. After this, the net is pulled together with a special rope to prevent the fish from escaping from underneath the net. The upper part of the net with the fish is pulled into the boat, allowing the fish to be manually picked, one by one. Fish that try to escape remain entangled in the nets' meshes, which makes it possible for fishermen to remove them by hand. Only fish larger than a certain size remain in the net, while the smaller fish can slide through, thereby preserving the next generation of fish. For some species, such as sardines, the attraction for sources of light is also used to benefit the catch—sardines are attracted by bright lights, powered by gas, that attract the fish to the boat and make them easier to catch.

Although fishing in the Mediterranean Sea is hard work and is not blessed with a high return, fish here remains among the most valued and expensive foods. Immediately after the catch, fish are selected and prepared for market. Packed in ice, they quickly move on to the fish market.

For all coastal inhabitants, passing by the fish market is part of the daily morning shopping routine, and the vividly colored, friendly, and loud environment should not be missed by the selective tourist. As to concerns about the "stench of fish," there is truly no basis to it, since fresh fish smells only of the ocean, and not of something that should make us hold our noses.

For regional cuisines, not only are saltwater fish important but so are freshwater fish from rivers and lakes, especial-

Top: The seafood selection is vast and multicolored. In the Mediterranean Sea there over 20 varieties of bass, as well as scampi, *a name that refers to crustaceans that we call either prawns or shrimps.*

Above: Although coastal demand and consumption of fish is high, fewer and fewer fishermen drive out to the water to fish with small boats.

ly in Northern Italy and throughout the alpine regions.

Amazingly enough, Italian cuisine is also full of recipes that call for dried cod (called *baccalà* introduced by Normans throughout the Mediterranean. In the old days, this was the only way to bring saltwater fish to the menus of inhabitants of the interior regions. Today, these dishes have more of a traditional value, especially on Friday and during Lenten meals.

Unless flown in directly for special purposes, few fresh Meditearranean fish typical of Italian cuisine reach our average supermarket or fish market. There are, however, plenty of American fish from the Atlantic or the Pacific Ocean that can replace Mediterranean fish without too much loss of that real Italian flavor, and many frozen varieties, such as squids, cuttlefish, smelts, flounder, and tuna.

Above, top: Onboard a cutter, a fisherman mends his nets. The fish are caught in the nets, and they can rip the thin threads. The large drum on the left side is used for pulling up the heavy nets.

Above: It takes a special skill to mend the torn nets. The nets are expensive and are a big investment for the fisherman.

Above: To fish with a line is labor-intensive. During the afternoon hours, the nylon lines are untangled and the hooks are baited. For easy access, they are stuck into the foam rubber rim of a basket.

In general, Italians cook their fish simply and naturally. No heavy sauces are used, only simple cooking methods such as grilling, broiling, baking, or stewing. Even the fish soups follow this basic principle. Usually, various pieces of fish are simmered in a tomato-based broth with garlic and herbs. Fine varieties of fish are used, and the side dishes, often soups, are prepared with a base of bread; after all, this was the daily food of fishermen, since the most valued fish was sold. Small fish and seafood are fried in oil and served with only lemon on the side.

Pure, refined luxury—today, as 2000 years ago in ancient Rome—are the oysters, farmed even in those days in manmade oyster beds. Simple folks had numerous shellfish at their disposal, available in abundance throughout the whole coastal area. As important as mussels are clams (called *vongole* in Italian, the famous ingredient for *spaghetti alle vongole*). Small tellins, triangle-shaped edible wedge clams that are found in colonies under banks of sand, are enjoyed raw. Unusual in shape, like short wooden sticks, are the razor clams, especially delicious when sautéed with garlic.

Not hard to find on our market are the cuttlefish with their elongated bodies, perfect for stuffings, and squid (sepia) with their short cigar-shaped bodies that emit ink to distract pursuers. They are used in many chowders as well as prepared grilled or stewed. Culinary favorites also include the prickly sea urchins, which are cut open with scissors and spooned out raw. In many restaurants of coastal cities in Sicily, swordfish, whose firm and mild meat is reminiscent of veal, is offered in many variations.

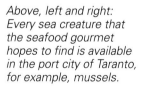

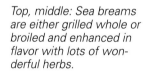

Above, left and right: Every sea creature that the seafood gourmet hopes to find is available in the port city of Taranto, for example, mussels.

Above, middle: All kinds of shellfish. The small triangle-shaped tellins are usually consumed raw.

Above: Various fish for chowders are prepared here.

Top, middle: Sea breams are either grilled whole or broiled and enhanced in flavor with lots of wonderful herbs.

Above, middle: The larger mullets with their firm and flavorful flesh are favorites. Sardines and anchovies (in the boxes) are usually prepared right away.

Right: Scampi (prawns) belong to the lobster family and have claws. On our market, they are also sold under the name of saltwater crawfish, Dublin Bay prawns, langoustine, or Norway lobster.

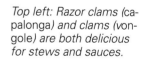

Top left: Razor clams (ca-
palonga) and clams (von-
gole) are both delicious
for stews and sauces.

Middle, left: Embedded
here in algae are the in-
gredients for a fish-chow-
der.

Left: As a special cus-
tomer service, fish are
cleaned immediately after
purchase.

Above, top: The fish mar-
ket in Naples.

Above: Dried cod, called
baccalà, *is also popular
throughout the coastal
regions.*

Campagna and Basilicata

Volcanoes and Beaches:
Like a god of ancient times: Vesuvius.

The Regions and Their Products

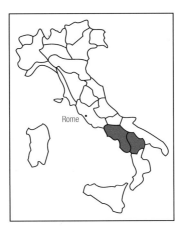

To many, Campagna is Naples and the country-side around it, or Mount Vesuvius, a volcano that is like a god of ancient times, violent

Above, top: The soil of the plain surrounding Mount Vesuvius is very fertile because of volcanic ash.

Above: The port of Naples lives off fishing and transporting people to and from the islands of Ischia and Capri.

and unpredictable. Ischia and Capri, perennial favorite vacation spots in the Mediterranean, also belong to the region of Campagna. Here, the mild climate is unmistakably felt, and it makes lemon trees and fields of flowers grow.

Although poor and fairly isolated, Basilicata, called Lucania, touches the sea in two areas and is open to tourism: on its western tip that stretches forth from the Campagna region, and on the eastern side as a piece of the boot that is the long and sandy coast on the Ionian Sea. The back country is rough and mystic; here, too, there is a volcano: Mount Vulture.

Campagna's cuisine is rather simple; it is made from ingredients that are basic but original and spicy. There have been disagreements on whether Sicily or Campagna was the first region to create pasta: so far, Sicily still seems to be ahead. However, the choice and varieties of pastas that are

Above, right: Vegetables and fruit play the most important role in Campagna's way of cooking; meat seems relegated to use as a side dish. In small orchards located around Vesuvius, tomatoes, artichokes, onions, and zucchini are frequently planted.

Right: Naples has not been touched by consumerism as much as other cities in Italy. Here, you can still find the small delis with different varieties of hams and cheeses that can satisfy anyone's palate.

popular in Campagna seem to indicate that the product found a fruitful home in this region. Spaghetti, macaroni, penne, rigatoni, and vermicelli are in tune with the Neapolitan temperament, which tends to be impatient and hectic and dislikes waiting too long before being served food. Except on Sunday. Then there are dishes that require a long preparation time, such as *fritto misto*, seafood dipped in batter and deep-fried, fish, and vegetables. Or a ragù that is left simmering for hours and hours.

Two ingredients above all mark Campagna's cuisine: cheese and vegetables. Cheese is eaten every day—mozzarella, pro-

volone, caciocavallo, and many other varieties are available in this region. Vegetables are lovingly grown in small orchards. Potatoes, peppers, artichokes, and fennel are cultivated, especially throughout the plain surrounding Mount Vesuvius. And, of course, tomatoes, since it was Naples that began the tomato canning industry that made the fruit popular throughout Northern Italy. Naples is also home to pizza, especially the classic Pizza Margherita, which was created in 1889 to honor Italy's queen and inspired by the colors of the national flag, with green basil, white mozzarella, and red tomatoes.

Basilicata also has its two culinary staples: the pig and the *peperoncini*. Many families throughout the countryside keep their own pigs especially for making sausages. These sausages are not only made for the family's own use, but are also sold to increase household income, since the farming industry's yield is not very high here. The local cuisine does not include many expensive ingredients; it produces dishes that are simple and naturally flavored. The use of peperoncini, as well as of spicy sausages, is common. As in Campagna, pasta is also important here, as are such cheeses as provolone, caciocavallo, and fresh varieties like ricotta.

Above: A farmer displays his freshly harvested onions with pride, since their flavor is especially remarkable due to the volcanic soil.

Left: Less fine cuts of meat are also favorites in Campagna. The tripery sells tripe, stomachs, heads of veal, and pigs' feet.

Above: The mild climate favors the growth of citrus fruits in abundance. Orange and lemon plantations are especially numerous on the peninsula of Sorrento.

People, Events, Sightseeing

ancient woods and streams that foam into the sea between the occasional fishing villages and tourist spots, and the old ruins of the ancient Greek city of Elea.

Although small, Basilicata's coast on the Tyrrhenian Sea offers rock formations with caves and bays in which luxury yachts often drop anchor. The most famous beach resort is Maratea, with its exclusive hotels, pensions, and villas. Here, too, there is layer after layer of history; over remainders of Lucanic cities lay the ruins of Greek building, which, in turn, became foundations for Medieval castles.

Campagna's cities and villages are the gigantic backstage for a play that changes its scenes daily. This should come as no surprise, since the area itself has had exposure to tourism for over 2000 years. After all, there was hardly an historic event in the Mediterranean area in which this region did not somehow take part. The coastal regions appear to be especially favorite holiday spots with their wide beaches or small bays, active and inactive volcanoes, fruit orchards and woodlands, hotels, villas, ports and ancient excavations, noble spa locations with thermal springs, and restless villages. And in the center, the Gulf of Naples with its bubbly, frightening, and at the same time fascinating metropolis, and its people famous for their astuteness. This character is most evident throughout the Forcella, Naples's smuggler center located near Via Duomo, where tourists can never be sure to take home what they had just seen being wrapped in paper before their own eyes. Often enough, the great buy turns out to be nothing but an old brick! Worth visiting in Naples is the Virgini district, with its multicolored open-air markets.

Located on the west side of Naples is Pozzuoli, where stopping on the quay of the port on Sunday morning for the fish market should not be missed. Ideal for those who love authentic mozzarella are the surroundings of Sorrento and Sant'Agata. A visit to the small town of Ravello, built on a rock with an amazing view, is worth a trip to the interior. Not far away is Vesuvius with its most recent intimidating volcanic crater, and Pompei, the largest and most impressive city of the ancient world, dug up from the ashes. Through the mist above the water is the island of Capri, a living picture of southern joy of living. You could still believe that you can hear the singing of sirens in the caves if you are fortunate enough to visit these places without being escorted by an army of tourists.

Throughout Campagna, the historic past and today's modern life are very tightly interconnected, with layers of cultures intertwined, as in Pompei, Paestum, and Palinuro. From Salerno on, the coast begins to gently slope and appear golden. Located there is the temple of Paestum, closed in by ancient walls.

Finally, toward the foot of the mountains of Cilento, there are

Naples is not a city that has cleaned up its act for the tourist; however, it is fascinating, with its old narrow streets, left and right, along Spaccanapoli, a road that dates from Greek Naples' times.

Above, top: Pompei is being dusted. Of course, visiting these gigantic ruins from ancient times is a "must" for the serious Campagna visitor.

Above: Naples is famous for its coffees—and for its coffeeshops. According to hearsay, the special flavor of the coffee is due to the water and to the unique way of preparing it in special espresso machines.

From Maratea the road leads to the interior, up on the high plateaus, where wild sage and thyme grow.

The capital of the Basilicata region is Potenza, located high above the Basento Valley, an important commercial center for agricultural products from the surrounding areas. The old city has a lovely farmer's market that is worth visiting.

The Ionian coast also has plenty of summer resorts. Ancient Achaeans landed here in the eighth century B.C. and built Metapontum with amazing constructions, of which fifteen Palatine Tables, columns of the temples of Hera and Apollo, are still found to this day. The interior also has its own remarkable places that are worthy of sightseeing. Especially renowned is Matera with its Sassi, countless stone apartments, and hundreds of churches dug into the rocky mountain. This cultural monument with its caves and narrow streets that served as a backdrop for Pasolini's famous Gospel according to Matthew movie is now being restored with enormous amounts of money. To the south, is the majestic range of mountains called Pollino, with its peaks covered with snow throughout the year. Overall, this is a region where there is still plenty to discover, except for the traffic of tourism.

The events: San Bartolomeo in Galdo (Campagna), on the day of the Immaculate Conception at the beginning of December, celebrates a sausage and polenta festival. Many typical regional specialties are prepared during this culinary event.

In Roccanova (Basilicata), in the middle of November, a fall festival in honor of Saint Rocco is held, during which wine, food, and folklore are at the center of the festival's attention.

Above, top: The Sassi, old cave apartments recently rediscovered by tourists, have more than once served as a background for movies.

Above: Naples' teenagers are developing a lifestyle of their own.

Above: In spite of the worldwide presence of bakers of Neapolitan pizza, the best is still the taste of the original baked in a wood oven.

Above: Another aspect of Naples. Throughout the surrounding districts, life is fun; there are many trees and a lighthearted joy of life.

Above: The quiet mood of old age makes us easily forget that people in this region work since childhood to provide income for the entire family.

The Wines

Campagna has always been a red wine region with a long-standing tradition. Since ancient times, *Falerno* wine was praised for its "full-bodiedness, strength, and its fieriness." Today, the wine lives on with the *Falerno*, dark red and almost sweet, originally from the area of Caserta located north of Naples. The leading grape here is the Primitivo mixed with other grape varieties. Aging turns it into a good, dry, slightly vanilla-perfumed wine that is a fine accompaniment for meat with dark gravies.

Naples' surroundings also account for remarkable white wines: the *Capri Bianco*, a light yellow, dry, and refreshing wine suitable for fish dishes, and the *Lacrimae Christi* from the vineyards along Mount Vesuvius. Several legends exist regarding the literal translation of its name, "tears of Christ." The origin is associated with the Jesuits, who owned vineyards in this area and who searched for a suitable-sounding name for the wine made from Aglianico grapes. Truly good Lacrimae Christi is rare; it is similar to the Capri Bianco and is best if consumed with fish. Both are also available as red wines recommended for roasted meats.

Three notable wines originate from Ischia: *Ischia Rosso, Ischia Bianco*, and *Ischia Bianco Superiore*, usually refreshing and best suited for early consumption. The red is made from Guarnaccia and Piedirosso grapes and is not only recommended for meats, but also for fish and seafood. The light, refreshing white wine, made from Forastera and Biancolella grapes, can be labeled Superiore if certain conditions are met and if its alcoholic content is at least 12 percent.
Throughout coastal Amalfi, valuable wines are also found, such as the *Ravello* as white, rosé, and red. The rosé, light red, is especially good with vegetable dishes and seafood for its well-balanced and refreshing bouquet.

From the province of Benevento is the *Solopaca*, white or red, of which the white is especially aromatic, dry, and velvety, and the ruby red with an intense bouquet, dry, and elegant. The *Taurasi*, among the great classic old red wines, is made from overripe Aglianico grapes and has a typical scent of violets. While young, it is ruby, and later it tends to have a dark brick-red color. Its almost bitter aroma mellows and softens in time with aging. It is a classic wine for venison.

A tradition throughout Campagna is preparing, on Saint John's Day in June, the starters for *Nocillo*, a liqueur made from green walnuts flavored with cinnamon, cloves, sugar, and alcohol, to which each family adds its own special ingredients. Before a tasting can occur, the liqueur must mature at least until the day of Saint Lawrence in August.

Basilicata is, above all, a region of sausages and pork meats. And only a few wines go truly perfectly with hams, bacons, and headcheese. The typical wines of this region are rather simple red wines that are rich in alcohol content; they go well with regional specialties, but are not very well known abroad.

Exceptions to this rule are those wines made throughout the areas of Mount Vulture's craters. Aglianico grapes are grown here to produce a full-bodied, garnet red wine, the *Aglianico del Vulture*, which has a delicate scent and has a high tannic content while still young. If its alcohol content is at least 12 percent, and if the wine has been aged for at least three years, it is legally allowed to be labeled *Riserva*. These wines are often compared with the *Barbera* wines, since they mellow out, lose some of the tannic content, and become almost velvety with age. Actually, these long-lasting wines should not be consumed before five years after being made. Then they are remarkable wines perfect for elegant roasts and dark braised meats and venison.

From the area of Matera, Irsina, and Tricarico is another wine made from Aglianico grapes, the *Aglianico dei Colli Lucani* or *di Matera*, very similar to the Vulture, but labeled as "table wine," according to the geographical area of origin.

Above, left: The ancient Romans knew that grapes grow well on Campagna's volcanic soil. However, many winemakers from throughout Naples' region don't seem to have the sense of quality-oriented wine production.

Left: A few winemakers, however, produce outstanding wine from classic varieties like the Aglianico grapes. The Taurasi made by the Mastroberardinos in Atripalda becomes smooth and velvety after several years of aging.

Regional Recipes

Pizza margherita

Pizza Margherita (with Mozzarella, Tomatoes, and Basil) (Campagna)

Serves 2

<u>For the dough:</u>
1/4 fresh compressed cake of
   yeast or 1 1/4-ounce envelope active dry yeast
1 1/2 cups all-purpose flour +
   flour to roll out
1 pinch granulated sugar
1/4 teaspoon salt

<u>For the topping:</u>
1/2 bunch fresh basil
5 ounces or 2 small balls mozzarella cheese
2 tablespoons freshly grated
   romano or Parmesan cheese
1 14 1/2-ounce can or about 8
   peeled plum tomatoes
4 tablespoons olive oil
Salt and freshly ground pepper

<u>Approximate preparation time:</u>
   *45 minutes
   (+ 1 1/2 hours rising time);
   790 calories per serving.*

This simple, almost Spartan
bread wheel of the past, which
was topped only with olive oil,
herbs, and cheese, has long
since become a symbol of Italian
cuisine; undoubtedly, no other
specialty has been more acclaimed. Many rather peculiar
variations circulate worldwide, all
of which carry the name of pizza,
but they are, unfortunately, more
to the disgrace than to the glory
of the pizza's inventor.

• Throughout Naples, fortunately,
everyone knows even today the
secret to a good pizza: The
dough should be thoroughly
kneaded and allowed to raise
very slowly, and baked preferably
in a wood oven at very high temperature. The finished pizza
should be brought to the table
right away and served immediately.

• The topping for the pizza should
be selected from good quality ingredients put together with good
sense, similar to the method
used in 1889 by the inventor-bak-
er who pulled out of the oven the
version that is still a favorite today.

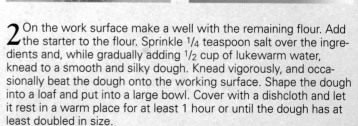

1 For the pizza dough: In a
small bowl mix the yeast
with 1 pinch of sugar and 2 tablespoons of lukewarm water.
Add 2 tablespoons of the all-
purpose flour and allow the
starter to rise in a warm place
for 30 minutes.

2 On the work surface make a well with the remaining flour. Add
the starter to the flour. Sprinkle 1/4 teaspoon salt over the ingredients and, while gradually adding 1/2 cup of lukewarm water,
knead to a smooth and silky dough. Knead vigorously, and occasionally beat the dough onto the working surface. Shape the dough
into a loaf and put into a large bowl. Cover with a dishcloth and let
it rest in a warm place for at least 1 hour or until the dough has at
least doubled in size.

3 Preheat the oven to 425°F. Brush a pizza pan with 1 tablespoon of olive oil. Vigorously knead the dough once more. Roll out the dough, place it in the pizza pan, and, by hand, finish stretching by pressing it into the pan, leaving it thicker around the rim.

4 Drain the canned tomatoes and set the juice aside. Slice the tomatoes, distribute them evenly on top of the pizza, and crush them lightly with a fork. Leave a 1-inch-wide rim around the walls of the pan. Thinly slice the mozzarella and layer the slices over the tomatoes. Season with salt and freshly ground pepper.

5 Place the pizza on the lowest rack in the preheated oven and bake for 15 minutes. Remove the pizza and sprinkle it with the grated cheese and fresh basil. Drizzle the basil with oil. Return the pizza to the middle rack of the hot oven, bake for 10 more minutes, and serve hot.

Calzone
Stuffed Pizza (Campagna)

Serves 2 to 4

<u>For the dough:</u>
1/4 fresh compressed cake of
  yeast or 1 1/4-ounce envelope active dry yeast
1 1/2 cups all-purpose flour +
  flour to roll out
2 tablespoons olive oil
1 egg yolk to brush
1 pinch granulated sugar
1/4 teaspoon salt

<u>For the stuffing:</u>
4 ounces or 4 slices sliced
  prosciutto ham (or Italian
  salami)
5 ounces or 2 small balls
  mozzarella cheese
3/4 cup ricotta cheese
2 tablespoons freshly grated
  Parmesan cheese
1 sprig fresh oregano (or 1
  teaspoon dried)
2 eggs
5 tablespoons olive oil
Salt and freshly ground pepper

<u>Approximate preparation time:</u>
  50 minutes
  (+ 1 1/2 hours raising time);
  690 calories per serving.

These too belong to the classics of pizza history, stuffed pockets of pizza that bake on the baking sheet until they are crispy or that are fried as mini pizza pockets.

In the stuffing for the calzone, various cheeses, prosciutto, salami, herbs, and vegetables can be used. In some regions (Apulia or Basilicata), meatless and spicy sauces are preferred, such as combining lots of onions with tomatoes, garlic, green capers, and anchovies.

1 For the dough: In a small mixing bowl, combine the yeast with 1 pinch of sugar, 2 tablespoons of lukewarm water and 2 tablespoons all-purpose flour. Cover, and set aside for about 30 minutes. On a work surface, make a well with the remaining flour. Add the starter, 2 tablespoons of olive oil, and 1/4 teaspoon of salt to the flour. Gradually adding 1/2 cup of lukewarm water to the flour, knead until you get a smooth and silky dough. Knead vigorously, shape the dough into a loaf, and set aside, covered, in a warm place for at least 1 hour, or until the volume has at least doubled in size.

2 In the meantime, prepare the stuffing: Cut the ham or salami into thin strips and dice the mozzarella. Press the ricotta through a fine strainer into a medium bowl. Cream together with the eggs. Fold the ham strips, the diced mozzarella, and grated Parmesan cheese into the mixture. Season with salt, pepper, and oregano.

3 Preheat the oven to 425°F and brush a large baking sheet with 1 tablespoon of oil. On the floured work surface, knead the risen dough once more, cut it in half, and roll out both pieces to make large wheels of dough. Brush each wheel of dough with 1 tablespoon of oil.

4 Evenly top each wheel with some stuffing, leaving a large rim of dough around the border. Fold each wheel in half and firmly pinch the borders together. Brush each pizza pocket with 1 tablespoon of oil and egg yolk and place them on the greased baking sheet. Bake in the oven for 20 minutes.

5 Variation: Before baking, brush each calzone with well-seasoned tomato puree, with freshly grated romano or Parmesan cheese, and oregano. Always serve the calzone very hot.

Pizzette alla napoletana
Fried Mini Pizzas, Naples Style (Campagna)

Mozzarella in carrozza
Fried Mozzarella "Couched" in Bread (Campagna)

Serves 4

For the dough:
1/4 fresh compressed cake of
  yeast or 1 1/4-ounce envelope active dry yeast
1 1/2 cups all-purpose flour +
  flour to roll out
2 tablespoons olive oil +
  enough oil to fry
1 pinch granulated sugar
1/4 teaspoon salt

For the sauce:
1 bunch fresh basil
1 tablespoon fresh oregano
  leaves, minced (or 1 teaspoon dried)
28 ounce can peeled tomatoes
3 cloves garlic, minced
2 tablespoons olive oil
Salt and freshly ground pepper

Approximate preparation time:
  45 minutes;
  480 calories per serving.

1 Prepare the dough according
   to the calzone recipe on
page 248.

2 Sauce: Drain the tomatoes
   (keep the juice) and chop. In
a saucepan, heat the oil and
sauté the garlic. Add the
oregano and tomatoes, and
season with salt and pepper.
Add the tomato juice and simmer.

3 Punch down and knead the
   risen dough, then roll it out
1/4 inch thick. Cut out rounds of
about 4 1/2 inches.

4 Heat oil to fry, and fry the
   mini pizzas until golden
brown. Keep warm and drain,
each fried wheel of dough on
paper towels until all are fried.

5 Cut half of the basil leaves
   into thin strips, stir these into the sauce, and season.
Serve the sauce with the
pizzette, and garnish with basil
leaves.

Serves 4

5 ounces or 2 small balls
  mozzarella
8 slices one-day-old white
  bread, suitable for toasting
1 tablespoon fresh oregano (or
  1/2 teaspoon dried)
2 eggs
2 tablespoons flour
2 tablespoons milk
Salt and freshly ground pepper
Enough oil to fry

Approximate preparation time:
  25 minutes;
  600 calories per serving.

1 Cut the mozzarella into thin
   slices and cut off the crust
of the bread. On each slice of
bread, place 2 slices of mozzarella, leaving some space
around each bread slice. Season with salt, pepper, and
oregano. Sandwich together all
bread-mozzarella slices, dip the
edges of the bread briefly into
iced water, and pinch them
firmly together.

2 Beat the eggs with the milk,
   salt, and pepper. Lightly dust
each sandwich with flour and
place them on a large shallow
dish. Pour the milk-egg mixture
over the sandwiches and set
aside until the bread has absorbed all liquid. Turn the bread
sandwiches over once.

3 Heat enough oil in a large
   frying pan to fry the sandwiches. Fry them until golden
and crispy on both sides. Place
them on paper towels to allow
any excess fat to drain, and
serve immediately.

• A similar specialty, called
Pandorato, is also included in
Roman cooking (see recipe
on page 178).

Crostini alla napoletana

Toasted Bread Slices, Naples Style (Campagna)

Serves 4

2 small, fresh, ripe tomatoes
11 ounces mozzarella
1 tablespoon fresh oregano
   leaves (or 1 teaspoon dried)
6 to 8 canned anchovy fillets,
   drained
4 slices white toast
2 ounces or 3 tablespoons
   butter
2 tablespoons oil for the baking
   sheet
Salt and freshly ground pepper

Approximate preparation time:
   20 minutes;
   480 calories per serving.

1 Rinse the tomatoes and cut them first in slices and then in strips, removing the stem portion. Cut the mozzarella into 8 slices. Rinse the anchovies, pat dry with paper towels, and cut each in half.

2 Preheat the oven to 350°F and brush a baking sheet with 2 tablespoons of oil. Cut the slices of bread into halves and spread them evenly with butter.

3 Line each bread slice with 1 slice of mozzarella, a few strips of tomato, and 1 or 2 pieces of anchovy. Sprinkle each slice with oregano and pepper, and if necessary, with salt (the amount of salt will depend on the saltiness of the anchovies), and place them on the baking sheet. Bake in the preheated oven for 10 minutes and serve hot.

• These small slices make a wonderful appetizer; you may serve these with a dry Martini on ice, with a Campari soda, or with an Aperol with lemon.

Caprese

Mozzarella and Fresh Tomatoes, Capri Style (Campagna)

Serves 4

4 medium large, fresh, ripe
   tomatoes
1 bunch fresh basil
11 ounces or about 4 small
   balls mozzarella
8 tablespoons olive oil
Salt and freshly ground pepper

Approximate preparation time:
   15 minutes;
   380 calories per serving.

1 Rinse the tomatoes and cut them into slices, removing the stem portions. Slice the mozzarella balls.

2 Prepare 4 large plates and place the slices of mozzarella and tomatoes to fit the plate, alternating the slices as if you were to cover the center of the plate with a roof of shingles. Season with salt and freshly ground coarse pepper. Drizzle with the olive oil. Serve garnished with fresh basil leaves.

• Together they are unsurpassable, tomatoes and mozzarella, the two ball-shaped prominent ingredients of Campagna's cuisine. As an ancient topping for pizza, they are old, established culinary classics; as appetizers, they have recently sparked the interest of more than one international chef. And, as with many secular pleasures, heaven and hell are near each other. It is easy to describe an ingredient, but it is not as easy to fulfill the ingredient's promise. The tomato will need to taste like a tomato, the mozzarella will have to carry a label with a buffalo, the basil will need to have the scent of freshness, and the olive oil will have to be one of the finest varieties.

Maccheroni alla napoletana

Macaroni with Meat Gravy, Naples Style (Campagna)

Serves 6 to 8

About 2 pounds beef for
    stewing
2 ounces or 4 tablespoons
    vegetable oil
1 bunch fresh basil
1 carrot
2 stalks celery
11 ounces caciocavallo or
    mozzarella cheese
2 onions
2 cloves garlic, minced
2 cups dry white wine
1 pound macaroni or rigatoni
4 tablespoons tomato paste
3 tablespoons olive oil
2 tablespoons butter
Salt and freshly ground pepper

<u>Approximate preparation time:</u>
    3 ³/₄ hours;
    700 calories per serving.

This is a variation of a classic
recipe in which the meat is
stewed for several hours in order to flavor the gravy for the
noodles.

The meat can be served later,
as a warm second course, or
you can allow the flaky meat to
cool off, slicing it later, and
preparing it as a rich and flavorful salad with green capers,
onions, peppers, and an-
chovies.

Another authentic but less
time-consuming Neapolitan
method: Instead of cooking the
meat, prepare a spicy tomato
sauce. Alternate layers of macaroni with thin slices of cheese
(caciocavallo, mozzarella, or
scamorza) and layers of tomato
sauce, and bake until the top is
golden and crispy.

1 Tie the piece of beef with a
kitchen string to make a suitable shape. In a Dutch oven,
heat the vegetable oil, add the
meat, and brown it evenly on all
sides.

2 Thinly slice the carrot, celery, and onions. Add these
vegetables to the meat with
the garlic, and sauté, stirring
constantly. Season the vegetables and meat with salt and
pepper to taste.

3 Gradually, in small splashes,
moisten the meat with the
white wine; allow the liquid to
evaporate, add more liquid, let
it evaporate, and so on. Stir in
the tomato paste and add about
2 cups of water (the meat
should be barely covered).

4 Partially cover and simmer on low heat for at least 3 hours, allowing the meat gravy to boil only periodically. Toward the end
of the meat cooking time, bring 3 quarts of salted water to a boil in
a large pot. Add the macaroni or rigatoni and cook until al dente or
until still firm to the bite (about 5 minutes). Brush a large baking
dish with 1 tablespoon of oil and preheat the oven to 400°F.

5 Slice the caciocavallo or mozzarella cheese. Prepare the basil leaves, shredding the larger ones. Drain the noodles and mix with 2 tablespoons of oil. Line the baking dish with a layer of noodles.

6 Remove the meat from the Dutch oven and set aside in a warm place to be served later as a second course, if so desired. Bring the gravy once more to a rapid boil and season if necessary; it should be dark, velvety, and strong in flavor. Before using it, you can mash the vegetables in the gravy with a fork.

7 Generously cover the noodles with the gravy and top with slices of cheese and basil. Top this layer with another layer of noodles, gravy, cheese, and basil until no more ingredients remain. Set a few leaves of basil aside.

8 Finish with a layer of gravy and evenly distribute 2 tablespoons of butter. Bake the noodles in the preheated oven for 10 minutes, garnish with fresh basil, and serve very hot.

253

Fusilli alla napoletana
Corkscrew Pasta with Tomato Sauce (Campagna)

Serves 4 to 6

4 ounces or 4 slices bacon
3 large or 8 small fresh, ripe
  plum tomatoes (you may substitute one 14 $1/2$-ounce can
  of peeled, diced tomatoes)
1 stalk celery, minced
1 carrot, minced
About $1/2$ cup ricotta cheese
$2/3$ cup freshly grated romano
  or Parmesan cheese
1 sprig fresh oregano (or 1
  teaspoon dried)
1 onion, minced
1 clove garlic, minced
$1/2$ cup dry white wine
11 ounces fusilli (corkscrew-
  shaped pasta)
Salt and freshly ground pepper

Approximate preparation time:
  1 hour;
  430 calories per serving.

1 Dice the bacon. Combine
the celery, carrot, onion, and
garlic in a large pot and gradually sauté on low heat until
glossy and limp.

2 Moisten with the white
wine. Blanch, peel, seed,
and chop the tomatoes. Add to
the ingredients in the large pot.
Season with salt and pepper
and simmer until you get a
smooth sauce.

3 In the meantime, bring 3
quarts of salted water to a
boil in a large pot. Add the fusilli
and cook for 8 to 10 minutes or
until still firm to the bite. Crumble the ricotta cheese.

4 Drain the cooked fusilli and
fold immediately into the
sauce with a few spoonfuls of
the noodle water, if necessary.
Sprinkle with 1 tablespoon of
grated romano cheese, crumbled ricotta, and oregano
leaves. Season again with salt
and pepper. Serve the remaining romano cheese on the side.

Spaghetti alle vongole
Spaghetti with Clam Sauce (Campagna)

Serves 4 to 6

2 pounds small clams in their
  shells (14 ounces canned
  clams)
2 bunches fresh Italian parsley,
  minced
1 small onion, minced
3 cloves garlic, minced
1 cup dry white wine
About 1 pound spaghetti
6 tablespoons olive oil
2 tablespoons softened butter
$1/2$ lemon (about 2 tablespoons
  of juice)
8 peppercorns
Salt and freshly ground pepper

Approximate preparation time:
  70 minutes;
  430 calories per serving.

1 Thoroughly clean and brush
the fresh clams under running water; discard all clams
that remain open when tapped
with a finger. Put the closed
clams into a large pot, moisten
with the white wine, and bring
to a boil.

2 Cook for 5 minutes or until
the shells have opened. Discard those clams that have not
opened and set the others
aside, allowing them to cool.
Pour the clam juice through a
fine strainer and set aside for
later use (if you use canned
clams, keep the juice).

3 Heat 4 tablespoons of olive
oil in a large saucepan, add
one bunch of minced parsley,
and the minced onion and garlic, and sauté stirring constantly. Add the clam juice and allow
it to reduce by a half (if you use
canned clams, mix the juice
with $1/2$ cup wine).

4 Bring 4 quarts of salted water to a boil in a large pot.
Add the spaghetti and cook until al dente (8 to 10 minutes).

5 Pick out the clean meat
from the shells and add it to
the sauce, allowing the meat to
heat without cooking! Stir in

Spaghetti alla puttanesca
Spaghetti with Tomato, Olives, Anchovies, and Green Caper Sauce (Campagna)

the butter, lemon juice, salt, and pepper. Mince the remaining parsley. Crush the 8 peppercorns in a mortar with a pestle.

6 Drain the spaghetti and fold in 2 tablespoons of olive oil and the clam sauce. Distribute on preheated plates, sprinkle with parsley and pepper, and serve.

• Visually impressive (and less work): Use the clams with the shells.

• An old classic Neapolitan specialty that is now commonly prepared throughout many Italian regions.

Serves 4 to 6

About 5 medium large or 8 fresh, ripe plum tomatoes (or one 14 1/2 ounce can, peeled, diced)
1/2 bunch fresh Italian parsley
3 1/2 ounces or 40 small pitted black olives, minced
3 tablespoons green capers
3 cloves garlic, minced
3 canned anchovy fillets, drained
1 hot red chili pepper
2 tablespoons tomato paste
1 pound spaghetti
6 tablespoons olive oil
Salt and freshly ground pepper

Approximate preparation time:
    40 minutes;
    410 calories per serving.

1 In a large pot, blanch the tomatoes in boiling water, drop them into iced water, and peel them. Seed and chop them.

2 Rinse the anchovies, pat dry, mince, and reduce to a paste with a fork. Open and seed the hot red pepper, and slice it into thin strips (be careful to thoroughly wash your hands afterward!).

3 Heat the olive oil in a large saucepan. Sauté the garlic and the hot chili pepper, stirring constantly. Stir in the tomatoes, tomato paste, and anchovy paste. Simmer for 15 minutes in the uncovered saucepan.

4 Bring to a boil 4 quarts of salted water in a large pot. Cook 1 pound of spaghetti until al dente.

5 Stir the capers and olives into the sauce and season with salt and pepper. Drain the spaghetti and fold immediately into the sauce. Sprinkle with the parsley. You can serve

freshly grated Parmesan cheese with this dish.

• Use salt sparingly, since anchovies, capers, olives, and tomato paste are already salted.

255

Fritto misto di mare
Mixed Fried Fish and Seafood (Campagna)

Serves 4

1 pound small fresh squid (or
   frozen and thawed)
4 small red mullets (you may
   substitute any suitably sized
   mullet-type fish or orange
   roughy)
About 1 pound fresh sardines
   or smelts (or frozen and
   thawed)
9 ounces large shrimp
2 to 3 lemons
2 cloves garlic
Enough flour to dust
Enough olive oil to fry
Salt

<u>Approximate preparation time:</u>
   1 ¹/₂ hours;
   720 calories per serving.

Fried bite-size delicacies, these
are cherished by Italians. There
is hardly anything that has not
yet been fried at some point in
this superlative cuisine, from
tender pieces of calf's meat to
innards, brain, blanched vegetables, rice balls, or birds and
poultry.

Very important in the case of
fish: Use first-quality, super-
fresh ingredients, prepare them
accurately, and serve them very
hot!

1 Thoroughly clean and rinse
the squid; peel off the membranes, remove the cuttlebone,
tentacles, and innards from the
body, and cut off the heads.
Slice the tentacles and discard
the innards and the heads. For
larger squids, cut the mantle
into strips.

2 Scale the red mullets and
cut off the heads and fins.
Rinse the fish under running
water and pat dry with paper
towels. Sprinkle with salt.

3 Clean and scale the sardines
or smelts. Cut off all fins except the tail (if you use very
small sardines or smelts, leave
the heads on; you can eat
those too). Thoroughly rinse all
the fish and pat dry with paper
towels. Sprinkle with salt.

4 Prepare the shrimp by leaving on the tails and the shell,
and by removing the heads and
the dark intestinal vein (or, completely, peel the shrimp out of
their shells, including the tails
and heads) and lightly dust with
flour before frying. Preheat the
oven to 300°F.

5 Heat enough olive oil in a
large frying pan to fry the
fish and drop the peeled garlic
cloves into the hot oil. For the
temperature test: Dip a wood-
en spoon in the oil; as soon as
small bubbles rise to the surface, you may begin frying the
fish. Before frying, remove the
garlic from the oil.

6 Dust the squid very lightly
with flour and gradually drop
into the hot oil and fry until
golden and crispy. Keep warm
on paper towels to allow the
excess fat to drain.

7 Also lightly dust the red mullets (or any suitably sized mullet-type fish or orange roughy), gradually fry them in portions until crispy (mullets 3 to 4 minutes, fresh sardines or smelts 2 minutes). With a slotted spoon, remove the fried fish, place on paper towels, and keep warm with the squid. Fry the shrimp in their shells in the hot oil until they are crispy (or fry the shelled shrimps lightly dusted with flour, see step 4). Place them on paper towels to allow the excess fat to drain.

8 Prepare a large serving platter lined with a clean white napkin. Place all fried fish and seafood decoratively on the napkin. Sprinkle with salt. Cut lemons into wedges, add these to the platter, and serve immediately.

Polpi alla napoletana
Braised Squid with Tomatoes, Naples Style (Campagna)

Serves 4

1 ³/₄ pounds small squids
(either fresh or frozen and
thawed)
About 1 pound or 8 fresh, ripe
plum tomatoes
1 bunch fresh Italian parsley,
minced
¹/₂ lemon (about 2 tablespoons
of juice)
2 ounces or 20 small, green,
pitted olives, minced
¹/₂ cup white wine
2 onions, minced
4 cloves garlic, minced
5 tablespoons olive oil
Salt and freshly ground pepper

<u>Approximate preparation time:</u>
1 ¹/₂ hours;
310 calories per serving.

1 Thoroughly clean and rinse
the fresh squid and peel off
the membranes. Remove the
cuttlebone, innards, and tentacles from the body. Cut off the
heads of the squid (use the tentacles and the mantles; discard
everything else). Turn the mantle inside out, rinse thoroughly,
and slice. Pat everything dry
with paper towels. If using
frozen squid, thaw it ahead of
time, cut it up, rinse, and pat
dry with paper towels.

2 Blanch the tomatoes in boiling water in a large pot,
peel, and cut in half. Remove
the seeds with a spoon. Chop
the tomatoes.

3 Heat the tablespoons of
olive oil in a large saucepan.
Add the squid and stir-fry until
golden brown. Season with salt
and pepper. Stir in the onions
and sauté until glossy. Drizzle
with the lemon juice.

4 Stir in the minced garlic and
the tomatoes. Bring to a rapid boil and moisten with the
white wine. Cover and simmer
on low heat for 45 minutes.

5 As soon as the squid is
done and tender (test with a
toothpick), uncover the
saucepan, and bring the sauce
to a rapid boil, allowing it to reduce. Add the minced olives
and parsley, and season with
salt and pepper.

• Named after Naples' district
of Santa Lucia, this dish is also
called Polpi alla luciana if the
squid is allowed to cook together with a spicy chili pepper. Instead of squid, octopus, with
its strong tentacles, is also often used; in this case, allow the
octopus to cook longer than either squid or cuttlefish, both of
which are less tough. Of
course, do not forget to test for
doneness here!

Sgombri alla marinara
Herbed Mackerels, Mariner's Style (Basilicata)

Serves 4

4 fresh mackerels (about 11
  ounces each) (you may substitute whitefish)
1 bunch fresh mint, minced
1 bunch fresh Italian parsley
Mixed herbs to garnish
1 lemon (3 to 4 tablespoons of
  juice)
2 bay leaves
2 garlic cloves, minced
$1/2$ cup white wine vinegar
4 tablespoons olive oil
$1/2$ teaspoon black peppercorns
Salt and freshly ground pepper

Approximate preparation time:
  1 hour (+ about 24 hours for
  marinating);
  480 calories per serving.

1 Preheat the oven to 400°F.
Scale, clean, and thoroughly
rinse the mackerels. Put in a
large baking dish, season with
salt, and top with the bay leaves
and peppercorns. Drizzle with the
lemon juice and enough water to
barely cover the mackerels.

2 Bake in the preheated oven
for 10 to 15 minutes. Re-
move the fish from the pan
juices and drain. Slice the still
warm mackerels open lengthwise and remove their skin. Set
them aside to cool off and,
when cold, remove their bones
to make fillets. Prepare a shallow serving platter.

3 Cut the mint leaves into thin
strips. Mix the mint, parsley,
and garlic with the white wine
vinegar, and stir in the olive oil.
Season with salt and pepper.

4 In a shallow serving platter,
lay several mackerels side by
side, and brush them with some
of the herbed marinade. Lay the
remaining fillets over the first
layer of fish and drizzle more
marinade on everything. Cover
the platter and refrigerate for at
least one day to allow the liquid
to seep into the fish. Before
serving, garnish with fresh
stemless leaves of mixed herbs.

• A valued fish with a very dis-
tinct flavor and aroma that is a
favorite in Apulia's cuisine.
While preparing these fish, the
fillets can easily fall apart when
they are freed from their bones,
especially if the fish is warm.
Do not be bothered by this es-
thetic detail, since the delicious
flavor will reward you for putting up with this minor flaw.

Bistecchine alla napoletana

*Braised Small Beef Steaks, Naples Style
(Campagna)*

Serves 4

8 small thin steaks of beef
   (each about 3 ounces)
4 ounces to 4 to 6 slices
   prosciutto
11 ounces or about 18 small to
   medium fresh white or baby
   portobella mushrooms
1 bunch fresh Italian parsley
1 1/2 lemons (4 to 5 tablespoons juice)
3 tablespoons olive oil
Salt and freshly ground pepper

Approximate preparation time:
   40 minutes;
   330 calories per serving.

1 Season the steaks on both
sides with pepper, drizzle
with 2 tablespoons of lemon
juice, cover, and set aside.

2 Cut the prosciutto into thin
strips. Thoroughly clean the
mushrooms and slice thin.
Mince 1/2 bunch of parsley. Preheat the oven to 400°F.

3 Heat 1 tablespoon of olive
oil in a large frying pan, stir
in the prosciutto, and sauté for
2 minutes. Stir in the mushrooms and parsley, and sauté
for 2 more minutes. Season
with salt and pepper, and flavor
with 1 to 2 tablespoons lemon
juice. Put all ingredients into a
large baking dish.

4 Place the marinated steaks
on the mushroom mixture.
Bake in the preheated oven for
20 minutes. After 10 minutes,
turn the meat over, season with
salt and pepper, and drizzle
with 2 tablespoons of olive oil
and 1 tablespoon of lemon
juice.

5 Serve the steaks on serving
plates, topped with mush-
rooms and ham. Garnish with
stemless small leaves of
parsley.

• An easy-to-prepare meal from
the oven.

Pollo alla lucana

Stuffed Chicken, Lucania Style (Basilicata)

Serves 4

1 young chicken (about 2
   pounds)
7 ounces chicken livers
4 ounces or 4 slices lean country ham
2 ounces or 2 slices bacon
1 bunch fresh Italian parsley
2/3 cup freshly grated romano
   or Parmesan cheese
1 sprig fresh rosemary (or 1
   teaspoon dried)
2 eggs
Salt and freshly ground pepper

Approximate preparation time:
   1 3/4 hours;
   690 calories per serving.

1 Dice the ham and bacon.
Heat both in a medium frying pan and sauté until the fat
has rendered and the bits are
crispy. Remove the bacon bits
and set aside. Add the chicken
livers to the rendered fat and
brown evenly on all sides.
Season with salt and pepper,
remove chicken livers from the
pan, and allow them to cool off.
Dice the chicken livers, and,
mix them with the bacon bits in
a mixing bowl. Keep the rendered bacon fat in the pan.

2 Beat the 2 eggs and pour
over the chicken liver mixture. Add the minced parsley.
Add the grated cheese and mix
everything thoroughly. Season
with salt (keep in mind the saltiness of the bacon, ham, and
cheese!) and pepper.

3 Preheat the oven to 425°F.
Rinse the chicken inside and
out and pat dry with paper towels. Season with salt and pepper, stuff it with the liver mixture, and sew the chicken
opening with kitchen thread, or
close with toothpicks. Tie the
wings and the legs to the body,
including the sprig of rosemary
(if you use dried rosemary, add
it to the stuffing).

Costolette alla pizzaiola
Tomato and Garlic Braised Pork Cutlets, Pizza Maker's Style (Campagna)

4 Reheat the bacon-ham fat in the pan. Brush a large Dutch oven with 1 tablespoon of fat. Put the stuffed chicken in the middle of the Dutch oven and brush it on all sides with the bacon-ham fat. Bake uncovered in the preheated oven for about 1 1/4 hours or until golden and crispy. Turn the chicken over at least twice while you bake it, and occasionally baste it with the pan juices.

• With this chicken you can serve roasted potatoes with onions and mushrooms, or a tangy refreshing cauliflower salad (see recipe on page 264).

Serves 4

4 pork cutlets (7 ounces each)
17 1/2 ounces or 5 medium large or 10 fresh, ripe plum tomatoes
1 tablespoon fresh oregano leaves (or 1 teaspoon dried)
3 to 4 cloves garlic, sliced thin
1/2 cup red wine
2 tablespoons tomato paste
3 tablespoons olive oil
Salt and freshly ground pepper

<u>*Approximate preparation time:*</u>
40 minutes;
500 calories per serving.

1 Blanch, peel, seed, and chop the tomatoes.

2 Heat 2 tablespoons of olive oil in a large frying pan with a cover. Add the cutlets and brown evenly on both sides. Remove the meat, season it with salt and pepper, and set it aside.

3 Pour off any excess of fat from the pan, leaving only a glossy surface. Add 1 tablespoon of olive oil, heat, and sauté the garlic slices. Sprinkle the garlic with half of the oregano and stir in the chopped tomatoes. Moisten with the red wine and bring to a vigorous and rapid boil. Allow the sauce to thicken, stirring constantly. Season with salt and pepper.

4 Place the cutlets in the sauce, cover, and simmer for about 15 more minutes, turning once. Remove the cutlets from the pan and prepare them on preheated plates. Top the meat with tomato sauce, sprinkle it with oregano, and serve.

• When the cutlets are set aside after browning, plenty of meat juice will gather around the meat; be sure to use that juice by adding it to the tomato sauce.

• *Alla pizzaiola* is a culinary method that implies the use of fish or meat together with tomato sauce. You may substitute these pork cutlets with veal or beef cutlets, or even slices of fish.

Parmigiana di melanzane
Eggplant Parmesan (Campagna)

Serves 4 to 6

2 pounds medium-large fresh
   eggplants
2 pounds fresh, ripe tomatoes
1 bunch fresh basil
1 + $2/3$ cup freshly grated
   Parmesan cheese
11 ounces or 3 to 4 balls
   mozzarella
2 hard-boiled eggs
2 cloves garlic, crushed
Enough oil to bake and to brush
   the baking dish
Salt and freshly ground pepper

Approximate preparation time:
  1 $1/2$ hours (+ 1 hour for
  "debittering" of the slices
  of eggplant);
  430 calories per serving.

There is plenty of disagreement, especially in the south of Italy, about what region should be credited for the creation of this famous and delicious dish: fried crispy, thin slices of eggplant, prepared with a flavorful tomato sauce, basil, garlic, mozzarella, freshly grated Parmesan cheese, layered and then baked until golden and crispy.

Around the area of Naples, where there no one doubts the local origins of this specialty, the dish is also sometimes prepared with bitter chocolate.

If you cannot find freshly grated Parmesan cheese in your supermarket, you may substitute romano cheese or any other flavorful hard cheese of your choice. However, try to stay away from the prepackaged and pregrated packages of Parmesan cheese, since those cheeses have very little in common with the original Parmesan cheese. This rule should also be applied to all other recipes in this book calling for Parmesan cheese.

1 Rinse the eggplant, cut off the stems, and cut lengthwise in $1/4$-inch-thick slices. Sprinkle with salt, layer on a large plate, cover with another plate of similar shape and size, and set firmly in place with something heavy. Set aside and leave at least 1 hour to allow the bitter eggplant juices to drain out.

2 Sauce: Blanch, peel, seed, and chop the tomatoes. Heat them in a medium saucepan. Slice the leaves of basil into thin strips, and add, with the garlic, to the tomatoes. Simmer until you get a velvety and smooth sauce and season with salt and pepper. Stir occasionally.

3 In the meantime, briefly rinse the eggplant slices under running water, let them drain, and pat them dry with paper towels. In a frying pan, heat enough olive oil to fry the eggplant, and gradually fry the slices until golden brown. Place the slices on paper towels to allow the excess fat to drain.

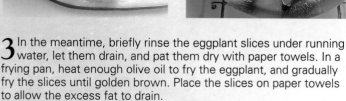

4 Brush a large baking dish with oil. Cut the remaining basil into thin strips and slice the mozzarella and the hard-boiled eggs. Preheat the oven to 350°F.

5 Line the baking dish with a layer of eggplant slices. Sprinkle with Parmesan cheese. Top with slices of eggs and mozzarella, and cover with some tomato sauce and a few leaves of basil. Cover with eggplant slices, and repeat the layer sequence (keep 2 tablespoons of Parmesan cheese for the final top layer). Finish with tomato sauce.

6 Place the eggplant casserole into the preheated oven and bake for about 40 minutes. Ten minutes before removing from the oven, sprinkle with the remaining grated Parmesan cheese. Serve the dish not hot, but rather lukewarm (this dish is also wonderful almost cold).

Insalata di rinforzo
Cooked Cauliflower with Tangy Salad Dressing (Campagna)

Serves 6

1 small fresh cauliflower (about 1 pound)
1 small, fresh red pepper
2 ounces or 20 small black pitted olives
2 ounces or 20 small green pitted olives
4 canned anchovy fillets, drained
4 pickled, green, mild Italian peperoncini (you may substitute pickled jalapeños)
1 tablespoon green capers
3 to 4 tablespoons wine vinegar
6 tablespoons olive oil
Salt and freshly ground pepper

Approximate preparation time:
30 minutes;
150 calories per serving.

1 Thoroughly clean and rinse the cauliflower and divide it into florets. In the meantime, bring salted water to a boil in a large pot, and blanch the cauliflower for 5 minutes. With a slotted spoon, remove, drop into iced water, and drain.

2 Rinse the red pepper and cut it in halves. Seed and remove the internal membranes and cut into very thin strips or dice the remaining pepper parts. Cut in halves both the green and black pitted olives. Rinse the anchovies, pat dry, and slice in thin strips. Seed the peperoncini (or pickled jalapeños), and cut them either in rings or in strips.

3 Place the cold cauliflower in a bowl, add all the prepared vegetables, and the capers. Season with salt and pepper, and dress with the wine vinegar and olive oil. Toss all ingredients well and, if necessary, season some more with salt and pepper.

• A pinch of powdered red chili or cayenne pepper will give a pleasant kick to these very interesting florets.

Zucchine marinate
Marinated Zucchini (Campagna)

Serves 4

1 pound small zucchini
1/2 bunch fresh mint
1/2 bunch fresh basil
1/2 bunch fresh Italian parsley, minced
3 cloves garlic, minced
About 1/3 cup aromatic wine vinegar
Enough olive oil to fry
Salt and freshly ground pepper

Approximate preparation time:
20 minutes
(+ 3–4 hours to marinate);
140 calories per serving.

1 Thoroughly clean and wash the zucchini. Slice them 1/4 inch thick, sprinkle with salt, and set aside to allow the zucchini water to drain out. Pat dry.

2 Heat enough olive oil to fry in a frying pan. Gradually fry the zucchini slices on both sides. Remove the zucchini from the oil with a slotted spoon and place on paper towels to allow the excess fat to drain.

3 Cut both the mint and the basil leaves into thin strips. Dilute half of the mint, basil, parsley, garlic with the wine vinegar and drizzle over the fried zucchini slices. Sprinkle with the remaining herb mixture and refrigerate for at least 3 to 4 hours.

Cianfotta
Potatoes and Eggplants (Basilicata)

Serves 4 to 6

1 ⅓ pounds fresh eggplants
2 fresh, red peppers
1 ⅓ pounds fresh, ripe toma-
    toes
2 pounds potatoes (preferably
    red or waxy)
1 bunch fresh Italian parsley,
    minced
1 tablespoon fresh oregano
    leaves (or 1 teaspoon dried)
2 onions, minced
3 cloves garlic, minced
6 tablespoons olive oil
Salt and freshly ground pepper

Approximate preparation time:
    1 ½ hours;
    260 calories per serving.

1 Trim, clean, and dice the
eggplants into 1-inch pieces.
Sprinkle with salt and set aside
for about 30 minutes.

2 In the meantime, clean,
trim, seed, and dice the peppers. In boiling water, blanch

the tomatoes. Peel, seed, and
chop them. Wash, peel, and
cube the potatoes.

3 Briefly rinse the eggplants
and pat them dry with paper
towels. Preheat the oven to
400°F. Heat 6 tablespoons of
olive oil in a large saucepan.

4 Add and stir in the potatoes
and brown them evenly on
all sides. Add the minced
onions and gradually, while stirring periodically, add the diced
eggplants and the diced peppers. Season with 1 tablespoon
of oregano, minced garlic, salt,
and pepper. Add the chopped
tomatoes, thoroughly mix all ingredients, and cover.

5 Place everything in a large,
greased baking dish. Cover.
Bake in the preheated oven for
45 minutes. Fold the minced
parsley into the vegetable cian-
fotta before serving. Season
with salt and pepper.

• This dish is not only ideal as a
side dish for lamb, pork, or
beef, but as a vegetarian main
course (3 to 4 servings in this
case). It is somehow reminiscent of French *ratatouille*.

• Instead of baking this dish,
you can also sauté it on top of
the stove, enhancing it with
green olives, zucchini, or ribs of
celery, and sprinkling fresh basil
leaves over it before serving.

Grano dolce
Sweet Wheat (Basilicata)

Serves 4

1 pomegranate
1/2 lemon (peel)
2 tablespoons walnuts
1/2 cup whole wheat berries
1/2 cup semidry white wine
2 tablespoons honey
2 ounces semi-sweet chocolate

<u>Approximate preparation time:</u>
45 minutes
(+ 12 hours to soak);
240 calories per serving.

1 Soak the kernels of wheat in water overnight. The next day, drain the wheat berries, rinse them with fresh water, and cook them in fresh water for about 30 minutes. Drain them, put them in a small bowl, and set them aside to cool off.

2 Finely chop the walnuts. Heat and briefly stir-fry the nuts without any fat, then add to the wheat.

3 Cream the wheat to a smooth mixture with the wine and honey. Cut the pomegranate in halves (be careful, the juice contains a very strong coloring agent!). With a spoon, remove the seeds from the fruit and add them to the wheat mixture. Add and mix in the grated peel of 1/2 lemon.

4 Place in a small serving bowl and refrigerate. Shortly before serving, garnish with chocolate shavings.

• This very unique and delicious dessert unmistakably shows its Arab origins. A similar dessert is prepared with cooked wheat, honey, nuts, chocolate, and cinnamon, served traditionally around Christmastime, in Sicily (*cuccia*) and in Apulia (*grane cuotte*).

Coviglia di caffè
Chilled Coffee Cream (Campagna)

Serves 6 to 8

1 cup very strong coffee or
espresso
1 cup milk
1/2 pint or about 1 1/4 cups
whipping cream
1 vanilla bean
4 egg yolks
8 tablespoons granulated sugar
Coffee beans to garnish

<u>Approximate preparation time:</u>
45 minutes
(+ 3–4 hours freezing);
330 calories per serving.

1 Dissolve 4 tablespoons of sugar in the freshly brewed coffee and allow it to cool off. In a small saucepan, heat up the milk. Cut open the vanilla bean and drop with the internal scrapings and the bean husk into the hot milk. Allow the flavor to seep into the milk, but do not allow the milk to boil!

2 Place a round heat-resistant bowl in the middle of a warm water bath, add the egg yolks and 4 tablespoons of sugar, and beat to a foamy mass with a whisk (you can also use a double boiler in this step).

3 Remove the vanilla bean from the milk. While still whisking constantly, gradually pour first the cold coffee and then the milk into the egg mixture. Remove the foamy cream from the heat, place it in a cold water bath, and, still whisking constantly, allow the cream to cool off.

4 Beat the whipping cream to a stiff peak and fold two–thirds of it into the coffee cream. Cover and refrigerate the remaining whipped cream for later use to garnish the dessert. Freeze the cream for about 3 to 4 hours to allow it to solidify.

5 Remove the cream from the freezer 20 minutes before

Zuppa inglese alla napoletana
Ricotta, Chocolate, and Liqueur Trifle, Naples Style

serving. Fill a pastry bag with the remaining whipped cream and squeeze small dots on the surface of the chilled dessert. Garnish with coffee beans.

• Variation: *Granita di caffé*, a refreshing chilled drink specialty, which is available in bars throughout southern Italy. It is basically a type of water ice-cream, made from coffee and sugar, that is crushed or pureed before being served topped with whipped cream. Even more thirst-quenching is the *granita al limone*, made from chilled mixed lemon juice and sugar syrup.

Serves 4 to 6

1 ready-to-use sponge cake (see recipe on page 160)
1 pound or 2 cups ricotta cheese
2 ounces semisweet chocolate in bar or square form
1 tablespoon + 1 teaspoon Amaretto (almond liqueur)
About 3 tablespoons rum
1 vanilla bean
1/2 cup milk
3 eggs
3/4 cup granulated sugar

Approximate preparation time:
1 1/2 hours
(+ 2 hours refrigeration);
550 calories per serving.

1 In a saucepan, heat but do not boil the milk with 1/4 cup of sugar. Slice the vanilla bean open lengthwise, scrape out the inside, and drop it with the whole bean into the milk. Keep the vanilla in the milk for 10 minutes, then remove the milk from the heat source and allow it to cool off.

2 In a mixing bowl, beat 2 eggs with 1 egg yolk and 1/2 cup of sugar to a fluffy consistency. Remove the vanilla bean from the cold milk, and gradually add it to the egg mixture, beating constantly until you get a smooth cream.

3 Press the ricotta cheese through a fine strainer and add to the egg cream. Grate the chocolate and fold the shavings into the cream. Flavor with the Amaretto.

4 Cut the sponge cake into 2-inch-thick slices. Line the bottom of a large rectangular baking dish with one third of the slices of sponge cake. Drizzle with the rum and top with one third of the cream. Repeat the layers of ingredients in the same sequence (this should result in three layers).

5 Refrigerate for at least 2 hours to allow all the flavors

to combine and the dessert to cool off.

6 Shortly before serving, preheat the oven to 475°F. Beat the remaining egg white to a stiff peak. Fill a pastry bag with the egg white mixture, and, using a flat decorating tip, garnish the surface of the dessert. Bake very briefly in the hot oven, or until the topping begins to show golden brown patches. Serve immediately.

• If you have experienced this *zuppa* being prepared in a different way, it is probably the variation made in Emilia-Romagna. Unlike in Naples (or in Rome) this version is prepared without the egg white topping, and it is layered in a dish with slices of cake alternating with vanilla and chocolate cream. Another favorite is a vanilla cream speckled with finely chopped candied fruits.

Pasta—Pure Passion

In its length and its width lies the essence of pasta. In shapes of curves and bumps, snail shells, small hats and little ears, curls, feathers, and spirals, wagon wheels and golden nests, butterflies, stars, pearls, and angels' hair…

Pasta, the fantastic phenomenon, is made up of noodle creations of flour, water, or egg, oil and salt. Naturally, with almost neutral taste, Maccheroni and Company turn out to be masters in the kitchen of multifaceted flavors. It is not only important that all ingredients be the right ones, but also what shape of pasta dough creations we are dealing with.

Pasta is available in at least 300 different shapes, and every type seems to be created for a certain type of topping that is either *sugo* or *ragù* (meat sauce), melted butter, or fresh olive oil.

Sugo, one of the magic terms in pasta cuisine, is the ideal complement to many varieties of pasta—translated as "sauce" with a certain oversimplification. In one term, the word *sugo* incorporates various regional variations such as minced root vegetables, a small portion of meat, fish, or seafood with spices, herbs, wine, or stock, and more often whole or pureed tomatoes. While the meaning of *ragù* is associated with a hearty, patiently simmered meat sauce, the sugo requires less time; sometimes it is sufficient to begin cooking the sugo as soon as the water for cooking the pasta has been set up to boil.

The more delicate the type of pasta, the more subdued and refined the topping sauce should be; in extreme cases,

some melted butter or a bit of olive oil will do. Small filled pasta is often served in the Northern Italian regions *in brodo*, in a clear homemade broth that allows the flavors of the filling to come out in their full aroma. *Pasta asciutta*, on the other hand, is the term that is used to label all noodles that are not served in liquid, that is, that are used "dry" and prepared with sauce or cheese. Strangely shaped pasta varieties with holes and indentations, such as *conchiglie* or *lumache*, drink up a lot of sauce. Grooves in noodles such as *rigatoni*, *ditali*, and *tortiglioni* have the same function. Rich and heartier mixtures, or thick meat ragus, go well with pasta that have wider surfaces or large empty spaces such as *pappardelle*, *cannelloni*, *lasagne*, or *maccheroni*.

However, the art of Italian pasta making does not have much in common with the thin Oriental noodles, still considered by Marco Polo's followers the noodle's precursors. It is more likely that it was originally Sicily, the triangular island in the South, where this cult began with inhabitants who cooked and ate for a long time under Arab domination. Unusual documents about this origin can be found in a small place along the Ligurian coast—the Spaghetti Museum in Pontedassio (Imperia), lovingly cared for by the Agnesi family, which presents pasta as life's ultimate purpose. There, a visitor can learn everything about pasta, from the small Etruscan flour satchel to the most modern pasta design.

Even without its being the location of pasta's origin, Naples is still addicted to noodles. Open street noodle cooking stands, and sunny squares and streets where pasta hung like laundry

set out to dry were common scenes that marked the image of the city and its surrounding areas up to the beginning of this century. It was here that the foundations of industrial pasta production were laid and only from here did pasta find its way as a favorite dish throughout the entire country.

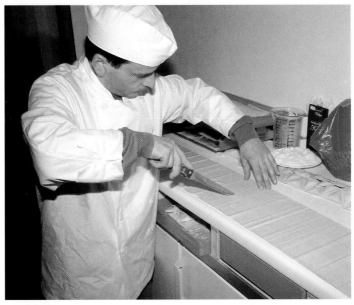

Far left: As early as 2000 years ago the precursors of today's pasta utensils served as models for engravings on Etruscan columns. Today, these utensils find their way into the best kitchens of the world—pasta rolling pins, pasta cutters, and other implements for the production of pasta.

Above: The newer models of noodle-making implements are simple but efficient; the rolled-out sheets of dough are released as either narrow or wide strips of pasta, according to the placement of the drums.

Middle: Over and over, human intervention by hand is required, especially when making homemade ravioli. To ensure that the pasta pockets are sealed well, the rolled-out sheet of dough needs to be processed right away.

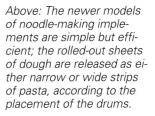

Left: Pasta secca are labeled "noodles," from spaghetti to fusilli to farfalle, made from hard wheat, sold in bags or packages. Manufacturers from throughout Italy engage in truly esthetically pleasing, creative, and exciting competition.

The legal basis for the unparalleled Italian pasta quality was set in Genoa, in Liguria, about 500 years ago—it must be hard wheat! The high content of gluten protein makes this wheat an especially suitable ingredient for pasta, especially for *pasta secca*, the industrially manufactured noodles, which include only flour (in this case, hard wheat semolina flour) and water, but without any eggs. For centuries, the robust and remarkably dense hard wheat was grown along the shores of the Black Sea, especially throughout the fertile area of Taganrog, and was shipped to Italy's pasta capitals. The 1917 revolution put a stop to this commercial enterprise, creating a new whirlwind around the spaghetti cooking methods. Fortunately, new techniques were found, with new growing areas in Italy itself, on the extreme southern part of the boot, *grano duro* is now grown on fields along the sea. Hard wheat is also grown in Sicily and, more recently, also in Central and Northern Italy.

The secret of pasta secca is the mixture of a certain type of wheat, milled as coarse semolina, with pure water. The remarkable aspect of *pasta fresca*, on the other hand, lies in the individual touch. The dough for these homemade egg noodles, also called *pasta all'uovo* or *pasta fatta in casa*, is made from fine wheat flour and eggs. According to each recipe, the dough is also further refined or colored, for example, flavored with aromatic olive oil, pureed spinach, minced herbs or tomato paste, saffron or chili pepper, with the intense juice of the red beet, or with flavorful grated cheese. Salt can, but does not need to be, added to the dough—the flavor will surely be added later during the cooking and with the topping sauce. It takes strength, as well as patience and a good sense of humor, when it comes to kneading, rolling out, shaping, and cutting the pasta fresca. For a larger family, in order to obtain fairly quickly either a thin or almost transparent sheet of

dough, a pasta machine should be among the basic noodle-making requirements. Whether one makes ribbon-shaped noodles or small filled pasta pockets (ravioli) can be decided spontaneously; it is above all the cutting technique that counts here. However, if you choose filled pockets, you will have to begin right away, while the dough is fresh and still moist. For cutting flat noodles, the dough should actually be slightly dry.

The love of homemade and rather time-consuming egg noodles is spread, above all, throughout Northern Italy. From Rome southward, it is the pasta secca that cooks in the pasta pot. And here, we have reached the subject of pasta cooking. Especially important for cooking pasta is the quantity of water: In a large pot, which should be filled only three quarters of

Above: Not fine flour, but coarsely milled hard wheat semolina, is used for making pasta secca, *with a dough that has a maximum water content of 12 1/2 percent.*

Middle: The authentic pasta dough made from hard wheat flour is slightly yellow, even without any eggs. This method makes it possible for the annual consumption of pasta to be as high as 55 pounds per person in Italy.

Left: Fresh scraps left over from pressing dough into various shapes go back again into the large mixing machine to be kneaded together with raw dough.

the way, 4 quarts of salted boiling water for every pound of pasta.

In the case of pasta secca, time instructions on the packages are useful; however, always check in advance whether the noodles have reached the cooking stage of *al dente*, that is, whether the heart of the noodles is still firm to the bite, since overcooked pasta is the worst of sins in this noodle paradise. For homemade egg pasta and filled pasta pockets, the same requirement of checking for doneness applies. Additionally, the sticking of the noodles can be prevented with a splash of oil in the boiling water. Pasta cooked al dente should be poured at once, well drained, and should never be sprayed with cold water. In a mixing bowl, mix the very hot noodles with the prepared sauce, or drizzle with some olive oil, and Pronto! The only thing left to say is: "Buon Appetito!"

In Summary: The Most Important Varieties of Pasta

Agnolotti – filled with meat, vegetables, and cheese; Piedmont

Anolini – filled half-moons, in chicken broth; Emilia-Romagna

Bigoli – thick spaghetti made from whole wheat flour; Veneto

Bucatini – tube-shaped, thick spaghetti with a hole in the middle; Latium

Cannelloni – tubes of pasta that are stuffed with various fillings and oven-baked

Capellini – very thin type of spaghetti, also called angel hair, *capelli d'angelo*

Cappelletti – small hats filled with meat and cheese; Emilia-Romagna

Conchiglie – shell-shaped noodles

Culingiones – round, filled pasta pockets; Sardinia

Ditali – short, ribbed tube noodles; Liguria

Farfalle – butterfly-shaped pasta, made with a fluted pastry wheel

When it comes to cutting the noodles, not only are accurate mixing skills required, but the pasta roll must also be properly set in place.

On a moving conveyor belt, tagliatelle are moved away from the machine; they are perfect in length and in width and are folded for the next step.

Flat noodles are placed to dry on well-ventilated fine meshed screens before being packaged automatically.

Even for some filled varieties of pasta, like the ravioli shown here, the modern spirit of technology takes care of filling, cutting, and packaging.

After the ravioli machine has done the work, scraps shaped like punch cards of dough remain as leftovers; these are thoroughly re-kneaded and rolled out.

Machine-made and dried tortellini can undoubtedly be sent worldwide; however, gourmets still prefer homemade fresh pasta.

Fettuccine – narrow flat noodles

Fusilli – long or short corkscrew-shaped noodles; Campagna, Calabria

Gnocchi – small dumplings made from various types of dough: semolina flour, or potatoes made industrially in Sardinia also as pasta secca

Lasagne – large, wide sheets of pasta that are used in alternating layers with sauce and cheese in a baking dish and oven-baked

Linguine – narrow, flat noodles, also called *bavette*

Lumache – snail shaped pasta

Maccheroni – macaroni – long or short thick tubes of pasta; originally a generic term for many types of pasta

Maccheroni alla chitarra – Abruzzi's specialty (see page 209), narrow, flat pasta made with a guitar-shaped implement

Malfatti – differs according to regions, usually unevenly shaped dumplings

Malloreddus – homemade small dumplings; Sardinia

Orecchiette – time-consuming ear-shaped pasta; Apulia

Pansooti – herb-filled pasta pockets; Liguria

Pappardelle – very wide ribbon pasta; Tuscany

Penne – short, diagonally cut noodles with a hole in the middle

Ravioli – filled pasta pockets; the most famous variation comes from Liguria

Rigatoni – short, ribbed noodles with a hole in the middle

Spaghetti – the ultimate for all pasta lovers; literally translated: small ropes or threads

Spaghettini – very thin spaghetti

Tagliatelle – flat noodles; Emilia-Romagna

Tortellini – small, round filled pasta pockets; for Emilia-Romagna, it is Bologna's culinary marker

Tortelloni – large, round, filled pasta pockets

Tortiglioni – long ribbed noodles with a hole in the middle

Trenette – long, narrow, flat noodles; Liguria

Trofie – spiral-shaped homemade pasta; Liguria

Vermicelli – very thin string-shaped pasta

Calabria and Sicily

Hills and Islands:
Patchwork fields throughout Calabria's hilly landscape.

The Regions and Their Products

The heart of Calabria's cuisine throbs in the mountainous interior of the elongated tip of the boot. People did not settle permanently along the unsafe coast. Even today, 387 of the region's 408 villages are located throughout the protected hills and mountains. Every small handkerchief of land is used here for growing vegetables, among which eggplant and tomatoes are favorites. Potatoes, cauliflower, peppers, onions, legumes, and artichokes are also harvested here in abundance. The valleys of Gioia Tauro, Lamezia, and Sibari, created by the formation of rivers and streams flowing from the mountains, are fertile. The mountains are often located very near the shores, as on the coasts of Diamante and Cirella, which then break as steep rocky cliffs into the sea. The gray gives way to green where lemon orchards find a refuge.

Sicily: Similar to the neighboring region of Calabria, the largest island of the Mediterranean region is covered throughout four-fifths of its approximately 9200-square-mile area by hills and mountains, and is bounded by the Ionian, Tyrrhenian, and Mediterranean seas. A crown of islands belong to Sicily; in the North, the Eolie or Lipari Islands, and in the South, the Palegie Islands and Pantelleria. As diverse they may wish to be, they all have in

Above, top: Many towns are located like fortresses on the tops of mountain peaks, such as Altomonte in Calabria.

Above: In the mountainous regions, milk is obtained from goats and sheep, and is the basic ingredient for many hearty cheese varieties.

Above, right: Citrus fruits grow along Messina's road.

Middle, right: Olives and pickled vegetables accompany almost every meal.

Right: Swordfish is part of a favorite gourmet meal.

common good wine and a very rich tuna industry.

The large triangular island of Sicily is not easily classified by one unique common denominator. While the vegetation is influenced by the hot breath of African air along the southern coast where almond trees thrive, in the islands' chain of mountains there are trees and plants reminiscent of the North, such as the whin, the walnut, and the edible chestnut. The east coast, protected by Etna, remains green all year round, while around the high plateaus near Enna and Caltanisetta, in the island's interior, there are green oceans of cereal fields that turn into golden wheat, and later, during the summer, only the leftovers of cut stems and dried out yellow dirt remain. The western part of the island, between Palermo and Marsala, belongs almost exclusively to wine.

Along the coasts of Calabria and Sicily, on both sides of the Straits of Messina, swordfish, one of Southern Italy's basic foods, is caught between March and September. Calabria's interior offers venison and mushrooms, trout from the lakes and streams of the Sila, with acorn- and chestnut-fed pigs, from which come hearty sausages. During the dry summers, sheep and goats still find enough nourishment to provide milk for the *butirri* and cheese

from butter cream. In Sicily's Ragusa Province, cheese is also produced from cows' milk. Among the wonderful ingredients produced here that flavor many pasta dishes is the indispensable ricotta for *cassata siciliana* or for the filling of *cannoli*, the crispy sweet pastries. Both famous specialties represent only a fraction of the sweet delicacies prepared for yearly festivities, and the fact that the recipes were left as a souvenir by Muslims of Arabia has not bothered anyone on Sicily.

Above, left: Sunday market in Randazzo on Mount Etna, with cheese available from areas throughout Sicily—canestrato made from sheep milk, fresh or oven-dried ricotta, provola, and pecorino.

Middle: The famous Sicilian sweets are made from almonds, such as pasta di mandorla, baked from marzipan.

Left: Along with tomatoes and peperoncini, eggplants are especially important in Calabria's cuisine, with innumerable ways to prepare them.

Above: Herbs, mushrooms, and small wild artichokes, as well as wild-grown small pink onions, are gathered by Calabria's women in the mountains and woods. Pickled in oil and vinegar, the cipudazzi are not only an appetizer for the home table, but also an item for export. They are available on the market in glass jars.

People, Events, Sightseeing

Calabria was never easy on its inhabitants. The extended tip of the boot that lies between the Tyrrhenian and the Ionian seas was not only a challenge for them, but also for other domination-minded Mediterranean cultures. The locals were repeatedly forced to pull back from contact with the sea and to find refuge in the interior of the land. Instead of crawling back into valleys, and in order to protect themselves from unpleasant surprises and to be nearer to their saints, Calabrians glued their cities and towns on top of difficult and rocky mountains. They made a living as shepherds, farmers, and artisans. The traces of the hard life made their faces stern and closed. However, similar to the springtime that covers gray rock landscapes with carpets of yellow flowers, red poppies, and white daisies, the people here lose their timidity when others reach out for contact and friendship. The rare tourists who cross Calabria and who meet the occasional shepherds and farmers are welcomed with touching openness.

Sicily, the triangle in the Mediterranean Sea, has always been a melting pot of people and cultures. Those interested in discovering them can learn the most from their cuisine. Were we to mix everything that can be found here in a huge cooking pot, we would need to combine the sea's breezes with the

Above: The panoramic view of Mount Etna and the coast is incredible from the ancient theater overlooking Taormina. Festivals are held here, as well as in the theaters of Segesta, Tindari, Selinunta, and Syracuse (Siracusa), in the spring and summer.

Top, right: The celebration of Sicilian regional costumes in May in Taormina.

Right: Fishing boats with lobster cages in the port of Syracuse (Siracusa). Fishermen honor their patron, Saint Peter, with a festival held in June.

scents of Arabia, the bitter flavor of wild herbs with the rich smell of sun-ripened tomatoes and sweet oranges, or with the oil from centuries-old olive trees. We would also need to include the pungency of cheeses and sausages, the sweetness of honey, raisins, and almonds, and, last but not least, the bouquet of wines made from grapes matured in the sun near the fire of Etna.

The personality of the Sicilian is also marked by a variety of influences, like a rich mixture of wonderful ingredients. In the Sicilian are paired a lively, sparkling, creative fantasy with a languid Oriental mood. Poverty and the will to survive have often forced island inhabitants to emigrate, and have given them a strong work ethic, reliability, and sternness, while reinforcing the love of the homeland and the desire to maintain family and archaic traditions.

Culinary highlights throughout the year in Calabria include the swordfish festival celebrated every July in Bagnara with a ship parade. Vibo Valentia celebrates its homemade noodles on July 26 with the *dei Fileia* festival. In August in Pilinga, the Nduja (tripe) festival, is held. It features tripe prepared in a spicy pot with pork tongue. Soveria Mannelli includes in its August schedule of events the festival market of the potatoes. On September 15 in Soverato, there is the festival and market of the eggplants, while in January there is a festival of citrus fruits with a big parade in Corigliano Calabro.

In Sicily, almond blossoms are celebrated with an international celebration in Agrigento in February. In June, Castelbuono celebrates the blessing of the cherries, and on June 29, for the name day of their patron, there is great cooking and good eating in all the fishing communities. On the Monday of Pentecost, for the festival of San Liberante in Trapani, squid with beans simmer in huge kettles along the streets and in the squares. During All Souls, children are given gifts of sweet, hard candy shaped like the bones of the dead, the *ossa dei morti* that were brought secretly by dead relatives—at least, that's what children are being told.

Top: Corso Umberto, Taormina's casual meeting place and walking street. A paper artist put up his portable easel here.

Middle: Frutti della martorana, *fruits, vegetables, and even fish and seafood that look almost as if they were alive are shaped by pastry and candy makers.*

Above: Summer breakfast Sicilian style: granita di caffe with whipped cream, and a brioche pastry. It is dipped in the iced coffee specialty. It can also be followed, according to taste, by an espresso.

Far left: The noble knight of the Sicilian puppet theater is waiting for a customer in front of a souvenir shop.

Near, left: Where there is a festival, either in Calabria or in Sicily, there is also a band.

The Wines

It is believed that Calabrian athletes from the Greek colonies were celebrated with *Krimis* when they came back triumphantly from the ancient Olympic games. Whether or not it was the oldest wine in the world is still left open to discussion; however, it surely must have been among the first wines in Europe. Its grapes grew along the Ionian coast in today's province of Cosenza.

Even if not of such ancient nobility, today's locally grown *Cirò* is the most famous of the Calabrian wines. The grape used for the *Cirò Rosso* and *Rosato*, as well as for the other Calabrian red wines, is the Gaglioppo. The Cirò takes at least four years in the barrel, with a yearly transfer, to reach full maturity and a balanced bouquet; however, it never reaches a completely dry stage and always maintains a sweet touch. The white Cirò is made from Greco di bianco, a very old grape variety, which produces not only brilliant dry wines that are pleasantly refreshing, but also such rich dessert wines as the *Greco di Bianco* that is velvety with a delicate orange blossom aroma.

The mountainous tip of the boot of Italy predominantly has cool and rugged slopes, and big harvests are not to be expected. It is quality, therefore, that counts

here. Near Castrovillari, the red *Pollino* is made from different varieties of grapes. While the wine is young, it is suitable as table wine to hearty dishes. A characteristic of many Calabrian wines is a semidry tone and a relatively high alcohol content from 14 to 17 percent alcohol (28 to 34 proof). Currently, however, there are efforts directed toward the production of lighter table wines to complement the established old-style wines.

Additional products that are remarkable: *Cerasuolo di Scilla*, a cherry red local wine from Scilla along the road from Messina; *Donnici* from the hills surrounding Cosenza, ruby to light red, fruity, and aromatic. *Palizzi* and *Pellaro*, the Reggio Calabria province's most renowned wines, go best

with flavorful meat dishes after suitable aging. Vineyards spread throughout wide areas; the province of Trapani produces almost half of all Sicilian wines. The most prominent is the *Marsala* wine that originated during the short duration of the Phoenicians' stay on the island. A straw yellow wine with high sugar content, Marsala is made from local grape varieties: Grillo, Cataratto, and Inzilio. With the addition of other wine factors, nectars from the same area, and long aging in oak barrels, the big competitor of the famous port, sherry, and *Madeira* wines develops here. Marsala wines are available from dry to sweet in various scents and flavors. The dry variety is worth tasting with the province's specialty, the *Cuscusu*, similar to the

Arab *couscous*, with fish and lobster. Among the great dessert wines of this region is the island of Pantelleria's *moscato*, made from Zibibbio grapes. The province also produces, in a controlled vineyard area around Alcamo, excellent table wines: the *Bianco d'Alcamo*, a good accompaniment to fish, the interesting *Rapitalà*; and lesser-known grape varieties. In the province of Agrigento, leading wines include the *Libecchio Bianco* and *Rosso*, with labels created by the famous painter Renato Guttuso; in addition, there are the *Settesoli Bianco* with a refreshing aroma, and the *Rosato* with a fruity bouquet. The vineyard area around Palermo produces the most renowned wine, the *Corvo*, which comes as white, and goes well with fish and seafood, and as red for all meat dishes. Produced by the Donnafugata estate and made famous by Tomaso di Lampedusa's "Leopard" is the wine with the same name. The province of Caltanisetta produces the *Regaleali* and Catania produces the *Etna* wines, which are dry red and white wines full of character, best suited for regional fish and vegetable dishes. The provinces of Ragusa and Messina produce small quantities of wine that are, however, of excellent quality. Still produced here with great pride is the *Mamertino*, the wine cherished by Julius Caesar. Outstanding *Malvasia* wines are produced throughout the island of Lipari, and especially on the small island of Salina, which is also known for excellent table wines.

Erika Casparek-Türkkan

Top: Wine has been made in Sicily since ancient times. It is said that the god of wine, Bacchus himself, brought it to the island; out of his footsteps came the vines. The ancient Greeks also made wine in Calabria.

Left: All flavor nuances are represented on Sicily's wine list, from sweet to dry, from the Marsala to the Rapitalà, while Calabria is 90 percent focused on red wines. The remaining 10 percent is mainly made up of sweet dessert wines.

Regional Recipes

Arancini di riso
Stuffed Rice Fritters (Sicily)

Yield: 8 to 10 Pieces

3 1/2 ounces boneless turkey
   breast
3 1/2 ounces lean ground beef
1/3 cup fresh peas (or frozen
   and thawed)
1 stalk celery
1 bunch fresh Italian parsley
1/2 bunch fresh basil
2/3 cup grated romano or
   Parmesan cheese
11 ounces or 1 1/2 cups
   short/round-grain Vialone, Arborio, or Avorio risotto rice
2 tablespoons tomato paste
3/4 cup hot beef stock
2 eggs
3 tablespoons butter
3 tablespoons olive oil + olive
   oil (or butter) for frying
1 onion, minced
4 tablespoons unseasoned
   breadcrumbs
2 tablespoons flour
1 pinch powdered red chili peppers
1 envelope saffron (1/2 to 1 teaspoon saffron in bulk)
Salt and freshly ground pepper
Bay leaves to garnish (they can
   also be fresh)

Approximate preparation time:
  2 hours; for 10 pieces—
  300 calories per piece

Arancini—golden and round, as the meaning of the name indicates, they indeed remind us of tiny oranges. They are, however, fried rice balls that deliciously surprise us with their own flavored fillings.

In Sicily, the stuffing is traditionally made from a mixture of poultry and meat combined with fresh vegetables and grated hard cheese.

A similar recipe exists in Latium, where these crispy rice balls are called either *supplì alla romana* or *supplì al telefono* and have a soft heart of mozzarella (recipe on page 179).

Tip: Prepare a double portion of meat ragù that includes all the ingredients that are left over from making these balls, and serve it as a sauce-type side dish to the stuffed rice fritters.

1 Mince 1/2 bunch parsley. Dice the turkey breast and celery. In a large saucepan, heat the oil and melt 1 tablespoon of butter. Add the onion and sauté until glossy. Add the turkey and ground beef and brown evenly. Stir in the celery and parsley, and sauté briefly. Season with salt, pepper, and powdered red chili peppers. Mix the tomato paste into the beef stock; add the stock to the meat mixture together with 1/3 cup of fresh peas (or frozen and thawed). Cover the saucepan and simmer on low heat.

2 Bring 2 cups of salted water to a boil in a large saucepan. Add the risotto rice in a stream and cook on low heat, stirring frequently. If necessary, add some water. When the rice is almost done, dissolve the saffron in 2 tablespoons of hot water and stir into the rice. When ready, the rice should be still firm to the bite and not mushy. Fold 2 tablespoons of butter and the grated romano or Parmesan cheese into the hot rice. Set aside to cool, and when cold, stir 1 egg into the rice.

3 Mince the remaining parsley and cut 1/2 bunch of fresh basil into thin strips. Make sure that the liquid of the meat mixture has evaporated and that the mixture has a firm consistency. Remove the meat mixture from the heat, fold the herbs into it, and season with salt and pepper.

4 In a small mixing bowl, beat 1 egg and season with salt and pepper. Remove about 10 small orange-size portions from the cold rice and shape each into a ball. In each rice ball, press an indentation with your fingers and fill it with 1 tablespoon of meat mixture with your fingers; then seal the rice balls. Dust the balls with flour, roll them first in the beaten egg and then in breadcrumbs. Set the balls aside on a clean dishcloth.

5 In a large frying pan, heat enough olive oil or butter for frying. Fry all the rice balls until they are crispy on all sides. Set them aside on paper towels to allow any excess fat to drain, and keep them warm. To garnish, stick a bay leaf into each rice ball.

Olive fritte
Stir-fried Olives (Sicily)

Serves 4

9 ounces or 2 cups small, pitted, black olives
1 sprig of fresh oregano (or 1 to 2 teaspoons dried)
3 cloves garlic, thinly sliced
3 tablespoons olive oil
6 tablespoons white wine vinegar
Freshly ground pepper

<u>Approximate preparation time:</u>
10 minutes;
280 calories per serving.

1 Drain the olives and pat them dry.

2 Heat the olive oil and sliced garlic in a medium frying pan. Add the olives and stir-fry for 3 minutes. Sprinkle with half of the oregano.

3 Moisten with the white wine vinegar and 2 to 3 tablespoons water, bring to a rapid boil, and allow the liquid to evaporate.

4 Stir in the remaining oregano and season with freshly ground pepper. Serve the olives out of the pan.

• Serve with a lot of crispy white bread that you can dip into the olive pan juices.

• Calabria is full of recipes for pickled or preserved olives; however, all call for the fresh ripe fruits. Usually, olives are soaked in water for 24 hours and marinated in layers with flavorful ingredients like garlic, oregano, peperoncino, olive oil, wine vinegar, salt, and pepper.

Insalata di arance
Orange Salad (Sicily)

Serves 4

2 juicy oranges
1 fresh, small fennel bulb
2 small white onions, thinly sliced
1 teaspoon fresh stemless rosemary (or 1/2 teaspoon dried)
1 tablespoon white wine vinegar
4 tablespoons extra virgin olive oil
Salt and freshly ground pepper

<u>Approximate preparation time:</u>
15 minutes;
140 calories per serving.

1 Peel the oranges, making sure to also remove the white skin. In a small mixing bowl, keep any juice that drips. Slice the oranges 1/4 inch thick and, if necessary, remove the seeds. Place the orange slices on a large serving platter.

2 Thoroughly clean the fennel and trim the woody and hard parts. Set aside the green feathery fennel tops for later use. Chop the tender inside of the fennel.

3 In the mixing bowl, combine any juice from the oranges with the white wine vinegar and olive oil. Mince the rosemary and add to the dressing. Season with salt and pepper.

4 Drop the chopped fennel into the dressing, make sure that everything is well coated, remove the fennel, and distribute it evenly over the orange slices. Top with the onion slices and drizzle the entire salad with the dressing. Season with coarsely ground pepper and garnish with the feathery fennel greens.

• You may leave out the fennel or substitute black olives, and you can add more onions.

Insalata di mare
Seafood Salad (Calabria/Sicily)

Serves 4

1 pound squid (either fresh or
   frozen and thawed)
3 1/2 ounces cooked shelled
   shrimp
2 lemons
1 bunch fresh Italian parsley,
   minced
1 teaspoon fresh oregano (1/2
   teaspoon dried)
1 to 2 red pickled chili peppers
2 cloves garlic, minced
5 tablespoons of extra virgin
   olive oil
Salt and freshly ground pepper

Approximate preparation time:
   50 minutes
   (+ 2 hours for marinating);
   220 calories per serving.

1 Prepare the squid: Rinse under running water, peel off
the membranes, cut off the
heads, and turn the mantles inside out.

2 In a large pot, bring 4 cups
of water to a boil with the
juice of 1/2 lemon and 1/2 teaspoon of salt. Drop the cleaned
squid into the boiling water and
cook covered for about 30 minutes (test the doneness with a
toothpick). Remove the squid
from the water and drain well.
Cut the tentacles into small
pieces and slice the mantle into
rings. In a large mixing bowl,
combine the squid with the
shrimps.

3 For the marinade, seed and
slice the pickled chili peppers. In a small mixing bowl,
whisk 2 to 3 tablespoons of
lemon juice with the olive oil
and season with salt, pepper,
and oregano. Add to the chili
peppers and garlic.

4 Drizzle the squid and the
shrimp with the marinade,
mix thoroughly, and refrigerate
for at least 2 hours to allow the
juices to seep into the seafood.

5 Remove the salad from the
refrigerator about 15 minutes before serving. Stir in the
fresh parsley. Season the salad
again with salt and pepper to
taste. Garnish with lemon
wedges.

• Another way to prepare squid
salad: Sauté cleaned and prepared squid in olive oil and season with garlic, oregano, powdered dried chili peppers, salt,
and pepper. Moisten with white
wine and simmer. Set aside to
cool in its juice, or while still
warm, dress like a salad with
cold-pressed olive oil, herbs,
and lemon juice. The salad will
be even more flavorful and brilliant in color if you add chopped
tomatoes, strips of red pepper,
and grated lemon peel.

Cannelloni
Stuffed Pasta (Sicily/Calabria)

Serves 4 to 5

For the dough:
1 cup + 2 tablespoons all-purpose flour + flour to roll out
1 cup semolina flour
2 eggs
Salt

For the filling:
1 pound braised roast beef with a flavorful gravy (for example, prepared according to recipe on page 68, (Brasato alla milanese)
3 ½ ounces caciocavallo or romano cheese in one piece for grating
Nutmeg
Salt and freshly ground pepper

Other ingredients:
Salt
2 to 3 tablespoons oil
5 tablespoons olive oil
2 eggs

Approximate preparation time:
2 hours
(prepare the roast ahead!);
480 calories per serving.

For a faster variation, use pre-cooked, prepackaged cannelloni. Be careful that the rolls don't fall apart during the filling step.

To save time, the filling can also be prepared with ground beef.

Delicious Italian alternatives to the meat filling: a filling of ricotta and spinach leaves, or a flavorful *sugo* of tomatoes with diced mozzarella and herbs. The stuffed crepes are also often baked with a thick layer of white béchamel sauce (as in the recipe on page 60).

1 Dough for the noodles: On a work surface, mix and make a well with the all-purpose and semolina flour. Add the eggs and ½ teaspoon of salt, moisten with ⅓ cup + 2 tablespoons of lukewarm water, and knead to a smooth and silky dough. Cover with a clean dishcloth for 20 minutes.

2 On the floured work surface, roll out the dough to a ¹⁄₁₆-inch-thick sheet. Cut out dough rectangles 4 inches in length. Bring 3 quarts of salted water mixed with 2 to 3 tablespoons of oil to a boil in a large pot. One by one, cook each sheet of dough for 5 minutes. Remove with a slotted spoon, dip into iced water, let drain well, and place on a clean dishcloth.

3 Pass the ready-to-use roast beef through a meat grinder or chop the meat into small dice. Place the meat into a large saucepan together with half of the pan juices, and simmer until you get an evenly sautéed meat mixture. Season with salt, pepper, and freshly ground nutmeg.

4 Brush a large baking dish with 3 tablespoons of oil. Preheat the oven to 400°F. Grate the caciocavallo cheese. On one side of each dough rectangle, place 2 tablespoons of the meat mixture, lengthwise, and sprinkle the meat with 1 tablespoon of cheese. Roll up each rectangle of dough. Place the stuffed crepes side by side in the prepared baking dish. Distribute any leftover sauce over the crepes and sprinkle with the remaining cheese. Drizzle 2 tablespoons of oil over the crepes.

5 Place the baking dish in the preheated oven and bake the cannelloni for 15 minutes. Beat the eggs, pour the mixture over the cannelloni, and bake for 5 additional minutes until the surface is golden brown.

Maccheroni alla calabrese

Macaroni with Prosciutto, Calabrian Style (Calabria)

Serves 4 to 6

4 ounces or 4 slices prosciutto
   (or raw country ham)
2 pounds fresh, ripe tomatoes
1 bunch fresh Italian parsley
1/2 bunch fresh basil
3 1/2 ounces caciocavallo or
   romano cheese in one piece
   for grating
1 pound maccheroni or bucatini
   noodles
5 tablespoons olive oil
1 dried chili pepper
1 onion, minced
2 to 3 cloves garlic, minced
1/2 teaspoon black peppercorns
Salt and freshly ground pepper

<u>*Approximate preparation time:*</u>
   70 minutes;
   500 calories per serving.

1 Blanch, peel, seed, and chop
tomatoes. Cut the prosciutto
into thin strips.

2 Heat 3 tablespoons of olive oil
in a medium saucepan. Sauté
the onion and chili pepper. Add

and stir in the garlic and ham,
sauté, and add the tomatoes.
Simmer this sauce for about
45 minutes while stirring
periodically.

3 Bring 3 quarts of salted water
to a boil in a large pot. Break 1
pound of maccheroni or bucatini
into shorter pieces and cook for
about 8 minutes or until still firm
to the bite.

4 Grate the caciocavallo
cheese, mince the parsley,
and cut the bunch of basil into
strips. Season the tomato sauce
with salt and pepper. Remove
the chili pepper. Fold three quarters of the parsley into the sauce.
Crush 1/2 teaspoon of peppercorns.

5 Drain the maccheroni and fold
in 2 tablespoons of olive oil
and the crushed peppercorns.
Add and combine the cheese and
the tomato sauce. Sprinkle with
the remaining minced herbs.

Pasta con le sarde

Noodles with Anchovies, Sardines, and Fennel (Sicily)

Serves 4 to 6

1 pound fresh sardines (or
   smelts or small whitefish)
1 fresh fennel bulb with greens
1 lemon (juice + peel)
1 bunch fresh Italian parsley
4 canned anchovy fillets,
   drained
1/2 cup raisins
2 tablespoons pine nuts
1 pound bucatini or maccheroni
1 teaspoon fennel seeds
1 medium onion, minced
3 cloves of garlic, minced
About 1/3 cup + 2 tablespoons
   olive oil
Salt and freshly ground pepper

<u>*Approximate preparation time:*</u>
   1 3/4 hours;
   600 calories per serving.

1 Clean the fish, remove the
bones, and cut off the
heads. Rinse and pat dry. Sprinkle with salt, drizzle with lemon
juice, and refrigerate.

2 Soak the raisins in water.
Clean, trim, and remove all
hard parts of the fennel. Set
aside the feathery green tops.
In a saucepan, bring salted water to a boil and cook the fennel
for 10 minutes. Drain and set
aside the fennel water. Dice the
fennel.

3 Mince 1/2 bunch of parsley.
Rinse the anchovies, pat
dry, and mince. In a mortar with
a pestle, crush the parsley, anchovies, garlic, grated lemon
peel, and fennel seeds with 4
tabelspoons olive oil.

4 Heat 2 tablespoons of oil in
a frying pan. Sauté the
onions. Stir in the fennel and
sauté. Reduce the temperature,
stir in the anchovy mixture, the
raisins with their liquid, a few
spoonfuls of fennel water, and
the pine nuts.

5 Add enough water to the
fennel water to make 3

Fusilli alla siracusana
Corkscrew Pasta with Vegetables and Capers, Syracuse Style (Sicily)

quarts and bring to a boil with salt in a pot. Add the noodles and cook until al dente. Drain and fold in 2 tablespoons of olive oil.

6 In a frying pan, heat 4 table-spoons of olive oil. Pat dry the sardines, fry for 2 minutes on both sides, and season with salt and pepper. Chop parsley and the fennel greens.

7 Layer the noodles length-wise in a preheated dish and season with salt and pepper. Drizzle each layer with the anchovy sauce, then top with fried sardines. Sprinkle chopped parsley and fennel greens over each layer and drizzle with 2 to 3 tablespoons of olive oil.

• In Sicily, this dish is baked with wild fennel, sometimes also with tomatoes.

Serves 4 to 6

1 small fresh eggplant (7 ounces)
2 fresh small yellow sweet peppers
1 2/3 pounds fresh, ripe tomatoes
1 bunch fresh basil
2 ounces caciocavallo or ro-mano cheese in one piece for grating
4 canned anchovy fillets, drained
2 ounces or 20 small, pitted black olives
2 tablespoons green capers
2 cloves garlic, thinly sliced
1 pound fusilli noodles
6 tablespoons olive oil
Salt and freshly ground pepper

<u>Approximate preparation time:</u>
1 3/4 hours;
440 calories per serving.

1 Cut the eggplant into 1/2-inch dice. Put the diced eggplant in a colander, sprinkle with salt,

and set aside to allow the juices to drain.

2 Cut the peppers into halves, seed, and remove the mem-branes. Roast or bake the pep-pers either under the broiler or in the oven (425°F) until the skin of the peppers has blisters and begins to turn dark. Re-move the peppers from the broiler/oven, cover with a clean, damp dishcloth, and peel. Chop the peppers after they have cooled.

3 Blanch, peel, seed, and chop the tomatoes. Rinse the 4 anchovies, pat them dry with paper towels, and mince. Chop the pitted olives.

4 Briefly rinse the diced egg-plant and pat dry. In a large frying pan, heat 4 tablespoons of olive oil. Stir-fry the eggplant and garlic. Add and stir in the anchovies and tomatoes. Sea-son with salt and pepper. Cover

and simmer for about 15 min-utes. Grate the cheese.

5 Bring 3 to 4 quarts of salted water to a boil in a large pot. Cook the fusilli for about 8 to 10 minutes or until al dente.

6 In the meantime, fold the chopped peppers, olives, and green capers into the sauce and continue simmering, uncovered, until the fusilli are done. Drain the noodles and fold in 2 tablespoons of olive oil.

7 Season the sauce with salt and pepper. In a large, pre-heated serving bowl, fold the sauce into the fusilli. Sprinkle with fresh shredded basil leaves and serve with grated cheese on the side.

• Fusilli—a corkscrew-shaped noodle that is also a favorite throughout Calabria.

Cuscusu
Couscous with Fish (Sicily)

Serves 4 to 6

10 ½ ounces or 1 ⅔ cups
   couscous
1 envelope saffron (or ½ to 1
   teaspoon saffron in bulk)
1 pinch powdered cloves
1 pinch cinnamon
Nutmeg
Salt and freshly ground pepper

For the fish stock:
2 pounds mixed fish (such as
   bass, mullet, sardines, and
   haddock)
1 pound or 5 medium large or
   10 fresh, ripe plum tomatoes
2 stalks celery
1 bunch fresh Italian parsley
1 onion, minced
3 cloves garlic, minced
1 bay leaf
5 tablespoons olive oil
2 whole cloves
Salt and freshly ground pepper

Approximate preparation time:
   3 hours;
   520 calories per serving.

Oriental fairy tales flavor this
chapter of Sicilian cuisine; the
traces of the Arabian past have
aromas of cinnamon, nutmeg,
cloves, and saffron.

Couscous, tiny kernels of hard
wheat flour or millet seeds, is
usually prepared in the areas of
its origins with mutton, poultry,
and chick-peas (garbanzo
beans); Sicilians combine it
mainly with fish and seafood. A
variation with lamb is also included on the island's list of
dishes.

If couscous is traditionally
steamed, it will be pleasantly
fluffy, soft, and still grainy. A
"couscoussière" is the original
cooking implement for making
this dish; however, you may also use a large pot with a sieve
or colander insert and a cover.

• Important: Periodically fluff up
the couscous with a fork and,
when it is done, crush the
lumps with your fingers.

1 For the fish soup, clean, rinse, and fillet the fish, or cut them into pieces. According to the type of fish you use, be sure to scale
the fish first (this goes especially for fresh bass and haddock; scale
sardines only lightly). Refrigerate the fish fillets for later use. For
the soup, use only the fish trimmings.

2 Blanch, peel, seed, and chop
the tomatoes. Mince ½
bunch of fresh parsley. Heat 5
tablespoons of olive oil in a
large saucepan. Add and sauté
the celery, onion, garlic, and
parsley.

3 Add the fish trimmings, the
tomatoes, and bay leaf. Season with salt and pepper. Add 6
cups of water, cover, and simmer for 30 minutes. Drain the
fish stock and return about 4
cups of stock to the pot. Pour
the remaining stock into a deep
pot to cook the fish.

4 Dissolve the saffron in a few
spoonfuls of stock. Moisten
the couscous with this liquid.
Bring the fish stock in the pot
to a boil. Place the couscous in
a large heat-resistant sieve or
colander over the boiling fish
stock and cover. Steam for
about 10 minutes, periodically
fluffing up the couscous.

5 Turn the couscous out onto a large platter, fluff it up with a fork, and let it cool. Again place the couscous in the colander and repeat the steaming operation over the fish stock for 10 more minutes.

6 In the meantime, bring the remaining stock (about 2 cups) to a boil in the deep pot. Place the fish in the stock and simmer on medium heat for 5 to 10 minutes. Chop the remaining parsley.

7 Season the couscous with salt, pepper, powdered cloves, cinnamon, and grated nutmeg, and place on a preheated platter. Top the couscous with the pieces of fish, sprinkle with the chopped parsley, and serve immediately.

• Tip: Cook down the remaining fish stock, season it with powdered dried chili peppers, and drizzle like a sauce over the couscous (keep the couscous warm until you serve it and top it with fish immediately before serving).

Nasello alla palermitana

Baked Hake with Rosemary, Palermo Style (Sicily)

Serves 4

*1 fresh hake (about 2 pounds)
ready to use (you may substitute rockfish)
2 small fresh sprigs of rosemary
2 lemons
6 canned anchovy fillets,
drained
2 cloves garlic, minced
4 tablespoons unseasoned
breadcrumbs
About 1/2 cup olive oil
Salt and freshly ground pepper*

<u>Approximate preparation time:</u>
*1 hour;
500 calories per serving.*

1 Have the hake prepared at
your fish market for kitchen
use (scaling, emptying, and removing gills). Before preparing
the fish, rinse it thoroughly under running water and pat it dry
with paper towels. Sprinkle the
inside and outside with salt and
pepper.

2 Brush a large, flat baking
dish with 2 tablespoons of
olive oil and add the rosemary.
Preheat the oven to 300°F.

3 Thoroughly rinse the anchovies, pat them dry, and
mince. In a small saucepan,
heat them up in 2 to 3 tablespoons of olive oil. Press and
crush them to a paste with a
fork, and cream them with the
oil. Stir the garlic into the anchovies. Add 2 to 3 tablespoons of olive oil.

4 Brush the inside of the fish
with some of the anchovy
mixture. Place the fish in the
baking dish on top of the rosemary and drizzle with the remaining anchovy mixture.
Sprinkle the fish with the breadcrumbs and the remaining olive
oil. Bake in the preheated oven
for about 40 minutes. Garnish
with slices of lemon and serve.

Tonno alla marinara

Braised Tuna, Mariner's Style (Sicily/Calabria)

Serves 4

*4 slices of fresh tuna (about 1/2
pound each)
2 pounds fresh, ripe tomatoes
(or a 28-ounce can of peeled
tomatoes)
1 bunch fresh basil
Fresh mint leaves
1/2 cup dry white wine
20 small pitted black olives
2 tablespoons green capers,
minced
1 small onion, minced
2 cloves garlic, crushed
6 tablespoons olive oil
Salt and freshly ground pepper*

<u>Approximate preparation time:</u>
*1 hour;
720 calories per serving.*

1 Rinse the tuna, and pat dry
with paper towels. Rub all
sides of the tuna with the
crushed garlic. Season with salt
and pepper. Preheat the oven
to 350°F.

2 Blanch, peel, seed the tomatoes (drain the canned tomatoes thoroughly and save the
juice). Mince the peeled tomatoes. Chop the olives. Cut the
fresh leaves of basil and mint
into thin strips.

3 Brush a large baking dish
with 4 tablespoons of olive
oil. Put the tuna side by side in
the baking dish and drizzle with
1/2 cup of white wine. Top the
tuna slices with the chopped
tomatoes, onion, olives, capers,
and half of the herbs, and drizzle with the remaining 2 tablespoons of olive oil. Season with
salt and pepper.

4 Bake in the preheated oven
on the middle rack for 20 to
30 minutes. Sprinkle with fresh
herbs and serve.

Braciole di pesce spada
Grilled Swordfish Rollups (Sicily)

Serves 4

4 long, thin slices of swordfish
   (about 6 1/2 ounces each)
2 ounces provolone cheese
   (you may substitute mozzarella)
1/2 bunch fresh parsley, minced
1 teaspoon fresh thyme (or 1/2
   teaspoon dried)
1 tablespoon green capers,
   minced
3 tablespoons unseasoned
   breadcrumbs (preferably
   freshly grated)
1 onion, minced
2 cloves garlic, minced
5 tablespoons olive oil
1 pinch cayenne pepper
Salt and freshly ground pepper

For the sauce:
2 lemons (7 to 8 tablespoons
   juice)
1/2 bunch fresh parsley
1 teaspoons fresh oregano (or
   1/2 teaspoon dried)
1/2 cup extra virgin olive oil
Salt

Approximate preparation time:
   1 hour;
   500 calories per serving.

1 Rinse the swordfish, and pat
dry. Sprinkle with salt and refrigerate.

2 Heat 2 tablespoons of olive
oil in a small frying pan.
Sauté the onion and garlic. Stir
in the breadcrumbs and stir-fry
until golden brown. Remove
the frying pan from the heat
and fold in the herbs and the
capers. Season the mixture
with salt, pepper, and cayenne
pepper.

3 Thinly slice the cheese.
Evenly sprinkle the herbed
breadcrumb mixture over the
swordfish slices, top the slices
with cheese, and make the
swordfish rollups. Close the
rollups with a toothpick.

4 Brush a griddle with 1 tablespoon of olive oil and heat.

Place the fish rollups on the
griddle, drizzle with the remaining oil, and grill on medium heat
on all sides (about 7 to 8 minutes).

5 In the meantime, prepare
the sauce. With a reamer,
press out the juice of the
lemons into a small bowl.
Mince 1/2 bunch of parsley and
1 teaspoon of oregano. Dissolve 1/4 teaspoon of salt in 1/2
cup of warm water. Put 1/2 cup
of olive oil in a second small
mixing bowl and place the mixing bowl in a bowl with warm
water. In a stream, gradually
pour and whisk the salted water and lemon juice into the oil.
Add the herbs and serve with
the swordfish. Season the fish
with freshly ground pepper.

• This dish also can be prepared with slices of shark.

Farsumagru

Mock Lean Roast Roll (Sicily)

Large roasts, made from beef or veal, are rare in Sicilian daily cooking; this rich roast roll is a classic, especially because of its typical and hearty filling.

• If this meat is sliced thin, it is also delicious either cold or lukewarm; it can serve as snack or an appetizer.

Serves 4 to 6

1 large, about 1 ¼-inch-thick lean piece of beef (about 1 ⅓ pound for example, such as a flank steak or a chuck steak from the shoulder)
7 ounces ground beef
5 ounces mild Italian sausage, without the casing
3 ½ ounces raw prosciutto (or raw country ham)
1 bunch fresh Italian parsley, minced
1 teaspoon fresh rosemary leaves (or ½ teaspoon dried)
1 teaspoon fresh thyme (or ½ teaspoon dried)
3 tablespoons freshly grated romano or Parmesan cheese
3 ½ ounces provolone or mozzarella cheese

1 roll without crust
3 eggs (2 of which are hard-boiled)
2 egg yolks
4 tablespoons milk
2 cups red wine
1 28-ounce can peeled tomatoes
1 bay leaf
2 cloves garlic, minced
1 onion, coarsely chopped
6 tablespoons of olive oil
Salt and freshly ground pepper

Approximate preparation time:
   3 hours;
   830 calories per serving.

1 Butterfly the meat horizontally (cut a deep horizontal pocket into the meat without cutting the meat through to the other side), open the two sides, press them down, and beat until both sides are no thicker than ½ inch.

2 Shred the roll into tiny crumbs. Beat 1 whole egg with 2 egg yolks and the milk. Soak the bread in this mixture. Mince the rosemary.

3 For the filling, combine the ground beef and the sausage in a large mixing bowl. Add the egg and bread mixture, 3 tablespoons of the grated romano cheese, the parsley, garlic, rosemary, and thyme. Mix everything thoroughly and season with salt and pepper.

4 Place the meat on a flat working surface and, with wet hands, evenly spread the filling mixture over the meat. Leave a 1-inch space without stuffing around the edges of the meat.

5 Cut the provolone cheese into thin slices, and slice the prosciutto into thin strips. Peel 2 hard-boiled eggs and slice. Place the ground beef on the open meat with an evenly spread layer of cheese slices, strips of prosciutto, and hard-boiled egg slices.

6 Roll up the slab of meat and carefully tie with a kitchen string. Preheat the oven to 350°F. Heat up 6 tablespoons of olive oil in a large Dutch oven.

7 Add the roast roll to the hot oil, brown evenly on all sides, and remove it when it is brown. Sauté the onion in the Dutch oven. Moisten with 2 cups of red wine, bring to a very rapid boil, and simmer until it is cooked down at least to half. Return the roast to the Dutch oven.

8 Chop the canned tomatoes and distribute the juice and the tomatoes around the meat in the Dutch oven. Season with salt and pepper and add the bay leaf. Cover. Bake in the oven for about 2 hours. When the roast roll is ready, slice it and serve with the tomato sauce.

Scaloppine al marsala
Veal Cutlets in Marsala Wine (Sicily)

Serves 4

4 large boneless veal cutlets
   (5 ounces each)
2 tablespoons clarified butter
About 1/2 cup Marsala
   (Sicilian sweet wine)
1 clove garlic
2 tablespoons cold butter
Salt and freshly ground pepper

<u>Approximate preparation time:</u>
   30 minutes;
   310 calories per serving.

1 Butterfly the veal cutlets and, with the smooth side of a meat mallet, pound them carefully until they are somewhat thinner. Rub the cutlets on both sides with pepper.

2 Peel the garlic. In a large frying pan, slowly heat the clarified butter. Add the garlic and sauté for about 2 minutes on medium low heat. Remove the garlic. Increase the heat.

3 Place the cutlets into the hot butter and brown on both sides for about 5 minutes. Remove the meat, place it on a preheated serving plate, and keep warm.

4 Pour the excess fat out of the pan, moisten the pan juices with Marsala wine, and allow the liquid to reach a rolling boil. Drop the cold butter into the sauce and let it melt. Season with salt and pepper. Place the cutlets in the sauce and rapidly heat once more before serving.

• Garlic lovers can roast more than one clove of garlic with the cutlets and serve the meat with the garlic.

• Potatoes and vegetables (for example, fresh broccoli) are suitable side dishes.

Morseddu
Meat Pie (Calabria)

Serves 4

<u>For the dough:</u>
1/2 fresh compressed cake of yeast, or a 1 1/4-ounce envelope active dry yeast
1 3/4 cups all-purpose flour + flour to roll out the dough
1 pinch salt

<u>For the filling:</u>
1/4 pound fresh boneless pork shoulder chop or picnic ham
5 ounces fresh pork liver
5 ounces fresh veal liver
4 tablespoons pureed tomatoes (or tomato paste)
2 tablespoons vegetable oil
1 peperoncino or any chili pepper
1 onion, minced
2 cloves garlic, minced
1 teaspoon dried oregano
Salt and freshly ground pepper

<u>Other ingredients:</u>
Olive oil to brush a pan and dough
1 teaspoon oregano to sprinkle over the pie

<u>Approximate preparation time:</u>
   2 hours
   (+ 30 minutes rising time);
   600 calories per serving.

1 For the dough, mix the yeast with 2 tablespoons of lukewarm water and 2 tablespoons of flour. Place the remaining flour in a bowl, make a well, and add salt and the dough starter. Cover with a clean dishcloth and let the starter rest for 30 minutes in a warm place. Moisten the flour mixture with 1/2 cup lukewarm water. Knead to a dough. Cover and let rise for about 1 hour or until the volume of the dough has increased in size.

2 Prepare the pie filling: Cut the pork and the liver into 1/2-inch dice.

3 Heat the oil in a saucepan and brown the pieces of liver. Remove the liver. Add the minced onion, garlic, and peper-

oncino and sauté until limp.

4 Brown the diced pork evenly on all sides. Season with the oregano, salt, and pepper. Dissolve the pureed tomatoes into 4 tablespoons of water, and stir into the meat. Cover and simmer for about 10 minutes. Add the liver and cook for 10 more minutes. Remove the cover and simmer again. Remove the peperoncino and season with salt and pepper.

5 Preheat the oven to 350°F. Brush a 10-inch baking pan with olive oil. On a floured work surface, roll out two-thirds of the dough to 1/4-inch thickness. Line the pan with this dough, and roll the overlapping dough outward around the walls of the pan. Top the dough with the filling and fold the overlapping dough inward.

6 Roll out the remaining dough to a wheel suitable

for covering the pie. Cover the pie and the filling. Pierce the top of the dough and brush with olive oil. You also can sprinkle the pie with oregano. Bake in the oven for about 50 minutes.

• In Sicily, meat pies are also favorites, such as the *pasticcio di carne* prepared with a flaky dough made from flour, shortening, and eggs, and a filling of pork combined with almonds, cinnamon, and pistachios.

Pollo alla messinese
Chicken with Tuna Sauce (Sicily)

Serves 4

1 fresh chicken (about 2 1/2 pounds)
1 carrot, cubed
2 stalks celery, cubed
2 lemons (juice)
1 bunch fresh Italian parsley
1/2 bunch fresh basil
1 can tuna in spring water (about 6 ounces)
1 tablespoon green capers
1 egg yolk
1 onion, cubed
1/2 cup + 1 tablespoon olive oil
Salt and freshly ground pepper

<u>Approximate preparation time:</u>
about 2 hours;
670 calories per serving.

1 Bring 3 quarts of salted water to a boil in a large pot. Add the carrots, celery, and onion to the boiling water. Pour in the juice of 1 lemon. Rub the chicken on all sides with pepper, lower it into the boiling water, and simmer on the lowest cooking heat (time will vary according to

the type and size of chicken —1 to 2 hours).

2 In a small bowl, mash the tuna with the capers and 2 tablespoons of olive oil. Mince 1/2 bunch of parsley and 1/2 bunch of basil.

3 In a medium mixing bowl, cream 1 egg yolk with 1 pinch of salt and 2 tablespoons of lemon juice. While gradually pouring the remaining oil in a stream, beat all the ingredients with a hand mixer to a mayonnaise.

4 Stir the herbs, the tuna, and a few spoonfuls of chicken broth into the mayonnaise. Season with salt and pepper, and if necessary, more lemon juice.

5 Remove the chicken from its broth and let it cool. Remove the skin. Place the chicken on a serving platter and serve with the tuna sauce.

Pomodori alla siciliana
Stuffed Tomatoes, Sicilian Style (Sicily)

Serves 4

4 large, fresh, ripe tomatoes
1/2 lemon (about 2 tablespoons
 of juice)
1 bunch fresh Italian parsley
4 tablespoons freshly grated romano or Parmesan cheese
1 can (3 1/2 to 4 1/2 ounces) sardines (preserved either in
 spring water or in olive oil)
10 to 15 small, unpitted black
 olives
2 tablespoons green capers
2 onions, minced
2 cloves garlic, minced
1 dry stale roll (or 4 tablespoons
 unseasoned breadcrumbs)
6 tablespoons olive oil
Salt and freshly ground pepper

Approximate preparation time:
 1 1/2 hours;
 290 calories per serving.

• In Calabria there are also flavorful recipes for stuffed tomatoes,
traditionally prepared either with
noodles and herbs or with
ground beef, grated pecorino
cheese, breadcrumbs, and parsley.
• Stuffed tomatoes make a wonderful side dish for roasted meat
or fish; they can also be served
as an appetizer or as a snack
with fresh, crispy white bread.

1 Thoroughly rinse the tomatoes, cut off the tops, and
seed them with a spoon. Remove the inside meat of the
tomato and chop fine. Season
the insides of the tomato with
salt and, to allow the excess
juice to drain, turn them over in
a colander.

2 Drain the sardines and chop.
Drizzle with the lemon juice.
Grate the roll into crumbs. With
a small knife cut the pulp off
the olive pits. Mince 1/2 bunch
of fresh parsley.

3 Heat 1 tablespoon of olive oil in a large frying pan. Sauté the
onions until glossy. Stir in the minced garlic and parsley and
continue sautéing. Add the chopped sardines and chopped tomato
meat, sauté, and simmer until the liquid has evaporated. Stir in the
pieces of olives and the capers. Continue simmering. Season with
pepper and, if necessary, with salt, and remove the pan from the
source of heat.

4 Preheat the oven to 350ºF and brush a large baking dish with 1 tablespoon of olive oil. Place the well-drained whole tomatoes side by side in the baking dish with their openings facing up.

5 Heat 2 tablespoons of olive oil in a small frying pan and brown the breadcrumbs until golden. Mix 3 tablespoons of the grated romano or Parmesan cheese and half of the toasted breadcrumbs into the prepared filling. Season with salt and pepper. Fill the empty tomato shells with the filling. Add to the baking dish.

6 Sprinkle the stuffed tomatoes with the remaining breadcrumbs and 1 tablespoon of cheese, and drizzle with the remaining 2 tablespoons of olive oil. Bake in the preheated oven for about 30 minutes. Mince 1/2 bunch of parsley and sprinkle it over the tomatoes. Serve hot.

Peperonata
Stewed Peppers (Sicily)

Serves 4

3 large, fresh, sweet peppers
   (red, green, and/or yellow)
1 pound or 5 medium or 10
   fresh, ripe plum tomatoes
2 medium large onions
2 cloves garlic
4 tablespoons white wine
   vinegar
4 tablespoons olive oil
1 pinch cayenne pepper
Salt and freshly ground pepper

<u>Approximate preparation time:</u>
   1 hour;
   130 calories per serving.

1 Cut the peppers into halves, and seed and remove the internal membranes. Rinse the pepper halves and cut each half into four pieces.

2 Blanch, peel, and quarter the tomatoes. Remove the seeds with a spoon. Coarsely chop the tomatoes.

3 Cut the onions into halves, and slice them thin. Thinly slice the garlic.

4 Heat the oil in a large frying pan. Sauté the onions until glossy. Add and stir-fry the peppers and the garlic.

5 Drizzle the vegetables with the wine vinegar and rapidly bring to a boil. Season with salt, pepper, and cayenne pepper. Add and stir in the peeled tomatoes. Reduce the heat, cover the pan, and simmer the pepper mixture for about 20 minutes. The peppers should be done but should not fall apart. Season with salt and pepper.

• Serve hot, lukewarm, or cold as a side dish for meat.

Patate al marsala
Roasted Potatoes with Marsala Wine (Sicily)

Serves 4

1 ²/₃ pounds potatoes, preferably small and evenly sized
   (red or waxy variety; if available, use new potatoes)
1 bunch fresh basil
1/2 cup dry Marsala (Sicilian
   sweet dessert wine)
4 tablespoons olive oil
3 tablespoons butter
Salt and freshly ground pepper

<u>Approximate preparation time:</u>
   1 hour;
   310 calories per serving.

1 Rinse and peel the potatoes. Heat the olive oil in a large frying pan and melt 1 tablespoon of butter. Add the potatoes and brown for 10 minutes on medium heat.

2 Turn the potatoes over, add 1 tablespoon of butter, and brown for about 5 more minutes.

3 Moisten the potatoes with the dry Marsala, and rapidly bring to a boil. Reduce the heat, add 1 more tablespoon of butter to the potatoes, and season with salt. Continue browning for 20 to 25 minutes (time will vary according to the size of the potatoes). Occasionally, turn the potatoes over. Sprinkle the crispy potatoes with fresh basil leaves, season with freshly ground pepper, and serve immediately.

• Important: Use only dry *Marsala*, and not a sweet variety. You may substitute with dry sherry.

• The method of preparing these potatoes can be applied to other types of vegetables; for example, carrots (*carote al marsala*) are a well-known variation.

Insalata mista
Mixed Salad (Calabria)

Serves 4

1 fresh, young fennel bulb
   (7 ounces)
1 fresh, sweet red pepper
   (5 ounces)
5 ounces young carrots
2 small zucchini (about 5
   ounces)
4 fresh stalks celery
7 tablespoons olive oil
2 to 3 tablespoons white wine
   vinegar
Salt and freshly ground pepper

Approximate preparation time:
   45 minutes;
   210 calories per serving.

1 Clean the fennel and trim all
the woody and hard parts.
Slice the heart of the fennel paper thin. Set aside the feathery
green parts of the fennel.

2 Cut the peppers into halves;
seed and remove the internal membranes. Rinse the pepper halves and cut them into
thin strips.

3 Peel the carrots and rinse
the zucchini and celery
(keep the young celery leaves).
Slice these vegetables either
paper thin or in thin strips (julienne).

4 Mix all the ingredients in a
large bowl. Add the celery
leaves and the feathery fennel
tops.

5 For the dressing, in a small
bowl, whisk the olive oil,
white wine vinegar, salt, and
pepper. Drizzle the dressing
over the salad and serve immediately.

• Important: Use aromatic extra
virgin oil and vigorously whisk
the vinegar and the seasonings.
You can increase the amount of
vinegar or enhance the flavor
with lemon juice to taste.

Caponata
Sweet-and-Sour Eggplant Relish (Sicily)

Serve 4 to 6

1 1/3 pounds fresh eggplant
3 stalks celery
1 medium onion (preferably a
    sweet variety, such as Vi-
    dalia or Spanish), coarsely
    chopped
1 bunch fresh basil
1 28-ounce can peeled toma-
    toes
20 small, pitted green olives
2 tablespoons green capers
5 to 6 tablespoons aromatic
    white wine vinegar
About 1/3 cup + 2 tablespoons
    olive oil
1/2 teaspoon sugar
Salt and freshly ground pepper

Approximate preparation time:
    1 1/2 hours;
    240 calories per serving.

1 Dice the eggplant (1/2 inch) and place into a fine strainer. Sprinkle with salt and set aside for about 1 hour to allow the bitter juices to drain off.

2 Clean the celery and cut into 1 1/2-inch-long pieces. Set aside the tender top leaves. Drain the tomatoes and chop. Set the tomato juice aside to be used later (for example, for tomato soup). Cut the olives into halves.

3 Heat 4 tablespoons of olive oil in a large frying pan. Sauté the onions until glossy. Add the celery and stir-fry. Sprinkle with the sugar and season with salt and pepper. Stir in the tomatoes, olives, and capers. Simmer in the uncovered pan on low heat for 15 minutes. Stir occasionally.

4 In the meantime, rinse the diced eggplant and pat dry with paper towels. Heat the remaining olive oil in another large frying pan, and brown the eggplant dice until golden and crispy on all sides. Place the eggplant on paper towels to allow the excess fat to drain.

5 Add the eggplant dice to the other vegetables in the first large frying pan. Moisten with the white wine vinegar and simmer everything for 15 more minutes. Season with salt and pepper, and more vinegar if desired. Sprinkle with chopped celery and basil leaves.

• Especially delicious lukewarm. Goes well as an appetizer with bread and rice, as a side dish with grilled meat, or as a main course, for example, with hard-boiled eggs or with a small squid dish.

Involtini di melanzane con salsa di pomodoro

Eggplant Rollups in Tomato Sauce (Calabria)

Serves 4 to 6

For the eggplant rollups:
2 large, elongated eggplants (about 1 ¹/₃ pounds)
1 bunch fresh Italian parsley, minced
1 bunch fresh basil, minced
5 ounces or 2 small balls mozzarella
4 tablespoons freshly grated romano or Parmesan cheese
2 cloves garlic, minced
3 tablespoons unseasoned breadcrumbs
About 6 tablespoons olive oil
Salt and freshly ground pepper

For the tomato sauce:
2 pounds fresh, ripe tomatoes
1 peperoncino (or any hot chili pepper)
1 onion, minced
2 cloves garlic, minced
2 tablespoons olive oil
¹/₂ cup red wine
Salt and freshly ground pepper or cayenne pepper

Approximate preparation time:
80 minutes;
290 calories per serving.

1 For the rollups, rinse and trim the eggplant. Slice them lengthwise ¹/₄ inch thick. Sprinkle the slices of eggplant on both sides with salt, and place, side by side, on a clean dishcloth. Set aside for about 1 hour to allow the bitter juices to drain off.

2 In the meantime, prepare the sauce. For this step, blanch the tomatoes in boiling water in a large pot. Peel, seed, and mince the tomatoes. Heat the olive oil in a large saucepan. Sauté the onion and garlic until limp. Stir in the peperoncino, ¹/₂ cup of red wine, and the chopped tomatoes. Season with salt and pepper and continue simmering on low heat.

3 Rinse the eggplant slices and pat them dry with paper towels. In a small saucepan, heat 1 tablespoon olive oil and brown the breadcrumbs. Mix the breadcrumbs with the parsley, basil, garlic, and grated cheese. Moisten the mixture with the olive oil and season with salt and pepper. Thinly slice the mozzarella.

4 Spread the herbed breadcrumb mixture evenly on the slices of eggplant, and line each slice with slices of mozzarella. Roll up and keep in place with a toothpick.

5 Brush a griddle with olive oil and heat. Grill the eggplant rollups on the hot griddle until they are evenly golden brown and somewhat crispy. If necessary, brush the griddle with more oil. Season with freshly ground pepper.

301

Cassata alla siciliana
Molded Dessert, Sicilian Style (Sicily)

Serves 12

For the sponge cake (preferably prepared ahead of time):
1/2 lemon (peel)
4 eggs, separated
1/2 cup + 2 tablespoons granulated sugar
1 cup + 2 tablespoons all-purpose flour
1 pinch salt

For the filling:
1 3/4 pounds (or 2 small 15 ounce containers) ricotta cheese
3 tablespoons + 3 teaspoons Maraschino liqueur
5 ounces semi-sweet chocolate
1/2 cup shelled unsalted pistachio nuts
5 ounces or 3/4 cup candied fruit
1 1/2 cups granulated sugar

To decorate:
1 cup or 1/2 pint whipping cream
1 teaspoon vanilla sugar
9 ounces candied fruit to use sliced or whole to decorate

Approximate preparation time:
2 hours
(+ 3 hours refrigeration);
670 calories per serving.

With the exception of the candied fruit, the popular Italian ice cream dessert called *cassata* has nothing in common with the original Sicilian cassata featured here. For the inhabitants of the island, cassata has a special meaning. It is often the final center-stage touch to a grand festive meal, such as the Easter meal or a wedding reception.

• Good and fresh authentic Italian ricotta cheese is not available everywhere; if you use the commercial American variety, pay attention to the expiration date on the packages and make sure to drain it well.

• Variation for decorating: You may also glaze the cake with chocolate glaze, or you can simply dust the cake with confectioners' sugar.

1 Sponge cake: Preheat the oven to 350°F. In a small mixing bowl, beat the egg whites to a stiff peak with a pinch of salt. In a stream, gradually add the granulated sugar and the grated lemon peel. Fold in and mix the egg yolks and all-purpose flour. Line a 9-inch, round springform pan with parchment paper. Pour in the batter and spread out evenly.

2 Bake in the preheated oven for about 24 minutes. Remove the sponge cake from the oven; turn the cake over on a cooling rack, and let cool off completely. When the cake is cold, cut it into 3 layers with a cake knife.

3 Filling: Cream the ricotta cheese in a mixing bowl. In a small saucepan, mix the granulated sugar with 1/2 cup of water, heat, and let the sugar melt into a light syrup. Remove from the heat and let cool. Fold the syrup into the ricotta cheese with 2 tablespoons of Maraschino liqueur, and mix.

4 Coarsely chop the chocolate, pistachio, and candied fruit. Fold these ingredients into the ricotta cream.

5 Return one layer of sponge cake to the springform pan and drizzle with 2 teaspoons of Maraschino liqueur. Top the flavored layer of sponge cake with half of the ricotta cream, spread the filling evenly, and cover the cream with another layer of sponge cake. Drizzle this layer of cake also with liqueur, topping it with the remaining cream and covering the cream with the last sponge cake layer; drizzle the last layer with the remaining liqueur.

6 Refrigerate the cake for at least 3 hours, allowing it to become firm. Later, place the cake on a cake server and carefully open the springform pan.

7 Whip the whipping cream with the vanilla sugar to a stiff peak. Cover the cake with three-quarters of the whipped cream; fill a pastry bag with the remaining whipped cream and decorate. Distribute the fruits attractively while decorating the cake. Serve as soon as possible.

Vecchiarelle
Honey Fritters (Calabria)

Serves 6

1/3 cup blanched almonds
1/3 cup very fluid honey
1/2 fresh compressed cube or
    1 1/2 1/4-ounce envelopes ac-
    tive dry, or 3 1/2 teaspoons
    of active dry yeast
1 cup confectioners' sugar
3 cups + 3 tablespoons all-pur-
    pose flour
1 pinch salt
1 pinch powdered cloves
1/4 teaspoon powdered cinna-
    mon
Enough vegetable oil to fry

Approximate preparation time:
    30 minutes (+ 1 hour resting
    time for the dough);
    430 calories per serving.

1 Chop the almonds and roast
them until golden in a frying
pan.

2 Dough: In a bowl, make a
well with the flour. Dissolve
the yeast in 2 tablespoons of
lukewarm water. Add the yeast,

almonds, and confectioners'
sugar to the flour well.

3 Mix all the ingredients with
1/3 cup + 2 tablespoons of
lukewarm water, and knead into a smooth, dough. Cover with
a clean dishcloth, and set aside
in a warm place for 1 hour or
until the volume has increased
in size. Refrigerate.

4 On a floured work surface,
knead the dough and cut it,
like French fries (1/2 inch x 2 to
2 1/2 inches). In a frying pan or
an electric fryer, heat enough
oil to fry. Fry the dough sticks
until golden and crispy. Remove
them, place them and on paper
towels to drain. Drizzle with
honey.

• In the original recipe, these
fritters are fried and then
dumped into the honey; our
version is less rich and sticky.

Pesche ripiene
Stuffed Peaches (Sicily)

Serves 4

4 large, ripe, yellow peaches
3 ounces or 6 double-wrapped
    or 12 single Amaretti
1/3 cup + 2 tablespoons Marsala
2 tablespoons lemon juice
1 egg yolk
8 blanched almonds
1 to 2 tablespoons granulated
    sugar
2 to 3 tablespoons butter
1 tablespoon confectioners'
    sugar

Approximate preparation time:
    35 minutes;
    380 calories per serving.

1 Blanch and peel the peaches, cut them into halves, and
remove the pits. Scrape out
some peach pulp from the center of the halves, put the pulp in
a large mixing bowl, and mash
it with a fork. Preheat the oven
to 400°F.

2 Crush the Amaretti and drizzle with Marsala. Add this
mixture to the peach pulp in the
mixing bowl, together with the
sugar, lemon juice, and egg
yolk. Mix thoroughly. Fill each
peach with this stuffing, and
top each stuffed peach with a
blanched almond.

3 Put the peaches in a large,
buttered baking dish, dot
with butter, and drizzle the remaining Marsala on top.

4 Bake in the oven for about
15 minutes. Lightly dust
with confectioners' sugar.

• The deliciously sweet *Marsala*
wine is a product of this island;
in Sicily, the wine is not only
served as an alcoholic drink, but
is also enthusiastically used in
sweet or sweet-and-sour dishes. The dry variation of this
wine (secco) is the most suitable for this dessert.

Budino di ricotta

Ricotta Pudding (Sicily)

Serves 6

15 ounces ricotta cheese
1 lemon (peel)
3/4 cup milk or water
4 eggs
2 tablespoons raisins
1 tablespoon + 1 teaspoon rum
1 ounce each of candied lemon
  and candied orange peel
3 tablespoons semolina
4 tablespoons confectioners'
  sugar + sugar for dusting
1/4 teaspoon powdered cinnamon
Baking spray and flour for the
  pan
Candied fruits to garnish

Approximate preparation time:
· *1 1/2 hours;*
   260 calories per serving.

1 Soak the raisins in the rum
and mince the candied lemon
peel and candied orange peel.

2 Heat the milk in a saucepan
and, while stirring constantly, pour in the semolina. Simmer until the semolina has
thickened.

3 Remove the semolina from
the heat, pour it onto a plate
that has been rinsed with cold
water, and let it cool off. Preheat the oven to 350°F.

4 In a large bowl, mix the ricotta, sugar, 1 whole egg, 3 egg
yolks, minced lemon and orange
peel, soaked raisins, cinnamon,
and the grated peel of 1 lemon.

5 Beat 3 egg whites to a stiff
peak. Stir the cold semolina
into the ricotta. Fold the beaten
egg whites into the mixture.

6 Grease pudding mold (about
1 1/2 quart) and dust it with
flour. Pour the ricotta mixture into it. Bake in the oven in a water bath for about 1 hour. When
the pudding is done, turn it over
on a plate, and dust with sugar.
Garnish with candied fruits.

Mantecato di melone

Melon Sherbet (Sicily)

Serves 6

1 honeydew melon (about 1 3/4
  pounds)
1 lemon (about 4 to 5 tablespoons juice)
6 tablespoons granulated sugar

Approximate preparation time:
   20 minutes
   (+ 3–4 hours freezing);
   140 calories per serving.

1 In a small saucepan, gradually heat the granulated sugar
with 6 to 8 tablespoons of
water until the sugar has dissolved. Simmer for a few minutes on medium heat, then remove from the heat and cool.

2 Peel and seed the melon,
cut the pulp into small
pieces, and puree in a food
processor. Mix the lemon juice
into the puree.

3 Mix the cold sugar syrup into the melon mixture and

pour everything into a freezer-
safe bowl.

4 Freeze the sherbet until it
has reached a semisolid
consistency (about 1 hour). Remove from the freezer, stir vigorously, return to the freezer,
and allow to solidify some
more.

5 About 1/2 hour before serving, remove the sherbet and
briefly thaw. Vigorously stir
once more and serve in small
dessert bowls or attractive
glasses.

• This is a refreshing all-purpose dessert that, in Sicily,
sometimes is made from wa-
termelon instead of honeydew,
or is enhanced with pine nuts,
raisins, candied lemon peel,
and cinnamon.

Tomatoes—A Cherished Southern Treasure

Tomatoes, today undoubtedly a synonym for Italy's cuisine, play a major leading role in the southern regions of Italy's boot and in Sicily. The gift from America to the Old World, brought by the Spaniards in the sixteenth century, has revolutionized the entire culinary scene in Italy. It would be hard to imagine how today's Italians could cook without their "golden apples."

In the southern climate, tomatoes find their indispensable 120 sunny days a year, during which the ripening and the building of their full aroma can unfold. Either as a main dish or side dish, or as a flavoring, they impart their unique flavor, aroma, and color to Italian dishes. During harvest time in many locations, as in Francavilla di Sicilia, a small town at the foot of Mt. Etna, it is easy to spot women gathered to can and preserve the summer blessings in bottles and glass jars for the winter.

The region around Etna is very fertile. In addition to wine products, fruit and citrus growers take advantage of the mineral – rich soil resulting from the still – smoking volcano that periodically spits up fire, ash, and lava. Squeezed in between the rows or among the perennially green orange trees, vegetables are grown for daily use on very closely monitored spaces: artichokes, beans, onions, potatoes, broccoli, eggplants, and peppers, but above all, tomatoes.

When the tomato foliage begins to wilt and brown, from the middle of August until the end of September, the fully ripened plump tomatoes are even more visible. Under their shiny skins, a wonderful mixture of well – balanced acidity and sweetness with a remarkable aroma has developed over the summer. They hang on their vines in large clusters, using only the support of cages or poles. Harvesting them is easy. Only those fruits still green around the stem stay behind for a slow, complete ripening that happens gradually, until the southern wind signals the end of the season.

Throughout Mt. Etna's surroundings, the egg- or pear-shaped San Marzano, a fleshy variety low on seeds, is widely grown. This variety is cherished in the neighboring region of Calabria on the other side of the *stretto*, the road from the Straits of Messina, as well as in the heart of the Sicilian tomato region in the province of Ragusa. It is the tomato industry here, throughout the plains of Sicily, that harvests the peeled fruit or the raw material for concentrates for cans and tubes.

A common landscape throughout the South of Italy are fields of tomatoes as far as the eye can see. Not only do the numerous single users harvest the tomatoes here, but the entire industry also cherishes the flavorful fruits.

Above, top: Cases filled with brilliant fruit—with this sign, the vegetable peddler has it easy. The southern gold sells well directly from a truck either with or without a picturesque panoramic background.

Above: Jars filled to the rim contain the valued food that the Italian family stocks up on for the whole year. Tomatoes are the most important culinary basis for daily meals and extraordinary specialties—there is hardly anyone who cooks without them.

Italy's north, the rest of Europe, (and America), can also enjoy the Sicilian tomatoes. Compared to their less flavorful relatives from other areas and countries or from greenhouses, even canned Southern Italian tomatoes have no competitors.

Instead of using industrial products, women in Sicily and Calabria remain attached to home canning, not only because home – canned tomatoes taste better, but for economical reasons as well. A well – stocked reserve of tomatoes not only guarantees a certain independence, but also financial security in case the money occasionally runs out. After all, according to the size of a family, a supply of at least 150 quarts of peeled tomatoes preserved in jars and bottles is required during the year until the next harvest. No day passes in which pastas, soups, risottos, meat, vegetable, or fish dishes do not call for the addition of tomatoes, not to mention using them in *antipasti*.

It is also, therefore, not hard to understand why women rely on their friends in the neighborhood to process the mountain of tomatoes, while the favor is later reciprocated. The occasion becomes an opportunity to exchange news and gossip, and for pouring out one's soul to friends. To agree on a date for the meeting, several important questions must be settled. Monday is usually a bad day because tomatoes canned on this day seem to be under a bad spell. Further, no woman would touch a glass during her monthly critical days, and if a wedding is announced, the tomatoes just have to wait. Once the canning day is agreed on, the fruits are picked in the morning, the tools and implements for the canning stand ready, and everything runs as smoothly as ever, with great excitement, through the crowd that will be busy until late in the evening, with the washing, peeling, and pureeing of tomatoes.

Above: The tomatoes are set to dry in the open air on a very simple meshed metal grate. The result is a precious miracle of flavors.

Above: Canned pelati *from Sicily exported worldwide. Even as a concentrate, the sun-dried aromatic fruit overshadows its northern tomato relatives.*

The start of a long working day: The tomatoes are harvested early in the morning—only the fully ripe ones. All others are left behind on the vine and will have to wait for the next harvest.

Two women are extremely busy; they gradually lift the tomatoes out of the water bath, drain them, and put them into larger processing bins.

At home, the harvest is washed in large tubs; this water is also joyously used for playtime by the children.

Before deciding whether to remove the tomatoes or not, a few are fished from the water and tested to see whether the peel is beginning to lift.

A selection of tomatoes is still possible at this stage; those not fully ripe will remain in the kitchen and will be used in a few days.

At home, a small group is ready to sterilize the glass jars and bottles; other neighbors sit around the bins filled with hot tomatoes and begin to peel.

The process goes on in the courtyard: A huge copper kettle is filled with water and placed on a tripod, the blanching water for the washed tomatoes.

Large bunches of basil are readied for use, the tomatoes peeled first are already placed in layers in the glass jars, and, together with the fresh herbs, they begin to give out their scent.

Although rare, one of the men of the group can unexpectedly appear, with the assumption that making fire is actually a man's job.

The conversation begins to be more animated while the peeling, seeding, and draining of tomatoes is done.

As soon as the water boils, the first bunch of tomatoes are quickly dipped into the kettle for blanching.

Red juice drips off the womens' hands when the tomatoes are put into the glass jars and pressed down with a spoon to prevent the formation of air bubbles. The next step will include the sterilizing; in the meantime, evening has long since arrived.

After this step is finished, the canning is far from complete. Large plates of tomato purees are set out under the sun; the tomato paste that comes to us in cans and tubes is created with this drying process.

Especially in Calabria, jars of dried tomatoes preserved in olive oil are part of the winter home pantry supply. As time permits between house chores and errands, some pear-shaped tomatoes or small, dark Napolitana tomatoes are cut into halves and sprinkled evenly with sea salt on the exposed surfaces. The next day, the cut-open plump tomatoes that have flattened and become oval-shaped are visible outside the door, spread out under the sun on the rectangular metal meshed frames. No more than one or two days are needed for the fruit to lose its excess liquid while developing an intense flavor in one single slice. There is hardly anything more flavorful than these tomatoes, especially if they are put in clay pots or glass jars with not only olive oil, but also with capers or anchovies, or with a little spicy peperoncino, black pepper, or a pinch of oregano, as is customary in Calabria for appetizers or to combine with bread and cheese. These *pomodori secchi* also flavor pasta dishes with their marvelous tomato aroma, especially if enhanced by olive oil. For city residents, who are not able to dry tomatoes, weekly farmers' markets offer partially processed products, dried tomatoes that can later be put in oil; this is a prerogative that is common among all housewives of either Sicily or Calabria.

Erika Casparek-Türkkan

During the winter it is possible to maintain a supply of fresh and juicy fruit thanks to a unique tomato variety, the pomodoro a grappolo. *On cool, ventilated, shady balconies, the round and especially thick-skinned tomatoes are left hanging attached to their stems.*

Wonderfully flavorful po-modori secchi—under the bright southern sun, it takes no more than two days for the salt-rubbed tomato halves to lose their juice and turn into wrinkled gourmet food items.

Dried tomatoes tower near marinated olives, strips of eggplant preserved in vinegar, oil, garlic, and basil, the famous slightly small, bitter onions, and flavorful marinated wild mushrooms, precious treasures with which gourmet fans in the South equip themselves for special culinary events.

Index and Glossary from A to Z

Listed here are the English/American and the Italian recipe titles, once in alphabetical order and once under the dishes' main ingredients. Also included and marked with an asterisk (*) sign are the pages with the regional introductions, as well as the explanations of dishes and ingredients.

The numbers that appear next to a description signify that an explanation is included on the corresponding page.

Recipe Index
from Appetizers to Desserts

Regional recipes are listed here according to menu course sequence; the recipes are listed in alphabetical order according to the Italian name, accompanied by the English/American name.

Antipasti · Appetizers

Pizza e pane · Pizzas and Savory Breads

Primi Piatti – First Courses
(Pasta, Rice, and Soups)

Minestre – Soups

Risotto e polente – Rice and Polenta

Paste asciutte – Noodle and Pasta Dishes

Dolci · Desserts and Cakes

Italian Culinary Terms

Abbacchio: Suckling lamb
Aceto: Vinegar
Aglio: Garlic
Agnello: Lamb
Al dente: Generic term to
    describe pasta cooked until
    still firm to the bite inside
Al forno: Baked in the oven
Alla griglia: Grilled
Anguilla: Eel
Arrosto: Roasted
Arancia: Orange
Arista: Pork roast
Asparagi: Asparagus

Baccalà: Dried cod
Biscotti: Cookies
Bistecca: Steak
Bollito: Boiled meat
Brasato: Stew
Budino: Pudding

Calamari: Squid
Carciofi: Artichokes
Carne: Meat
Carole: Carrots
Casalinga: Homemade
Cavolfiore: Cauliflower
Cavoto: Cabbage
Ceci: Chick-peas (Garbanzo
    beans)
Cinghiale: Boar
Cipolla: Onion
Coniglio: Rabbit
Costoletta: Cutlet
Cotechino: Pork sausage
Cotto: Cooked
Cozze: Mussels
Crudo: Raw

Fagiano: Pheasant
Fagioli: Dried beans
Fagiolini: Green beans
Fegato: Liver
Fichi: Figs
Finocchio: Fennel
Formaggio: Cheese
Fragole: Strawberries
Frittata: Omelet
Fritto: Fried
Frutti di Mare: Seafood
Funghi: Mushrooms

Gelato: Ice cream
Gnocchi: Dumplings
Gratinato: Baked or broiled until
    golden and crisp

In agro: Pickled
In agro dolce: Pickled sweet-
    and-sour
In brodo: In broth
In marinata: Marinated
In padella: Out of the pan
In umido: Stewed or braised
    with gravy
Insalata: Salad
Involtini: Filled rollups

Latte: Milk
Lenticchie: Lentils
Lepre: Hare
Limone: Lemon
Lingua: Tongue

Magro: Lean
Maiale: Pork
Manzo: Beef
Mela: Apple
Melanzane: Eggplant
Merluzzo: Cod
Minestre: Soups

Nasello: Hake
Noci: Nuts

Olio: Oil
Orzo: Barley

Pane: Bread
Panna: Whipped cream
Patate: Potatoes
Peperoncini: Hot chili peppers
Petti di pollo: Chicken breasts
Pernici: Partridges
Pesce spada: Swordfish
Pesche: Peaches
Pesci: Fish, fish dishes
Piselli: Peas
Pollame: Poultry
Pollo: Chicken
Polpi: Squid
Pomodori: Tomatoes
Porchetta: Suckling pig on a spit
Porcini: Porcini or cepes
    mushrooms
Prosciutto: Ham

Quaglie: Quails

Ricotta: Italian cottage cheese
Ripieno: Filled, stuffed,
    or stuffing
Riso: Rice

Sarde: Sardines or anchovies
Scaloppine: Boneless cutlets
Scorzonera: Scorzonera
Sedani: Celery
Sgombri: Mackerels
Sogliola: Sole or flounder
Spinaci: Spinach

Tonno: Tuna
Triglie: Mullets
Trippa: Tripe
Trote: Trout

Uova: Eggs or egg dishes

Verdure: Vegetables
Visciole: Tart cherries
Vitello: Veal
Vongole: Clams

Zucca: Pumpkin or winter
    squash

Authors and Photographers

Professor Franco Benussi

His involvement is not only limited to his profession—a native of Milan, attorney, and professor of law, he is also devoted to music, liberal arts, and the study of ethnic traditions. As a director of the Munich delegation of the Accademia Italiana della Cucina, he is particularly dedicated to the preservation of the Italian culinary culture. He has written the introduction for this book and has been a competent consultant.

Reinhard Hess

His culinary interest began at an early age; however, the hobby became a profession only after he completed studies in German culture and geography in 1979, when he became the editor of the largest cooking magazine in Germany. During those years, he worked on cookbooks and as a freelancer with a wine magazine. Conceptual work for new cookbooks became his specialty. For four years, he has worked exclusively as an author for Gräfe und Unzer.

Sabine Sälzer

She brought her culinary taste from her home state of Baden, Germany, and her scientific background for everything that is associated with food and drink from her studies at the Technical University of Munich. After five years of magazine editorship, she followed the call of book publishing. Since 1988 she has been an exclusive author for Gräfe und Unzer, where she is in the creative pool for new projects.

Erika Casparek-Türkkan

The roots of her culinary interest lie back in a country inn located in the Rhine region, where her grandmother was the head of the kitchen. She combined her hobby with her love of traveling. As a journalist and freelance writer of cookbooks and travel guides, she now lives and works on Lake Starnberger in Germany. She photographed and wrote the text for the chapters on Calabria and Sicily, including the article on tomatoes.

Food Photography Eising

Pete A. and Susanne Eising specialize in food photography and have created a very mood-filled and personal style. Together with Pete A. Eising and Susanne Eising, Martina Görlach also has worked on this book. She was in charge of the requirements and worked on the photography layout. Chefs were Reinhold Apfelbeck and Tina Kempe.

Gottfried Aigner

He is a freelance journalist and photographer in Munich, Germany, but can more often be found traveling in the South, especially throughout Italy. His reasons: people, landscapes, and the everyday life; all this he describes in a direct and genuine way.

Wolf Heider

He is a photojournalist for magazines and newspapers, for which he captures actual life on film. Trying to convey with mood-filled snapshots the culinary personalities of the land and people of less renowned regions in Italy has been, for him, an interesting assignment.

Photography

Cover and photography of recipes: Foodfotografie Eising. All other photographers are listed in alphabetical order. The pages in which the photographers' pictures appear are listed after the photographer's name. Page numbers alone indicate that all the photographs on these pages were made by that photographer, and page numbers followed by a number in brackets indicate the location the photographer's work on that page, according to the diagram (picture reference is the top left corner of the picture).

1	2	3	4
5	6	7	8
9	10	11	12
13	14	15	16
17	18	19	20
21	22	23	24

Gottfried Aigner: page 10, 11, 12 (7), 13 (17), 14, 15, 16 (2), 16 (12), 42, 45 (11), 46, 47, 48, 49, 50 (15), 51(5), 51 (6), 51 (14), 52 (3), 5 (11), 53, 54 (2), 54 (12), 82 (1), 82 (4), 82 (20), 83 (2), 85 (6), 85 (8), 87 (12), 90 (6), 91 (7), 91 (17), 92 (6), 92 (17), 93 (9), 93 (17), 94 (2), 94 (10), 94 (11), 126, 127, 128 (13), 129 (17), 130 (13), 130 (19), 131 (1), 131 (17), 164 (5), 167 (1), 167 (9), 171 (11), 173 (9), 204 (9), 204 (10), 204 (13), 204 (17), 204 (18)
Archive Aigner: page 82 (12), 87 (16), 90, (17)
Nina Aigner: page 12 (15), 13 (9), 44, 45 (3)
Antrazit/Brigitte Kraemer: page 129 (19)
Azienda di Promozione Turistica

(APT) della Provincia di Reggio Emilia: page 80
Azienda di Promozione Turistica Parma-Salsonmaggiore Terme: page 51(9)
Wilfried Becker: page 91 (15), 91 (16)
Erika Casparek-Türkkan: page 83 (18), 272, 273, 274, 275, 276, 277, 278, 306, 307, 308, 309
Consorzio del Formaggio Parmigiano Reggiano/Dr. Mario Zannoni: page 81
Consorzio del Gallo nero: page 132 (3), 164 (19), 164 (20), 165, 166
Consorzio del Prosciutto di Parma: page 85 (5), 85 (13), 85 (14)
Hans-Joachim Döbbelin: page 128 (11), 128 (9), 129 (9), 129 (11), 164 (3), 167 (17), 268
Eising: page 13 (6), 51 (17), 86 (5), 87 (14)
Bildagentur Eising AG, Schweiz: Cover picture
Marlene Fetzer: page 130 (3), 131 (12), 131 (16)
Robert Gigler: page 52 (13), 52 (14), 269 (2), 269 (10)
Wolf Heider: page 6, 82 (9), 84 (6), 85 (16), 86 (4), 86 (12), 86 (14), 86 (20), 170 (19), 171 (1), 171 (17), 172, 173 (16), 174 (10), 203, 204 (2), 204 (4), 204 (12), 205, 206, 207, 208, 209, 210, 211, 212, 234, 235, 236, 237, 238, 239, 240, 241, 242, 243, 269 (18)
Calle Hesslefors: page 93 (1), 93 (7), 93 (15), 94 (18), 244
Christian Michel: page 90 (19)
Klaus-D. Neumann: page 12 (13), 170 (3), 170 (11), 170 (13), 171 (3), 173 (1), 173 (17), 174 (18), 174 (19)
Herman Rademacker: page 2, 3, 83 (10), 129 (1), 167 (3)
Franz Roth/V-Dia: page 50 (13)
Franz Roth/V-Dia/Tjörben: page 88, 89, 90 (8), 92 (19)
Franz Roth/V-Dia/Tjörben/Pavla Chrapek: page 270, 271
Sabine Sälzer: page 84 (15), 87 (6), 87 (7)
Lothar Schiffler: page 12 (17), 13 (5), 50 (7), 128 (3), 130 (11), 202 (3)
Ulrike Schlüter/Peter Wellnitz: page 16 (17), 54 (17), 132 (17)
Silvestris/Gerhard Palinkas: page 168, 169
Verlag und Druckerei Meininger GmbH: page 122, 123, 124, 125, Georg Weindl: page 82 (17), 82 (24)

Thank you

and Grazie to all of those who helped us:

Azienda di Promozione Turistica
Agenzia Regionale di Promozione Turistica Emilia-Romagna, Katja Schmale
Azienda di Promozione Turistica Parma-Salsonmaggiore Terme
Consorzio del Formaggio Parmigiano Reggiano, Dr. Mario Zannoni
Consorzio del Prosciutto di Parma Parma Alimentare
Consorzio del Gallo nero, Dr. Lucia Franciosi
I.C.E. Düsseldorf, Gertrud Schmitz
Tourist Office in Reggio Calabria, Gabriella Romeo
Tourist Office of the Province of Catanzaro, Roberto Ianni
To the women of Francavilla di Sicilia, and to the local Chamber of Commerce
Elisabeth Koppelberg ua Bambara, Taormina
Elisabetta Lampe, Mailand
Tourist Office in München

Imprint:

Published originally under the title *Die Echte Italienische Küche*. Typische Rezepte und kulinarische Impressionen aus allen Regionen.

© Copyright 1991 by Gräfe und Unzer Verlag GmbH, München. English translation © Copyright 1998 by Gräfe und Unzer Verlag GmbH, München.
United States edition © Copyright 1999 by Barron's Educational Series, Inc.
English translation and U.S. adaptation by Elisabetta A.G. Castleman.

All inquiries should be addressed to:
Barron's Educational Series, Inc.
250 Wireless Boulevard
Hauppauge, NY 11788
http://www.barronseduc.com

International Standard Book Number 0-7641-5159-2
Library of Congress Catalog Card Number 99-72142
Printed in Germany

98765432